Ultimate Web Authentication Handbook

Strengthen Web Security by Leveraging Cryptography and Authentication Protocols such as OAuth, SAML and FIDO

Sambit Kumar Dash

Orangeava.com

First published: October 2023

Published by: Orange Education Pvt Ltd, AVA™

Address: 9, Daryaganj, Delhi, 110002

ISBN: 978-81-19416-46-2

www.orangeava.com

Dedicated to

My Beloved Parents

and

My Loving Wife

Foreword

In today's interconnected world, web authentication stands as a crucial pillar of digital security. As technology continues to advance at an unprecedented pace, it is paramount that we equip ourselves with the knowledge and skills to navigate the intricate landscape of authentication protocols and standards. It is with great pleasure and anticipation that I introduce this exceptional book, a comprehensive guide to advanced web authentication, focused on programming and hands-on understanding of authentication protocols, authored by an esteemed industry expert in the field.

I have had the honor of working alongside the author during our tenure together at Symantec, growing Symantec's strong authentication services to have been serving tens of millions of users worldwide. Sambit, as a brilliant product management leader, spearheaded our flagship authentication product line, which provided comprehensive strong authentication methods and protocols. His exceptional product guidance and expertise were instrumental in driving solutions that ensured the utmost security and reliability for our clients.

Through our work together, I witnessed firsthand Sambit's unwavering dedication and unparalleled knowledge in the realm of authentication. His deep understanding of the subject matter, combined with his ability to translate complex concepts into practical implementations, positioned him as a true authority in the field.

This book strikes a perfect balance between theory and practice, delving into the fundamental concepts of authentication protocols and standards while emphasizing their practical implementation through programming. By emphasizing the hands-on application of protocols rather than relying on wrapped third-party libraries, one can truly gain a solid grasp of the subject matter. The Flutter client framework and sample server code in the Go Language are especially well chosen for learning and use in one's own application.

This book caters to the critical needs of a broad audience, ranging from computer programmers, and web application designers, to architects who are eager to embrace authentication best practices in their applications. While network security experts undoubtedly possess invaluable knowledge in the field, they may find that existing resources often lack the level of detail required to configure enterprise authentication tools. Similarly, many Identity Management Products predominantly focus on server components, leaving developers of client integrations without comprehensive guidance.

As someone who has witnessed the author's extraordinary expertise in managing and building real-world authentication products, I wholeheartedly endorse this book as an invaluable resource for aspiring developers, security professionals, and anyone seeking to advance their knowledge of advanced web authentication.

May this excellent book inspire you to push the boundaries of what is possible in the realm of digital security, and may it empower you to create robust and reliable authentication systems that safeguard the digital world.

– MINGLIANG PEI

Distinguished Engineer, Broadcom

Technical Co-chair of Open Authentication (OATH) and an author of multiple RFCs in the field of authentication

About the Author

Sambit Kumar Dash is passionate about bringing technology product ideas to reality. He has over 25 years of experience in product and business management, architecture, and research and development. His interests in technology expand to document technologies, computer security, artificial intelligence, and natural language processing. Sambit has conceived and developed a PDF reader library in the Julia language. This library is available on GitHub (**https://github.com/sambitdash/PDFIO.jl**). He is passionate about developing new technologies and has eight patents in document technologies, computer security, virtualization, and human-computer interfaces. Additionally, he provides product management consultancy to start-ups and early-stage ventures through Lenatics Solutions Private Limited.

About the Reviewer

Gopal Sharma is a hands-on senior technology leader and software architect in Enterprise Software, Digital Technologies, and Data Engineering, with over 25 years of proven experience in building innovative solutions to challenging business opportunities and building R&D teams. He is adept at collaborating with cross-functional teams to deliver innovative solutions that meet business requirements. He is also a freelance writer of technical articles in Big Data, Data Science, and Enterprise Tech.

In the dynamic realm of technology, Gopal's journey is a testament to the enduring pursuit of knowledge. Starting as a mechanical engineer, Gopal's life has been marked by a remarkable transformation, ultimately leading him to his current role as a book reviewer.

Raised in Kolkata, India, Gopal embarked on his academic path at the prestigious Indian Institute of Technology, Kharagpur, graduating in 1995 with a Bachelor of Technology (Honours) in Mechanical Engineering. His early career was firmly rooted in the mechanical domain, where he honed his skills in machinery, design, and manufacturing.

However, Gopal's curiosity and openness to change soon drew him towards the world of software engineering. With determination and a deep desire to learn, he transitioned from mechanical engineering to software development. Starting as a developer, he progressed to roles such as senior developer and tech lead, all the while embracing new challenges with humility.

Gopal's ability to grasp complex software concepts and craft elegant solutions stood him in good stead. His journey exemplified his adaptability and unwavering commitment to self-improvement.

As the years passed, Gopal's career evolved, with him assuming key roles as an architect and software security expert. His dedication to safeguarding digital assets and his deep knowledge of security protocols helped him immensely.

The vast landscape of data science and big data beckoned to Gopal, and he eagerly explored these domains, leveraging data to drive innovation and decision-making.

His passion for data was evident in most works he undertook, from analyzing extensive datasets to uncovering valuable insights.

Gopal's reviews offered a unique perspective and a wealth of knowledge. Beyond mere evaluations, they were heartfelt explorations of the books he encountered, demonstrating his authentic passion for learning and his aspiration to impart wisdom to others.

Acknowledgement

Writing an acknowledgment for a book on technology is always challenging, primarily because you are building on top of someone else's work. This book disseminates the ideas and research of hundreds of technologists. Firstly, I would like to express my gratitude to all of them for producing such remarkable pieces of technology. I have provided reference notes for most of their works, but to err is human. Hence, I request readers to report any omissions,as they are purely unintentional.

Secondly, I thank Mingliang Pei for finding confidence in me and encouraging me to take up this audacious step of writing a book on a technology he masters. Your encouraging foreword means a lot to me. Gopal Sharma and Shashi Bhushan Kumar painstakingly went through every piece of technology discussed in the book and provided their invaluable feedback, making the book better in every respect. Srinath Venkataramani's inputs on digital identity and Krishnan Rajagopalan's on foundational identity and MOSIP enriched the contents further. A casual discussion with Ashutosh Chandra added significant updates to the Zero Trust Principles. I thank them all for their contributions. While all these industry leaders have provided well-intentioned inputs, all omissions and errors should only be attributed to me.

Thirdly, I thank Subha and Sonali for being the editors of this book and the entire Orange AVA team for their remarkable support in making this work see the light of day.

Lastly, I want to express my gratitude to you for choosing this work for your learning. We hope you enjoy it as much as we enjoyed putting it all together. Please do not forget to share your comments and suggestions to help us improve the book further.

Preface

The COVID-19 pandemic affected not only approximately 640 million people worldwide but also resulted in 6.6 million casualties[1]. The disease spared no one,affecting people from developing nations to the most developed ones. Despite all lockdowns and travel restrictions, the world has moved on. Life has not come to a stand still. The pace at which the world embraced digital technologies added to overcoming some need for physical interaction. People could work from home, share personal and private information, and continue communicating securely. Industries not used to remote working opened to employees working from home. The internet was a great enabler in all these. However, the ability to trust the person accessing the corporate resources is equally important. Organizations deployed authentication systems, and they helped in providing secure access.

India launched a massive vaccination program to inoculate its 1.3 billion population. To date, 2.2 billion dosages of the vaccine have been administered[2]. The vaccination must reach all the deserving people based on priority with tracking of dosage. A vaccine management platform COWIN developed by the Govt of India was used to track patients and medical practitioners. SMS OTP-based authentication is used for the COWIN portal.

India has only about 60% smartphone penetration[3]; a sophisticated authentication platform could not have reached the masses. As much as networking and the internet have become a need for digitization, there is a growing need to keep information and user identities secured in this connected world. Computers and user authentication have always run together. However, technologies are constantly evolving. Today, almost all our transactions are carried out using the web as the communication interface. Only a few books provide a holistic view of all the user authentication platforms relevant to web authentication. We endeavor to bring a ready reckoner for programmers to understand the authentication

1. World Health Organization Statistics as of 1st Dec 2022 **https://covid19.who.int/**

2. Ministry of Health and Family Welfare, Government of India as of 1st Dec 2022 **https://www.mohfw.gov.in/**

3. India to have 1 billion smartphone users by 2026: Deloitte report, **https://www.business-standard.com/article/current-affairs/india-to-have-1-billion-smartphone-users-by-2026-deloitte-report-122022200996_1.html**

protocols and work on them to integrate them into their application development. The book is composed of the following chapters:

Chapter 1: The World Wide Web has evolved organically. It started as a simple platform for information exchange. However, today it has become the backbone of Internet commerce, business, education, governance, etc. If we were to design a system as complex, keeping so much extendibility in mind, it would have been almost impossible. The underlying protocol of Internet HTTP is stateless. It did not have any native security model in place. The state architecture was established at the application layer using some constructs like headers and cookies. Similarly, there are restrictions placed on the protocol to ensure that browser communications remain secure. In this chapter, we will explore some classic security aspects of Web Architecture.

Chapter 2: HTTP, although developed for information exchange, did not have many safeguards for state and user management. The transport protocols for HTTP did not have any default protection on information exchange. TCP/IP sends a packet to all the network devices without restriction. The network device that is the only intended recipient analyses the network packet and consumes it, while others ignore it. In such an open communication world, for any information to be protected, the data itself should be encrypted such that a non-intended audience cannot decipher the message. We will review some of the encryption technologies in this chapter.

Chapter 3: In the earlier chapters, we discussed how we can encrypt information. We did not show the application in exchanging information. Fortunately, the network protocol designers realized this complexity and solved it with two distinct architectures. One is in the transport layer called Transport Layer Security (TLS), and the other at the IP layer called IPSec. While both technologies utilize similar encryption techniques, the protocols and usage are very different. We will be focusing on TLS in this chapter. HTTP over TLS as transport is known as HTTPS and is used in most browser communication today.

Chapter 4: So far,we have only discussed individual services the users are connecting to, authenticating themselves, and getting access to the system. However, in an organization, there are several systems based on functions or roles. An employee connects to the HR system for leave application, the payroll system for salary, or an IT incident management system for reporting the failure of a laptop. An HR team member will have administrative rights over the HR system, while even the CEO may have user-level rights. These granular policy controls are hard to maintain in every individual service. It started the domain of Identity and Access Management (IAM). IAM is a complex domain. It caters to applications and network configurations, one of the significant complexities seen was with Web Applications in terms of session management. A user who has logged in once to the organization servers does not have to reauthenticate for access to any other server. This concept is called Single Sign-On (SSO). SAML was one of the most used protocols for Web SSO.

Chapter 5: While SAML started to solve the SSO problem for enterprises, there was a need for mutual trust between the service provider (SP) and identity providers (IdP). In the Web 2.0 world, this was quite limiting. Users wanted to show their Twitter and Facebook feeds on their web pages as mashup content. While such content is viewable on web pages, it should not be editable. A new paradigm of access control or authorization was needed to address this. In SAML, some attributes or membership of groups are good enough to establish access control for a user. OAuth started as an authorization protocol with restricted access to a resource by the owner. However, it got extended as an authentication protocol with the Open Identity Connect (OIDC) protocol. We will see some aspects of the OAuth and OIDC protocols and review Java Web Token (JWT) to transmit authentication and authorization information.

Chapter 6: Passwords are open to brute-force or social engineering attacks. Hence, the industry is trying to move to a password-less model. However, the investment in passwords is so significant that moving away may take a few more years. In the past few decades, other factors of authentication as something you have (tokens) and something you are (biometric authentication) have developed. They are used alongside password-based authentication providing another layer of authentication. This is known as Multifactor Authentication (MFA). We saw one such technique with digital certificates. We will delve deeper into two standards: Open Authentication (OATH) and Fast ID Online (FIDO) based WebAuthn.

Chapter 7: We have discussed users producing credentials to justify a claim on their identity. An identity represents a human being,and the biometric, possessory, or knowledge attributes are mere credentials. There is a need to justify if the identity is in existence supported by government records or documentation. This process is called identity proofing. Earlier, ID-proofing systems depended on physical verification by agents and manual approval. With advances in AI, such systems have moved into automated document feature extraction, face recognition, and other biometric data collection mechanisms. Governments have started developing citizen ID databases containing biometric information for verification. In industries where Know Your Customer (KYC) is a policy requirement, faster digital eKYC systems are in use. The KYC systems provide an authoritative database for identity. Additionally, network and device insights and assessment from security practice are making organizations use a Zero Trust Network Security, where authentication is becoming the backbone.

About the Questions

The questions provided at the end of the chapters are for leading you to understand the topic in depth. It is perfectly alright if you cannot answer them satisfactorily in the first reading of the book. Some questions may not have answers within the chapter where they appear. They can create a lingering doubt to be answered in a later chapter. Some of them may need resources outside of the book. As most practitioners quest, some of the questions may not have a concrete answer, especially when it comes to system design, making them open to discussions and debates.

Downloading the code bundles and colored images

Please follow the link to download the
Code Bundles of the book:

https://github.com/OrangeAVA/Ultimate-Web-Authentication-Handbook

The code bundles and images of the book are also hosted on
https://rebrand.ly/k90i95c

In case there's an update to the code, it will be updated on the existing GitHub repository.

Errata

We take immense pride in our work at **Orange Education Pvt Ltd,** and follow best practices to ensure the accuracy of our content to provide an indulging reading experience to our subscribers. Our readers are our mirrors, and we use their inputs to reflect and improve upon human errors, if any, that may have occurred during the publishing processes involved. To let us maintain the quality and help us reach out to any readers who might be having difficulties due to any unforeseen errors, please write to us at :

errata@orangeava.com

Your support, suggestions, and feedback are highly appreciated.

DID YOU KNOW

Did you know that Orange Education Pvt Ltd offers eBook versions of every book published, with PDF and ePub files available? You can upgrade to the eBook version at **www.orangeava.com** and as a print book customer, you are entitled to a discount on the eBook copy. Get in touch with us at: **info@orangeava.com** for more details.

At **www.orangeava.com**, you can also read a collection of free technical articles, sign up for a range of free newsletters, and receive exclusive discounts and offers on AVA™ Books and eBooks.

PIRACY

If you come across any illegal copies of our works in any form on the internet, we would be grateful if you would provide us with the location address or website name. Please contact us at **info@orangeava.com** with a link to the material.

ARE YOU INTERESTED IN AUTHORING WITH US?

If there is a topic that you have expertise in, and you are interested in either writing or contributing to a book, please write to us at **business@orangeava.com**. We are on a journey to help developers and tech professionals to gain insights on the present technological advancements and innovations happening across the globe and build a community that believes Knowledge is best acquired by sharing and learning with others. Please reach out to us to learn what our audience demands and how you can be part of this educational reform. We also welcome ideas from tech experts and help them build learning and development content for their domains.

REVIEWS

Please leave a review. Once you have read and used this book, why not leave a review on the site that you purchased it from? Potential readers can then see and use your unbiased opinion to make purchase decisions. We at Orange Education would love to know what you think about our products, and our authors can learn from your feedback. Thank you!

For more information about Orange Education, please visit **www.orangeava.com**.

Table of Contents

CHAPTER 1
Introduction to Web Authentication

Introduction

While authentication is the primary focus of our discussion, we cannot look at it in isolation. There is a need to understand the fundamentals of computer networking and its history to appreciate the development of authentication protocols. It is probably secure to have a point-to-point network where communication is confined to two systems only. Such systems are not scalable as you cannot technically wire every pair of devices. The International Standard Organization (ISO) Open Standards Interconnection (OSI) is the backbone of all computer networking. The design prioritized data redundancy, communication assurance, and packet transmission over secured communication. Here is a basic explanation of the communication protocol. The electrical signals are exchanged across the internetworked computer in conceptual packets of electrical pulses. The electrical pulses do not differentiate any device. However, the pulse packets have a destination network address encoded in them. When a computer receives the pulse packet, it matches the address to its own assigned address. If the match is successful, the pulse packet is accepted.

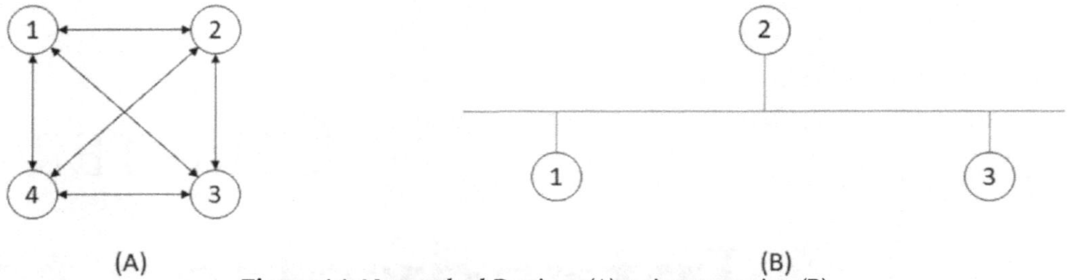

Figure 1.1: *Networked Devices (A) point-to-point (B) A bus network: signal will reach all devices on the network*

In the OSI model, physical and datalink layers are for low-level signal management. The network layer assigns the address for the pulse packets. Internet Protocol (IP) is the protocol of choice today. The computers may have an IPv4 address (32-bit) written as four numbers separated by dots (198.168.1.1). An IPv6 network uses a 128-bit address instead. Hexadecimal numbers are separated by a colon (:) for this representation; for example, 2001:0db8:85a3:0000:0000:8a2e:0370:7334. Due to the nature of transmission, the pulse packets are not delivered in a consistent order. The pulse packets are collected at the network devices and reordered to reconstruct meaningful messages. The transmission layer of the OSI stack handles these scenarios. The most common transmission protocols are the User Datagram Protocol (UDP) and Transmission Control Protocol (TCP). UDP is acceptable for low-latency networks where applications are tolerant to intermittent data loss. TCP is a connection-oriented protocol with guaranteed data delivery. Packets lost are retransmitted as part of TCP. Web interactions utilize TCP as the network transmission protocol. Hence, we will discuss TCP-IP for all network-related discussions in this book.

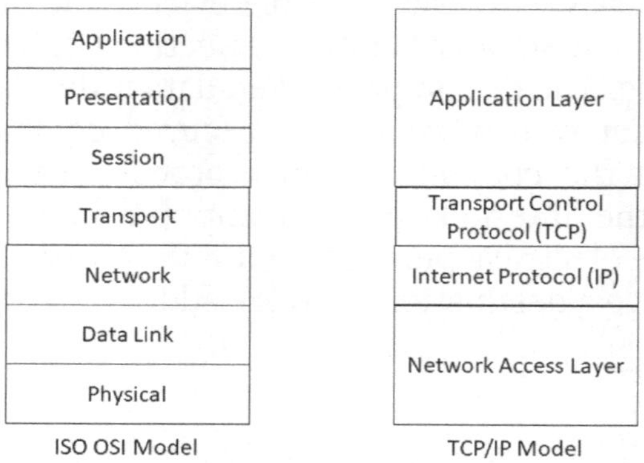

Figure 1.2: *ISO OSI Layers vs TCP/IP Layers: While authentication belongs to the session layer in the OSI model or application layer in the TCP/IP model, authentication can be implemented as part of transport and network layers as TLS and IPSec VPNs, respectively.*

Networking has not always been an open and standards-based domain. For example, Novell Networking used a proprietary IPX protocol as its networking protocol. Initially, Apollo computers provided the Network File System (NFS) for their networks. As time progressed, organizations realized the need to collaborate to develop open standards for better interoperability. Most web development today is based on open standards. While TCP-IP became the lingua franca of networking, the other OSI layers, namely, session, presentation, and application, never got the buy-in from the organizations to standardize. The applications implemented these layers as per their convenience. Hence, they are considered application layers in the TCP/IP stack. For example, the HTTP protocol is an application layer protocol. Authentication should have been in the session layer in the OSI stack.

Structure

In this chapter, we will cover the following topics:

- Tools and Resources
- HTTP Protocol Basics
- Web Architecture
- Introduction to Authentication
- Authentication over HTTP
- Limitations
- Conclusion

Tools and Resources

We will work with web applications in this book. We will look at HTTP and other internet protocols. We will need some tools to study the network data. Today, most browsers provide great developer tools to trace HTTP data. They have excellent tools for the HTML Document Object Models (DOM) and analyzing embedded JavaScript. We suggest readers use some of these tools to understand the HTTP traffic.

MDN Web Docs

MDN, earlier known as Mozilla Developer Network[1], provides excellent documents and training material for web developers. We suggest you review those for a better understanding of HTTP, HTML, CSS, JavaScript, and so on. We do not consider the knowledge of these technologies a prerequisite for this

1 MDN **https://developer.mozilla.org/en-US/**

book; a web developer will learn them with experience. We will introduce the required concepts for this book as the need arises.

Google Chrome

Google Chrome started as a developer-friendly browser that tried to use standards-compliant HTML specifications and had one of the fastest JavaScript engines. Today, it dominates the browser market with almost 65 percent market share leaving its distant second competitor at about 11 percent. All browsers ship with excellent developer tools for easier debugging and analysis of web technologies. We use Flutter as a frontend technology for our samples; Google Chrome provides better support for such environments. Moreover, developers have written large numbers of extensions that help analysis in the browser. Google Chrome is available for Windows, Mac OS, and Linux platforms.

CURL

CURL is a set of open-source libraries and command-line tools for accessing URLs. These tools are available on almost all well-known operating platforms; you can download them from **https://curl.se**. We are interested in the command line tool here so that we can compose custom HTTP requests to better our understanding while reading this book.

OpenSSL

In the area of cryptography or transport-level security, there is hardly any other tool that can boast of such coverage in the market. OpenSSL has the most elaborate cipher suites, certificate management, and transport layer security protocols. It also has an extensive command-line tool that exposes all the relevant functionality to be tried and tested. With strict FIPS compliance practices implemented, OpenSSL is one of the most sought-after tools in the domain. Just as we suggested CURL for connectivity debugging, we will be using OpenSSL for debugging the cryptographic and transport layer security issues. You can download the tool from **https://www.openssl.org/source/** [2].

Go Language

Designed by Robert Griesemer, Rob Pike, and Ken Thompson, working for Google, Go Language is a modern C-like general-purpose programming

---

2 Due to security regulations around cryptography, the community does not distribute the OpenSSL in binary form. However, most operating systems like Linux and Mac distributions have OpenSSL available. On Windows, you can use the embedded version of OpenSSL already installed in the system with another tool. The author uses OpenSSL from a Git installation found at **`C:\Program Files\Git\usr\bin`.**

language. Yet the language, with just a decade of existence, has become the language of choice for web application designs due to its concurrency, ease of programming, ecosystem, and support by large organizations. Developed and maintained as an open-source project, the resources for the language can be accessed from **https://go.dev**. People with relatively less experience with the tool can look at *Appendix A: The Go Programming Language Reference* for a simplified introduction and installation instructions. However, the presentation is only rudimentary. We expect the readers to learn the Go language from other language resources.

Flutter Framework

While the Go Language provides the backend of a web application, you need the client libraries to render the content on a browser or a mobile application. Developed by Google as an open-source project, the Flutter application framework provides easy-to-use mechanisms to build applications for the web, Windows, Linux, iOS, and Android platforms. Since authentication requires integration with the application UI, we shall be developing some of the applications on Flutter where user interface can be of paramount importance. You can download the Flutter framework resources from: **https://flutter.dev**. *Appendix B: The Flutter Application Framework* provides an introductory understanding of the framework.

HTTP Protocol Basics

As organizations were developing more and more applications for desktop computers, the general framework was to bring a file or resource from the remote machine locally before using it. There were hardly any applications that rendered the content while downloading it from a remote resource; the concept known today as browsing. The exchange of text as electronic mail was prevalent. File transfer protocol (FTP) was the most common technique to download non-text content and view it locally. Tim Berners Lee, a scientist at the European Council for Nuclear Research (CERN), developed a telnet-friendly service to download research data and results. Eventually, this became the Hypertext Transfer Protocol (HTTP). Initially started with only the **GET** as the command, more commands and mnemonics were added to the protocol.

```
telnet google.com 80

connecting to… 142.XXX.XXX.XXX

GET /

<<Hypertext Response>>

Connection to host lost
```

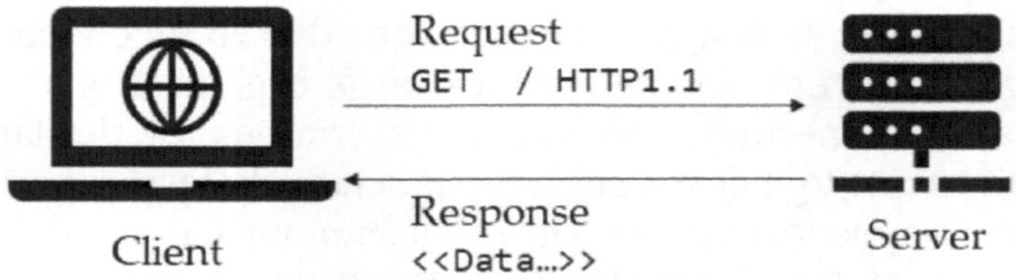

***Figure 1.3**: An HTTP client requesting a server for a specific resource*

Hypertext Markup Language (HTML) was developed to link text and images in a single view. The National Center for Supercomputing Applications (NCSA) developed the first browser Mozaic. Netscape and Microsoft built their commercial versions of the browsers Navigator and Internet Explorer (IE) respectively by licensing Mozaic technology. The protocol was kept very simple. Open a connection to a server, request the information you require, and close the connection. There was no concept of a state or resuming the activity where you had left. The protocol remained simple and generic, but it did not give the ability to deliver state management.

Headers

HTTP started as a protocol without any state management controls. However, the client and server needed additional directives for communication. Request for a specific URL or resource was not enough for reliable communication. Let us try to connect to **`http://google.com`** with **`curl`** and understand the data exchange.

In the **`curl`** command, the **`-v`** option prints the detailed communication exchange. In the print, the outputs are classified into four sets. Sentences beginning with:

- * Are explanations from actions of CURL
- > Information sent from the client to the server
- < Information received from the server
- Nothing - A dump of the data received.

```
C:\>curl -v http://google.com
*   Trying 2404:6800:4009:82b::200e:80...
* Connected to google.com (2404:6800:4009:82b::200e) port 80 (#0)
```

Along with the **GET** request, **curl** sent a few data values. These name-value pairs separated by a colon (:) are headers. Headers help in exchanging control information[3] between the client and server.

```
> GET / HTTP/1.1

> Host: google.com

> User-Agent: curl/7.83.1

> Accept: */*

>
```

Header **User-Agent** tells the name and version of the client software used to connect the server. The **Host** header tells the server and port (optional) that shall receive the request. The **Accept** header tells the MIME types the client can understand. These are only a few that **curl** sends for this minimal example. Browsers send a lot more headers as default. One can review a complete list of standard HTTP headers from this MDN site: **https://developer.mozilla.org/en-US/docs/Web/HTTP/Headers**. These are not all. The communication across custom clients and servers can use custom headers as well.

As **curl** sent a few headers, the site google.com also replied with a few HTTP headers along with the response. The response here is a **301 error** stating the site contacted has moved. And, the user agent must connect to the site as per the value of the **Location** header. The Location header points to the site **http://www.google.com/**.

```
* Mark bundle as not supporting multiuse

< HTTP/1.1 301 Moved Permanently

< Location: http://www.google.com/

< Content-Type: text/html; charset=UTF-8

< Cross-Origin-Opener-Policy-Report-Only: same-origin-allow-popups;
report-to="gws"

< Report-To: {"group":"gws","max_age":2592000,"endpoints":
    [{"url":"https://csp.withgoogle.com/csp/report-to/gws/other"}]}

< Date: Thu, 08 Dec 2022 15:21:46 GMT

< Expires: Sat, 07 Jan 2023 15:21:46 GMT

< Cache-Control: public, max-age=2592000

< Server: gws

< Content-Length: 219
```

3 Protocols like SMTP and FTP use separate control and data channels for communication, while Telnet and HTTP use only one channel for data and control signal exchange.

```
< X-XSS-Protection: 0
< X-Frame-Options: SAMEORIGIN
<
```

`Content-Length` is a very useful header that tells how many bytes shall be downloaded as part of the response. Here, 219 bytes of content follow the headers.

```
<HTML><HEAD><meta http-equiv="content-type" content="text/
HTML;charset=utf-8">
<TITLE>301 Moved</TITLE></HEAD><BODY>
<H1>301 Moved</H1>
The document has moved
<A HREF="http://www.google.com/">here</A>.
</BODY></HTML>
* Connection #0 to host google.com left intact
```

If you plan to download only the HTTP headers and no content, you could use the **`curl`** command line:

```
curl --head -v http://google.com
```

There is a lot of information on HTTP headers one needs to learn to be a good web developer. However, we will leave those for the readers to explore for themselves.

Cookies

In HTTP, there is no way to track the continuity of requests. Every request is an independent exchange of data. The server can send a client key-value pairs to remember, and the client can send the same key-value pairs in a subsequent request. These kinds of exchanges are known as cookies in HTTP. The information exchanged in cookies is small chunks of data only.

```
C:\>curl --cookie-jar cookies.txt -v http://www.google.com


*   Trying 2404:6800:4007:81f::2004:80...
* Connected to www.google.com (2404:6800:4007:81f::2004) port 80 (#0)
> GET / HTTP/1.1
> Host: www.google.com
> User-Agent: curl/7.83.1
```

```
> Accept: */*
>
* Mark bundle as not supporting multiuse
< HTTP/1.1 200 OK
< Date: Thu, 15 Dec 2022 07:55:39 GMT
…

< Set-Cookie: 1P_JAR=2022-12-15-07; expires=Sat, 14-Jan-2023 07:55:39
GMT; path=/; domain=.google.com; Secure
< Set-Cookie: AEC=AakniGMJBryHGiLz0B-1QnVwN91aqzJeWcfrpw2hO_
idwaRhjCMeJ6mNHA; expires=Tue, 13-Jun-2023 07:55:39 GMT; path=/;
domain=.google.com; Secure; HttpOnly; SameSite=lax

*Added cookie NID="511=tOdOEL2UXQFjj2IUhgV1wrFmW9Hs_eIacoHSD9lVeUoSg
LOGF9gYObvKzw5q0h3BR2OnbKnzlcaSDy0QeamKxFJnWXh3gnpPY38lOFyHIvjhxGq_-
eQU5OggdCcTmGOJEFeq0alI-VxhPhhmYunoC949t9abiWu9UK-0_jKVjYs" for domain
google.com, path /, expire 1686902139
< Set-Cookie: NID=511=tOdOEL2UXQFjj2IUhgV1wrFmW9Hs_eIacoHSD9lVeUoSgL
OGF9gYObvKzw5q0h3BR2OnbKnzlcaSDy0QeamKxFJnWXh3gnpPY38lOFyHIvjhxGq_-
eQU5OggdCcTmGOJEFeq0alI-VxhPhhmYunoC949t9abiWu9UK-0_jKVjYs; expires=Fri,
16-Jun-2023 07:55:39 GMT; path=/; dcmain=.google.com; HttpOnly
…
```

Here the **curl** command contacts the server with the option (**--cookie-jar <filename>**) to save the received cookies. The server sends a response with three headers of **Set-Cookie**. **Set-Cookie** as a directive to the client to cache the cookie values and send them to the server in the subsequent request. If you open the **cookies.txt** file, you will see the following data:

```
# Netscape HTTP Cookie File
# https://curl.se/docs/http-cookies.html
# This file was generated by libcurl! Edit at your own risk.

#HttpOnly_.google.com     TRUE   /      FALSE  1686902139   NID
511=tOdOEL2UXQFjj2IUhgV1wrFmW9Hs_eIacoHSD9lVeUoSgLOGF9gYObvKzw5q0h3BR2O
nbKnzlcaSDy0QeamKxFJnWXh3gnpPY38lOFyHIvjhxGq_-eQU5OggdCcTmGOJEFeq0alI-
VxhPhhmYunoC949t9abiWu9UK-0_jKVjYs
```

Out of the three cookies suggested by the server, only one is saved by the client. Let's look at the Set-Cookie headers closely.

```
Set-Cookie: 1P_JAR=2022-12-15-07; expires=Sat, 14-Jan-2023 07:55:39 GMT;
path=/; domain=.google.com; Secure
```

Along with the key and value pair, we have other directives like:

- **`expires`**: The time when the cookie expires. Browsers need not store a cookie after the expiry
- **`domain`**: the domain to which the cookie is bound
- **`path`**: the path where the cookie shall be used. A **`'/'`** shall mean any path after the domain name as in this case.
- **`Secure`**: This cookie shall be exchanged in a secured HTTPS exchange channel. On an HTTP channel, such a cookie shall not be sent.

It is this secure directive that ensures the cookie is not saved in the cookie jar file[4]. We shall now use **`curl`** with the option **`-cookies`** to send the cookie in the HTTP request.

```
C:\>curl --cookie cookies.txt -v http://www.google.com
*   Trying 2404:6800:4009:823::2004:80...
* Connected to www.google.com (2404:6800:4009:823::2004) port 80 (#0)
> GET / HTTP/1.1
> Host: www.google.com
> User-Agent: curl/7.83.1
> Accept: */*
> Cookie: NID=511=tOdOEL2UXQFjj2IUhgV1wrFmW9Hs_eIacoHSD9lVeUoSgLOG
F9gYObvKzw5q0h3BR2OnbKnzlcaSDy0QeamKxFJnWXh3gnpPY38lOFyHIvjhxGq_-
eQU5OggdCcTmGOJEFeq0alI-VxhPhhmYunoC949t9abiWu9UK-0_jKVjYs
>
```

As expected, **`curl`** sent the cookie to the server in the request headers.

Session Management

Cookies serve three purposes in HTTP:

- Session Management – Storing logged-in users, shopping cart information, a continuation of the previous step, navigation history, and so on.
- Personalization - Storing user preferences, themes, and so on.
- Tracking - analyzing user behavior.

4 We suggest the readers to review the details of the Set-Cookie header from the MDN. **https://developer.mozilla.org/en-US/docs/Web/HTTP/Cookies**

Here we will be focusing on the first aspect only. Suppose we want to count the number of times a user has visited a website. The server can send the client a **`Set-Cookie`** header to store a counter. On the subsequent request, the server can receive the counter from the client, increment the counter, and send back a **`Set-Cookie`** header with the incremented value of the counter. The following diagram explains the process.

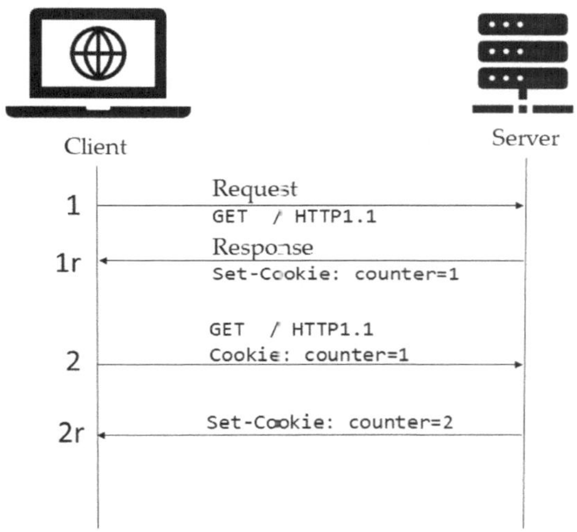

***Figure 1.4**: Cookies used to count the number of visits*

We shall use Golang[5] to develop the series of samples showing the session management. Each part has a separate handler function for easier understanding. The server can be launched by going into the **`chapter-1`** folder and using the command:

```
PS C:\work\HOWA\chapter-1> go run .\main.go
```

Minimal Web Server

We use the go language tools and HTTP package[6] to code our use cases. There are more advanced libraries available in the framework. However, we prefer the HTTP package due to its native availability in the Go language framework. The following code block initializes a web server over port 8080.

5 While we provide code snippets of Golang in this chapter, *Appendix A: The Go Programming Language Reference*, provides a brief overview of the language. However, readers are encouraged to learn the Go language for their professional use.

6 Package **`http`** provides HTTP client and server implementations. **https://pkg.go.dev/net/http**

```
func addHelloHandler() {
  helloHandler := func(w http.ResponseWriter, req *http.Request) {
    io.WriteString(w, "Hello, World!\n")
  }
  http.HandleFunc("/hello", helloHandler)
}

func main() {
  addHelloHandler()
  log.Fatal(http.ListenAndServe(":8080", nil))
}
```

By connecting to **http://localhost:8080/hello** you will get a response of:

```
Hello, World!
```

Counter Cookie

As shown in *Figure 1.4*, the server sets the cookie for the counter. The user agent (browser) honors the server directive and sends the cookie to the server. The server looks for the cookie and increments the counter. It sets the cookie again and sends it back to the browser. The following code block shows the above concept in action.

```
func addCountHandler() {
  countHandler := func(w http.ResponseWriter, req *http.Request) {
    count := 0
    if c, err := req.Cookie("count"); err == nil {
      if count, err = strconv.Atoi(c.Value); err != nil {
        log.Default().Print(err)
        count = 0
      }
    }
    count += 1
    http.SetCookie(w, &http.Cookie{
      Name:  "count",
      Value: strconv.Itoa(count),
    })
    str := fmt.Sprintf("You have visited: %d times.", count)
```

```
    log.Default().Print(str)
    io.WriteString(w, str)
  }
  http.HandleFunc("/count", countHandler)
}
```

By connecting to **http://localhost:8080/count**, you will be able to see the number of times the client connected to the server.

```
You have visited: 7 times.
```

The browser sends the state parameter of computation (**count**) that the server trusts for subsequent business logic. While this architecture is reasonable for a trusted client and server, a rogue client can manipulate the server's behavior. We want the control to be maintained on the server. Most servers will keep the business logic opaque to the client. They only notify the client to keep a reference to the session. The continuation of the session can be maintained, while the actual data needed is maintained on the server.

Session Cookie

The session cookie[7] is an opaque reference to the session data. The actual data is stored on the server in a local variable such as a map or a database. The server sets the session cookie on the client. The client can send this cookie to the server for subsequent computations. The following code snippet explains this concept.

```
func addSessionHandler() {
  cmap := map[string]int{}
  sessionHandle := func(w http.ResponseWriter, req *http.Request) {
    uid := ""
    if cookie, err := req.Cookie("session"); err != nil {
      uid = uuid.NewString()
      log.Default().Printf("No session found. Creating a new session:
%s", uid)
```

7 This is a toy solution to a larger problem. There are quite a few issues associated with session management. A few of them are: persisting the session data across load-balanced application servers, securing the session id at the client and validating the session id at the server, associating the session id to a specific client identity, storing multiple data structures against a session, and so on. Go has many advanced libraries for session management. One of them is SCS: HTTP session management for Go. **https://pkg.go.dev/github.com/alexedwards/scs/v2@v2.5.0** . We will not be able to delve into all these issues in this book but readers are suggested to review other relevant texts on these.

```
      http.SetCookie(w, &http.Cookie{
        Name:  "session",
        Value: uid,
      })
      cmap[uid] = 0
    } else {
      uid = cookie.Value
    }
    cmap[uid] += 1
    str := fmt.Sprintf("You have visited: %d times.", cmap[uid])
    log.Default().Print(str)
    io.WriteString(w, str)
  }
  http.HandleFunc("/session", sessionHandle)
}
```

We use the **cmap** variable to store a mapping from the session id to the actual counter. The session id is a globally unique random value. If the session id is not transferred by a rogue client, it will be hard to guess the session ID. Capturing the session ID of another client session is called session hijacking. Web applications use various security architectures to ensure the application is protected against session hijacking. The job of authentication is to ensure that access to the session data is provided to an authorized entity or user.

Protecting the Cookies

Cookies can be sensitive attributes that a server sends to the client for safe protection and use. Web servers expect a trustworthy user agent must securely keep cookies and use them within the restrictions of use. Cookies can have **Secured** and **HttpOnly** attributes set on them. The **Secured** attribute ensures that the cookie is only to be used in an HTTPS transport. Similarly, **HttpOnly** means the cookie cannot be manipulated on the client by JavaScript. The **SameSite** attribute controls how the cookie is to be used across sites. There are also time limits, domain, and path restrictions set on cookie usage. A trusted client should consider all these limitations while accessing the server. Security of cookies and sessions is a researched topic with many industry practices[8]. Is it desirable for a session cookie to have the **Secured** and **HttpOnly** attributes set?

8 The readers are suggested to understand the cookie parameters. **https://developer.mozilla.org/en-US/docs/Web/HTTP/Cookies**. We will review this topic in further detail when we discuss transport layer security (TLS).

Web Architecture

The web architecture we discussed was oversimplified. We connected a client with a server. The client could assume the working of the server and respond accordingly. We did not discuss the presence of hundreds of networking devices between the client and the server. Multiple physical devices can provide various functions for the server. Hence, what we see as a single server in a schematic could be a complex setup. The flexibility of the web architecture keeps all these transparent from the users and the clients. Server developers should not assume any specific functioning of the client, nor the client developers should be dependent on any architectural details of the servers. They should interact with each other using a standard protocol like HTTP or compliant extensions of the HTTP. For example, HTTP is a proxy-compliant protocol. An organization can configure a transparent HTTP proxy that can redirect all the outbound HTTP connections through the proxy server. The clients do not need any specific functionality to support proxy servers. Even if there are some specific activities to be carried out, they should be within the scope of the HTTP protocol and not vary depending on the type of proxy server used.

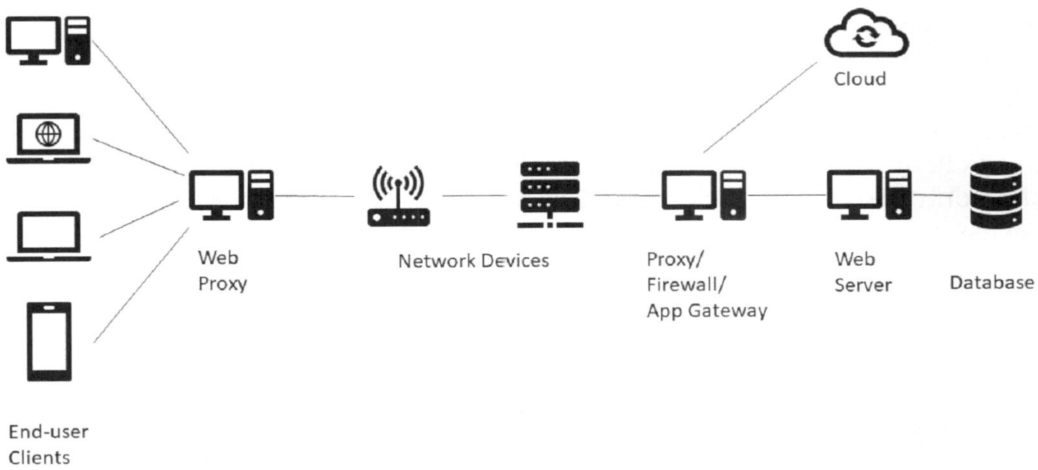

Figure 1.5: *A complex network in the web. All clients are redirected through a proxy. There are many network devices. An application gateway on the server side can control access to all the connections to the cloud services or the web server. The clients will not even be aware of the existence of a database server*

For a well-designed system for the web, the client does not need any specific functionality to be implemented if it is connecting to one server or a collection of servers. Following the network protocol properly shall automatically address such needs. Hence, there is a significant focus on using compliant protocols.

Web Application Architecture

As client-server applications became the norm of the industry, we started seeing clients that handled most of the presentation layer while data and business logic (application logic) were handled by the servers. This is known as the three-tier application architecture.

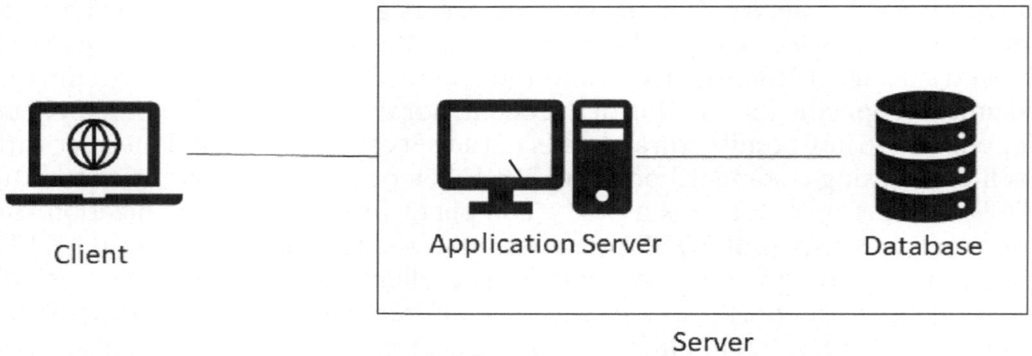

Figure 1.6: *Three-tier application architecture*

Web applications operate out of thin clients or browsers. Hence, the presentation layer was to be computed at the server as well. Clients are just meant to render the computed document object models (DOM) in the server presentation layer. Before web applications became mainstream, desktop applications or thick clients used Model-View-Controller UI models to present the data. View and controllers were implemented in the client, while the server provided the necessary model or data.

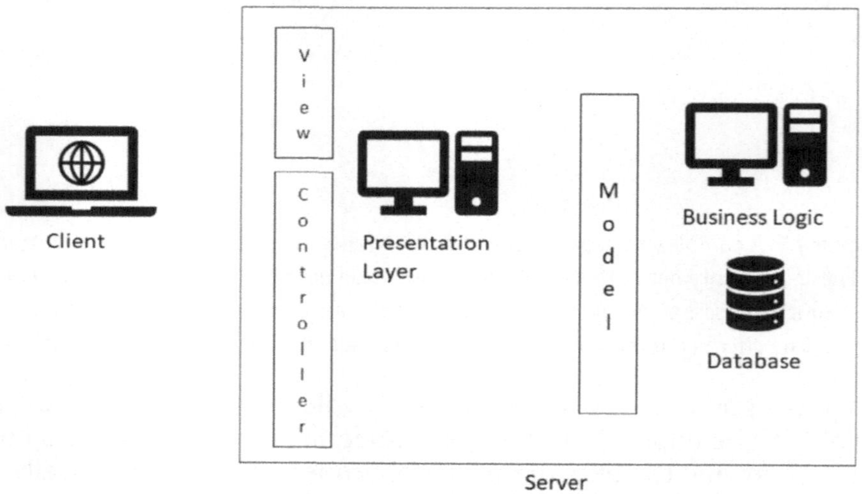

Figure 1.7: *MVC in a Web Application*

The adaptation of MVC architecture to the web applications was a mere extension of the client-server application with the view and controller residing on the server. The browser or the user agent renders whatever content is provided by the presentation layer. Even the controller events are posted to the presentation layer for subsequent updates. The computing power of the end-user devices could not be exploited in this model. The presentation layer became the front-end entry point for all communication with the browser.

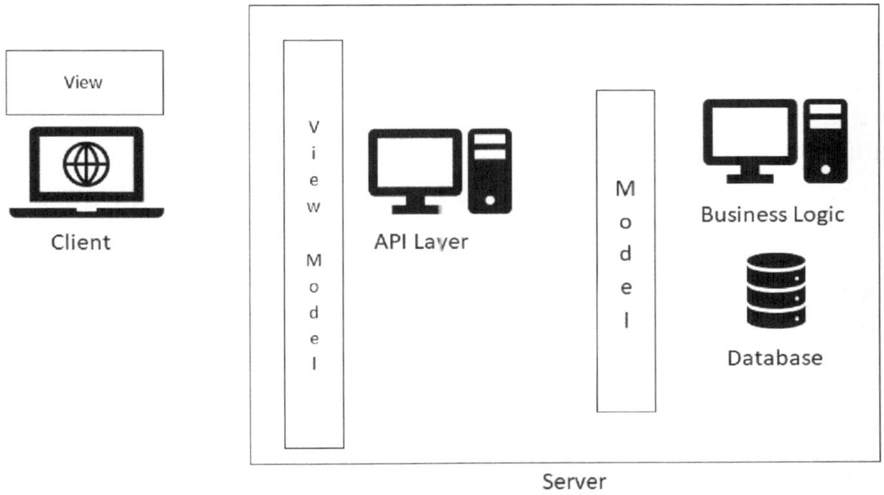

***Figure 1.8**: Model-View-View Model (MVVM) Web Architecture*

The Model-View-View-Model (MVVM) is a new kind of web application paradigm that is adopted by the most modern Single Page Architectures (SPA) like Flutter, Angular, React, and so on. The View is implemented as a SPA and is always loaded in the client. There is a continuous data exchange between the view layer and the view model layer. The view model is the presentation layer of the data that must be rendered in the view. View models are provided as APIs that the clients consume. Moreover, view models are continuously computed and updated from the model. Any update to the view models leads to the creation of new views in the client. The view layer and its associated HTML 5 resources are cached in the client. There is a need for such data to be protected and restricted against unauthorized access. The API layer of the MVVM is the real server entry point and should be properly access-controlled.

In our examples, we shall use Flutter for the view layer of the MVVM architecture. We will use Golang-based services for the API layer.

Introduction to Authentication

Authentication is an age-old field in technology. From the time there has been the existence of multi-user computing systems, we have been careful in protecting the distinction of work of one person from the other for various reasons. The technologies used in authentication are interdisciplinary and can be complex. We present a simplified aspect of authentication with these two anecdotes. Interestingly, every society has similar stories related to authentication.

The Sun temple of Konark, Odisha, India, was built in the 13th Century AD. It took 12 years to build the temple with the help of 1200 artisans. Bishu Maharana, the chief architect of the temple, left home when his son, Dharmapada, was still a toddler. In 12 years, the architect has never visited his home nor met his wife and son. When Dharmapada decides to meet his father on the construction site, his mother asks him to carry a piece of her jewelry and lemons from their backyard as artifacts to prove his identity to his father. Seeing both, Bishu Maharana recognizes his son.

The second story comes from Yadon Ki Barat, a movie of the 70s from the Indian movie industry, also known as Bollywood. The three sons of the family are separated young due to some unforeseen circumstances. They are in search of one another without the knowledge of any addresses. One of the sons is a singer in a hotel who keeps singing the first stanza of a family song they had been introduced to in their childhood by their parents, thinking someday one of his other brothers shall hear and complete the rest of the song. The same works and the family members are reunited.

In both these stories, the assertion of identities is impossible as appearances have changed from childhood to adulthood. Both are looking for some alternate artifacts that can establish a piece of circumstantial evidence. In short, we are in search of establishing authentication mechanisms. Digital authentication techniques are not entirely different from artifact matching. The category of artifact used for authentication varies based on who matches the artifacts and the purpose of artifact matching[9].

Credentials and access tokens

Let us look at a typical hiring process for an employee. We publish high-level requirements for candidates and start the interview process.

- The person should have an engineering degree from an institute of repute or institutions we have shortlisted.
- The person should have 5-10 years of experience from companies of repute (again, we have a list of reputed employers).
- The person should know some specific technologies.

9 Our introduction here is rudimentary. If you are looking for industry standard definitions of identity and authentication, you should refer to Digital Identity Guidelines, NIST, **https://doi.org/10.6028/NIST.SP.800-63-3**. We will introduce some of these concepts in later chapters as the discussions demand.

- His interpersonal skills were verified with discussions in the interview.

Finally, the company sent him an offer letter.

On the day of joining, an HR executive takes the offer letter, verifies all the necessary documents, and provides the access badge to the employee. All the information the candidate provided to the company is about his credentials. Interviewers and HR executives verified the credentials against a set of premises they had in mind. Suppose the HR executive doubted the document the candidate provided had been forged. The HR executive may escalate the matter to a document verification expert for authenticity. Depending on who is doing the verification, the credential may change. The HR department sent an offer letter. One can think of the offer letter as a **derived credential** based on the credential validation by the interviewers. Similarly, on the date of joining, the candidate will be given an access pass with a Photo ID to use organization resources. The automated access card provides the necessary access to the employee; the photograph helps the human security guard identify an authorized employee. The access card is an access token for the physical world.

Can an access token or card be a credential? In the limited sense, it is. For example, you show your ticket and passport at an international airport counter and receive a boarding pass. You have proven your credentials in terms of:

- You are a bonafide citizen trusted by your government.
- You have paid the necessary fees for the travel.

Based on this credential, the airline issues a boarding pass that allows you access to the flight. The boarding pass is an access token or a ticket and is not a credential.

Suppose you have an onward journey and take a connection to another mode of transport; the airline may not ask you to verify the ticket and passport but may allow you access using the boarding pass. The boarding pass is derived credential from your verified passport and travel ticket. In this book, we shall use credentials as proof of identity and use the term ticket or access token for the output of the verification process.

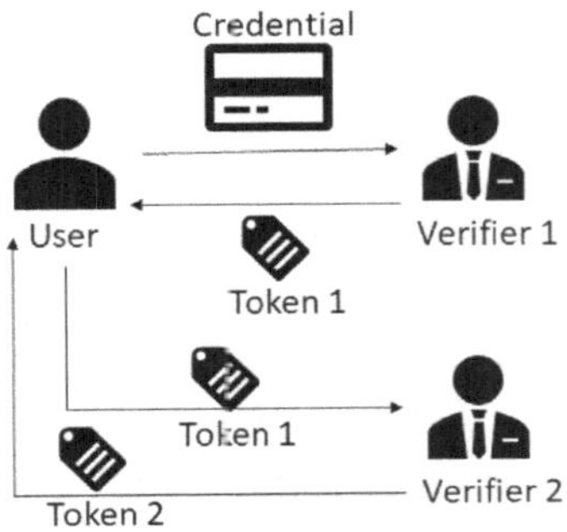

***Figure 1.9**: Credentials and tokens. Access tokens from previous steps can be used as derived credentials for future authentication steps in a workflow*

To summarize, authentication is about provisioning and verifying artifacts to ascertain the identity of a user or an entity. At least for most of this book, we will use this definition of authentication. However, each validation of an artifact can be complex and a domain of its own. We will discuss a few well-known types of artifact validation, but on a limited scale. In the digital world, password has been used as the most common form of credential. Initiatives like FIDO 2 and WebAuthn are proposed to switch to a password-less mode. We will discuss them later in this book. For the initial chapters, we will use passwords in many examples.

Authentication over HTTP

RFC 7235 defines the authentication protocol for HTTP. It provides a challenge-response architecture for authentication for client and server communication. The architecture is proxy-aware and can be additionally used to authenticate to HTTP proxy servers.

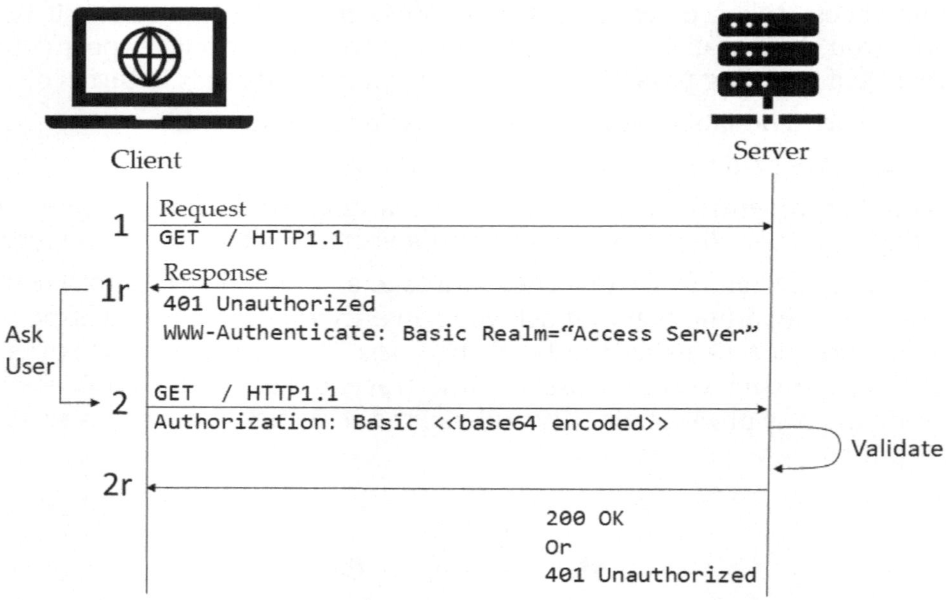

Figure 1.10: *HTTP Authentication. RFC 7235 describes this authentication scheme. While user name and password-based basic authentication are shown as an example in this workflow, any of the IANA-approved authentication schemes can be used here*

The following code snippet in Go implements the idea described in *Figure 1.10*. We use basic authentication as the authentication mechanism.

```
func addBasicAuthHandler() {
  pmap := map[string]string{"jdoe": "password"}
  basicAuthHandler := func(w http.ResponseWriter, req *http.Request) {
    if u, p, ok := req.BasicAuth(); ok {
      if pmap[u] == p {
        str := fmt.Sprintf("User %s authenticated.", u)
        io.WriteString(w, str)
        log.Default().Print(str)
      } else {
        str := fmt.Sprintf("User %s failed to authenticate.", u)
        w.WriteHeader(http.StatusUnauthorized)
        log.Default().Print(str)
      }
    } else {
     w.Header().Add("WWW-Authenticate", "Basic Realm=\"Access Server\"")
      w.WriteHeader(http.StatusUnauthorized)
      log.Default().Print("Basic authentication needed.")
    }
  }
  http.HandleFunc("/basicauth", basicAuthHandler)
}
```

When **ok** is **false**, there is no **Authorization** header in the request. The server responds with a **WWW-Authenticate** header, recommending the client send an **Authorization** header. The two scenarios are shown in the following **curl** commands.

```
C:\>curl -v http://localhost:8080/basicauth
*   Trying 127.0.0.1:8080...
* Connected to localhost (127.0.0.1) port 8080 (#0)
> GET /basicauth HTTP/1.1
> Host: localhost:8080
> User-Agent: curl/7.83.1
> Accept: */*
>
* Mark bundle as not supporting multiuse
< HTTP/1.1 401 Unauthorized
```

```
< Www-Authenticate: Basic Realm="Access Server"
< Date: Thu, 29 Dec 2022 18:05:08 GMT
< Content-Length: 0
<
* Connection #0 to host localhost left intact
```

In the next request, the browser should honor the **Www-Authenticate** header and send the base64 encoded user name and password as part of the **Authorization** header.

```
C:\>curl -v http://localhost:8080/basicauth -u "jdoe:password"
*   Trying 127.0.0.1:8080...
* Connected to localhost (127.0.0.1) port 8080 (#0)
* Server auth using Basic with user 'jdoe'
> GET /basicauth HTTP/1.1
> Host: localhost:8080
> Authorization: Basic amRvZTpwYXNzd29yZA==
> User-Agent: curl/7.83.1
> Accept: */*
>
* Mark bundle as not supporting multiuse
< HTTP/1.1 200 OK
< Date: Thu, 29 Dec 2022 18:08:34 GMT
< Content-Length: 24
< Content-Type: text/plain; charset=utf-8
<
User jdoe authenticated.* Connection #0 to host localhost left intact
```

Now, the user **jdoe** is authenticated. In a browser session, this username and password will be cached and will be sent in all sessions to the server. Authentication shall be carried out with every request. Basic authentication is not the only authentication method, there are other methods like Bearer, Digest, HOBA, and so on.[10]

10 A complete list of all supported authentication types prescribed by IANA can be found at: **https://www.iana.org/assignments/http-authschemes/http-authschemes.xhtml**

Limitations

Since HTTP headers are used for authentication here, these are known as header-based authentication. This authentication is helpful for network communication devices like proxies and servers, as most clients and browsers can understand the protocol.

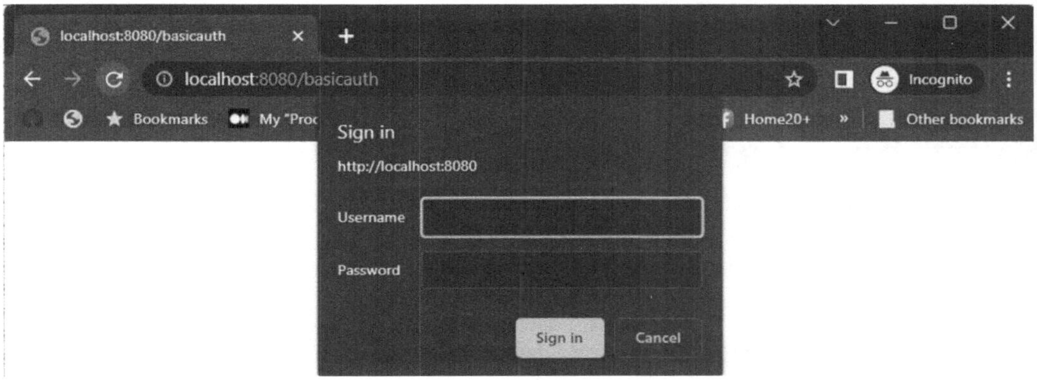

***Figure 1.11**: Basic authentication UI in Chrome. The authentication challenge is shown even before any parts of the page are shown*

However, the default behavior of the clients can be lacking. Firstly, they may not gel well with the application user interfaces.

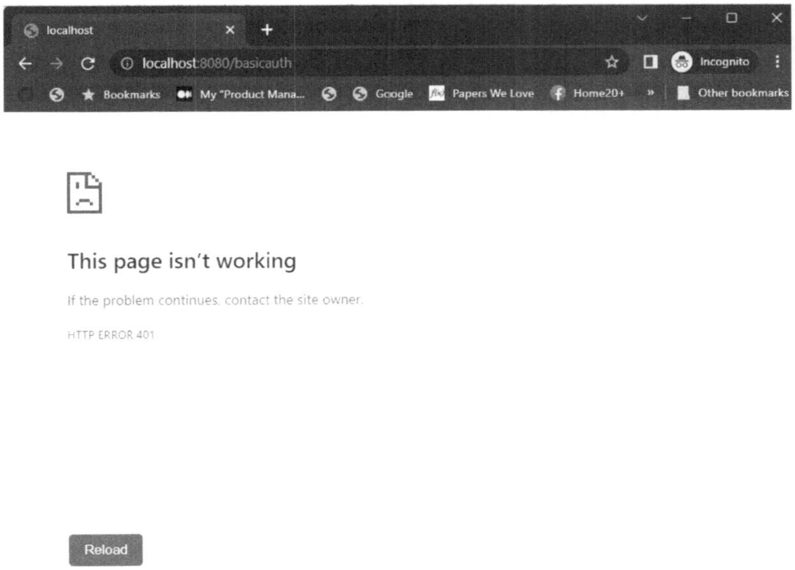

***Figure 1.12**: The default response of authentication failure. The response may not match the application user interface*

Secondly, this type of authentication requires every request to be validated. If the validation is to be carried out at a remote federated authentication server, it can slow down the server response time. However, some authentication schemes like the Bearer tokens[11] can be very fast if the bearer tokens can be locally validated without contacting the authentication servers. We shall review some of these in later chapters. Lastly, the password has to be stored and presented in clear text. When we discuss encryption, we will see how to store passwords safely. The examples are oversimplified to introduce the concepts of authentication. Using these in actual production environments is discouraged.

Form-based authentication

Form-based authentication is not a scheme from the HTTP specification but a crafty technique of utilizing HTTP cookies, session management, and HTML forms to make authentication UI work in conjunction with the application UI. *Figure* 1.13 outlines the authentication scheme.

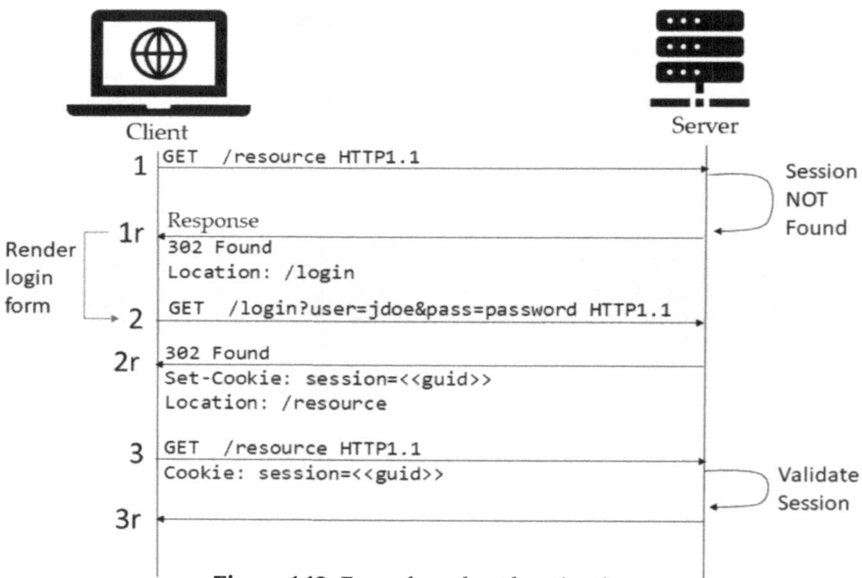

***Figure 1.13**: Form-based authentication*

The code block has two parts.

- An authentication guard that verifies the existence of a valid authenticated session and redirects to the **`/login`** page to authenticate the user.

11 Bearer tokens are authorization headers with the syntax **`Authorization: Bearer <<token>>`**. Some bearer tokens are signed and can be locally validated without contacting an authentication server.

```
  http.HandleFunc("/resource", func(w http.ResponseWriter, req
*http.Request) {
    if cookie, err := req.Cookie("session"); err != nil {
      w.Header().Add("Location", "/login")
      w.WriteHeader(http.StatusFound)
    } else {
      uid := cookie.Value
      user := smap[uid]
      if user != "" {
        str := fmt.Sprintf("User %s authenticated.", user)
        log.Default().Printf("Session %s found. Allowing user %s
to access", uid, user)
        io.WriteString(w, str)
      } else {
        w.Header().Add("Location", "/login")
        w.WriteHeader(http.StatusFound)
      }
    }
  })
```

- A **/login** page that shows the actual authentication form and sets a valid session cookie on successful authentication of the user.

```
func addFormBasedAuthHandler() {
  smap := map[string]string{}
  pmap := map[string]string{"jdoe": "password"}
  http.HandleFunc("/login", func(w http.ResponseWriter, req
*http.Request) {
    form := `<form method="GET" enctype="application/x-www-form-
urlencoded">
            <label for="user">Username:</label><br>
            <input type="text" id="user" name="user"><br>
            <label for="password">Password:</label><br>
            <input type="text" id="password" name="password">
            <input type="submit" value="Submit">
          </form>`
    user := req.FormValue("user")
    pass := req.FormValue("password")
```

```
    if user == "" || pass == "" {
      w.Header().Add("Content-Type", "text/html")
      w.Write([]byte(form))
    } else {
      if pmap[user] == pass {
        str := fmt.Sprintf("User %s authenticated.", user)
        log.Default().Print(str)
        uid := uuid.NewString()
        log.Default().Printf("No session found. Creating a new
session: %s", uid)
        http.SetCookie(w, &http.Cookie{
          Name:  "session",
          Value: uid,
        })
        smap[uid] = user
        w.Header().Add("Location", "/resource")
        w.WriteHeader(http.StatusFound)
      } else {
       str := fmt.Sprintf("User %s failed to authenticate.", user)
        log.Default().Print(str)
        w.Header().Add("Content-Type", "text/html")
        w.Write([]byte(form))
      }
    }
  })
...
}
```

The workflow is shown in the Chrome browser in *Figure 1.14*.

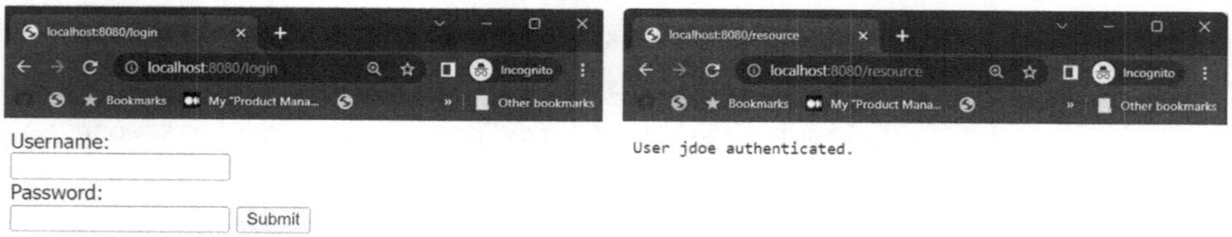

Figure 1.14: *The user interface for authentication. Username: jdoe, Password: password*

No elaborate verification of the `session` cookie is carried out. If a session cookie is found in the server, we assume the user is authenticated.

Conclusion

As an introduction to Web Authentication, we covered quite a bit of ground in the last few pages. We started with understanding the background context for the book, got an overview of the chapters and subject coverage, and moved on to learn a bit about the history of networking and web development. Toward the end, we introduced the header-based and form-based authentication schemes used in the industry today. Most readers have exposure to some form of web development and may not need that rigorous a treatment. However, relatively novice programmers should look at the suggested resources for a detailed understanding. In the next chapter, we will review some concepts of cryptography, which act as the technology foundation for authentication.

Questions

1. What is the difference between the ISO-OSI and the TCP/IP model in networking?
2. We discussed the GET command in HTTP in some detail in the book. Are there other HTTP commands supported? Why are they used?
3. What are credentials in authentication? How are they different from tokens or tickets?
4. What is header-based authentication in HTTP? What are some of the advantages and limitations of using header-based authentication?
5. Implement the example for Basic Authentication using Digest Authentication.

CHAPTER 2
Fundamentals of Cryptography

Introduction

In the previous chapter, we said web architectures are essentially unsecured for any practical business application. Maybe not in those clear terms, but quite close. We learned that the internet traffic travels to every device in the network, it does not have any privacy protection, and anyone can tap the wire and view all the exchange of traffic in the network. We mentioned that HTTP session management happens with cookies. Cookies flow over the wire like other network traffic. Hence, anyone tapping the wire can see them. The development in cryptography in the 70s to 90s led to finding some principles that can address these issues while keeping the underlying architecture simple. Unfortunately, cryptography is a complex subject, involves higher-level mathematics, and requires a steady focus to understand the nuances thoroughly. This chapter will only scratch the surface and highlight the principles of cryptographic operations. We will leave the details to the discerning readers to study other works on these subjects. We will provide a list of Reference Books toward the end of this chapter.

Security by Obscurity

Think of a lock box where you are hiding your secret document. You have two options: you hide the lockbox so that no one can ever find it, or you can keep the box in public but keep the combination secret code only available to trusted people. The combination system is foolproof; no one can open the lockbox unless she has the secret code. The first system will be a security system by obscurity. The security by obscurity is not reliable as there is always one person to whom the system is not obscure, for example the creator of the system knows the algorithm and can potentially access the documents. There is no test of strength of the security system as such systems may not have been subjected to formal cryptoanalysis. It is not scaleable to find a full proof secure algorithm for every user or implementation. We are interested in the second kind of systems here. The algorithms of cryptography should be known to everyone. The security of the system only relies on a key of binary data. Experts have analyzed the algorithms to ensure they cannot be intruded on in finite time and effort when keys are not available. Hence, the creator does not get any advantage with such a system.

Structure

In this chapter, we will cover the following topics:

- Message consistency
- Symmetric cryptography
- Password safety
- Asymmetric cryptography
- Digital signing
- Digital certificates
- Digital signing for authentication

Message Consistency

Let us say Alice wants to send some information to Bob[1] over the internet (refer to *Figure 2.1*). The internet has various communication devices that break the data into multiple electronic packets. Finally, the message that Bob gets is an aggregation of these electronic packets. Bob wants to know if he received what Alice wanted to send.

---

1 Alice, Bob, Carol, and so on, are standard actors in cryptographic protocol discussions in most texts. Some names have special meanings like Eve is an eavesdropper, Mallory is a malicious or man-in-the-middle user, Trent is a trusted advocate, and so on.

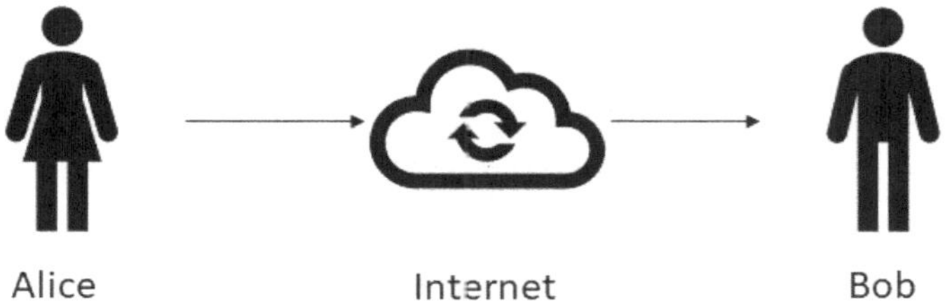

***Figure 2.1**: Alice is sending information to Bob. How can Bob be sure that he received the message Alice intended to send?*

Here is a possible scheme they adopt:

1. Alice creates a web page.
2. She lists the files that she wants Bob to download.
3. Against each of the files, she shows a CRC-32[2] value of the file.
4. Bob downloads the file.
5. He computes the CRC-32. If he gets the same value as Alice has stated on her website, Bob is sure he has received the correct file. There are no transmission errors.

A Cyclic Redundancy Check (CRC) is derived from the data to ensure the received data is transmitted properly. It determines the consistency of data. It is an electronic summary of the data, also known as the **digest**. Cryptographic digests have the following properties:

- From a digest, one should not be able to guess the message that produced it.
- If a message (M1) led to a digest (D1), finding a message M2 that will have the same digest should be computationally intractable.
- A small change in the message should produce a different digest.
- Using cryptographic **hash functions**, we can fulfill the digest properties. Some of the well-known hash functions are MD5, SHA-1, SHA-256, SHA-3, and so on.

```
C:\work\HOWA\chapter-2>openssl dgst -md5
The quick brown fox jumps over the lazy dog
```

2 Lammert Bies provides a website with an explanation of Cyclic Redundancy Check (CRC) and its application in identifying transmission losses in electronic communications. **https://www.lammertbies.nl/comm/info/crc-calculation**

```
(stdin)= 37c4b87edffc5d198ff5a185cee7ee09
C:\work\HOWA\chapter-2>openssl dgst -sha1
The quick brown fox jumps over the lazy dog
(stdin)= be417768b5c3c5c1d9bcb2e7c119196dd76b5570
C:\work\HOWA\chapter-2>openssl dgst -sha256
The quick brown fox jumps over the lazy dog
(stdin)=
c03905fcdab297513a620ec81ed46ca44ddb62d41cbbd83eb4a5a3592be26a69
```

MD-5, SHA-1, and SHA-256 generated hash values of 128-bit, 160-bit, and 256-bit respectively. Finding another message with the same hash value will be harder in the case of a 256-bit hash than a 128-bit hash function.

```
C:\work\HOWA\chapter-2>openssl dgst -md5
1234567890
(stdin)= 7c12772809c1c0c3deda6103b10fdfa0
C:\work\HOWA\chapter-2>openssl dgst -md5
1234567891
(stdin)= beac9407dc999ae35ba5e6851e28d7c5
```

While there is just a one-bit change in the message, the MD5 hash values for both messages are substantially different. This property is true for other hash functions as well. Ron Rivest developed MD5 at RSA, while scientists at the National Security Agency developed Secured Hash Algorithm (SHA-1). They had fixed bit length outputs, 128 and 160-bit, respectively. Later incarnations of SHA, like SHA-2 and SHA-3, can output 224, 256, 384, and 512-bit. After scientists at Google managed a birthday attack[3] (finding another message with the same digest as SHA-1), an algorithm that produces a 256-bit or higher strength output is generally considered safe. If the input message range is small, a malicious actor can always map the input messages to the digest values and store them. For example, if the cash transfer amount is the message, the malicious actor can precompute the hash from one to a hundred thousand. Using this kind of mapping, he can find the input message. A bonafide user can append a fixed length of random bytes to the input messages and increase the input message range. Thus, avoid these known plain text attacks.

Protection

Is there any information protection achieved with message consistency? The internet is full of malicious actors; some passively eavesdrop on the

3 **https://shattered.io/** the first full attack on a SHA-1 documents in 2017. NIST has discouraged the use of SHA-1 since 2011.

communication channel and look at the message. These kinds of actors can affect the privacy of the message, like Eve. The actor, like Mallory, is in line with communication and changes the message.

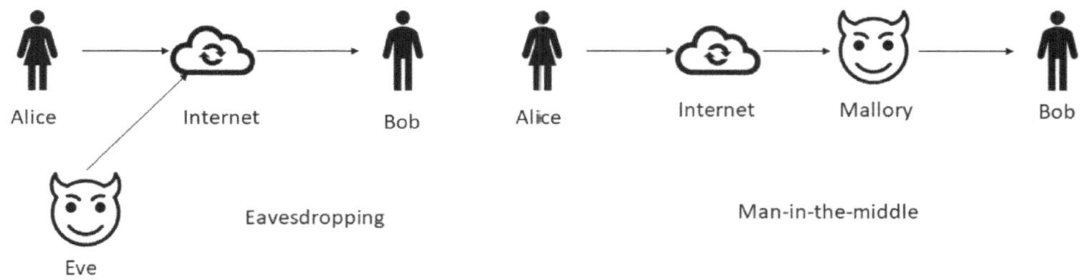

***Figure 2.2**: Eavesdropping and Man-in-the-middle*

Message consistency cannot protect against eavesdropping by design. However, there is partial protection against a message tampering attack. In the preceding example, if Mallory changes the message only, Bob will know someone has tampered with the text, and the digest is not the same as he has received from Alice. If Mallory modifies all the communication between Alice and Bob, he will change the digest value. Some people will advise sending the digest and the actual message via independent communication channels. Let us say the message is sent over the internet, while the digest communication is over SMS or email. So, spoofing one of the channels of communication shall not affect the other.

Symmetric Cryptography

In *Figure* 2.2, Eavesdropping and Man-in-the-middle, Eve and Mallory can access the whole communication. This is a breach of privacy for Alice and Bob. They decide to use the following scheme to communicate.

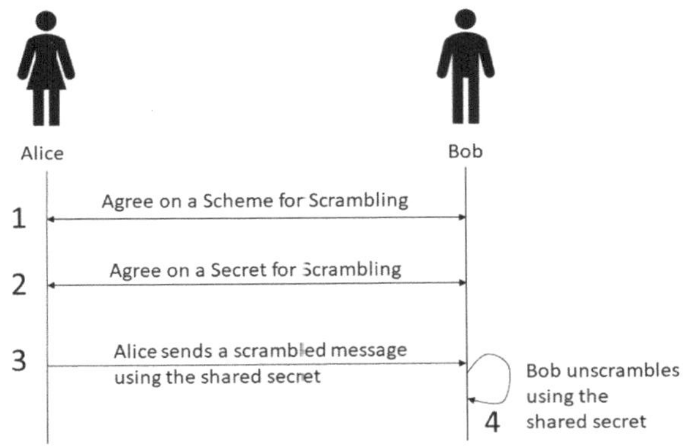

***Figure 2.3**: Symmetric Cryptography Scheme*

Let us review each step and find out the limitations they pose to communication.

1. Alice and Bob have never met. They are some nodes on the internet. There exists only one scheme that everyone uses on the internet. But it needs a key that establishes the trust between Alice and Bob.
2. Alice and Bob can never meet. A shared secret must be established between them using an out-of-band channel. Security depends on this step and can become the weakest link in the chain. The emphasis on out-of-band communication ensures Eve and Mallory listen to the main communication channel and cannot get access to the key.
3. Eve and Mallory see the scrambled message of the communication, but they cannot understand the message. This scrambled message is the cipher text, while the original message is the plaintext.
4. Bob uses the key to extract the information Alice has sent him. Since Alice has the key, only Alice and no one else has sent the message.

In the previous discussion, we used the word scramble in the most generic sense. If you have data that generates an output of n-bits, every bit pattern is equally likely unless you have the key with you. In the perfect cryptography world, all the values are possible. Cryptographic functions have a randomization property. If you want to reverse the results of cryptography, like decrypt or verify the cipher, you will need the key. That is why they are called **one-way functions**. In the presence of the key, computations can be carried out and cipher text can be obtained. In the absence of the key, the cipher text is all random values with no meaningful data. The bigger the random cipher data, the harder it is to guess the plain text from the cipher text. Since cryptography has a randomization effect, using a random algorithm with random steps does not necessarily produce the desirable randomness[4]. Hence, only use the algorithms that are cryptographically secured and mathematically established by experts.

While steps 3 and 4 in *Figure* 2.3 Symmetric Cryptography Scheme are part of the same scheme, they offer two distinct benefits.

- Step 3 is about **encryption**, which ensures the information is delivered only to the intended audience.
- Step 4 is about **decryption**, which helps Bob confirm the data came from Alice and has not been tampered with and that no one else other than he has seen the message.

4 Donald E. Knuth, The art of computer programming, volume 2.

Encryption

Here are a few misconceptions about symmetric cryptography that should be clarified.

- **An encryption operation generates the same number of bytes as the input**: Encryption scrambles the data and adds randomness to the information. Hence, most cipher texts are longer than the plaintext. Knowing this problem, someone may compress the data before encrypting to overcome this data bloat.
- **Encryption and decryption are the same algorithms**: Symmetric cryptography only requires the encryption and decryption operation to have the same key (K). The underlying algorithm for encryption and decryption can be completely different.

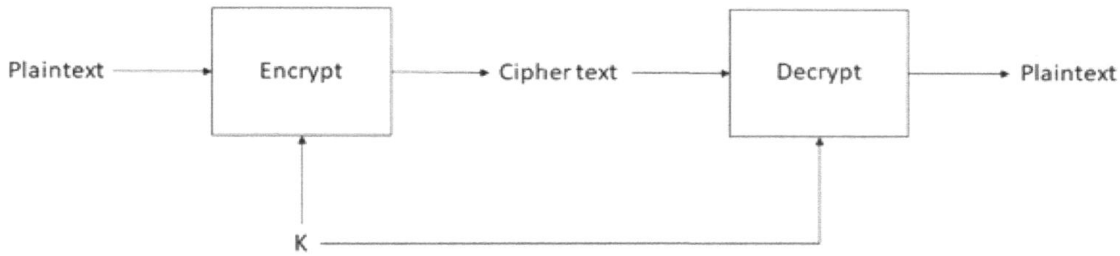

Figure 2.4: *Encryption and Decryption using symmetric cryptography*

We will use Advanced Encryption Standard (AES) as an example of an encryption method. AES can have 128, 192, and 256-bit key strengths. The initialization vector (IV) ensures the encryption output in different iterations does not generate the same result. In our example, we use the 128-bit version with the hex value of the text **`password (70617373776F7264)`** as the key.

```
C:\work\HOWA\chapter-2>openssl.exe
OpenSSL> enc -e -aes128 -K 70617373776F7264 -iv 0 -a -p
hex string is too short, padding with zero bytes to length
hex string is too short, padding with zero bytes to length
salt=C0C7FFFF00000000
key=70617373776F72640000000000000000
iv =00000000000000000000000000000000
The quick brown fox jumps over the lazy dog
zF/d9iGuL0gkG7gO3yQilEJH60X5xqwDmgmFytffJSrFe+ftHxZDyFCXfGLoV1VE
OpenSSL> enc -d -aes128 -a -K 70617373776F7264 -iv 0
```

```
hex string is too short, padding with zero bytes to length
hex string is too short, padding with zero bytes to length
zF/d9iGuL0gkG7gO3yQilEJH60X5xqwDmgmFytffJSrFe+ftHxZDyFCXfGLoV1VE
The quick brown fox jumps over the lazy dog
```

Keeping the same key by changing the IV, we get a different encryption output for the same input.

```
OpenSSL> enc -e -aes128 -K 70617373776F7264 -iv 1 -a -p
…
iv =10000000000000000000000000000000
The quick brown fox jumps over the lazy dog
4JDT9sLBZg5rKorlVqcZcxM+QT0hLiXpSs+67vkmKU/XSlCrD07wj04fIT5mgPEm
```

Using passwords as keys make the keys vulnerable to brute force attacks and hence seldom used. Keys derivation functions like Password-Based Key Derivation Function 2 (PBKDF2) are used extensively for these. OpenSSL provides PBKDF2 support to derive the key and IV from a password and should be preferred over directly supplying the key and IV.

```
OpenSSL> enc -e -aes128 -pbkdf2 -k password -a -p
salt=32FC211FC15C5D9E
key=E526355DF45714AC7586DF8B256533F0
iv =5D75D9AE602B29BC5207961AF8DCC9AD
The quick brown fox jumps over the lazy dog
U2FsdGVkX18y/CEfwVxdniJputAbFI+xBd/SKXq9ZlXF2iiQIA48lHVoLjq8pjvn
dskCjH6GnTVtviG/hd+bgg==
```

As seen here, the decryption operation generates the same key and IV. Thus, the intended decryption results are achieved.

```
OpenSSL> enc -d -aes128 -pbkdf2 -k password -a -p
U2FsdGVkX18y/CEfwVxdniJputAbFI+xBd/SKXq9ZlXF2iiQIA48lHVoLjq8pjvn
dskCjH6GnTVtviG/hd+bgg==
salt=32FC211FC15C5D9E
key=E526355DF45714AC7586DF8B256533F0
iv =5D75D9AE602B29BC5207961AF8DCC9AD
The quick brown fox jumps over the lazy dog
```

We will discuss more on PBKDF2 in the subsequent sections when we review passwords.

Signing

A signature to be valid should have the following properties[5]:

- **The signature is authentic.** The signature convinces the document's recipient that the signer deliberately signed the document.
- **The signature is unforgeable.** The signature is proof that the signer, and no one else, deliberately signed the document.
- **The signature is not reusable.** The signature is part of the document; an unscrupulous person cannot move the signature to a different document.
- **The signed document is unalterable.** Once the document is signed, it cannot be altered.
- **The signature cannot be repudiated.** The signature and the document are physical things. The signer cannot later claim that he or she did not sign it.

These accepted norms are valid for paper-based as well as electronic signatures. Let us build a document signing infrastructure that has the properties mentioned above.

- Only Alice and Bob know the shared secret. When the message comes from Alice, Bob can verify it.
- A hash algorithm can establish the authenticity of a message.
- A hash is unique to a message and cannot validate a different message.
- Once a hash is generated for a message, it gets tied to the message content. Any change in the message content shall fail validation.
- If we can use Alice's key in the hashing process, her providing the key is recorded.

Hashed Message Authentication Code (HMAC)[6] incorporates a user key in the hashing process and is a signing algorithm. The HMAC of the message is:

$$\mathrm{HMAC}(M) = H(K_1 + H(K_2 + M)) \quad \textit{where } K_1 = K \textit{ xor } B_{out} \textit{ and } K_2 = K \textit{ xor } B_{in}$$

5 Reproduced verbatim from Bruce Schneier, Applied Cryptography: Protocols, Algorithms, and Source Code in C, John Wiley & Sons (US) © 1996

6 HMAC can be computed with a variety of hash functions. The RFC 6234 US Secure Hash Algorithms provides a list of hash algorithms that are approved as per Federal Information Processing Standards (FIPS).

B_{in} *and* B_{out} are predefined byte arrays of fixed byte values. The symbol (+) is used for text concatenation. H is the hash function, for example, with HMAC-SHA1 it will be the SHA1 function. Here is an OpenSSL example:

```
OpenSSL> dgst -sha1 -hmac "password"
The quick brown fox jumps over the lazy dog
(stdin)= ac20b116a2aceeeed7447b8c4c775bfedb4c7d39
```

The output is a 20-bytes output as expected of an SHA-1 computation.

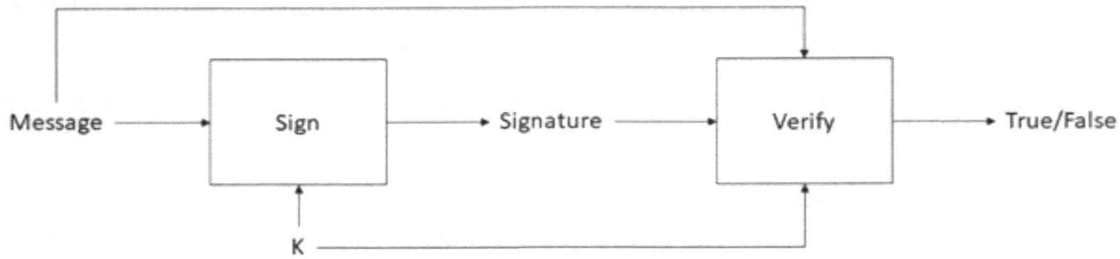

***Figure 2.5**: Sign and verify using symmetric cryptography*

has the same method for signing and verifying.

1. Alice sends the message (M), HMAC_SHA1(K,M), as a digest (D) to Bob.
2. Bob receives the message (M) and computes HMAC_SHA1(K,M'), and gets the digest value of (D').
3. If D = D', Bob knows the message M = M'; It can also confirm the message is from Alice.

Just like encryption, signing and verification do not have to be the same algorithm. However, both processes must use the same key. Is this scheme scalable? Let us add Carol and Dave to the communication. *Figure* 2.6 shows this situation.

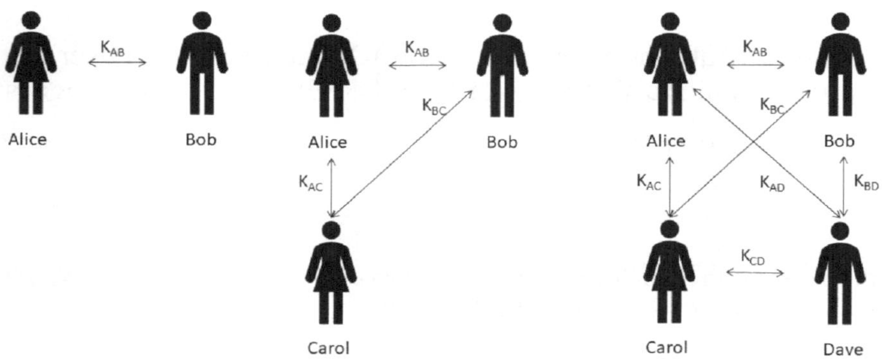

***Figure 2.6**: No of keys required is $O(n^2)$ when n is the number of people*

An alternative is to use a trusted attorney, Trent.

1. Alice will sign the message with her shared secret with Trent and send it to Trent.
2. Trent will certify that the message is from Alice, attach his certification information by signing it with Bob's shared key, and send it to Bob with the actual message.
3. Trent must repeat step 2 for Carol and Dave. So effectively, there is no broadcast, but the responsibility is transferred to Trent.

The scheme is shown in *Figure* 2.7.

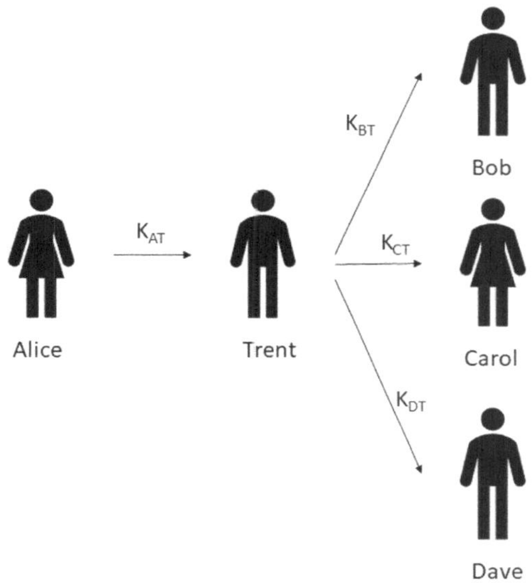

***Figure* 2.7**: *Communication using a trusted attorney. The number of keys is now O(n), but the scheme is very complex*

Symmetric cryptography has encryption as well as signing capabilities. However, the following are use cases that need a more effective solution.

1. In Step 2 of *Figure* 2.3, Symmetric Cryptography Scheme, an out-of-band communication channel was used for symmetric key exchange.
2. There is no easy mechanism to broadcast a message. Involving a trusted third party in every communication is a significant overhead.

With these limitations, symmetric cryptography is still preferred for its speed and for establishing a two-party trust; some well-known authentication schemes like symmetric keys-based OTP[7] or TOTP[8] are used in Google Authenticator.

Password Safety

HMAC_SHA1 is a great pseudo-random function. Some random number systems utilize truncated bits for applications like OTP generation[9]. Can we use it to generate random numbers of arbitrary lengths? In the section Encryption in Symmetric Cryptography, we used the ASCII values of the password to fill in the key. In the AES-128-bit example, we could have used a 20-byte key, but we padded the 12 bytes of zeros because *password* has only eight characters. Infusing randomness in passwords is hard. People coin passwords from words or names with some variability introduced with numbers and ASCII printable characters. It is hard to create uniform variability and randomness with them. Key derivation functions take the password as input and produce an arbitrary-length pseudo-random key. **PBKDF2** is a well-researched algorithm in the industry. It can utilize some keyed hash algorithms like HMAC_SHA1 to generate keys of arbitrary length. Readers interested in the details can find them in the reference text. We will not delve deeper into the exact algorithm. Here is a rough outline.

- A keyed hash is computed for a random value with the password as a key.
- A hash is further calculated for the output of the previous step while supplying the password as the key.
- The algorithm uses **xor** to aggregate all the computed hash values.

Sometimes the number of iterations used for **PBKDF2** is kept in the tens of thousands. Using iterations will slow down the computation and reduce the possibility of a brute-force attack. So far, we have just looked at deriving keys from passwords for better randomness. Ultimately, passwords are to be stored on the server for later comparison. In *Chapter 1, Introduction to Web Authentication*, Basic Authentication example, we saved the password of **jdoe** in the code. One can instead store the derived key. When someone provides the password, the derived key can be computed and compared with the stored value.

7 RFC 4226, **https://www.ietf.org/rfc/rfc4226.txt**

8 RFC 6238, **https://www.ietf.org/rfc/rfc6238.txt**

9 RFC 4226, **https://www.ietf.org/rfc/rfc4226.txt**

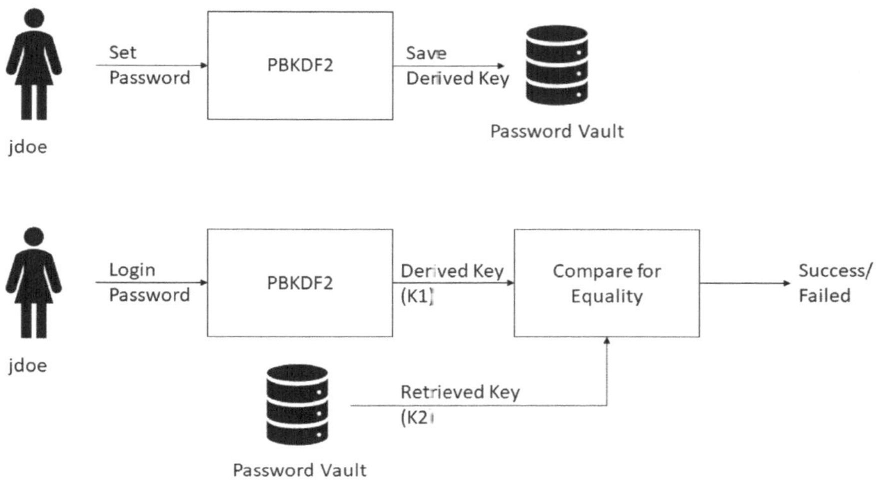

***Figure 2.8**: Password scheme used for login*

We provide a code snippet for the preceding scheme in the go language.

```
C:\work\HOWA\chapter-2>go run ./pbkdf.go password
1e69ed9b36e1a4231bb8d273090790d510f1404e
```

The relevant code for **pbdfk.go** is given here:

```
func main() {
  dk := pbkdf2.Key([]byte(os.Args[1]), []byte("12345678"), 4096, 20,
sha1.New)
  encodedString := hex.EncodeToString(dk)
  println(encodedString)
}
```

The derived key is computed with **"12345678"** as salt, **4096** as iterations, **HMAC_SHA1** as pseudo-random function, and **20** bytes key length. We take the hex dump of the derived key and store it in the **password.json** file.

```
{
 "jdoe":"1e69ed9b36e1a4231bb8d273090790d510f1404e"
}
```

We compare the derived keys now in the basic authentication code. The same can be seen in the **server.go** file.

```
func addBasicAuthHandler() {
  var pmap map[string]string
  if jsonFile, err := os.Open("password.json"); err == nil {
```

```
    byteValue, _ := ioutil.ReadAll(jsonFile)
    json.Unmarshal([]byte(byteValue), &pmap)
    log.Default().Print(pmap)
  } else {
    log.Fatal(err)
  }
  http.HandleFunc("/basicauth",func(w http.ResponseWriter,req *http.
Request) {
    if u, p, ok := req.BasicAuth(); ok {
      dk := hex.EncodeToString(
 pbkdf2.Key([]byte(p), []byte("12345678"), 4096, 20, sha1.New))
   if pmap[u] == dk {
      …
 })
}
```

You can run the code and access the website **http://localhost:8080/basicauth** and provide **`jdoe`** and **`password`** as username and password at the prompt. The server log is provided here:

```
C:\work\HOWA\chapter-2>go run ./server.go
2023/01/22 14:46:02 map[jdoe:1e69ed9b36e1a4231bb8d273090790d510f1404e]
2023/01/22 14:46:40 Basic authentication needed.
2023/01/22 14:46:53 User jdoe authenticated.
```

Printing the password vault in the sample code is for quick debugging and learning. Do not print passwords or derivatives to any output stream like a file, log, or console. Passwords are inherently unsafe. More so because they are hard to remember. When the same password is used on multiple websites, compromising the password on one website can make all other websites vulnerable. Hence, it is recommended to use some password policies. Here are some common ones:

- Passwords should have a minimum length (8 is commonly preferred).
- They should contain a combination of uppercase, lowercase, and numerals.
- They should contain non-English or punctuation characters like (#!~$= and so on).
- A user must change the password every X (30 commonly suggested) day.

- The new password should not match any of the Y (5 commonly suggested) previously set passwords.
- The password should not be saved on the disk or left in the memory in cleartext. Since strings are immutable in many programming languages, use byte arrays or streams while handling passwords.
- Always cover the keypad while typing passwords to avoid the surveillance cameras picking up the key sequences.
- Passwords should not be shown on the screen while typing.

In the later chapters, we will look at other means of authentication. Although passwordless authentication is becoming the new focus for many authentication providers, the password remains the most used authentication mechanism due to its reach and adoption.

Asymmetric Cryptography

Over the last few pages, Alice can send Bob a secret message. Bob can verify if Alice initiated the communication. This all happened with the assumption that Alice and Bob share a secret. However, we have not addressed how Alice and Bob securely shared the secret. This section can solve such needs. Asymmetric cryptography is about two keys. Data encoded with one can be decoded by the other. One of the keys is kept secret from the world, known as the private key. The other is part of a directory available to the whole world as the public key. Let us assume Alice and Bob have such keys assigned to them. K_{AV} is the private key of Alice and K_{AP} is the public key.

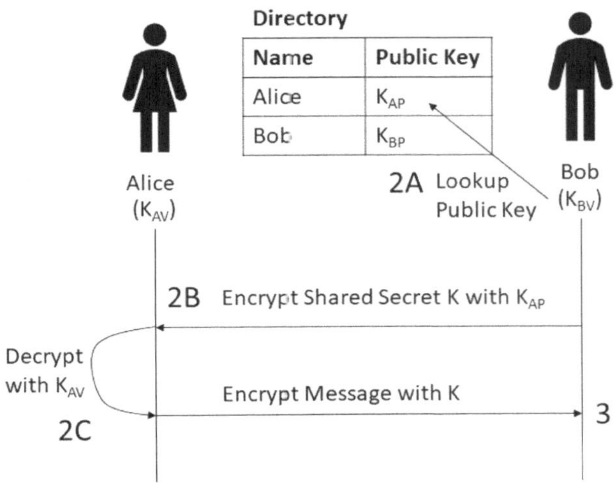

Figure 2.9: *Key exchange using asymmetric cryptography*

In Step 2 of *Figure* 2.3, Symmetric Cryptography Scheme:

1. Bob obtains the public key of Alice (K_{AP}).
2. He generates a symmetric key (K) of sufficient bit strength that they can use for encrypting messages. He encrypts the K with the public key of Alice (K_{AP}).
3. Alice uses her private key (K_{AV}) to decrypt the message. Since Alice has access to the private key, only Alice and no one else can access the symmetric key.
3. Alice uses the symmetric key (K) to encrypt the message and send it to Bob.

Step 2 is known as the key exchange protocol. There are many such protocols established. However, Diffie-Hellman is one of the oldest and most revered schemes. Diffie and Hellman are considered the inventors of modern asymmetric cryptography. We will continue the discussion on the protocol in the next chapter when we review transport layer security. With a key exchange protocol, Eve and Mallory cannot access the symmetric key. Some of the questions are still unanswered:

- Can a public directory be trusted when it is open to updating by everyone?
- Did Alice update her public key in the directory? If Mallory updates a spurious key as Alice's public key, Alice cannot be part of any secured transaction. It will be a denial of service.

Asymmetric encryption is open to known plaintext attacks because the public key is available to everyone. Assume the case of encrypting money transfer amounts. Malicious user Mallory will consider all the numbers from 1 to 100000 and generate the cipher text using the public key. Since the plaintext space is limited, he can maintain a lookup for cipher text to plaintext. Effectively, he can decode the message without decrypting it. In the case of asymmetric encryption, adding a random nonce makes the plaintext unique. The receiving party removes the nonce and uses the relevant information.

There are many asymmetric cryptography algorithms. Some notable ones are:

- RSA is by far one of the most popular and the oldest. It draws the mathematical principles from the factorization of a large number into two prime factors.
- Elliptic curve cryptography (ECC) is modern. It needs fewer bits for the same key strength as RSA. The infeasibility of finding discrete logarithms on a random elliptic curve element is the basis of such a scheme.

The mathematics in both cases is complex. There are code libraries available to compute these algorithms. Hence, we will not delve into the algorithms but use them qualitatively to meet our authentication needs.

Digital Signing

In *Figure* 2.9, Key exchange using asymmetric cryptography, we used the public key to encode the data. What will happen if we use the private key to encode the message? Let us look at the following workflow.

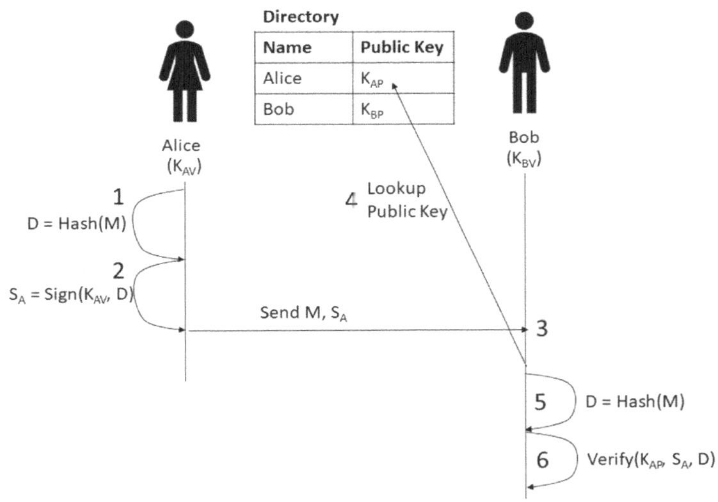

***Figure 2.10**: Signing using asymmetric cryptography*

1. Alice creates a digest of the message.
2. She signs the message using her private key.
3. She sends the message and the signature to Bob.
4. Bob, for that matter, anyone can obtain Alice's public key from the directory.
5. He computes the message digest.
6. Then, he can verify the signature and the digest using Alice's public key. Bob ensures Alice generated the message and no one has tampered with the message in the exchange.

Let us apply the principles of signing on the message.

1. **The signature is authentic.** The public key verifies the message and ensures it came from Alice.

2. **The signature is unforgeable.** The mathematics behind cryptography ensures a unique byte pattern of a message can generate a specific signature.
3. **The signature is not reusable.** The signature is only valid for the same digital byte pattern. It cannot match a message of a different byte pattern.
4. **The signed document is unalterable.** Once signed, any changes to the document will mean the byte pattern is not the same. Hence, the signature is not valid.
5. **The signature cannot be repudiated.** Only Alice has a private key. Any digital signature generated using her private key is with her consent.

In this communication, two people exchange information. If we extend the communication to more people, Alice does not need additional activities. She needs to send the same message and signature to another person. In short, this addresses the issue of broadcasting which we could not address in symmetric key signing. Symmetric key cryptography is fast and preferred for encryption. However, asymmetric key cryptography has a natural benefit in signing. Since the digest of the message is signed, there is no significant performance penalty. Asymmetric cryptography is ideal for key exchange and signing where the message is relatively short. If the plaintext space is small, concatenating a timestamp to the plaintext can make the message unique. Without a timestamp, a malicious actor can replay an older signed message, failing the non-repudiation claims of digital signing.

Just like encryption, signing with asymmetric cryptography utilizes various algorithms. Some popular ones are RSA, Digital Signing Algorithm (DSA), and Elliptic Cryptography Digital Signing Algorithm (ECDSA). RSA signing algorithms are very similar to the RSA encryption algorithm. You will need to use the private key instead of the public key. The verification process is like the signing process. DSA, though based on prime number factorization, is different from RSA. The signing and verification steps are also different algorithms in DSA. ECDSA is a modified version of DSA with elliptic cryptography. Is there a common understanding of the security of these algorithms on the basis of their key strength? This table can give some ideas[10].

10 *Table* 2, Recommendation for Key Management: Part 1 – General, NIST Special Publication 800-57 Part 1 Revision 5.

Security Strength	Symmetric Key Algorithms	FFC (DSA, DH, MQV)	IFC (RSA)	ECC (ECDSA, EdDSA, DH, MQV)
112	3TDEA	L = 2048 N = 224	*k* = 2048	*f* = 224-255
128	AES-128	L = 3072 N = 256	*k* = 3072	*f* = 256-383
192	AES-192	L = 7680 N = 384	*k* = 7680	*f* = 384-511
256	AES-256	L = 15360 N = 512	*k* = 15360	*f* = 512+

Table 2.1: *Equivalence of security strength across algorithms for various key sizes*

The directory of public keys has no custodian. Anyone can read and write into it. While reading is fine, writing and updating by a malicious actor can cause a denial of services. We entrust Trent to maintain the public keys directory. Trent maintains another column in the database having all the public keys signed with his private key.

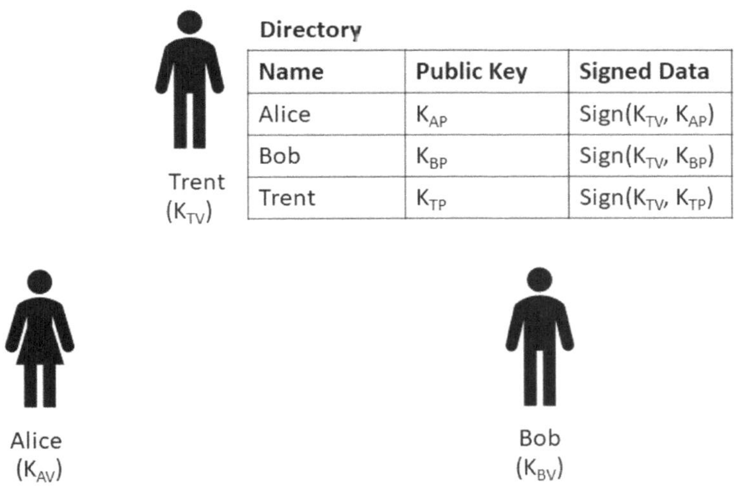

Figure 2.11: *Trent acting as a certifying authority*

Trent is acting as a certifying authority (CA). The CA signs all public keys of the directory using his private key. When Bob looks up Alice's public key, he should verify if Alice's public key is signed using the private key of Trent (CA). The last entry in the directory is Trent's public key, signed by his private key; it is called self-signing.

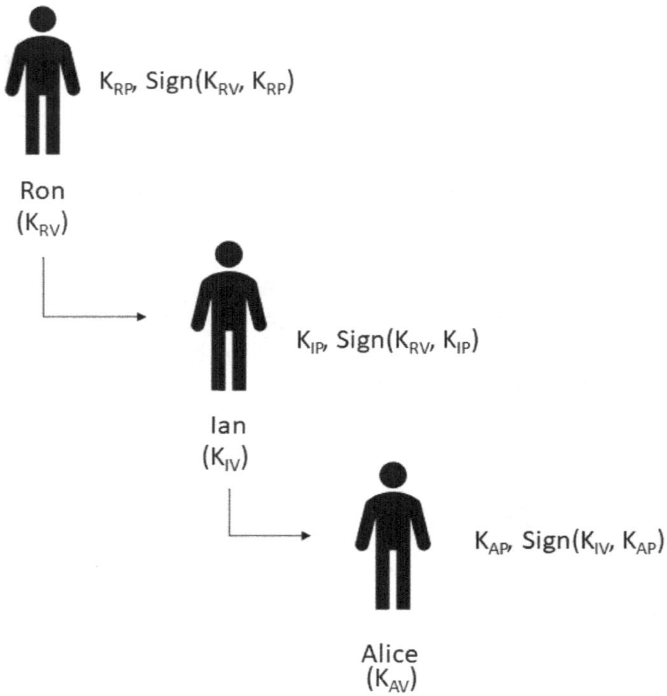

***Figure 2.12**: The Hierarchy of CAs and the chain of trust*

In *Figure* 2.12, Ron is the root CA. His public key is self-signed. Ian is an intermediate CA. Ron's private key signs Ian's public key. In turn, the intermediate CA (Ian) signs Alice's public key. To trust Alice, you must trust Ron and Ian. Hence, Ron, Ian, and Alice establish the complete trust chain. The next logical question is how will the signed public keys be shared. The digital certificates tried to address some of those needs.

Digital Certificates

International Telecom Union (ITU) was standardizing the concept of a directory under a collection of standards called X.500. One such standard is X.509. X.509 is about linking identity with a public key. Alternatively, it is also known as digital certificates. The standard came into existence in the late 1980s. Hence, X.509

certificates are ASN.1 based. The final presentation can be in PEM (Base64 ASCII) or binary DER format. With such a long history of technology, the tools are well-developed for these formats. We will use **OpenSSL** to create and manipulate x509 certificates in this chapter. Windows users can use **certutil**, or Java users can use **keytool** for certificate management functions. So far, we have mentioned certificates contain the public key of the asymmetric cryptographic algorithm. That is just the tip of the iceberg. Certificates can contain lots of additional metadata as complex ticket formats. The complete certificate and certificate extension profiles are available in RFC 5280[11].

Certificate Profile

Certificates are a collection of objects. We will mention only a few here for a conceptual understanding; an elaborate treatment is beyond the scope of this book.

- **Algorithm**: We have talked about three different algorithms used for signing. Several hash algorithms and varying bit strengths used hash generation. The certificate mentions algorithm details to remove ambiguities in working with them.
- **Subject:** A distinguished name (**DN**) in a certificate uniquely defines the subject of a certificate. The DNs can have hierarchies like common name (**CN**), organization (**O**), organization unit (**OU**), country (**C**), and so on. The association of certificates with X.500 directories is the driver for such subject names. **SubjectAlternateName** can be used to identify a subject. The format of this object can be any string, making it a very flexible entity for subject nomenclature.
- **Subject Public Key:** The certificate has an algorithm-specific public key associated with the certificate.
- **Issuer:** The subject of the CA that has signed the certificate.
- **Validity:** CA issues a certificate for a limited validity period. Time attributes **notBefore** and **notAfter** in the certificate provide the validity period.
- **Serial Number**: A non-negative integer that is unique to every certificate for a specific CA.
- **Signature Value:** A bit string that has signed the certificate using the private key of the CA.

11 **https://www.ietf.org/rfc/rfc5280.txt**

- **Revocation:** The CA can revoke the certificate before it has expired. The CA will need to publish a certificate revocation list and mention the URL in the certificate that the client can contact to collect the latest CRL information. Alternatively, if a CA implements the Online Certificate Status Protocol (OCSP), a client can query the OCSP responder if the certificate is valid.
- **Key Usage and Extended Key Usage:** Certificates are issued for a purpose. Certificates specifically issued for encryption should not be used for signing. Similarly, a TLS server certificate should not be used for TLS client authentication. These kinds of constraints can be configured through key usage and extended key usage extensions.

Issuance

For a CA to issue a certificate, the metadata and the public key should be presented in a specific format. This is called the certificate signing request (CSR). The following workflow outlines the process.

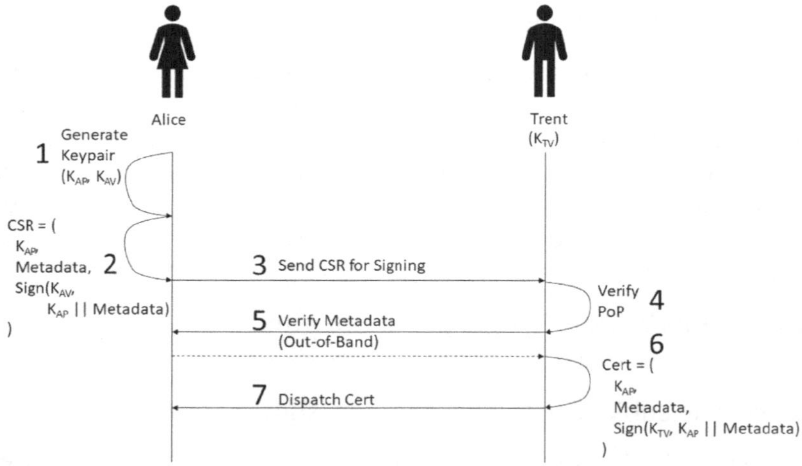

***Figure 2.13**: Certificate requisition process*

1. Alice generates a keypair using an asymmetric algorithm,
2. She creates a certificate signing request (CSR) by signing the keys and the metadata using the private key.
3. The CSR is sent to Trent (CA) for certificate issuance.
4. Trent uses the public key of the CSR to validate the signature of the CSR. It also affirms Alice is in possession of the private key. This process is known as proof of possession (PoP). PoP is achieved by self-signing.

5. Trent will verify the metadata, for example, the subject attributes. If the request is for issuing a certificate to a specific email address, Trent may send a verification email to that email address. While issuing SSL certificates, Trent will ask for a response from the DNS server.
6. Upon successful validation, Trent will create the certificate, sign it with his private key and dispatch it to Alice.

The private key never leaves Alice's computer. It is only the public key that is in transit. Validation Before using a certificate for signing or encryption, one must assert its validity. The validation process is application dependent. However, here are a few universal steps.

1. The current time must be within the certificate validity period, that is, the current time must fall within the **notBefore** and **notAfter** time.
2. To trust a CA, the CA certificate should be valid. This applies to the complete chain of roots and intermediate CAs.
3. The subject or subject's alternate name (SAN) should match the person who claims to own the certificate.

Examples

Here are some examples of certificate generation and manipulation with **OpenSSL**.

Self-Signed Certificate for CA

We create a self-signed certificate for Trent, the CA.

```
OpenSSL> req -newkey rsa:2048 -keycut trent.key -x509 -days 365 -out
trent.crt

Generating an RSA private key

...........+++++

.............+++++

writing new private key to 'trent.key'

Enter PEM pass phrase:

Verifying - Enter PEM pass phrase:

-----

You are about to be asked to enter information that will be incorporated

into your certificate request.

What you are about to enter is what is called a Distinguished Name or a
DN.
```

```
There are quite a few fields but you can leave some blank
For some fields there will be a default value,
If you enter '.', the field will be left blank.
-----
Country Name (2 letter code) [AU]:IN
State or Province Name (full name) [Some-State]:KA
Locality Name (e.g., city) []:Bangalore
Organization Name (e.g., company) [Internet Widgits Pty Ltd]:HOWA
Organizational Unit Name (e.g., section) []:CA
Common Name (e.g. server FQDN or YOUR name) []:Trent
Email Address []:trent@howa.in
```

Generating RSA Keypair and CSR

For Alice, we generate an RSA keypair as well as CSR to be signed by Trent.

```
OpenSSL> req -newkey rsa:2048 -keyout alice.key -out alice.csr
Generating an RSA private key
.........................................................................
..............................................+++++
.......................................+++++
writing new private key to 'alice.key'
Enter PEM pass phrase:
Verifying - Enter PEM pass phrase:
-----
You are about to be asked to enter information that will be incorporated
into your certificate request.
What you are about to enter is what is called a Distinguished Name or a
DN.
There are quite a few fields but you can leave some blank
For some fields there will be a default value,
If you enter '.', the field will be left blank.
-----
Country Name (2 letter code) [AU]:IN
State or Province Name (full name) [Some-State]:KA
Locality Name (e.g., city) []:Bangalore
Organization Name (e.g., company) [Internet Widgits Pty Ltd]:HOWA
```

```
Organizational Unit Name (e.g., section) []:Dev
Common Name (e.g. server FQDN or YOUR name) []:Alice
Email Address []:alice@howa.in

Please enter the following 'extra' attributes
to be sent with your certificate request
A challenge password []:Password
An optional company name []:
```

Signing the CSR with CA

We will sign the CSR generated for Alice using Trent's private key.

```
OpenSSL> x509 -req -CA trent.crt -CAkey trent.key -in alice.csr -out
alice.crt -days 365 -CAcreateserial
Signature ok
subject=C = IN, ST = KA, L = Bangalore, O = HOWA, OU = Dev, CN = Alice,
emailAddress = alice@howa.in
Getting CA Private Key
Enter pass phrase for trent.key:
```

The output will be the certificate **alice.crt**.

Viewing the Certificate

You can view the certificate with **OpenSSL**. You can also use Windows tools by clicking the certificate in **explorer**.

```
OpenSSL> x509 -text -noout -in alice.crt
Certificate:
    Data:
        Version: 1 (0x0)
        Serial Number:
            34:b9:4d:eb:e6:e2:b0:3b:d8:0d:60:b5:32:7e:2b:1c:b2:d1:70:b8
        Signature Algorithm: sha256WithRSAEncryption
        Issuer: C = IN, ST = KA, L = Bangalore, O = HOWA, OU = CA, CN =
Trent, emailAddress = trent@howa.in
        Validity
            Not Before: Jan 27 05:47:10 2023 GMT
            Not After : Jan 27 05:47:10 2024 GMT
```

```
        Subject: C = IN, ST = KA, L = Bangalore, O = HOWA, OU = Dev, CN
= Alice, emailAddress = alice@howa.in
        Subject Public Key Info:
            Public Key Algorithm: rsaEncryption
                RSA Public-Key: (2048 bit)
                Modulus:
                    00:a7:ff:dc:77:85:10:79:60:a2:93:5c:41:84:73:
                      …
                    bb:7f
                Exponent: 65537 (0x10001)
    Signature Algorithm: sha256WithRSAEncryption
         4b:28:27:74:54:8b:24:e7:f8:2a:f9:7b:14:40:56:a7:d3:da:
            …
         1b:c1:e0:38
```

We only used a subset of commands from OpenSSL in the examples. OpenSSL certificate management is quite extensive. We request readers to refer to OpenSSL documentation for further details.

***Figure 2.14**: Windows certificate viewer*

You can find a copy of the certificates and private keys generated in these examples in the **chapter-2/output** folder of the repository. We have used **password** for the password in encrypting the PEM files.

PKCS#12 Container

You can merge the key and certificate PEM files into one binary PKCS 12 container (.p12 or .pfx file).

```
OpenSSL> pkcs12 -export -in alice.crt -inkey alice.key -out alice.p12
-name Alice
Enter pass phrase for alice.key:
Enter Export Password:
Verifying - Enter Export Password:
The output will be alice.p12.
```

Encryption Using Certificates

We will use Alice's certificate to encrypt a message.

```
OpenSSL> rsautl -encrypt -inkey alice.crt -certin -in plain.txt -out
cipher.bin
```

We now decrypt the **cipher.bin** using the private key.

```
OpenSSL> rsautl -decrypt -inkey alice.key -in cipher.bin -out plain-out.
txt
Enter pass phrase for alice.key:
```

Signing Using Certificates

We will use Alice's certificate to sign the message.

```
OpenSSL> rsautl -inkey alice.key -sign -in plain.txt -out sign.bin
Enter pass phrase for alice.key:
```

We now decrypt the **sign.bin** using the public key. Remember that for RSA, the signing and encryption algorithms are the same.

```
OpenSSL> rsautl -inkey alice.crt -certin -verify -in sign.bin
The quick brown fox jumps over the lazy dog
```

Digital Signing for Authentication

The channel transports the password. Hence once compromised, a malicious actor can exploit it several times. Signing a new message every time means the response is changing. A replay is not as easy to orchestrate in such a case. Signing for authentication has been implemented in several strong authentication frameworks. Certificate-based authentication (CBA), mutual-Transport Layer Security (mTLS), OTP, CACs, and so on, use some form of signing mechanisms using symmetric or asymmetric cryptography. We will review them over several chapters in this book. A simple authentication protocol with signing is shown in the following figure.

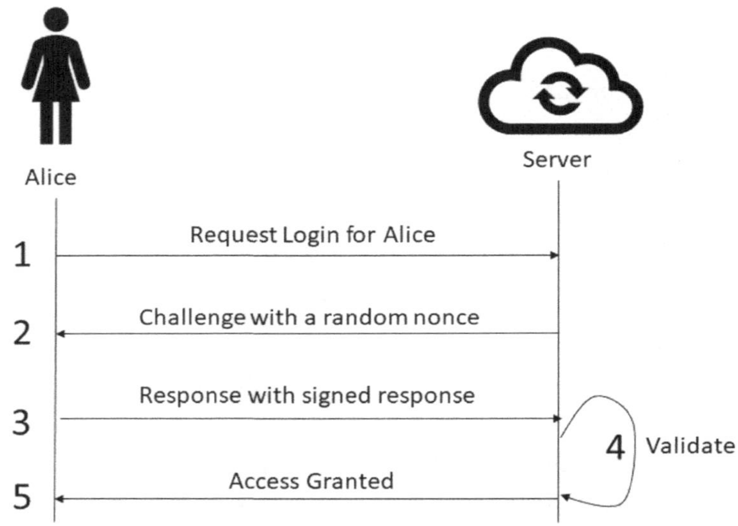

***Figure 2.15**: Authentication by Signing*

Conclusion

Cryptography is a complex subject with deep mathematical foundations. Our treatment here has been rudimentary, yet enough for conceptual appreciation. We expect readers to build on these foundations and learn further about cryptography. With enhanced computing power, the boundary of cryptography expands every few years. Quantum computing may render a few algorithms irrelevant. While we discussed a few algorithms, here are some key strengths that are safe for the next few decades[12].

12 Table 4, Recommendation for Key Management: Part 1 – General, NIST Special Publication 800-57 Part 1 Revision 5.

Security Strength	Through 2030	2031 and Beyond
< 112	Disallowed	Disallowed
112	Allowed	Disallowed
128	Allowed	Allowed
192	Allowed	Allowed
256	Allowed	Allowed

Table 2.2: *Safe security strengths for the future*

In the subsequent chapter, we shall explore transport layer security and securing the channel of communication.

Reference Books

In the 90s, some cryptographers understood the need to disseminate the knowledge on cryptography. They wrote some of the most admired books on this subject. Some are fundamental textbooks for undergraduate computer science and mathematics courses.

We can suggest a few in chronological order of publication:

1. Bruce Schneier, Applied Cryptography: Protocols, Algorithms, and Source Code in C, John Wiley & Sons (US) © 1996[13]
2. Alfred J. Menezes, Paul C. van Oorschot and Scott A. Vanstone, Applied Cryptography, CRC Press, 1996[14]
3. S.C.Coutinho, The Mathematics of Ciphers, A.K. Peters Ltd., 1999
4. J.H. Silverman, Jill Pipher, Jeffrey Hoffstein, An Introduction to Mathematical Cryptography, Springer, 2008
5. Bruce Schneier, Niels Ferguson, Tadayoshi Kohno, Cryptography Engineering: Design Principles and Practical Applications, John Wiley & Sons (US) © 2010
6. Aiden A. Bruen, Mario A. Forcinito, James M. McQuillan, Cryptography, Information Theory, and Error-Correction: A Handbook for the 21st Century, 2nd Edition, John Wiley & Sons (US) © 2021
7. David Wong, Real-World Cryptography, Manning Publications © 2021

13 The publishers republished a 20th-anniversary edition of this book in 2016.
14 Chapters of this book are available from: **https://cacr.uwaterloo.ca/hac/** with copyright restrictions.

Questions

1. In a communication channel, you will like to transmit compressed data. Should you do compression followed by encryption or vice versa, and why?
2. Build your authentication mechanism using HMAC. Is there a standard that already uses such a scheme?
3. *Figure* 2.12 establishes a trust chain of certificates. Using **OpenSSL**, create a set of digital certificates to establish the trust chain.
4. What changes are needed if you issue Alice an ECC-based certificate? Does this require a change in Trent's certificate?
5. What are intermediate CAs? Why are they needed?

CHAPTER 3
Authentication with Network Security

Introduction

In the previous chapter, we discussed cryptography, the building block on which computer security stands. The primitives of cryptography depend on algorithms and keys. Algorithms are standard; the secrecy of keys establishes the strength of the cryptographic exchange. If a computer system needs to connect to another, it announces the cryptographic algorithms it supports. The target end-point responds with the choice of protocol based on a handshake mechanism. All these complex exchanges use network protocols.

Network Protocols

It is time we look at *Figure* 1.2 OSI OSI Layers vs. TCP/IP layers again. The layers of two communication devices interact with each other. Introducing encryption in the IP layer or the transport layer keeps the application layer simple and unaffected by the effects of encryption.

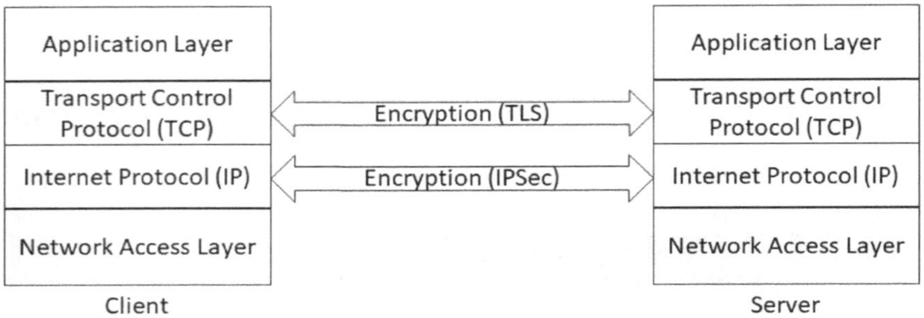

***Figure 3.1**: Encryption carried out in the IP layer leads to the secured IP protocol known as IPSec. Transport layer security (TLS) introduces security in TCP packets. IPSec is typically used in VPNs*

Effects vary based on the encrypted layer. For example, IPSec can encrypt the IP addresses of the destination computer. However, TLS can only encrypt the application data. The layer-wise data encapsulation controls the protection achieved.

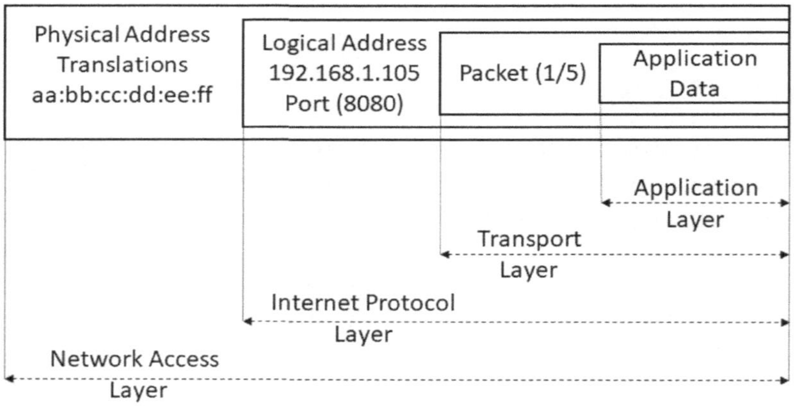

***Figure 3.2**: Every layer adds its own header to the transmitted packet. TLS can encrypt the application data but cannot encrypt the IP address. Such information can only be restricted with IPSec*

IPSec in tunnel mode can be used to encrypt IP headers; it can maintain the privacy of the IP addresses. However, IPSec in transport mode cannot accomplish the same[1]. SSH and SOCKS5 can establish proxy-based tunnels and hide destination information, hence are potential candidates to create privacy tunnels in the transport layer. We will only discuss the Transport Layer Security

1 Forouzan; B. A., TCP/IP Protocol Suite, Fourth Edition, pp.859, McGraw-Hill Company Ltd., 2010

(TLS) Protocol. There are two reasons: it is the most common security protocol used on the internet today and is the backbone of SSH, HTTPS, FTPS, etc. It has in-built user authentication support which is the core of this book.

Structure

In this chapter, we will cover the following topics:

- Transport Layer Security
- Server Authentication
- Client Authentication
- Web Browser Support

Transport Layer Security

Transport layer security (TLS) is the backbone of the internet today. It is considered one of the most complex protocols. The steps of the protocols are straightforward, yet the complexity arises due to many flexible cryptographic parameters in the exchange. The protocol lies in *Figure* 2.9, Key exchange using asymmetric cryptography. Conceived by Ralph Merkle and named after Whitfield Diffie and Martin Hellman, the Diffie-Hellman key exchange is one of the most used key exchange protocols. The explanation of the protocol is as follows.

1. Alice and Bob decide publicly to use g and p to exchange information.
2. Alice thinks of a private number a to herself and sends $A = g^a \ mod \ p$ to Bob.
3. Bob thinks of a private number b to himself, and sends $B = g^b \ mod \ p$ to Alice.
4. Alice takes B and computes $K_1 = B^a \ mod \ p$;

   Bob takes A and computes $K_2 = B^b \ mod \ p$;

   $K_1 = K_2 = K$ is the key for encryption.

Alice and Bob compute the Key (K), but no one with the knowledge of A, B, g, *and* p can come up with K as they will not know a or b . Hence, the computation is safe against the man-in-the-middle attacks of Mallory.

Let us try this with an example:

1. Suppose, $g = 2$ and $p = 29$.
2. If Alice keeps the private key a = 3, sends $A = 2^3 \ mod \ 29 = 8$

3. If Bob keeps the private key $b = 5$, sends $B = 2^5 \ mod\ 29 = 3$
4. Alice computes $K_1 = 3^3 \ mod\ 29 = 27$

   Bob computes $K_2 = 8^5 \ mod\ 29 = 32768 \ mod\ 29 = 27$

   Both get 27 which can be used as the encryption key.

In real implementations, g can be a small prime number like 2, 3, etc. However, p is a large number no less than 2048 bits. Instead of using K directly, it will be passed through a key derivation function like HKDF[2]. This ensures the derived key has sufficient entropy or randomness while it is of the desired length. TLS is a protocol to accomplish this exchange but with lots of variations and options. There are three unique DHE algorithms.

1. Finite field Diffie-Hellman Exchange (FFDHE) or Elliptic Curve Diffie-Hellman Exchange (ECDHE)
2. Pre-shared Key (PSK)
3. PSK with (EC)DHE.

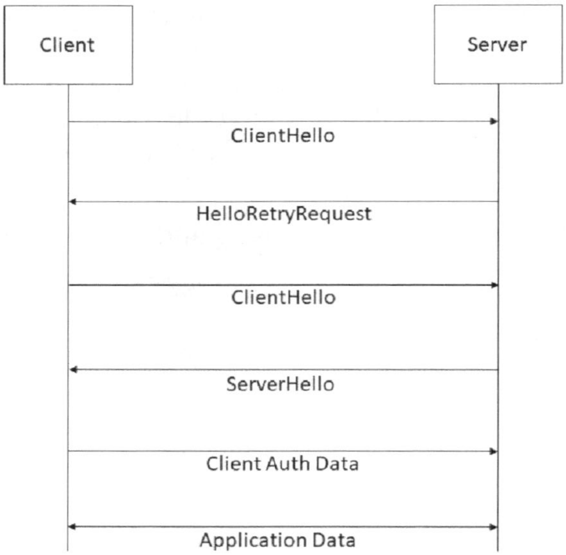

***Figure* 3.3**: A TLS 1.3 *full handshake with retry*

2 HMAC based expand and extract key derivation function (HKDF), **https://www.rfc-editor.org/rfc/rfc5869**

We overtly simplified the algorithm for explanation and illustration. The details are complex and we request you to review RFC 8446[3]. The protocol has gone over several iterations of addressing vulnerabilities.

1. The client sends a **`ClientHello`** message with the key info.
2. If the server does not agree with the key establishment algorithms, it asks the client to retry with another **`ClientHello`**.
3. The client sends another **`ClientHello`** with the shared key info based on the algorithm suggested by the server.
4. The server sends a **`ServerHello`** that contains a server certificate or a pre-shared key for authentication.
5. The client validates the server certificate and optionally sends its own certificate to authenticate.
6. In the process, the key is established at the client and server. It can be used to encrypt and decrypt the application data.

The authentication is carried out using four algorithms.

1. RSA
2. Elliptic Curve Digital Signature Algorithm (ECDSA)
3. Edward's Curve Digital Signature Algorithm (EdDSA)
4. Pre-shared Key (PSK)

The pre-shared key need not be established ahead of time. This can be established during the handshake protocol. PSKs are used to authenticate subsequent TLS connections after a full handshake establishes the initial connection. **`OpenSSL s_client`** is a great tool to connect to an SSL server and observe the handshake protocol with **`-debug`** option. You may use a binary editor to understand the handshake packet dumps.

Server Authentication

HTTPS is the HTTP protocol transmitted inside a TLS encrypted tunnel. HTTP clients and servers exchange information without encryption, hence such communication is unsecured. Today, finding a non-HTTPS webpage is very hard. All well-known websites support HTTPS as browsers mark all HTTP sites unsecured and warn the end-user. All websites, when connected using HTTP, will redirect to an HTTPS page. An end-user may not observe this as browsers silently load the redirected HTTPS page. Here is an under-the-hood observation using **`curl`** as a user agent.

---

3 The Transport Layer Security (TLS) Protocol Version 1.3, **https://www.rfc-editor.org/rfc/rfc8446**

```
C:\> curl -v http://w3c.org
*   Trying 217.70.184.38:80...
* Connected to w3c.org (217.70.184.38) port 80 (#0)
> GET / HTTP/1.1
> Host: w3c.org
> User-Agent: curl/7.83.1
> Accept: */*
>
* Mark bundle as not supporting multiuse
< HTTP/1.1 301 Moved Permanently
< Server: nginx
< Date: Thu, 02 Mar 2023 09:57:43 GMT
< Content-Type: text/html
< Transfer-Encoding: chunked
< Connection: close
< Location: https://www.w3.org
< Cache-Control: max-age=10800
< Vary: Accept-Language
<
...
```

The connection to **http://www.w3c.org** is redirected to **https://www.w3c.org**.

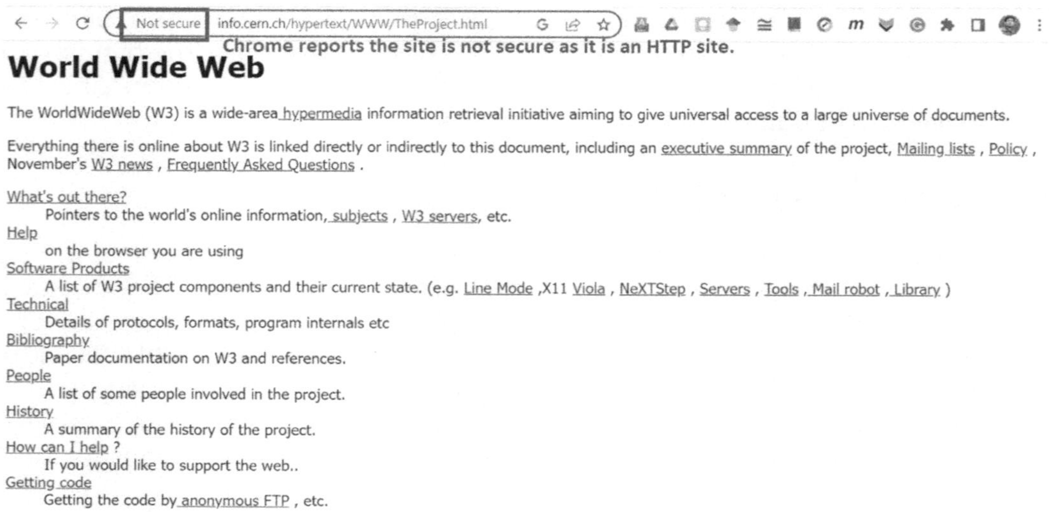

***Figure 3.4**: This CERN page is the first HTTP page created. As you can see, Chrome version 110.0.5481.178 (Official Build) (64-bit) reports it as unsecured*

A domain can have both secured and unsecured sites hosted on them. The following CERN site has an HTTPS URL and Chrome does not consider it unsecured.

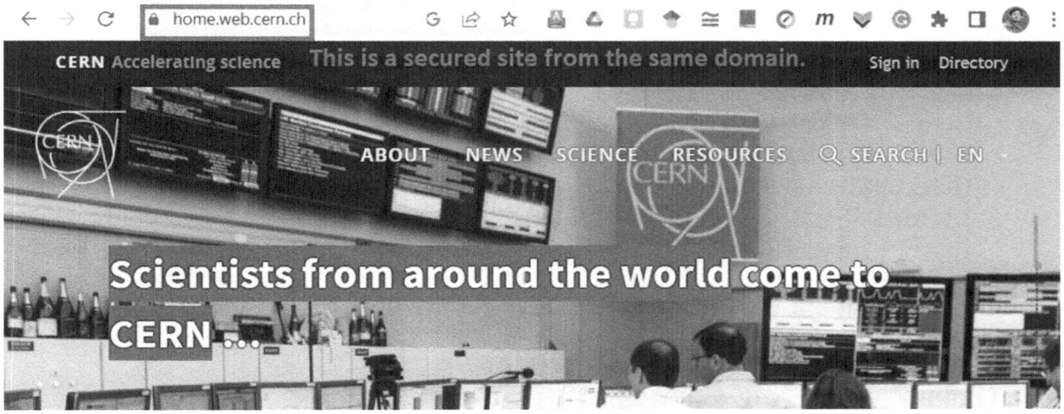

***Figure 3.5**: Modern CERN pages from an HTTPS site*

How does a client trust the server in the first place? During the TLS connection, the server presents a certificate to the client. The client trusts the server based on the details provided in the certificate. The associated sample code is available in the **`Chapter-3`** folder. The folder has certificates in the **`certs\server`** directory. **`mysrv.crt`** file has the annotated text of the certificate used for the SSL server. **`mysrv.p12`** contains the **`PKCS12`** certificate with the private key. We will be using **`PKCS12`** in the code snippets. However, you can use **`mysrv.crt`** to review the contents of the certificate.

- As documented in Chapter – 2, Digital Certificate → Validation section, the current time falls between the **`notBefore`** and **`notAfter`** time range of the end entity certificate and all the root certificates.
- The certificate is configured with the **`subjectAlternateName`** (SAN) **`DNS:mysrv.local`**.

  The client will connect to the server at: **https://mysrv.local** if the server is using this certificate. Hence, the DNS resolution on the client's computer should be configured to point to the server IP address. For the demo set-up, the author has configured the **`/etc/hosts`**[4] file to point to the loopback address[5]. The entry looks like this:

  ```
  127.0.0.5 mysrv.local
  ```

4 On Windows machines, the file is located at **%WINDIR%\system32\drivers\etc\hosts**

5 The CIDR network range of **127.0.0.0/8** can be loopback addresses

- The **mysrv.crt** has **Server Authentication** configured as extended key usage (EKU). The key usage has the following extensions: **Digital Signature, Non-Repudiation, Key Encipherment, Data Encipherment (f0)**
- The Intermediate CA that signs the server certificate has the basic constraints set as **Subject Type=CA, Path Length Constraint=0**. The root CA has the basic constraint **Subject Type=CA, Path Length Constraint=None.** While this is reasonable for some clients, some clients like **CURL** may require root certificates to provide certificate revocation details like CRL or OCSP. We provide the commands to create these certificates through **OpenSSL** in Appendix C: TLS Certificate Creation.

The hierarchy of **mysrv.crt** certificates are shown.

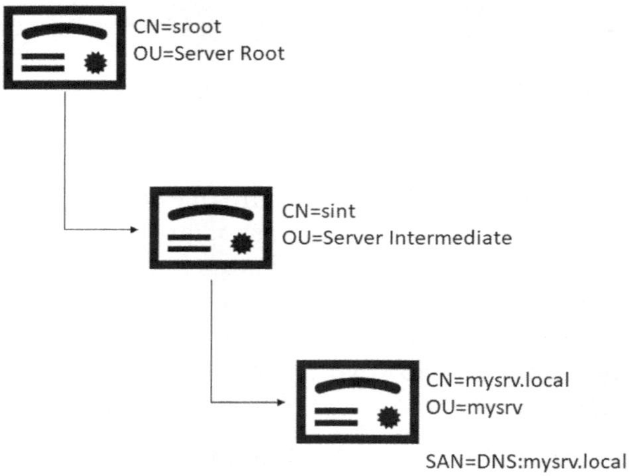

***Figure 3.6**: Server certificate hierarchy*

Let us set up a simple HTTPS server using the Go language.

```
func main() {
  // Assign false to turnoff client auth
  addHelloHandler()
  cert, err := getTLSCert()
  if err != nil {
    log.Default().Fatal(err)
  }
  tlsConfig := &tls.Config{
    ServerName:   "mysrv.local",
```

```
    MinVersion:   tls.VersionTLS13,
    Certificates: []tls.Certificate{*cert},
  }
  server := &http.Server{
    Addr:      ":8443",
    TLSConfig: tlsConfig,
  }
  log.Default().Fatal(server.ListenAndServeTLS("", ""))
}
```

We have already reviewed **addHelloHandler()** which adds a **/hello** endpoint to the server. There is no change introduced to that function when the TLS connection was added.

```
func addHelloHandler() {
  http.HandleFunc("/hello", func(w http.ResponseWriter, req *http.
Request) {
    log.Default().Print("Sending: Hello, World!\n")
    io.WriteString(w, "Hello, World!\n")
  })
}
```

The most important method for discussion here is **getTLSCert()**. The method opens the PKCS 12 envelope using the password, extracts the public certificate chain and the private key, and creates a **tls.Certificate** object to be used for TLS configuration for the HTTP connection.

```
/*
Server certificate
*/
func getTLSCert() (c *tls.Certificate, err error) {
  var (
    fdata  []byte
    blocks []*pem.Block
    cert   tls.Certificate
  )
  if fdata, err = os.ReadFile("certs/server/mysrv.p12"); err == nil {
    if blocks, err = pkcs12.ToPEM(fdata, "password"); err == nil {
      var pemData []byte
```

```
      for _, b := range blocks {
        pemData = append(pemData, pem.EncodeToMemory(b)...)
      }
      cert, err = tls.X509KeyPair(pemData, pemData)
        c = &cert
    }
  }
  return
}
```

We have configured the server to use TLS 1.3. We connect to the server using **OpenSSL s_client** TLS client.

```
OpenSSL> s_client -connect mysrv.local:8443 -CAfile sroot.crt
CONNECTED(00000004)
…
---
Certificate chain
 0 s:C = IN, ST = KA, L = BANGALORE, O = HOWA, OU = mysrv, CN = mysrv.local
   i:C = IN, ST = KA, L = BANGALORE, O = HOWA, OU = Server Intermediate, CN = sint
 1 s:C = IN, ST = KA, L = BANGALORE, O = HOWA, OU = Server Intermediate, CN = sint
   i:C = IN, ST = KA, L = BANGALORE, O = HOWA, OU = Server Root, CN = sroot
 2 s:C = IN, ST = KA, L = BANGALORE, O = HOWA, OU = Server Root, CN = sroot
   i:C = IN, ST = KA, L = BANGALORE, O = HOWA, OU = Server Root, CN = sroot
---
Server certificate
-----BEGIN CERTIFICATE-----
…
-----END CERTIFICATE-----
subject=C = IN, ST = KA, L = BANGALORE, O = HOWA, OU = mysrv, CN =
mysrv.local
issuer=C = IN, ST = KA, L = BANGALORE, O = HOWA, OU = Server
Intermediate, CN = sint
---
No client certificate CA names sent
Peer signing digest: SHA256
Peer signature type: RSA-PSS
```

```
Server Temp Key: X25519, 253 bits
---
SSL handshake has read 4381 bytes and written 377 bytes
Verification: OK
---
New, TLSv1.3, Cipher is TLS_AES_128_GCM_SHA256
Server public key is 3072 bit
Secure Renegotiation IS NOT supported
Compression: NONE
Expansion: NONE
No ALPN negotiated
Early data was not sent
Verify return code: 0 (ok)
---
---
Post-Handshake New Session Ticket arrived:
SSL-Session:
    Protocol  : TLSv1.3
    Cipher    : TLS_AES_128_GCM_SHA256
    Session-ID: A27A52743AE7C00A…BE16168E69CB1F513E81FD
    Session-ID-ctx:
    Resumption PSK: A4E02C7DBBF1F3949161DC88B6…9E0C245B0B7898189DA63049D5
    PSK identity: None
    PSK identity hint: None
    SRP username: None
    TLS session ticket lifetime hint: 604800 (seconds)
    TLS session ticket:
…
    Start Time: 1677862609
    Timeout   : 7200 (sec)
    Verify return code: 0 (ok)
    Extended master secret: no
    Max Early Data: 0
---
read R BLOCK
```

The connection presents the server certificates, negotiates the cryptographic algorithms, and completes the TLS handshake. In the command line, the OpenSSL screen will wait for HTTP requests to be sent through the TLS tunnel. We send a normal HTTP request to which the server will respond as shown.

```
GET /hello HTTP/1.1
Host: mysrv.local

HTTP/1.1 200 OK
Date: Fri, 03 Mar 2023 16:57:17 GMT
Content-Length: 14
Content-Type: text/plain; charset=utf-8

Hello, World!
```

This data is encrypted using AES-128. The server certificate helps in the following two ways:

1. The client can trust the server as it trusts the root certificate.
2. It establishes the necessary symmetric key to be exchanged for data encryption.

The client certificate, which is optional, authenticates the client. It plays no role in data encryption. *Can we use another authentication method to authenticate the client*? In the next step, we add **addBasicAuthHandler** to authenticate the client. The code is the same as shown in Chapter-1. When we use the **s_client** to request the basic authentication end-point we get as shown:

```
GET /basicauth HTTP/1.1
Host: mysrv.local
Authorization: Basic amRvZTpwYXNzd29yZA==

HTTP/1.1 200 OK
Date: Fri, 03 Mar 2023 17:57:27 GMT
Content-Length: 24
Content-Type: text/plain; charset=utf-8

User jdoe authenticated.
```

The **Authorization** header that contains the base-64 encoded username and password is encrypted in transit. Hence, communication is safe.

If you want to view the handshake messages in transit, use the **s_client** command with the **-debug** flag in **OpenSSL**.

Client Authentication

Unlike server trust, sending a certificate for client authentication is optional. We extend the previous example by adding client certificates to the configurations. At the very minimum, the server must trust the client CAs and validate the client certificates. The code snippet for the same is shown.

```
func configureClientAuth(tlsConfig *tls.Config) error {
  // Add certauth end point and handler
  http.HandleFunc("/certauth", func(w http.ResponseWriter, req *http.
Request) {
    if req.TLS == nil || req.TLS.PeerCertificates == nil ||
       len(req.TLS.PeerCertificates) <= 0 {
      str := "No client certificates. User failed to authenticate."
      w.WriteHeader(http.StatusUnauthorized)
      log.Default().Print(str)
    } else {
      str := fmt.Sprintf("User %s authenticated.\n",
               req.TLS.PeerCertificates[0].Subject.CommonName)
      io.WriteString(w, str)
      log.Default().Print(str)
    }
  })

  // Client CAs added to TLSConfig. Now, server can trust client certs.
  if data, err := os.ReadFile("certs/server/cint.crt"); err == nil {
    var block *pem.Block
    certpool := x509.NewCertPool()
    for block, data = pem.Decode(data);
        block != nil;
        block, data = pem.Decode(data) {
      if cert, err := x509.ParseCertificate(block.Bytes); err == nil {
        certpool.AddCert(cert)
      }
```

```
    }
    tlsConfig.ClientAuth = tls.VerifyClientCertIfGiven
    tlsConfig.ClientCAs = certpool
  } else {
    return err
  }
  return nil
}
```

Here we provide the **cint.crt** chain as client CAs. The file contains certificates for intermediate CA as well as the root CA. The hierarchy of the client certificate chain is as shown.

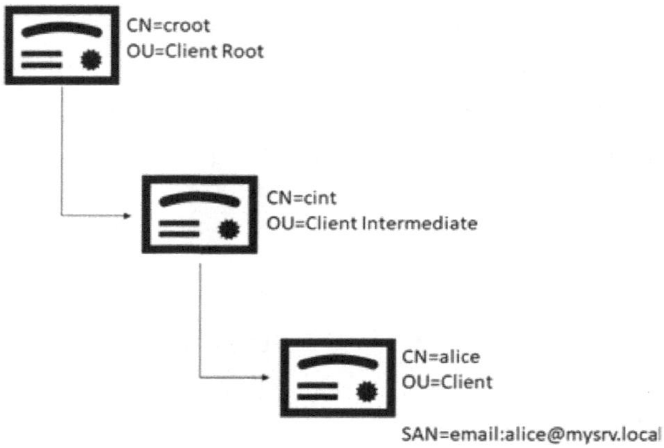

***Figure 3.7**: Client certificate hierarchy*

Just like server certificates, client certificates have certain constraints and key usages. Here are some of them.

- As documented in Chapter – 2, Digital Certificate → Validation section, the current time falls between the **notBefore** and **notAfter** time range of the end entity certificate and all the root certificates.
- The certificate is configured with the **subjectAlternateName** (SAN) **email:alice@mysrv.local**. This is not a hard requirement, unlike the server certificate. However, some servers may use email as the username.
- The **alice.crt** has **Client Authentication** configured as extended key usage (EKU). The key usage has the following attributes: **Digital Signature, Non-Repudiation, Key Encipherment, Data Encipherment (f0)**

- The Intermediate CA that signs the client certificate has the basic constraints set as **Subject Type=CA, Path Length Constraint=0**. The root CA has the basic constraint **Subject Type=CA, Path Length Constraint=None**.

We also create a **/certauth** endpoint to verify the TLS user record. Let us run the services and connect using **OpenSSL s_client**.

```
OpenSSL> s_client -connect mysrv.local:8443 -CAfile sroot.crt -cert
alice.crt -key alice.key

Enter pass phrase for alice.key:

CONNECTED(00000004)

…
---

Acceptable client certificate CA names

C = IN, ST = KA, L = BANGALORE, O = HOWA, OU = Client Intermediate, CN =
cint

C = IN, ST = KA, L = BANGALORE, O = HOWA, OU = Client Root, CN = croot

Requested Signature Algorithms: …

Shared Requested Signature Algorithms: …

Peer signing digest: SHA256

Peer signature type: RSA-PSS

Server Temp Key: X25519, 253 bits

---
…
---

read R BLOCK
```

The client certificate information was the only additional information exchanged in the TLS handshake. The HTTP request and responses are given as follows:

```
GET /certauth HTTP/1.1

HOST: mysrv.local


HTTP/1.1 200 OK

Date: Sun, 05 Mar 2023 10:26:35 GMT

Content-Length: 26

Content-Type: text/plain; charset=utf-8


User alice authenticated.
```

The user data is collected from the `TLS` object available in `HTTP.Request`. While what we have seen here establishes a custom HTTPS server and a client connecting to it, *will it work with a commercial web browser*?

Web Browser Support

We launch the simple TLS server with no client authentication enabled[6]. From a browser, we access the URL: **https://mysrv.local:8443/hello**. The browser reports that the website is not trusted and has errors. However, we do not see such errors on standard official websites. Normal websites use certificates from trustworthy CAs. The CAs and the companies developing browsers are part of a CA/Browser Forum[7]. The forum members provide best practices for TLS/SSL configurations and create awareness among all the browser manufacturers about the CAs that should be trusted by default. Since we used a custom certificate using OpenSSL using an untrusted root, we see these errors[8].

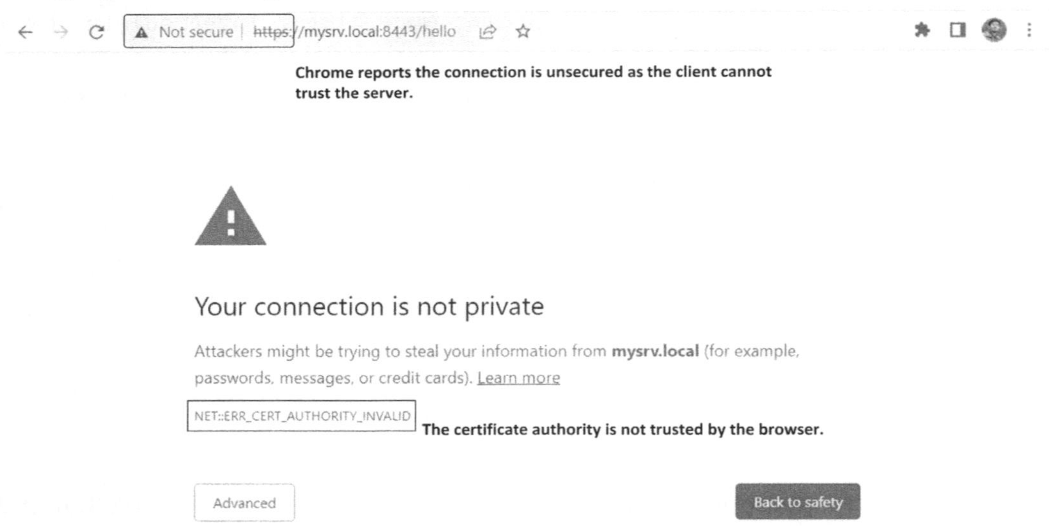

Figure 3.8: *Browser reports a security error when the certificate is from a trusted CA*

6 Setting **const CLIENT_AUTH = false** in the **main()** method turns off client certificate authentication.

7 CA/Browser Forum. **https://cabforum.com**

8 We used a Google Chrome browser on Microsoft Windows Platform.

To overcome this issue, the browser must be configured to trust the root CA. We accomplish this by accessing the certificate import through chrome settings.

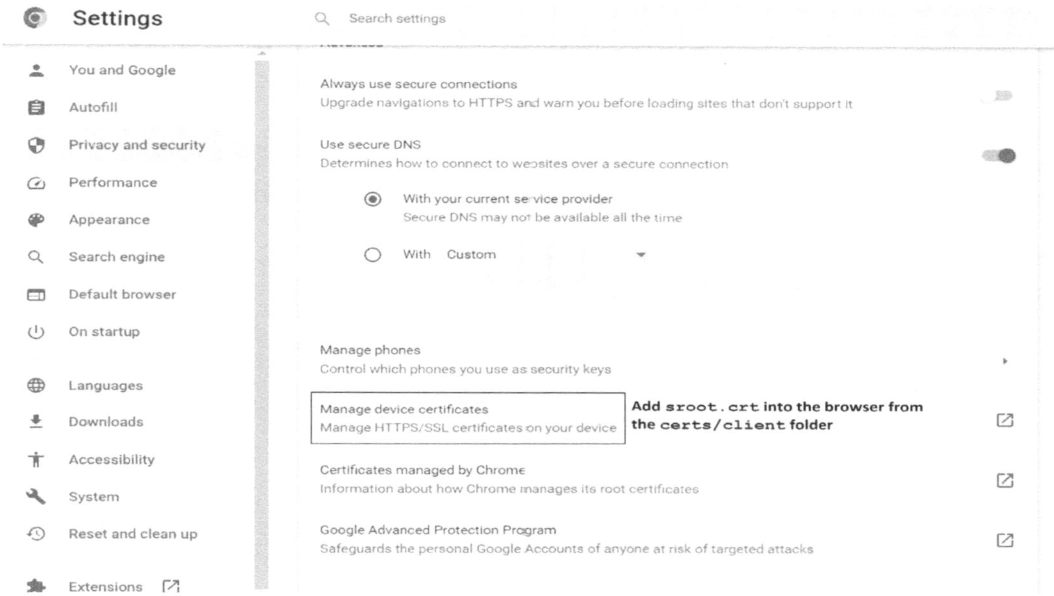

Figure 3.9: *Using the Chrome privacy and security settings to update the Windows device certificates*

Import the root certificate **`sroot.crt`** from the **`Chapter-3/certs/client`** folder. Ensure the certificate is imported into the Trusted Root Certificate Authorities of Windows.

Figure 3.10: *Adding trusted root CAs to the machine*

After importing the certificate, let's use the browser to access the server.

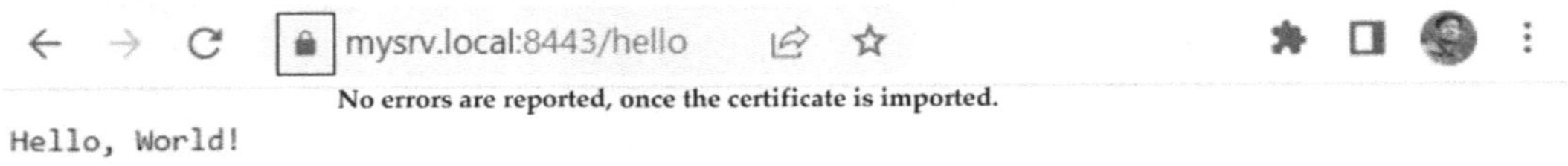

***Figure 3.11**: The browser after the certificate is imported*

If we access the **`/basicauth`** end-point, the browser challenges basic authentication.

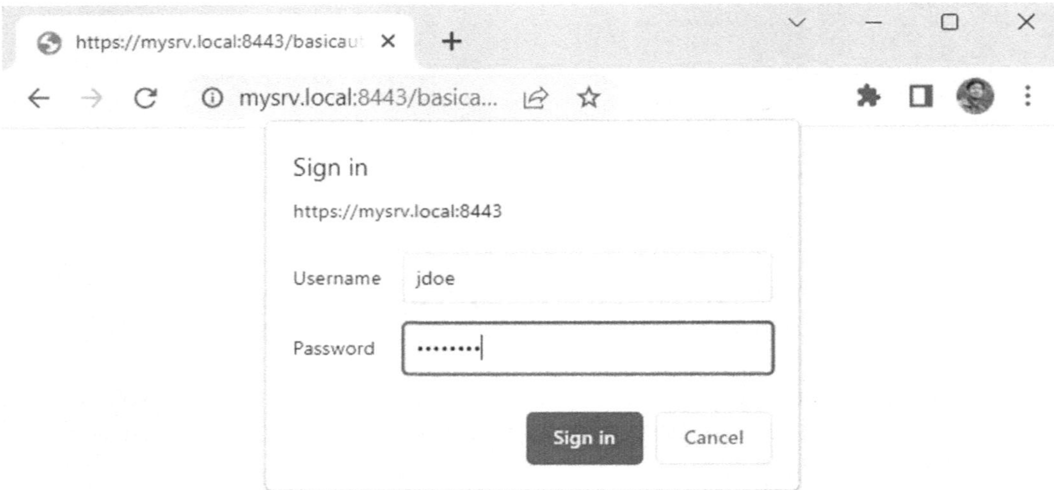

***Figure 3.12**: Basic authentication through TLS*

Client Certificates

Let us activate the client authentication in our demo server now. Setting **`const CLIENT_AUTH = true`** in the main() method turns on client certificate authentication. When we access the endpoint **https://mysrv.local:8443/certauth**, the authentication fails and the page cannot be accessed.

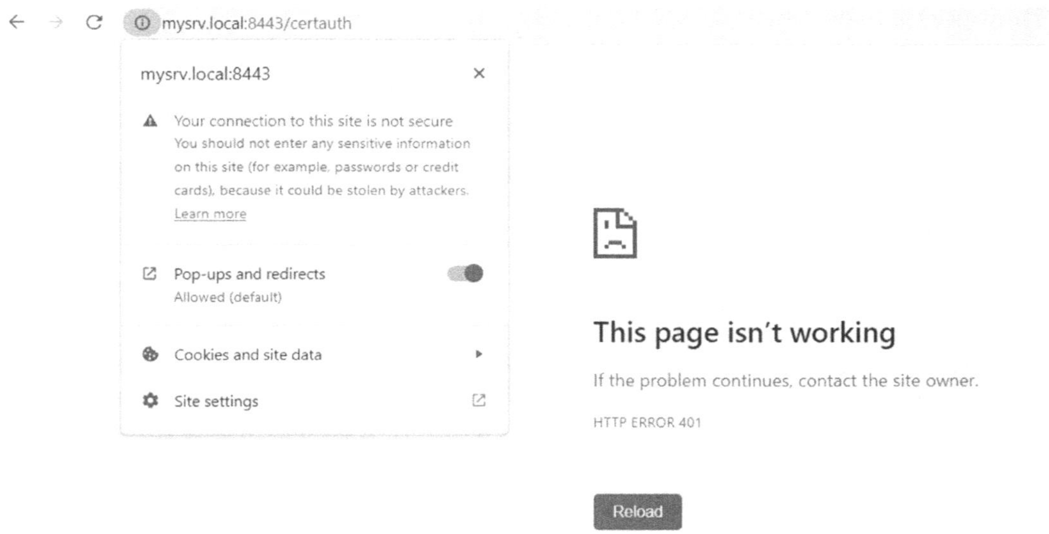

Figure 3.13: *The user could not be authenticated as the browser does not present a certificate*

The client certificate has to be imported into windows so that the browser can access the end-user certificates.

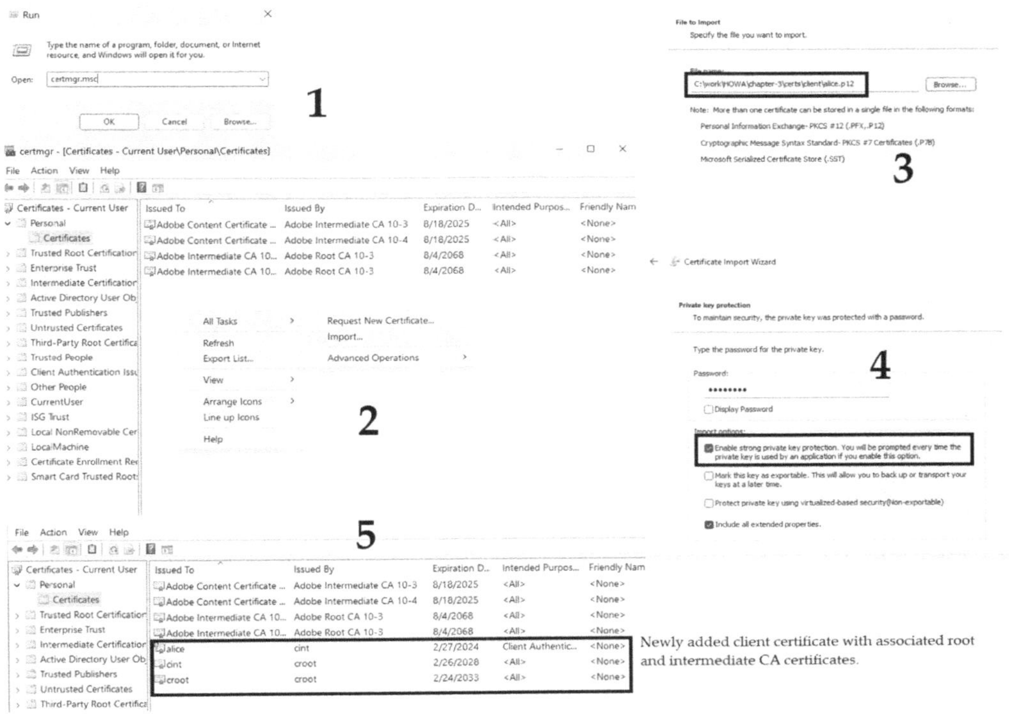

Figure 3.14: *Adding user certificate to the device*

To import a user certificate, follow these steps:

1. In the Run dialog launch the **`certmgr.msc`**.
2. Launch the certificate import wizard.
3. Import file **`Chapter-3/certs/client/alice.p12`**.
4. Provide a password and enable strong private key protection.
5. The end entity as well as all the CA certificates are imported into the personal certificates list.

The server is expected to verify the client certificate only when presented. It does not mandate the client to provide a certificate. This is accomplished by setting **`tls.VerifyClientCertIfGiven`** in **`TLSConfig.ClientAuth.`** As the server trusts a client certificate chain, whenever the server is accessed the client is challenged to provide a client certificate trusted by the server.

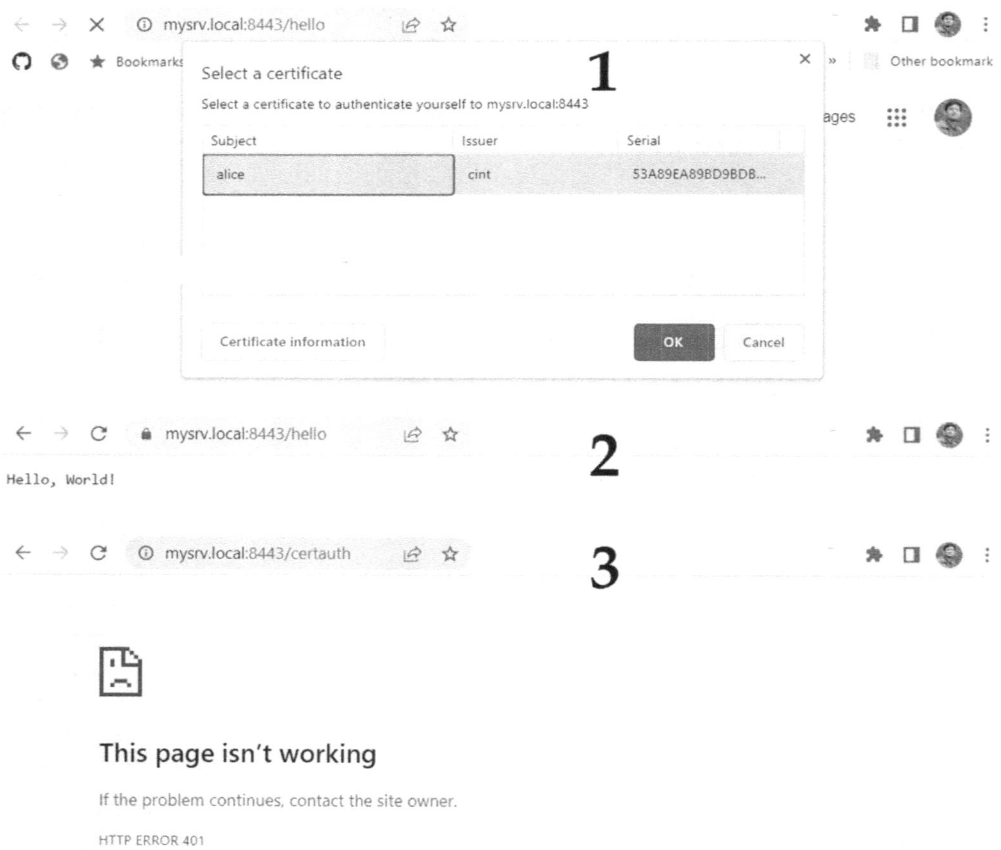

Figure 3.15: *Certificate presented when the server is contacted*

In the preceding figure:

1. A certificate to select is presented even though **`/hello`** endpoint does not need authentication.
2. When cancelled, the page is shown without any issues.
3. While accessing **`/certauth`** endpoint unauthorized error is displayed.

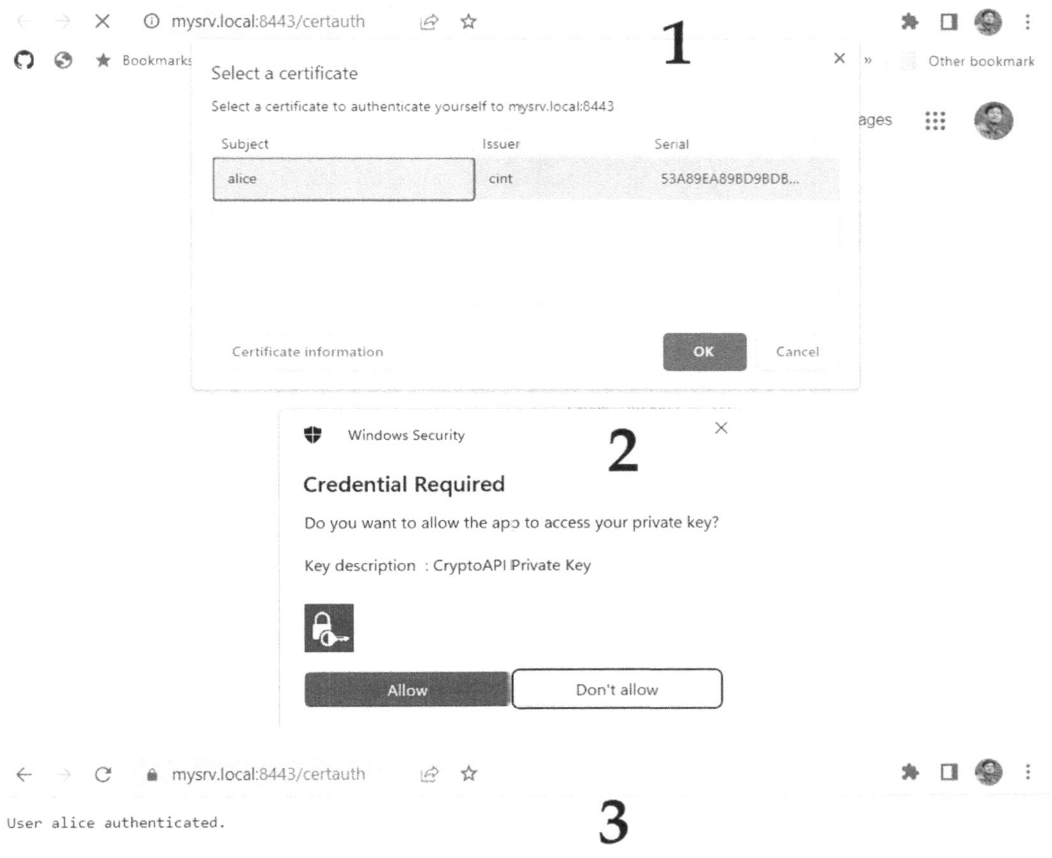

***Figure 3. 16**: Successful certificate-based authentication*

Close all browser sessions and launch the URL in a fresh browser session. When you access **`/certauth`**, the client certificate dialog is presented. Upon selecting the certificate of **`alice`**, the certificate is sent to the server. Since the chain is trusted by the server, the authentication is successful. Since strong private key protection is enabled, the user is prompted to accept access to the private key.

Non-TLS certificate-based authentication

In *Figure 3.15: Certificate presented when the server is contacted*, the HTTP connection returns an error when the user does not provide a certificate. The browser manages the HTTP error; the web application cannot take up any rendering. Sometimes, you need different authentication methods for every category of users; one set of users uses the password to authenticate, while the other set of users uses a user certificate.

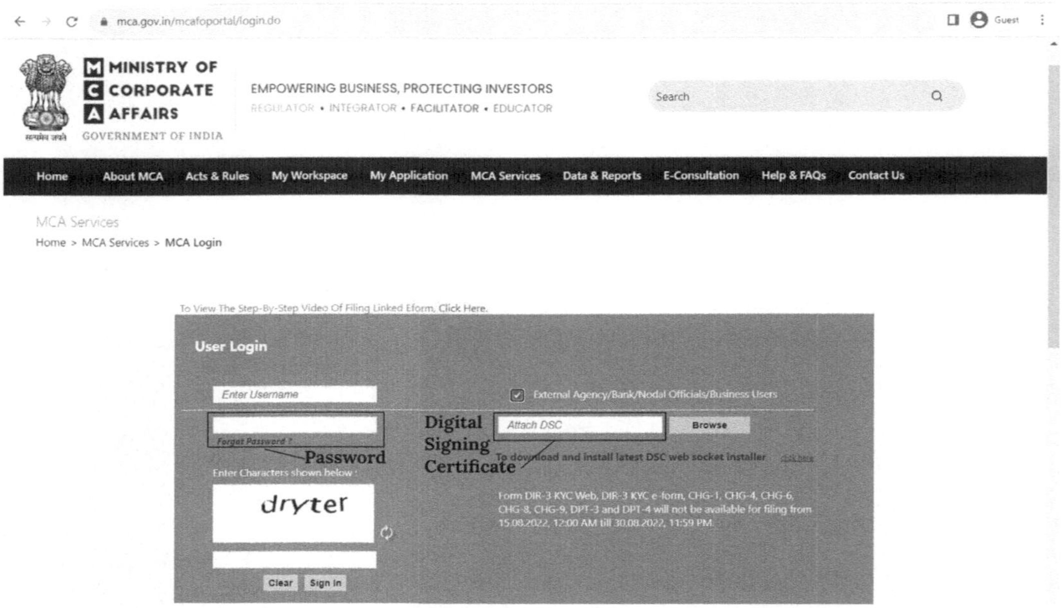

Figure 3.17: *Login form using both a password or a certificate to authenticate*

Browsers have limited access to the certificate stores of the operating systems. They can access the certificate stores to verify TLS connections or through plugin architectures like extensions. JavaScript on a web page cannot access a certificate private key to sign a payload. During authentication, a server sends a message hash to the client; the client signs the message hash and sends it to the server as the proof-of-possession. Since JavaScript in a web page cannot access the private key, such authentication requires some form of helper applications or browser extensions.

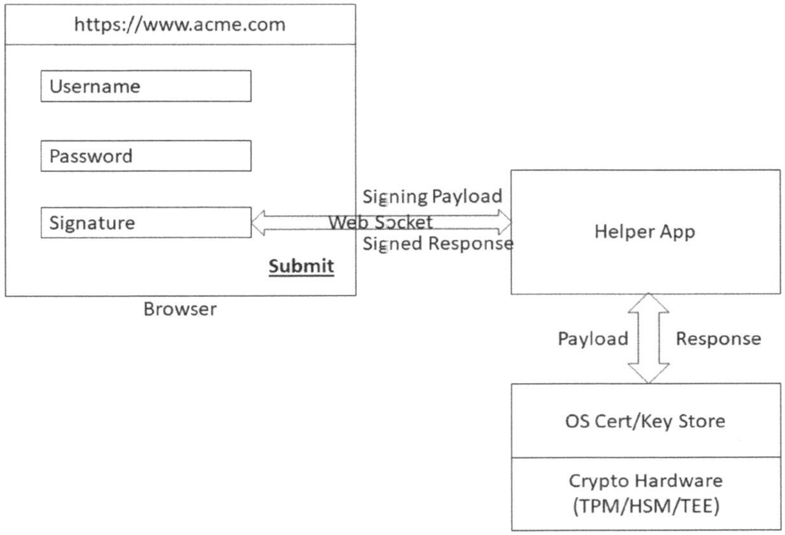

***Figure 3.18**: Web socket connector for signing browser payload*

Web sockets are like Unix sockets; however, a webpage can access web sockets. A helper application runs in the operating system and accepts connection on a web socket. The webpage receives the signing payload from the web server and sends it to the helper application to sign. The helper application passes the message to the operating system-managed cryptographic hardware to sign the payload. The webpage receives the signed response over the web socket. The scheme described is one of the many possible implementations. A variation of this architecture is used by the certificate authorities (CA) to provision certificates using browser enrollment. Every CA has its helper application workflow different from the competition. We suggest the readers learn them from CA-specific documentation based on their needs.

The support for passkeys with WebAuthn has made public key authentication easier without a separate helper application. We will discuss WebAuthn in a later chapter.

Conclusion

Finally, we ensured the data exchange between the client and the server was encrypted. Thus, the information is secured in transit. Cryptographically, the exchange is secured against any man-in-the-middle attacks. We also looked at a mutual TLS (m-TLS) handshake that ensures the client is authenticated with the server. However, m-TLS is not considered a preferred mode of authentication. The process is cumbersome and an untrusted client certificate leads to the termination of the connection. These steps make it hard to analyze failures from the browser. Secondly, the user experience is not friendly when some users need certificates to authenticate while others do not. Certificate management is complex for an end-user. m-TLS plays a crucial role in host-to-host connections. Moreover, TLS connections are terminated at applications or API gateways, freeing up backend services from handling any authentication overhead. With the advent of WebAuthn, PKI-based client authentication can be managed easily by the browser and OS combination effectively. We shall review the same in a later chapter. With network security in place, we will explore if authentication can be offered as a service. If any service needs user authentication, it can delegate responsibility to the specialized service. Federated authentication models address such problems and that will be the next direction of exploration.

Questions

1. What is Diffie-Hellman Exchange? Why is it needed in TLS?
2. Is a certificate a must to initiate a TLS connection? Are there any other mechanisms that clients and servers can use to establish a TLS connection?
3. From the TLS handshake protocol, find out how the browser determines the certificates to be displayed to the user for client authentication.
4. How does the browser behavior change when a server certificate is not trusted?
5. Provide a name to your machine and access it through network commands, like **ping**. Can you use this name on the certificate?

CHAPTER 4
Federated Authentication-I

Introduction

In our journey, we identified the need for authentication in web architectures, covered the basics of cryptography technology for all authentication systems, and protected the communication channel with TLS. On a timescale, we have covered several decades of development of these systems. The proponents of web architectures understood that authentication systems were becoming overly complex and independent services. Let us discuss this with an example. In an organization, there is an HR department that has a leave management system. While every employee can use the system to apply for leave, the employee's manager or an HR executive only can approve the leave. Mere employees logging in is not good enough; access levels they can reach are equally important. This access is known as authorization. While we look at simple authorization techniques, there are more complex authorization scenarios we will discuss in a subsequent chapter. A finance department manages a payroll application. The users can look at their payroll data from such an application, while the finance department will have payroll managers. A typical organization will have hundreds of such applications. If every application maintains user information in its independent database, an employee will have a username for every application of the organization. *How does an organization address such needs?*

Structure

In this chapter, we will cover the following topics:

- Federated authentication
- Single sign-on
- Authentication ticket or token
- Claims-based authentication
- SAML token
- An example
- Identity and access management

Federated authentication

We did a Google search on how many SaaS applications an average employee of a small organization uses. The numbers were in the tens range. Assuming every user had a username and password for each application, this situation is not scalable. The industry identified this need even in the pre-SaaS era, and organizations have been storing user information in a user store. LDAP servers like Microsoft Active Directory, Novell eDirectory, Oracle Directory Server, OpenLDAP, etc. provide such services for several decades. The servers stored identity information like usernames, passwords, group belongingness of the users, and other attributes relevant to the IT operations of the organizations in a consolidated location. LDAP provides an excellent query interface to search for users fast. However, it is not a web-based protocol.

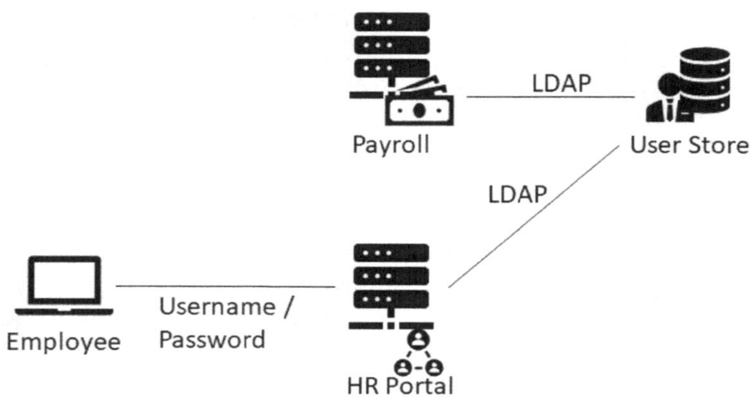

Figure 4.1: *LDAP as a User Store*

The on-premise IT applications are a thing of the past. Most organizations have data centers in the cloud and are connecting to some forms of cloud directories. Hence, instead of using LDAP as a query protocol, they can use REST APIs offered by cloud directories. While this addresses the issue of using LDAP as a protocol, every application should use the authentication methods of the directory service.

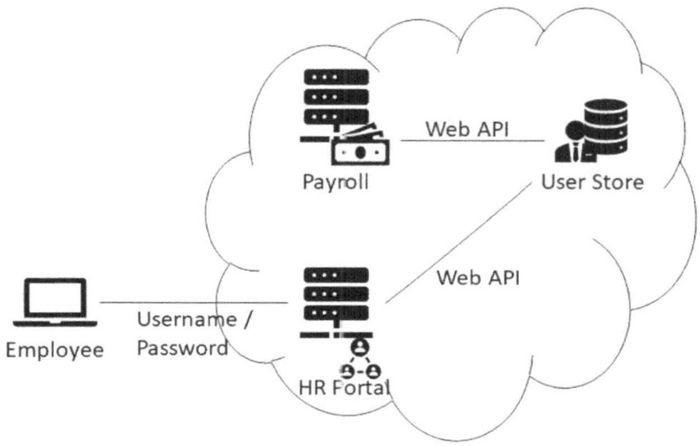

Figure 4.2: *Moving the user store to the cloud does not end the challenges*

Authentication is a specialized function. The industry realized a dedicated service should cater to the authentication needs of an organization. However, when a service collects user information like username and password from a user and presents it to an authentication server or identity store, it can store or cache the password. It can handle this private data in an unsecured manner. Since the service provider can be in a data center outside the enterprise's control, multiple network connections can transmit the password. Some of the transmissions can be beyond the security posture of the organization. This mode of authentication is called **delegated authentication**.

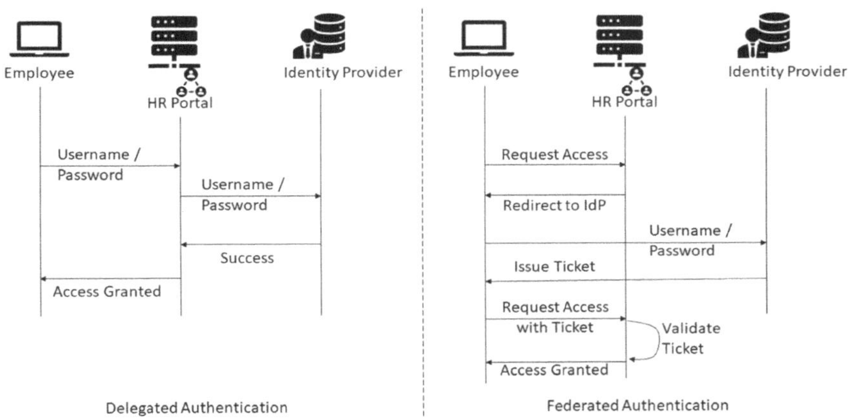

Figure 4.3: *Delegated vs Federated Authentication*

We have seen one of the downsides of using delegated authentication. The second issue is the variety of authenticators used. While username and password are the simplest form of authentication, an MFA authentication may require additional form fields to be added, like OTP. Every service provider in a delegation authentication workflow may need modification as soon as the enterprise uses a new authentication scheme. This is not scalable.

Federated authentication addressed these needs effectively. There is an exclusive authentication service that validates the user credentials and issues tickets consumed by other services. However, federated authentication is not a web paradigm. Kerberos-like protocols can be used effectively for federated authentication. We will not discuss Kerberos here as its use on the web is not as prevalent. However, interested readers can review RFC 4120[1]. Windows domain authentication utilizes Kerberos as a base with several extensions over the years. A federated authentication can be triggered by the service provider or the identity provider. We discuss both scenarios next.

Service provider initiated

The users contact the HR Portal, the service provider (SP), for access to a specific page. They are redirected to the identity provider (IDP). This scheme is often called a Service Provider (SP) initiated authentication. The use of the term redirection is colloquial here. It does not have to be an HTTP GET redirect request. One can simulate the workflow using HTTP POST requests as well. In the section on Binding, we will review how SAML can be used in both HTTP GET Redirect and HTTP POST context.

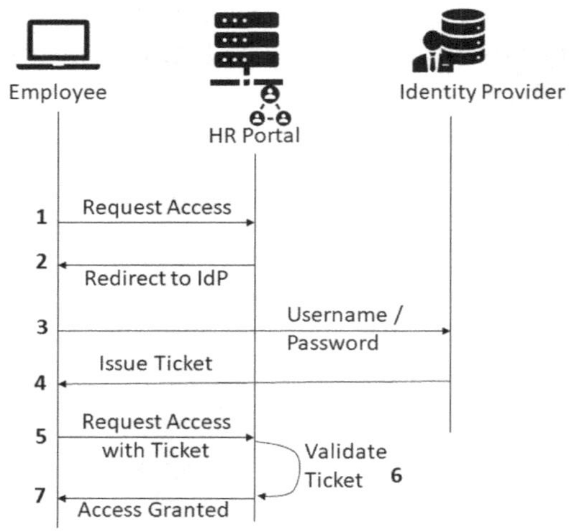

Figure 4.4: *SP-initiated authentication*

1 RFC 4120, https://www.ietf.org/rfc/rfc4120.txt

The potential authentication steps are:

1. The user agent (browser) tries to access a service provider (SP).
2. The service provider redirects the user to authenticate at an identity provider (IDP) and get an authentication ticket.
3. The user authenticates with the IDP.
4. The IDP issues the user a ticket.
5. The user agent (browser) presents the ticket to the SP and access request.
6. The SP validates the ticket.
7. The SP provides access to the resource.

IDP initiated

Let us contrast this with the IDP-initiated approach. Here, the users log into the IDP portal using their username and password. At the end of the authentication in step 2 in *Figure* 4.5: *IDP initiated authentication*, they land at a hyperlinked bookmark page of web applications. Clicking on a hyperlink will trigger step 3; the user can access the resource.

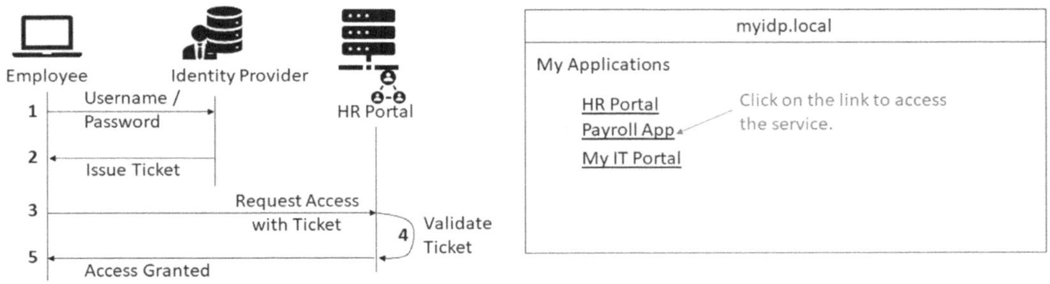

Figure 4.5: *IDP initiated authentication*

The user accessed the HR Application and provided a username and password once at the IDP login screen. Now, he goes to the payroll app. Does he have to present the login and password again?

Single sign-on

With only the Identity Provider, if we had authenticated using "Forms-based authentication", discussed in *Chapter 1: Introduction to Web Authentication*, we could have managed the authentication using a session cookie. If we could use the session cookie in all other services, we could have succeeded in single sign-on. The cookies are associated with a specific domain or sub-domains; you cannot share them across websites. An SP can offer a service from a different DNS domain than the DNS domain of the consumer enterprise. The access controls of the SPs can be different from one to the other. We will discuss this further in the next section. Sharing the cookie with all the SPs is not practical.

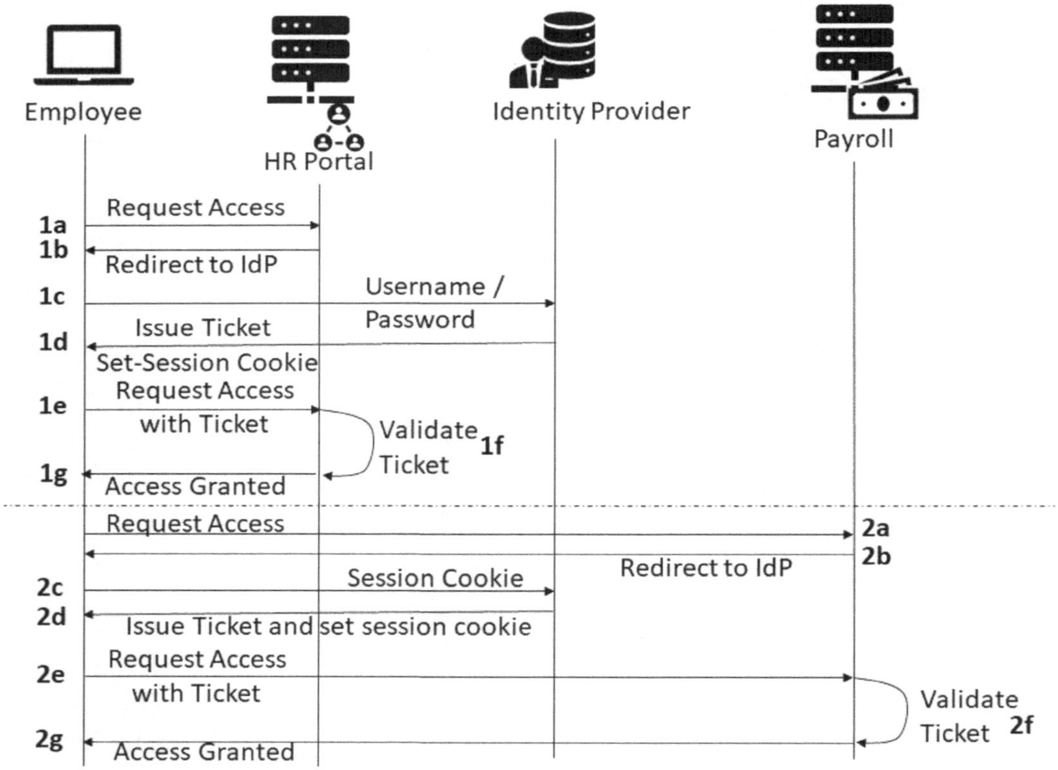

***Figure 4.6**: SSO with Federated Authentication*

In *Figure 4.6: SSO with Federated Authentication*, we have shown two SP-initiated authentication steps. The steps starting with '1' authenticate into the HR Portal, while the steps with '2' show authentication into the Payroll Portal. In step 1d, the IDP sets a session cookie in the browser on successful authentication. Step 2c utilizes the session cookie to authenticate into the IDP without providing the username and password. There is no requirement for a cross-domain cookie or any necessity for two SPs to use the same authentication ticket. The IDP maintains the session and issues separate tickets to both SPs.

Authentication ticket or token

In *Chapter 1, Introduction to Web Authentication*, we discussed access tokens. It is a good idea to extend that concept here. The users presented their credentials (username and password) to the IDP and obtained an access token. The access token should be trustworthy for the SP; the SP should ascertain the IDP issued it. If IDP signs this token, the SP can validate it. Should IDP sign with the same key pair for all the SPs? The IDP can use a different key pair for each of the SPs. Some prefer the second approach, as that ensures the token issued for SP_1 cannot be of any use to SP_2. Hence, there is no possibility of it getting misused. The ticket can have the following information:

- Subject or name identifying a user
- Issuer's identity
- Recipient's identity
- Time of issuance of the token
- The validity period of the token to be used:
    - not before
    - not after
- Revocation information of the token, if applicable
- Information on how and where to use the token

Looks familiar? We have seen some of this information with certificates in *Chapter 2: Fundamentals of Cryptography*. All this information is for the service provider to validate and confirm before using the token. For SSO, should a day-long ticket be issued to the SP? It depends on the SP. The tokens are issued for short durations, like 5-10 minutes, to ensure they are not affected by clock skews in distributed networks. Once a ticket is validated, the SP can decide when to revalidate with the IDP. A session cookie is maintained at the IDP by the user agent. Hence a new ticket can be issued to the SP as needed. Providing long-validity tokens may require token revocation procedures like in the case of certificates, which best be avoided. We looked at a token as a carrier of identity information, yet not all services require identity information for providing a service. Due to privacy concerns, some tickets have no identity or carry a pseudonymized identity. In some privacy-preserving blockchains, the transactions keep the public key of the user only, which is a form of pseudonymization.

Claims-based authentication

Let us continue with the pseudonymization example. An organization is setting up an application for whistleblowers to report on non-ethical practices. Such a service provider only needs to know if the person reporting is a bonafide employee of the organization. Their names, designations, or corporate identities are best not communicated to the service. In short, the SP is expecting the ticket provided by the IDP to claim if it belongs to an employee.

Contrast this to the example of the HR team having administrative rights on the HR Portal and the Finance team on the Payroll Application. Providing a group membership as part of the ticket is good enough for the SP to ascertain the level of access to the service. A user attribute on the token distinguishing full-time employees from contractors is another way to provide specific access. Claims can be considered a generalization over attribute-based or group-membership-based access control. The SP demands claims to be present in the token. The IDP fulfills them by deciphering the user information it has. Suppose a service requires the member to be above the age of majority; if the IDP sends the date of birth or the exact age of the user, it shares more information than expected. Merely reporting the user as not a minor is a good enough claim for the service to consume. It means the IDP will have a rules engine based on the user attributes and utilize them to fulfill claims needed for the SPs.

Do developers interested in federated authentication address all these complex scenarios? The answer is yes, but not by themselves. Fortunately, many vendors have understood these requirements and have developed identity and access management systems catering to such needs. You will seldom write code for an IDP but will consume tokens in SPs often. However, we will refrain from configuring IAMs in this book (we leave it as an exercise for you to try). There are many of them; they can be very complex to explain in this short book.

SAML token

Security Assertion Markup Language (SAML) is one of the most popular federated authentication schemes developed for web applications across domains. It will be a misnomer to call it just a ticket language. SAML has a well-defined authentication framework addressing all the scenarios we have discussed. SAML v2 standard came up in 2005. The language of choice was XML. Web Services and Simple Object Access Protocol (SOAP) were the popular standards for APIs. Hence, SAML is not strictly designed for REST APIs. SAML is still one of the most used Federated Authentication protocols for the web, hence the need to understand the design. Our focus will be on the conceptual aspects of SAML interactions. We will use a SAML library to manipulate any SAML constructs rather than manual editing.

The SAML specification has five broad parts.

- **Core**: Focuses on the protocol schema primitives.
- **Bindings**: Based on the underlying command of the HTTP protocol used (POST vs GET), the parameter structures of the communication change. Bindings define the parameter schema.
- **Profiles**: Common use cases the SAML protocol intends to address. It will vary based on client types, like web browsers vs. thick clients. We are interested in Web Browser SSO and the single logout profiles for this book.
- **Metadata**: The components of the SAML network, like the IDP and the SPs, need to communicate to each other their capabilities, signing and encryption certificates, connection endpoints, etc. They share this information as configuration metadata.
- **Conformance**: The required portions of the SAML protocol that the implementations should address for interoperability. When applications written using a standard can integrate without tweaking, the goals of the standard are met.

When using custom SAML integrations, it is a good practice to understand the SAML profile that is most relevant to you, identify the interacting parties in the protocol exchanges, and study the protocol primitives used from the core specifications. Reading a reference sample application addressing a similar example is another way to get the best out of the protocol. Reading the complete protocol text can be daunting. It can overwhelm any newbie programmer. Hence, we will discuss a few commonly used profiles, followed by parts of the primitives.

Metadata

Let us look at a simple IDP metadata to understand the concept. The metadata defines an IDP's service.

- There are two certificates, one for signing and the other for encryption.
- The IDP supports four encryption algorithms.
- The IDP supports a transient name ID or subject. It may not be meaningful outside of the transaction.
- The IDP only offers a single sign-on service at **/sso**. An SP can contact it through **HTTP-Redirect** (GET) or **HTTP-POST**.

```
<EntityDescriptor xmlns="urn:oasis:names:tc:SAML:2.0:metadata" validUntil="2023-04-10T06:34:43.761Z" cacheDuration="PT48H" entityID="/metadata">
  <IDPSSODescriptor xmlns="urn:oasis:names:tc:SAML:2.0:metadata" protocolSupportEnumeration="urn:oasis:names:tc:SAML:2.0:protocol">
    <KeyDescriptor use="signing">
      <KeyInfo xmlns="http://www.w3.org/2000/09/xmldsig#">
        <X509Data xmlns="http://www.w3.org/2000/09/xmldsig#">
          <X509Certificate xmlns="http://www.w3.org/2000/09/xmldsig#">MIIDBzCCAe+…=</X509Certificate>
        </X509Data>
      </KeyInfo>
    </KeyDescriptor>
    <KeyDescriptor use="encryption">
      <KeyInfo xmlns="http://www.w3.org/2000/09/xmldsig#">
        <X509Data xmlns="http://www.w3.org/2000/09/xmldsig#">
          <X509Certificate xmlns="http://www.w3.org/2000/09/xmldsig#">MIIDBzCCAe+…=</X509Certificate>
        </X509Data>
      </KeyInfo>
      <EncryptionMethod Algorithm="http://www.w3.org/2001/04/xmlenc#aes128-cbc"></EncryptionMethod>
      <EncryptionMethod Algorithm="http://www.w3.org/2001/04/xmlenc#aes192-cbc"></EncryptionMethod>
      <EncryptionMethod Algorithm="http://www.w3.org/2001/04/xmlenc#aes256-cbc"></EncryptionMethod>
      <EncryptionMethod Algorithm="http://www.w3.org/2001/04/xmlenc#rsa-oaep-mgf1p"></EncryptionMethod>
    </KeyDescriptor>
```

```
    <NameIDFormat>urn:oasis:names:tc:SAML:2.0:nameid-format:tran-
sient</NameIDFormat>
    <SingleSignOnService Binding="urn:oasis:names:tc:SAM-
L:2.0:bindings:HTTP-Redirect" Location="/sso"></SingleSignOnSer-
vice>
    <SingleSignOnService Binding="urn:oasis:names:tc:SAM-
L:2.0:bindings:HTTP-POST" Location="/sso"></SingleSignOnService>
  </IDPSSODescriptor>
</EntityDescriptor>
```

What about the SP? Does it also have metadata to describe its service description? Here is a sample service descriptor of an SP.

```
<EntityDescriptor xmlns="urn:oasis:names:tc:SAML:2.0:metadata"
validUntil="2023-04-06T13:24:10.714Z" entityID="http://local-
host:8000/saml/metadata">
  <SPSSODescriptor xmlns="urn:oasis:names:tc:SAML:2.0:metadata"
validUntil="2023-04-06T13:24:10.7142742Z" protocolSupportEnu-
meration="urn:oasis:names:tc:SAML:2.0:protocol" AuthnRequests-
Signed="true" WantAssertionsSigned="true">
    <KeyDescriptor use="encryption">
      <KeyInfo xmlns="http://www.w3.org/2000/09/xmldsig#">
        <X509Data xmlns="http://www.w3.org/2000/09/xmldsig#">
          <X509Certificate xmlns="http://www.w3.org/2000/09/xm-
ldsig#">…=</X509Certificate>
        </X509Data>
      </KeyInfo>
      <EncryptionMethod Algorithm="http://www.w3.org/2001/04/xm-
lenc#aes128-cbc"></EncryptionMethod>
      <EncryptionMethod Algorithm="http://www.w3.org/2001/04/xm-
lenc#aes192-cbc"></EncryptionMethod>
      <EncryptionMethod Algorithm="http://www.w3.org/2001/04/xm-
lenc#aes256-cbc"></EncryptionMethod>
      <EncryptionMethod Algorithm="http://www.w3.org/2001/04/xm-
lenc#rsa-oaep-mgf1p"></EncryptionMethod>
    </KeyDescriptor>
    <KeyDescriptor use="signing">
      <KeyInfo xmlns="http://www.w3.org/2000/09/xmldsig#">
        <X509Data xmlns="http://www.w3.org/2000/09/xmldsig#">
          <X509Certificate xmlns="http://www.w3.org/2000/09/xm-
```

```
ldsig#">…=</X509Certificate>
        </X509Data>
      </KeyInfo>
    </KeyDescriptor>
    <SingleLogoutService Binding="urn:oasis:names:tc:SAM-
L:2.0:bindings:HTTP-POST" Location="http://localhost:8000/saml/
slo" ResponseLocation="http://localhost:8000/saml/slo"></SingleL-
ogoutService>
    <NameIDFormat></NameIDFormat>
    <AssertionConsumerService Binding="urn:oasis:names:tc:SAM-
L:2.0:bindings:HTTP-POST" Location="http://localhost:8000/saml/
acs" index="1"></AssertionConsumerService>
    <AssertionConsumerService Binding="urn:oasis:names:tc:SAM-
L:2.0:bindings:HTTP-Redirect" Location="http://localhost:8000/
saml/acs" index="2"></AssertionConsumerService>
  </SPSSODescriptor>
</EntityDescriptor>
```

- There are two certificates, one for signing and the other for encryption.
- The SP supports four encryption algorithms.
- The SP only offers a single logout service at **/saml/sso**. An IDP can contact it through **HTTP-POST**.
- The SP provides assertion consumer service to receive the login tokens at **/saml/acs** as **HTTP-Redirect** and **HTTP-POST**.

The metadata of the SP should be configured in the IDP and vice versa. This way, the SP and IDP can know each other and communicate. However, the IDP or the SP does not need to publish their metadata.

Profiles

The Web Browser SSO profile is one of the most used SAML profiles and will be our subject matter of discussion here.

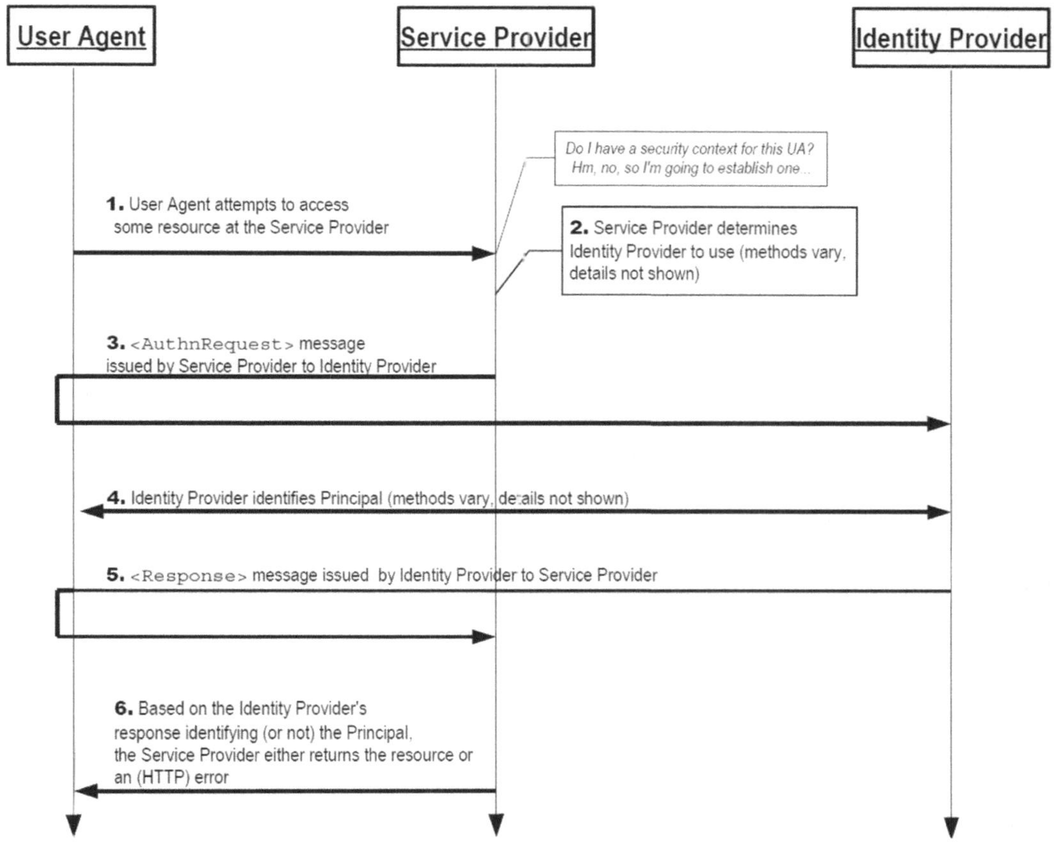

Figure 4.7: *Web Browser SSO Profile*
(Reproduced Figure 1: Profiles for the OASIS Security SAML v2)

A close look at *Figure 4.7: Web Browser* SSO *Profile* **(Reproduced Figure 1: *Profiles for the OASIS Security SAML v2*)** will ensure the scheme is not very different from *Figure 4.4: SP-initiated authentication.* In step 3, the service fills out an **`AuthnRequest`** for the user agent to submit to the IDP. Similarly, in step 5, the IDP issues a **`Response`** for the SP.

```
<?xml version="1.0"?>

<samlp:AuthnRequest
    xmlns:saml="urn:oasis:names:tc:SAML:2.0:assertion"
    xmlns:samlp="urn:oasis:names:tc:SAML:2.0:protocol"
    ID="id-691d0ed575bb8f812b6ac961a7b5f7a7d2a558a8"
    Version="2.0"
    IssueInstant="2023-04-08T12:50:25.879Z"
    Destination="/sso"
    AssertionConsumerServiceURL="http://localhost:8001/saml/acs"
    ProtocolBinding="urn:oasis:names:tc:SAML:2.0:bindings:HTTP-POST">
```

```
  <saml:Issuer
      Format="urn:oasis:names:tc:SAML:2.0:nameid-format:entity">
      http://localhost:8001/saml/metadata
  </saml:Issuer>
  <samlp:NameIDPolicy
      Format="urn:oasis:names:tc:SAML:2.0:nameid-format:transient"
      AllowCreate="true"/>
</samlp:AuthnRequest>
```

In step 3, there is an **AuthnRequest** sent to the IDP to validate the user. The request properties tell the IDP where to connect back to the SP using **HTTP-Post** binding. It also tells the IDP to create a user if the user does not exist. There is a mention of the issuer which is a URL to the metadata of the SP. It is not necessary for the IDP to access the SP at a predesignated **AssertionConsumerService** location defined in the metadata. The **AuthnRequest** can control that by providing an **AssertionConsumerServiceURL** explicitly.

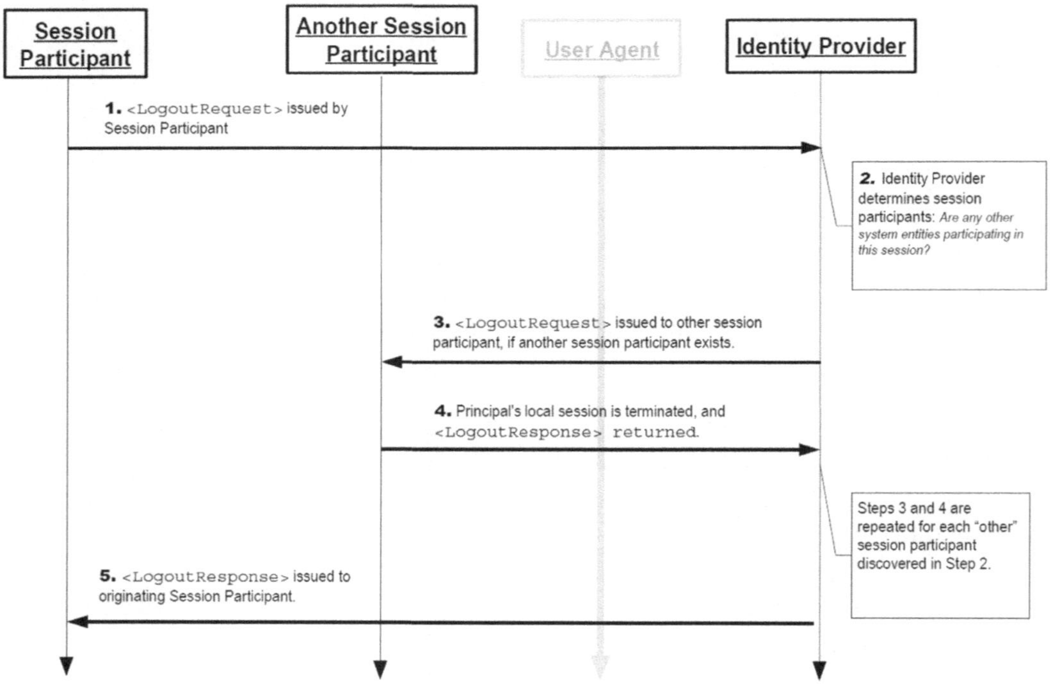

Figure 4.8: *Single Logout Profile (Figure 3: Profiles for the OASIS Security SAML v2)*

The single logout profile or SLO profile is another important profile. The idea here is simple. Since the IDP provides single sign-on service to all the service providers, it knows all the active service providers. If a user requests to log out from any service provider, the logout request can come to the IDP, and the IDP can create logout requests for all active service providers and send them. As simple as it may conceptually seem, there are some practical challenges. *What if the SPs are not on or in the middle of large transactions*? Such a request from a remote system can make the transactions inconsistent. Many libraries do not implement SLO properly. For example, the **crewjam/saml** package we use for the sample applications implements only the SP part of the SLO but not the IDP. If you use the SP library with an industry standard IDP, you can achieve SLO for your applications. A typical **LogoutRequest** looks like this[2]:

```
<samlp:LogoutRequest
    xmlns:samlp="urn:oasis:names:tc:SAML:2.0:protocol"
    xmlns="urn:oasis:names:tc:SAML:2.0:assertion"
    ID="d2b7c388cec36fa7c39c28fd298644a8"
    IssueInstant="2004-01-21T19:00:49Z" Version="2.0">
    <Issuer>https://IdentityProvider.com/SAML</Issuer>
    <NameID

        Format="urn:oasis:names:tc:SAML:2.0:nameid-
format:persistent">005a06e0-ad82-110d-a556-004005b13a2b</NameID>
    <samlp:SessionIndex>1</samlp:SessionIndex>
</samlp:LogoutRequest>
```

A response looks like this:

```
<samlp:LogoutResponse
    xmlns:samlp="urn:oasis:names:tc:SAML:2.0:protocol"
    xmlns="urn:oasis:names:tc:SAML:2.0:assertion"
    ID="b0730d21b628110d8b7e004005b13a2b"
    InResponseTo="d2b7c388cec36fa7c39c28fd298644a8"
    IssueInstant="2004-01-21T19:00:49Z" Version="2.0">
    <Issuer>https://ServiceProvider.com/SAML</Issuer>
    <samlp:Status>
        <samlp:StatusCode
Value="urn:oasis:names:tc:SAML:2.0:status:Success"/>
    </samlp:Status>
</samlp:LogoutResponse>
```

Binding

Profiles help us structure the data in a manner that can be transmitted using the underlying transport. In all the explanations, we have assumed the SPs and IDPs are interacting over HTTP GET-Redirect requests. In such a condition, the request can contain several parameters. When authenticating from an SP, a typical redirect to IDP looks like this[2].


```
https://idp.local:8443/idp/o?SAMLRequest=nJLNbtswDIBfReDdf7KbukJtI
GswLEC3BU22w26sxSwCLMkT6W55+yFph3aXDNhREj+Sn8hbRj9OZjnLITzQj5lY1C8/
nhw7mFExEdmwCemIjg9kuP94bnZcGmSmJiwHeINNlZkpR4hBHUOtVB85mN7a17b5a3J
RNU9PVQLXdP1atXjTa4r4q2+t6sWgqAvWVErsYOtB5CWrNPNM6sGCQDnSp66xsMn21K1
ujtdFVXl+330CtiMUFlDN5EJnYFIWzUz7GAUfTNk19OhbMEdTyj9FdDDx7Sl
tKT26gLw/3r/Ah5f7I6ek1Q1OczAscGNTmRfCdC9aF75d/4/E5iM2H3W6TbT5v
d9CfJ2LOekm9j8mjXE5yunE2259DDQVxcoT+n916ErQoeFu8Kdi/7MMn9LRebeLohu
N/NCEJAzsKAmo5jvHnXSIU6kDSTFD0zyX/3rr+dwAAAP//&RelayState=ODvy8cKq5l
MjwkXWiMjrVtCKL1hw2FdK6B9bPAV8AvaptB_lIgnDeump&SigAlg=http://www.
w3.org/2000/09/xmldsig#rsasha1&Signature=SQKdCaxXwqcEgan7u6026h+
KCPHn/2RMCGlKWzeuoZfdZKJkQ94h+DD2XhCWvT0u2QGHTJTn74QHanRp2q9iv6TIHt
s6gWEkvzS7iFUfFqOLQiupTNd9P82f8cLuFso9B/6/Re6yIXbY7JdnJshQeR4XHz
zk3Tnbwrx+yvACUPxZ2A95+Y43zIRQtRrzOpwDsGqnsARC4VcOWdFTN5uZDm6Y9y4
P0jWut3z9zzdsqbEboaM3pTU9lIUMb6d7VrOS3hUGJ2VxJk9zmXx231nTAJ+xED/j
bkI9QWIYJrKKfMnMayaqcnbhipgMOX0aismYQ7j0DoILvYP/fPeZiQI8ag==
```


There are four parameters in this URL.

1. **SAMLRequest**: The actual XML AuthnRequest object.
2. **RelayState**: A state information that the IDP can send back to the SP so that SP continues processing from that state after an authentication response from IDP.
3. **SigAlg**: The algorithm used to generate the signature.
4. **Signature**: The actual signature.

   XML data is compressed with the flate algorithm. The binary data is base64 encoded. The overall URL is URL encoded.

The actual XML of the **SAMLRequest** is:


```
<samlp:AuthnRequest
    xmlns:saml="urn:oasis:names:tc:SAML:2.0:assertion"
    xmlns:samlp="urn:oasis:names:tc:SAML:2.0:protocol"
    ID="id-9d8d8f1690443e5ce3dfb182642daf108736641e"
    Version="2.0"
    IssueInstant="2023-04-25T08:22:21.378Z"
    Destination="https://idp.local:8443/idp/sso"
    AssertionConsumerServiceURL=https://hr.mysrv.local:8444/saml/acs
    ProtocolBinding="urn:oasis:names:tc:SAML:2.0:bindings:HTTP-POST">
    <saml:Issuer
        Format="urn:oasis:names:tc:SAML:2.0:nameid-format:entity">
https://hr.mysrv.local:8444/saml/metadata</saml:Issuer>
    <samlp:NameIDPolicy Format="urn:oasis:names:tc:SAML:2.0:nameid-
```


2 Taken from the SAML Bindings Specifications.

```
format:transient"
        AllowCreate="true"/>
</samlp:AuthnRequest>
```

If the SP sends the **AuthnRequest** over **HTTP-GET Redirect**, the IDP does not need to respond on an **HTTP-GET**. The IDP can send the response as an **HTTP-POST** request. That is precisely mentioned in the above **AuthnRequest**. Here is a sample **AuthnRequest** using **HTTP-POST** binding[3].

```
<samlp:AuthnRequest
    xmlns:samlp="urn:oasis:names:tc:SAML:2.0:protocol"
    xmlns:saml="urn:oasis:names:tc:SAML:2.0:assertion"
    ID="pfx41d8ef22-e612-8c50-9960-1b16f15741b3"
    Version="2.0"
    ProviderName="SP test"
    IssueInstant="2014-07-16T23:52:45Z"
    Destination="http://idp.example.com/SSOService.php"
    ProtocolBinding="urn:oasis:names:tc:SAML:2.0:bindings:HTTP-POST"
    AssertionConsumerServiceURL="http://sp.example.com/demo1/index.
php?acs">
    <saml:Issuer>http://sp.example.com/demo1/metadata.php</saml:Issuer>
    <ds:Signature xmlns:ds="http://www.w3.org/2000/09/xmldsig#">
        <ds:SignedInfo>

      …

    </ds:Signature>
    <samlp:NameIDPolicy
        Format="urn:oasis:names:tc:SAML:1.1:nameid-format:emailAddress"
        AllowCreate="true"/>
    <samlp:RequestedAuthnContext Comparison="exact">
        <saml:AuthnContextClassRef>

urn:oasis:names:tc:SAML:2.0:ac:classes:PasswordProtectedTransport
        </saml:AuthnContextClassRef>
    </samlp:RequestedAuthnContext>
</samlp:AuthnRequest>
```

The signature and related information are part of one large XML envelope of the **AuthnRequest**. Similarly, the response XML in **HTTP-POST** contains one envelope with the assertion, response, and signed data. While requests and responses are communicated as several parameters in the **HTTP-GET** binding, in **HTTP-POST** binding only one large XML blob contains all the relevant parameters. We will look at the detailed response in the next example.

3 Example from OneLogin. **https://developers.onelogin.com/saml/examples/authnrequest**

An example

Enough of theory and conceptual discussions so far. Let us get to some implementations for real life. While real-life applications are complex and may need hundreds of application access, we simulate similar concepts with just three SPs and one IDP. We use the **crewjam/saml** Golang package to provide us with these functionalities. We use Flutter to render the user interface.

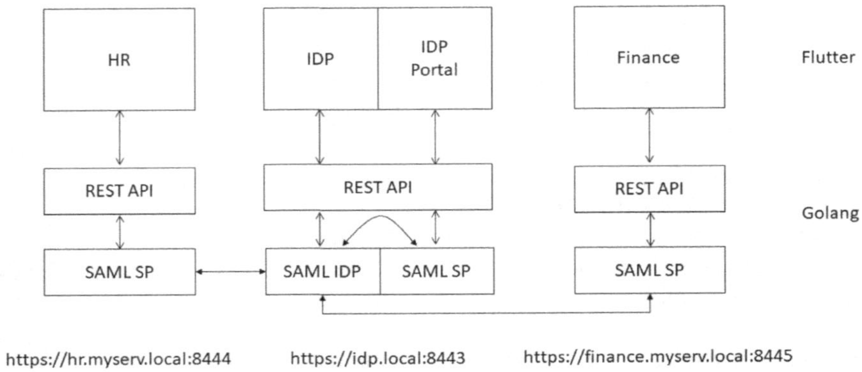

Figure 4.9: *Architectural Diagram of the Example*

In Chapter 4 folder of the sample code, you will find the sources of this example. There are hundreds of lines of code involved here. Hence, we will not be able to discuss all the source code. However, we will discuss the salient features of this code. The system comprises an IDP and three SPs. The three SPs are:

- HR App
- Finance App
- IDP Portal

We introduce the following changes in the **/etc/hosts** file such that all these apps can run on the same physical machine.

```
# Add these values to the /etc/hosts file.
# On Windows, the file can be: C:\Windows\System32\drivers\etc\hosts

127.0.0.5 mysrv.local
127.0.0.2 idp.local
127.0.0.3 finance.mysrv.local
127.0.0.4 hr.mysrv.local
```

```
The folder structure of the HR App is:
CHAPTER-4\HR
```

```
│   hr.go ← All backend implementation in Golang
├───certs
│   │   hr.p12 ← Certificate used for signing SAML Requests
│   └───ssl
│           hr.mysrv.local.p12 ← SSL certificate used for server
│
└───frontend
    ├───lib
            main.dart ← The frontend source code in Flutter/Dart.
```

Similarly, the structure of the IDP App is:

```
CHAPTER-4\IDP
│   idp.go
├───certs
│   │   idp.p12 ← Certificate used for signing SAML Responses
│   └───ssl
│           idp.local.p12 ← SSL certificate used for server
├───frontend
│   ├───lib
│   │       main.dart
└───sp ← Contains the metadata of all the service providers.
        finance.xml
        hr.xml
        idpportal.xml
```

The services are run on respective ports as shown in *Figure 4.9: Architectural Diagram of the Example*. The following code snippet is used to launch a TLS server using the **`Golang http`** module.

```
server := setupTLSServer("certs/ssl/idp.local.p12", "idp.local")
log.Default().Fatal(server.ListenAndServeTLS("", ""))
```

Configuring the identity provider

We use the **`crewjam/saml`** library and extend its capabilities to offer a minimal workable model for an identity provider. Since our focus is web authentication, we additionally provide single-sign-on capabilities to this application. The application UI has four tables showing:

- Users
- Service providers
- Shortcuts (used for IDP-initiated authentication)
- Active sessions

An IDP strictly does not require user authentication per se to the system. We like to provide IDP-initiated authentication that requires the links to be active when a user has logged in and a session exists. We call this service provided by the IDP the **IDP Portal**. The IDP must be started with the following command:

```
chapter-4\idp> go run ./idp.go
```

You can access it by reaching the website: **https://idp.local:8443/** on the browser.

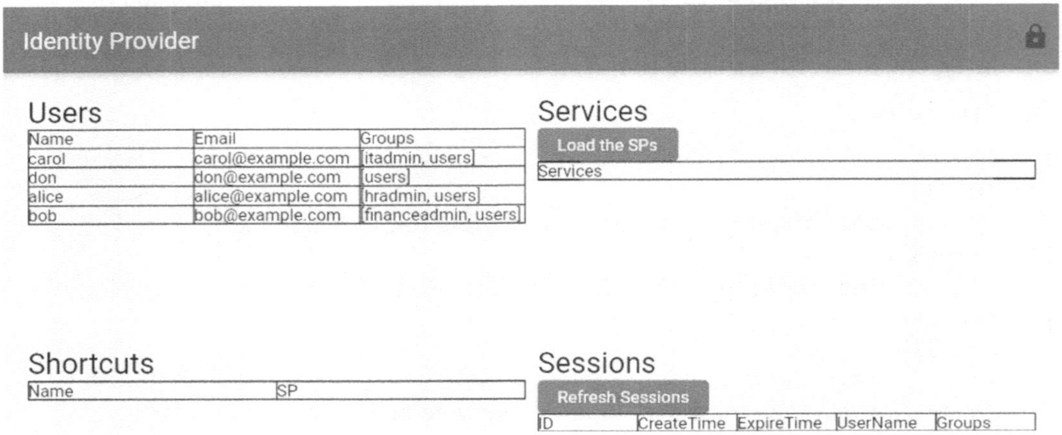

Figure 4.10: *IDP Initial Launch - No Service Provider is Loaded*

On the initial launch, service provider metadata are not loaded. Hence, the user can click the Load the SPs button to load the service providers. As the service providers are loaded, the login button in the top right corner gets active. The user can log in by clicking on the icon.

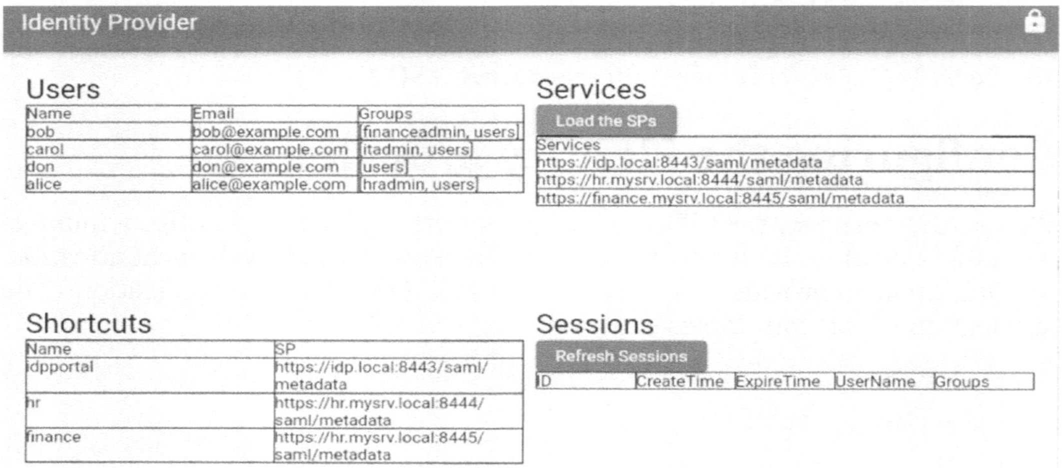

Figure 4.11: *SP Metadata is Loaded in the IDP*

Under the hood, the IDP attaches as a handler to the HTTPS server we started earlier. The following is the initialization code[4]:

```
if idpServer, err := samlidp.New(samlidp.Options{
    URL:         *baseURL,
    Key:         key,
    Certificate: cert,
    Store:       &samlidp.MemoryStore{},
}); err == nil {
    addUsers(idpServer)
    cors := cors.New(
       cors.Options{
           AllowedOrigins: []string{
          "https://hr.mysrv.local:8444",
          "https://finance.mysrv.local:8445"},
       })
    http.Handle("/idp/", cors.Handler(http.StripPrefix("/idp", idpServer)))
    http.HandleFunc("/", func(w http.ResponseWriter, r *http.Request) {
       http.SetCookie(w, &http.Cookie{
           Name:     "sploaded",
           Value:    strconv.FormatBool(sploaded),
           HttpOnly: false,
           Path:     "/",
       })
       invalidateIDPSession(w, r, idpServer)
       http.FileServer(http.Dir("frontend/build/web")).ServeHTTP(w, r)
    })
    http.HandleFunc("/addsps", addServiceProviders)
    addIDPAuth(idpServer, key.(*rsa.PrivateKey), cert)
}
```

As can be seen from the code:

1. The IDP service starts with a base URL, signing key, certificate, and memory store. There is no persistent store. Hence, every launch requires initialization.

4 Non-central concepts like error handling are not shown to keep the code simple.

2. Alice, Bob, Carol, and Don are the users. **`password`** is the password for all the users. The IDP loads this information.
3. The IDP is attached to the **`/idp`** virtual of the HTTPS server. Since SPs can redirect to IDP URLs, the permitted SPs should be white-listed. The Cross-Origin Resource Sharing (CORS) policy addresses these.
4. We serve the flutter-based frontend code at the root location. We also conduct some session cleanup as the user accesses the system.
5. We add a virtual **`/addsps`** as a trigger. All the SP metadata are loaded when the user clicks the **Load the SPs** button.
6. In the end, we attach the IDP Portal SP to the system.

The IDP exposes the following URLs. We use these extensively in the code to access the IDP[5].

```
/idp/metadata      - the SAML metadata
/idp/sso           - the SAML endpoint to initiate an authentication flow
/idp/login         - prompt for a username and password if no session is
established
/idp/login/:shortcut - kick off an IDP-initiated authentication flow
/idp/services      - RESTful interface to Service objects
/idp/users         - RESTful interface to User objects
/idp/sessions      - RESTful interface to Session objects
/idp/shortcuts     - RESTful interface to Shortcut objects
```

Once the IDP is configured and operational, we configure a Service Provider (SP) to authenticate a user.

Configuring the HR app service provider

HR App is a trivial pending leave view website. A user in the **hradmin** group can see the leave balance of all the users, while the users in the **users** group see the leave balances of theirs only. It provides a login button to log in to the system. To launch the application:

1. Make sure the IDP is running.
2. The SP metadata is loaded to the IDP.
3. Start the application by using the following command:

```
chapter-4\hr> go run ./hr.go
```

5 From the **`samlidp`** documentation. **https://pkg.go.dev/github.com/crewjam/saml/samlidp#Server**

4. Launch the browser and go to the URL: **https://hr.mysrv.local:8444**

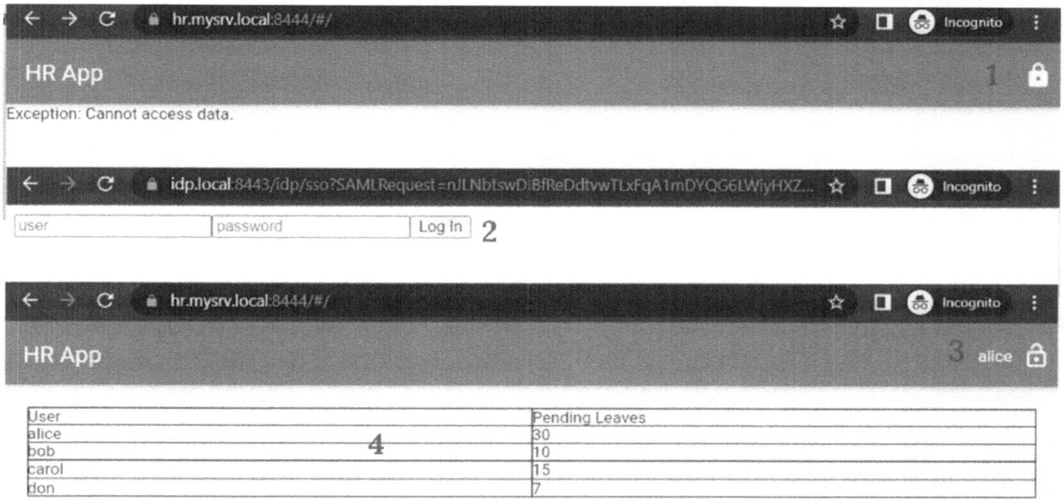

Figure 4.12: *User Alice accessing the HR App*

Once the user interface shows up, the steps are relatively simple.

1. Click on the lock icon in the top right corner.
2. The browser is directed to the **https://idp.local:8443/idp/sso** URL with a SAML request. Now, provide **alice** as the username and **password** as the password.
3. Authentication is successful. One sees the username and logout button in the top right corner.
4. As Alice belongs to the **hradmin** group, we see pending leaves of all the users.

We met the expectations of the application, *but how did it all work under the hood?*

In the code, we have configured a SAML service provider (**`crewjam/saml/samlsp`**) as shown[6]:

```
key, cert, _ := getProviderCertAndKey("certs/hr.p12")
idpMetadataURL, _ := url.Parse("https://idp.local:8443/idp/metadata")
idpMetadata, _ := samlsp.FetchMetadata(context.Background(),
                        http.DefaultClient, *idpMetadataURL)
samlSP, _ := samlsp.New(samlsp.Options{
    URL:                *rootURL,
```

6 Non-central concepts like error handling are not shown to keep the code simple.

```
    Key:               key,
    Certificate:      cert,
    AllowIDPInitiated: true,
    SignRequest:       true,
    IDPMetadata:       idpMetadata,
})

http.Handle("/saml/", samlSP)
http.Handle("/", http.FileServer(http.Dir("frontend/build/web")))
```

- We extract the key and the certificate from the **pkcs12** envelope and provide them to the initialization API.
- The initialization requires a few parameters like the **idpMetadata** that we directly fetch from the IDP by querying the metadata URL.
- The SP signs all the requests it sends to the IDP.
- The SP accepts IDP-initiated responses, which means the IDP can send responses to the SP without the SP sending an **AuthnRequest**. We will review this in a subsequent section.
- We bind the service provider to handle all requests coming on the **/saml/** virtual.
- We also want the frontend flutter code to be served from the **/** virtual.

Where is the authentication happening then? The authentication is bound to the **/auth** virtual. This is triggered when the lock button is clicked on the UI.

```
http.Handle("/auth/",
    samlSP.RequireAccount(
        http.HandlerFunc(func(w http.ResponseWriter, r *http.Request) {
            sProvider := samlSP.Session
            switch r.URL.Path {
            case "/auth/logout":
                // Session cleanup code goes here.
            default:
                // Session establishment code goes here.
            }
            http.Redirect(w, r, "/", http.StatusFound)
        }),
    ),
)
```

SAML libraries, like **crewjam/saml** hide all the protocol-level details. That is why you need to look at the network logs in the developer tool of the Chrome browser. Here, the **RequireAccount** call does all the magic. We will discuss this method in session management with further details. Let us relook at steps 1 to 4.

1. The IDP metadata tells the SP the availability of the Web SSO profile at: **https://idp.local:8443/idp/sso**.

```
<EntityDescriptor xmlns="urn:oasis:names:tc:SAML:2.0:metadata"
    validUntil="2023-04-29T03:40:35.161Z"
    cacheDuration="PT48H"
    entityID="https://idp.local:8443/idp/metadata">
 <IDPSSODescriptor xmlns="urn:oasis:names:tc:SAML:2.0:metadata"
     protocolSupportEnumeration="urn:oasis:names:tc:
                                SAML:2.0:protocol">
 <KeyDescriptor use="signing">
      ...
 </KeyDescriptor>
 <KeyDescriptor use="encryption">
      ...
 </KeyDescriptor>
 <NameIDFormat>urn:oasis:names:tc:SAML:2.0:nameid for-
mat:transient
 </NameIDFormat>
 <SingleSignOnService
     Binding="urn:oasis:names:tc:SAML:2.0:bindings:HTTP-Redirect"
     Location="https://idp.local:8443/idp/sso"/>
 <SingleSignOnService
    Binding="urn:oasis:names:tc:SAML:2.0:
                                      bindings:HTTP-POST"
     Location="https://idp.local:8443/idp/sso"/>
 </IDPSSODescriptor>
</EntityDescriptor>
```

2. Hence, the authentication request is sent as an **HTTP-redirect** to **https://idp.local:8443/idp/sso.** The URL is shown here:

```
https://idp.local:8443/idp/sso?
SAMLRequest=…&
RelayState=…&
SigAlg=…&
Signature=…
```

The **SAMLRequest** is shown below:

```
        <samlp:AuthnRequest
xmlns:saml="urn:oasis:names:tc:SAML:2.0:assertion"
            xmlns:samlp="urn:oasis:names:tc:SAML:2.0:protocol"
            ID="id-9d8d8f1690443e5ce3dfb182642daf108736641e"
            Version="2.0"
            IssueInstant="2023-04-25T08:22:21.378Z"
            Destination="https://idp.local:8443/idp/sso"
            AssertionConsumerServiceURL="https://hr.mysrv.
local:8444/saml/acs"
            ProtocolBinding="urn:oasis:names:tc:SAML:2.0:bindings:
HTTP-POST">
           <saml:Issuer Format="urn:oasis:names:tc:SAML:2.0:name
id-format:entity">
               https://hr.mysrv.local:8444/saml/metadata
           </saml:Issuer>
           <samlp:NameIDPolicy
               Format="urn:oasis:names:tc:SAML:2.0:nameid-
format:transient"
               AllowCreate="true"/>
        </samlp:AuthnRequest>
```

The IDP verifies the request with the Signature presented. The IDP has access to the metadata of the SP. Hence, it knows the public key of the signature. There is also a **RelayState** attribute sent along with the request. The IDP sends back this value to the SP as part of the **SAMLResponse**.

3. The IDP sends the response to the **AssertionConsumerServiceURL** of the SP. **AssertionConsumerServiceURL** is specified in the **AuthnRequest**. The IDP also sends the **RelayState** along with the response. The SP receives the response as an HTTP-Post. *Why*? Here are the relevant sections from the SP's metadata.

```
<AssertionConsumerService
    Binding="urn:oasis:names:tc:SAML:2.0:bindings:HTTP-POST"
    Location="https://hr.mysrv.local:8444/saml/acs"
    index="1"></AssertionConsumerService>
<AssertionConsumerService
    Binding="urn:oasis:names:tc:SAML:2.0:bindings:HTTP-Artifact"
    Location="https://hr.mysrv.local:8444/saml/acs"
    index="2"></AssertionConsumerService>
```

There is no definition of **AssertionConsumerService** (ACS) on an **HTTP-Redirect** binding. You may see **AuthnRequest** with **Assertion ConsumerServiceIndex** as an attribute. For example, the **AuthnRequest** could have **AssertionConsumerServiceIndex=1** in the attributes list. The SAML response has two form parameters. **SAMLResponse** and **RelayState**. In most cases, the **SAMLResponse** is a canonicalized XML document compressed using flate and encoded with the Base-64 algorithm[7]. The encoded form may look like this:

PHNhbWxwOlJlc3BvbnNlIHhtbG5zOnNhbWw9InVybjpvYXNpczpuYW1l
czp0YzpTQU1MOjIuMDphc3NlcnRpb24iIHhtbG5zOnNhbWxwPSJ1cm46b
2FzaXM6bmFtZXM6dGM6U0FNTDoyLjA6cHJvdG9jb2wiIHhtbG5zOnhzPS
JodHRwOi8vd3d3LnczLm9yZy8yMDAxL1hNTFNjaGVtYSIgSUQ9ImlkL
WI4MDdhYmYxYzY0OWQyYTE0Y2VjMjdiNDRiOTBiNmZiZWViMDU4ZjciIEluUmVzc
G9uc2VUbz0iaWQtOWQ4 …

HJpYnV0ZVZhbHVlPjxzYW1sOkF0dHJpYnV0ZVZhbHVlIHhtbG5zOn
hzaT0iaHR0cDovL3d3dy53My5vcmcvMjAwMS9YTUxTY2hlbWEtaW5zdGFuY2Ui
IHhzaTp0eXBlPSJ4czpzdHJpbmciPnVzZXJzPC9zYW1sOkF0dHJpYnV0ZVZhbH
VlPjwvc2FtbDpBdHRyaWJ1dGU+PC9zYW1sOkF0dHJpYnV0ZVN0YXRlbWVudD48L
3NhbWw6QXNzZXJ0aW9uPjwvc2FtbHA6UmVzcG9uc2U+

When decoded you see:

```
        <samlp:Response
xmlns:saml="urn:oasis:names:tc:SAML:2.0:assertion"
      … Attributes deleted
             Destination="https://hr.mysrv.local:8444/saml/acs">
        <saml:Issuer Format="urn:oasis:names:tc:SAML:2.0:nameid-
format:entity">
             https://idp.local:8443/idp/metadata</saml:Issuer>
        <ds:Signature xmlns:ds="http://www.w3.org/2000/09/
xmldsig#">
             … <!--- This is the signature of the response --->
        </ds:Signature>
        <samlp:Status>
     <samlp:StatusCode
Value="urn:oasis:names:tc:SAML:2.0:status:Success"/>
        </samlp:Status>
        <saml:Assertion
xmlns:saml="urn:oasis:names:tc:SAML:2.0:assertion"
             ID="id-cca9e5c45019296318fc0575edfe719b7785ba8f"
```

7 Many decoders are available in the market to decode such responses. We do not endorse any specific vendor nor recommend any such tools. We used the online tools freely available at: **https://www.samltool.com/online_tools.php**

```
            IssueInstant="2023-04-25T08:22:55.611Z"
            Version="2.0">
            <saml:Issuer
                Format="urn:oasis:names:tc:SAML:2.0:nameid-
format:entity">
                https://idp.local:8443/idp/metadata</saml:Issuer>
            <ds:Signature xmlns:ds="http://www.w3.org/2000/09/
xmldsig#">
                … This is the signature of the assertion.
            </ds:Signature>
            <saml:Subject>
                <saml:NameID
                   Format="urn:oasis:names:tc:SAML:2.0:nameid-
format:transient"
                   NameQualifier=https://idp.local:8443/idp/
metadata
                   SPNameQualifier="https://hr.mysrv.local:8444/
saml/metadata">
                   alice@example.com </saml:NameID>
                <saml:SubjectConfirmation
                   Method="urn:oasis:names:tc:SAML:2.0:cm:bearer">
                <saml:SubjectConfirmationData
Address="127.0.0.1:61849"
                   InResponseTo="id-9d8d8f1690443e5ce3dfb182642daf
108736641e"
                   NotOnOrAfter="2023-04-25T08:24:25.487Z"

                   Recipient="https://hr.mysrv.local:8444/saml/
acs"/>
                </saml:SubjectConfirmation>
            </saml:Subject>
            <saml:Conditions NotBefore="2023-04-25T08:22:21.378Z"
                NotOnOrAfter="2023-04-25T08:23:51.378Z">
               <saml:AudienceRestriction>
                  <saml:Audience>https://hr.mysrv.local:8444/saml/
metadata
             </saml:Audience>
               </saml:AudienceRestriction>
```

```
            </saml:Conditions>
            <saml:AuthnStatement
…
                <saml:AuthnContext>
                    <saml:AuthnContextClassRef>

urn:oasis:names:tc:SAML:2.0:ac:classes:PasswordProtectedTransport
                    </saml:AuthnContextClassRef>
                </saml:AuthnContext>
            </saml:AuthnStatement>
            <saml:AttributeStatement>
                <saml:Attribute FriendlyName="uid"
                    Name="urn:oid:0.9.2342.19200300.100.1.1"
                    NameFormat="urn:oasis:names:tc:SAML:2.0:attrna
me-format:uri">
                    <saml:AttributeValue
                        xmlns:xsi="http://www.w3.org/2001/
XMLSchema-instance"
                        xsi:type="xs:string">alice</
saml:AttributeValue>
                </saml:Attribute>
                <saml:Attribute
FriendlyName="eduPersonPrincipalName"
                    Name="urn:oid:1.3.6.1.4.1.5923.1.1.1.6"
                    NameFormat="urn:oasis:names:tc:SAML:2.0:attrna
me-format:uri">
                    <saml:AttributeValue
                        xmlns:xsi="http://www.w3.org/2001/
XMLSchema-instance"
                        xsi:type="xs:string">
                        alice@example.com</saml:AttributeValue>
                </saml:Attribute>
…
                <saml:Attribute FriendlyName="eduPersonAffiliation"
                    Name="urn:oid:1.3.6.1.4.1.5923.1.1.1.1"
                    NameFormat="urn:oasis:names:tc:SAML:2.0:attrna
me-format:uri">
```

```
                    <saml:AttributeValue
                        xmlns:xsi="http://www.w3.org/2001/XMLSchema-
instance"                               xsi:type="xs:string">hradmin</
saml:AttributeValue>
                    <saml:AttributeValue
                        xmlns:xsi="http://www.w3.org/2001/XMLSchema-
instance"                             xsi:type="xs:string">users</
saml:AttributeValue>
                </saml:Attribute>
            </saml:AttributeStatement>
        </saml:Assertion>
        </samlp:Response>
```

The response is composed of three parts:

- **Status**: This section lets the SP know if the authentication has succeeded.
- **Assertion**: This section states who has authenticated and the various attributes known about the subject.
- **Signature**: IDP has signed the response.

The assertion stands by itself and can be extracted from the response and validated. It has its signature section that signs the assertion section only. The assertion section has a few items that we like to highlight here.

- **Subject** - The name of the user in well-defined formats.
- **Subject Confirmation** - This specific assertion can be a bearer validation. In other cases, the relying party can demand additional assurance to thrust the assertion provider.
- **Conditions** - **`NotBefore`** or **`NotOnOrAfter`** stating the validity window of the assertion. This assertion is valid for only 90 sec.
- **AuthnStatement** - We bring your attention to the **`AuthnContextRef`**. The user provided username and password to authenticate. An AuthnRequest can specifically demand a particular authenticator as well.
- **Attributes** - The Assertion contains several attributes about the user.

4. For example, the groups attribute in the assertion (**`eduPersonAffiliation`**) has **hradmin** as a value. Hence, Alice sees the data of all the users.

Session management

The IDP issued an assertion to the bearer with a trust valid for 90 sec. The SP must keep the user authenticated for as long as he wants to work. The SP session management addresses this situation. The samlsp package takes the assertion and recreates another token using the JSON Web Ticket (JWT) format. We shall review the details of this format in the chapter on OIDC. JWT has three parts:

- **Header** - contains the signing algorithm details with the type, which is JWT.
- **Body** - Contains the subject and attributes, which we have seen in the assertion section.
- **Signature** - The SP issued it. Hence, signed by the SP's signature.

```
{
  "alg": "RS256", "typ": "JWT"
}
{
  "aud": "https://hr.mysrv.local:8444",
  "exp": 1682414575, ### Tue Apr 25 2023 09:22:55 GMT+0000
  "iat": 1682410975,
  "iss": "https://hr.mysrv.local:8444",
  "nbf": 1682410975, ### Tue Apr 25 2023 08:22:55 GMT+0000
  "sub": "alice@example.com",
  "attr": {
    …
    "cn": ["Alice Smith"],
    "eduPersonAffiliation": ["hradmin","users"],
    "eduPersonPrincipalName": ["alice@example.com"],
    "givenName": ["Alice"],
    "sn": ["Smith"],
    "uid": ["alice"]
  },
  "saml-session": true
}
//Signature section not shown
```

This data is normally encoded using Base-64 encoding[8]. The encoded string looks like this.


```
eyJhbGciOiJSUzI1NiIsInR5cCI6IkpXVCJ9.eyJhdWQiOiJodHRwczovL2hyLm15c3J2Lmx
vY2FsOjg0NDQiLCJleHAiOjE2ODI0MTQ1NzUsImlhdCI6MTY4MjQxMDk3NSwiaXNzIjoi
aHR0cHM6Ly9oci5teXNydi5sb2NhbDo4NDQ0IiwibmJmIjoxNjgyNDEwOTc1LCJzdWIiOiJhb
GljZUBleGFtcGxlLmNvbSIsImF0dHIiOnsiU2Vzc2lvbkluZGV4IjpbImUzNTFmZDk0Y2Q1M
WY5YTVkMDAwNzNkMDQyOWRjYjJmOTdjMzAwOTllNzZjYTgwOGI2NWFhNGIxZTY2ZGJjYzYiX
SwiY24iOlsiQWxpY2UgU21pdGgiXSwiZWR1UGVyc29uQWZmaWxpYXRpb24iOlsiaHJhZG1pbiIs
InVzZXJzIl0sImVkdVBlcnNvblByaW5jaXBhbE5hbWUiOlsiYWxpY2VAZXhhbXBsZS5jb20iX
SwiZ2l2ZW5OYW1lIjpbIkFsaWNlIl0sInNuIjpbIlNtaXRoIl0sInVpZCI6WyJhbGljZSdfS-
wic2FtbC1zZXNzaW9uIjp0cnVlfQ.n3WbxSXmXJ-Sh2-y2LMIrm_lrRZxZHL6y7WwAUk-
S1h6OX20KbNXtzhm6GViVoKXSlT78wfQ9tuCg8QVIyN-Jauuj0kS0MivClXgIBbraKpYDAgbg-
DUVskWgfy6fX8Q_6KP5GB2kK34BT8ykK_IdDJYe4YTWFYE-jTY7VK4ynQuMJ4662IaaXqrY7X-
tWc3WVtep3mwPjlRTym79jjgEEPPJrpyKuD9RtZhsn9rwFuwXiihyxu9lif44RnVyk2M7u8dFn_
bXGDspY1rGZ81DBPz7hElbZBqmqXNgXfkBU4UautXgm9SVwtnBnBu_-r7aG95NJ3YnHAclWW3_8T-
mQtbxQ
```


The issued JWT is for one hour while the original assertion was only issued for 90 secs. It is time to relook at the **`/auth`** handler again.

```
http.Handle("/auth/",
    samlSP.RequireAccount(
        http.HandlerFunc(func(w http.ResponseWriter, r *http.Request) {
            sProvider := samlSP.Session
            switch r.URL.Path {
            case "/auth/logout":
                sProvider.DeleteSession(w, r)
                // Delete the cookie named uid
            default:
                // set the cookie named uid
            }
            http.Redirect(w, r, "/", http.StatusFound)
        }),
    ),
)
```

The **`RequireAccount`** handler does all the session management activity here.

- The session management does not involve the IDP at all.
- The **`RequireAccount`** handler looks for a valid cookie with a name **`token`.** The cookie contains the actual JWT string. It checks the validity of the token.

8 Many decoders are available in the market to decode such responses. We do not endorse any specific vendor nor recommend any such tools. We used the online tools freely available at: **https://jwt.io**

- If no token is found or the token is invalid, it initiates the SAML Authentication workflow.
- On successful authentication, the handler creates a JWT token from the SAML assertion. This JWT token is signed with the SP's key and can be validated only with the SP's certificate. The token is marked **`HttpOnly`**. Hence, it cannot be accessed by JavaScript of the browser.
- We extract the **`uid`** from the token and set it separately. Now, the browser can render the logged-in user in the Flutter code.

```
appBar: AppBar(
  title: const Text('HR App'),
  actions: [
    Consumer<CookieRead>(
    builder: (context, cr, child) {
      if (cr.uid == null) {
        return IconButton(
          onPressed: () {
            launchUrl(
              Uri(scheme: "https", path: "/auth/"),
              webOnlyWindowName: "_self",
            ).then((_) => Provider.of<CookieRead>(context).
refresh());
          },
          icon: const Icon(Icons.lock),
          tooltip: "Login",
        );
      } else {
        return Row(
          children: <Widget>[
            Text(cr.uid!),
            IconButton(
              onPressed: () {
                launchUrl(
                  Uri(scheme: "https", path: "/auth/logout"),
                  webOnlyWindowName: "_self",
                ).then((_) => Provider.of<CookieRead>(context).
```

```
refresh());
                },
                icon: const Icon(Icons.lock_open),
                  tooltip: "Logout",
              ),
            ]);}})]),
```

The **CookieRead** is a **ChangeNotifier** that looks for a cookie by the name: **uid** and shows the username on the user interface.

- The logout implementation for the SP is local. This only clears the **token** cookie. The IDP token is not affected. No implementation of Single Logout (SLO) exists with the **samlidp** library. Hence, we have implemented a simple local logout only.

Protecting the APIs

With Flutter or React-based UI becoming central to web development, we need limited privacy protection in the user interface. REST APIs serve the View Models. We protect them with authentication guards. Here is how we protect the **/data** virtual.

```
http.HandleFunc("/data", func(w http.ResponseWriter, r *http.Request) {
    if session, err := samlSP.Session.GetSession(r); err == nil {
        attr := session.(samlsp.SessionWithAttributes).GetAttributes()
        var jsValue []byte
        bFound := false
        for _, v := range attr["eduPersonAffiliation"] {
            switch v {
            case "hradmin":
                jsValue, _ = json.Marshal(database)
                bFound = true
            case "users":
                uid := attr.Get("uid")
                jsValue = []byte(fmt.Sprintf("{ \"%s\" : %d}",
                                             uid, database[uid]))
            }
            if bFound {
                break
```

```
            }
        }
        w.Write(jsValue)
    } else {
        http.Error(w, "User not authenticated", http.StatusUnauthorized)
    }
})
```

Unlike **RequireAccount**, the **GetSession** method checks the existence of a valid token cookie. If the cookie does not exist, the authentication fails and an HTTP error is sent back as the response. **XMLHttpRequest** browser objects (Flutter **HttpClient**) access the REST APIs. These objects do not have access to the browser front end to redirect to an authentication form.

Single sign-on

We have launched the IDP, HR App, and Finance App. Now we access the HR App. We process the SP-initiated authentication sequence and access the HR App. Next, we access the Finance App by going to the URL: **https://finance.myserv.local:8445**. As expected, Alice is not prompted for any username and passwo]rd. She accesses the Finance App. The outline of the workflow is discussed in ***Figure 4.6: SSO with Federated Authentication***.

- The Finance App redirects to the IDP with an **AuthnRequest**.
- We suggest you go to the IDP page and open the developer tools. Under the applications tab, you will see a **session** cookie.
- When a browser sends this cookie to the website **https://idp.local:8443**, there is no authentication with a username and password required.
- The Finance App receives the relevant **SAMLResponse** on its **AssertionConsumerServiceURL**.
- The user logs in. Since Alice is not a member of the **financeadmin** group, she does not see the information of all the users.

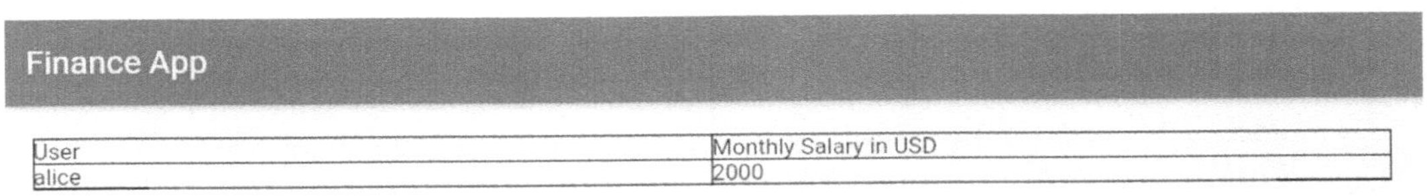

Figure 4.13: *SSO to the Finance App*

If you visit the IDP, you will still see the closed lock icon. However, clicking the icon will log in the user to the IDP Portal SP. There will be no need to provide a username and password.

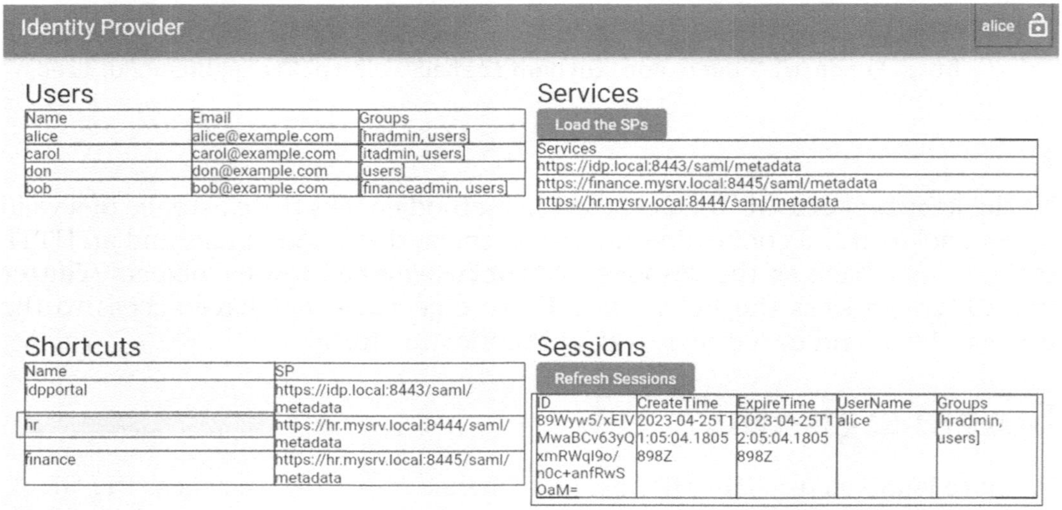

Figure 4.14: *IDP Portal on User Login*

You will observe the highlighted changes:

- Username and Logout buttons show up in the top right corner.
- In the Shortcuts section, the SP names will become clickable. We will be able to log in to these Apps by clicking on these cells. We will discuss this further under the IDP-initiated authentication.
- You will also see only one session in the Sessions section, while we logged into three applications.

If you go to the developer tools and view the cookies associated with this site, you will see these cookies:

- **`token`**: An IDP Portal SP cookie used to maintain the authentication in the IDP portal.
- **`session`**: This is the actual SSO session the IDP maintains. All the SSO authentications are carried out using this cookie.
- **`uid`**: The username cookie that is used to access the username in the Flutter sources.

The IDP initialization code had a line **`addIDPAuth(idpServer, key.(*rsa.PrivateKey), cert).`** This code sets up the IDP Portal authentication. The code is like what we have seen with the HR App.

- We set up a **`/saml`** virtual and associate it with the **`samlsp`** middleware.
- We associate a **`/auth`** virtual that manages the sessions and cookies for the SP.
- The IDP logout deletes the SSO **`session`** cookie. This means further authentications require a new authentication session.

IDP-initiated authentication

Before starting this, make sure you log out of any HR App screen open in the browser. And there is no residual **`token`** or **`uid`** cookie on the website: **https://hr.mysrv.local:8444.** Now, log in to the IDP as Alice. You will end up in ***Figure 4.14: IDP Portal on User Login***. There is an **`InkWell`** set around the SP names in the Shortcuts section. Clicking that will open the HR App in a new tab.

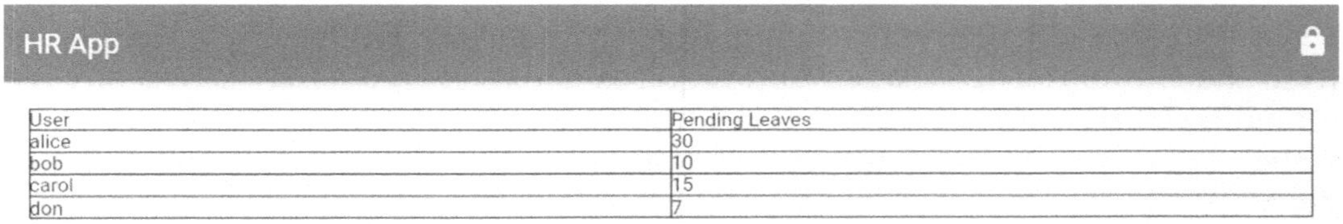

***Figure 4.15**: Clicking the IDP Link Led to Authentication in SP*

In the configuration of SP, we allowed IDP to send **`SAMLResponse`** directly without the SP requesting an **`AuthnRequest`**. If you look at the network logs in the browser developer tools, you will see a complete **`SAMLResponse`** form field posted to **https://hr.mysrv.local:8444/saml/acs**. Instead of clicking the cell, you could directly access the URL **https://idp.local:8443/idp/login/hr**. *Could you spot the error in the UI yet?*

You will see the lock is closed in the top right corner, yet the data is shown in the UI.

- As the user has logged in already in the IDP when the **`SAMLResponse`** reaches the ACS, the **`samlsp`** module creates a valid token.
- Since we check only for the **`token`** cookie in the **`/data`** virtual, the results are reported in the table.
- We create the **`uid`** cookie only when the **`/auth`** virtual is hit. Now try this URL in the browser: **https://idp.local:8443/idp/login/hr/auth**

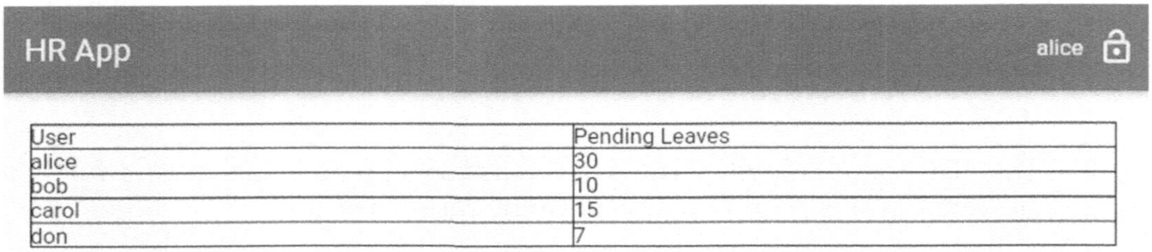

User	Pending Leaves
alice	30
bob	10
carol	15
don	7

Figure 4.16: *Accessing with the proper RelayState ensures authentication*

If you view the form data submitted to the ACS, you will realize **`/auth`** was sent as the **`RelayState`**. The **`samlsp`** is redirected to the RelayState once the authentication data is verified at the ACS.

Protected resources

Did you realize the authentication guard set up for the Finance App is different from the HR App? The Finance App requires a logged-in user to access any file including UI resources on the server, the authentication guard is set on the root virtual (**`/`**). While the HR App routes authentication through a specific virtual **`/auth`**. *What should be the approach in real life?* The browser does not require downloading all the files through a UI. With **`XMLHttpRequest`** (Flutter **`HttpClient`**) objects, some resources can be downloaded in the background. In such cases, redirection to authentication can fail. It can be detrimental when some resource files cannot be downloaded. Assume a background thread downloads a resource file. The client redirects to the login page. Since there is no UI, the user cannot authenticate. The user authenticates on the first file that downloads through the UI channel, like, an HTML file. There is a possibility that some resource files are lost when accessed by a background thread. With MVVM architecture, the UI or View layer may not need authentication protection. The real private data is available at the View Model (REST API) layer. Hence, a dedicated virtual, like, **`/auth`** in HRApp, can carry out the authentication. However, one must be careful of possible oversights we observed in our implementation of using the **`RelayState`** effectively.

Note:

*Separating the authentication to a specific URL, like **`/auth`**, helps the UI developers launch the URL in a popup or dialog window and complete authentication there. This way, the main application can continue to show the static view (without authentication) on the screen. If the authentication is successful in the popup window, the main application receives an updated view model to render the authenticated view. However, in all our sample code in the book, we use complete application redirection to reduce the UI complexity.*

Identity and access management

Whenever we attempt to explain something using simplified examples, we run the risk of trivializing the problem. Yet, a simple system helps to visualize problems seen in real life. In the example of IDP, HR App, and IT App, we discussed significant concepts of identity and access management (IAM). Let us take a closer look.

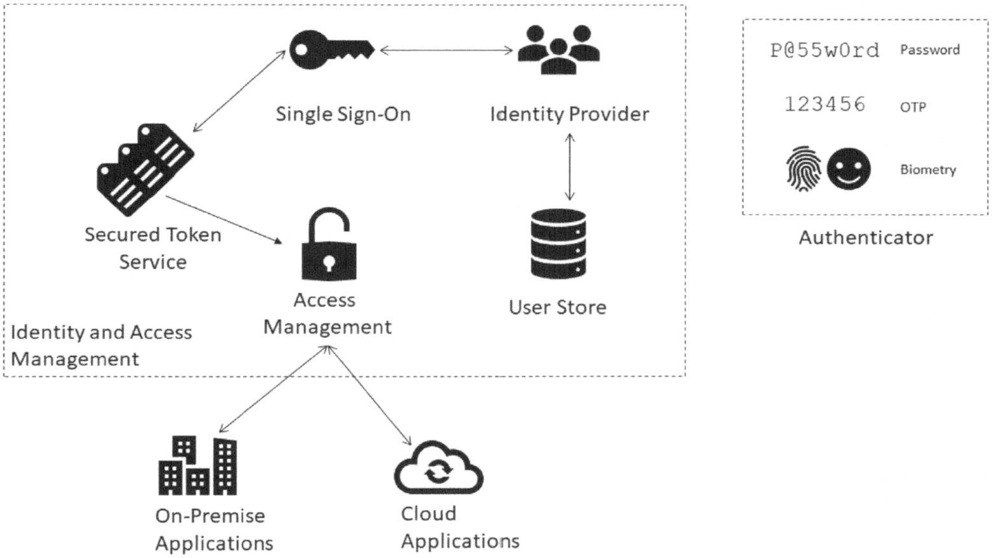

Figure 4.17: *Identity and Access Management*

We simplified the interaction into two categories: service providers (SP) and identity providers (IDP). There are several entities in the play. The IDP interacts with a user store for user information and authenticates with authenticators of many kinds. We simplified using a memory user store and used only a password as an authenticator. A user store could have been an LDAP server or a cloud-based user store using a REST interface. We had the IDP maintain the SSO session. SSO can be an independent component of the IDP. A vendor can offer only SSO, delegating authentication to a third-party IDP over SAML. We had the SPs mint the security tokens. Some IAM solutions provide Secured Token Servers (STS) that only issue and manage these tokens. Finally, access managers consume these tokens and give access to networks or specific applications with varying authorization. IAM platforms undertake one or more such responsibilities and delegate the others to upstream or downstream systems. Fortunately, several commercial IAM platforms address these responsibilities, reducing the scope of custom development. At the same time, what we discussed is in sync with the larger IAM framework.

Conclusion

We had quite a roller-coaster. We started with understanding federated authentication and got some understanding of SSO. We looked at the SAML protocol and its various conceptual frameworks. Subsequently, we moved to an example and looked at IDP and SPs. We showcased SP-initiated authentication, IDP-initiated authentication, assertions, attributes, SSO, and some code snippets as part of the learning. Did that cover enough of SAML? The standards have been in existence for more than a decade. They feature several extensions and addendums. It is not practical to cover all of it in one chapter. More importantly, one need not understand the standard in so much detail to use it through libraries and SDKs. We have discussed enough to help you understand the rationale of the protocol. You require additional exploration and applications to master the protocol. In this chapter, the enterprise had control over the SPs and IDPs. The IDP is trusted by all the SPs and vice-versa. IDP provided all the claims that a trusted SP asked for. *What happens when the user decides what information the IDP should share with the SP? What if the user does not want to share all the data in IDP's possession but wants to share a small subset? Can there be varying levels of access control provided?* All these are questions of the social networking era of authentication and our subject matter for the next chapter.

Questions

1. Pick up an open-source Identity and Access Management product of your choice. Write a SAML application and authenticate with the IAM system. Configure some claims and verify them in your application.
2. Can a certificate act as an authentication token? What are some of the downsides?
3. Open a SAML response in a text editor and identify various authentication token parameters in it.
4. Why does an SP sign a SAML **`AuthnRequest`**? Can an SP query for specific claims from the IDP through an **`AuthnRequest`**?
5. How do the SPs establish mutual trust with the IDP? Do the SPs need to trust each other for SSO?

CHAPTER 5 Federated Authentication-II

Introduction

In the previous chapter, we introduced federated authentication. We realized the need for enterprises to separate user authentication from other services in the organization. Users can authenticate at the identity provider (IDP), while service providers (SPs) can trust and extend access to the users. There are a few assumptions in this system. The SPs must trust the IDP, and the IDP trust all the SPs. It looks plausible in an organization, but extending beyond an organization can be limiting. Let us say there is a contractual employee or a partner organization whose employees are to access the organization's systems. The partner's IDP must be additionally trusted by the organization. These kinds of architecture have been there for some time now. Daisy chaining of IDPs or user stores is not unusual in a corporate context.

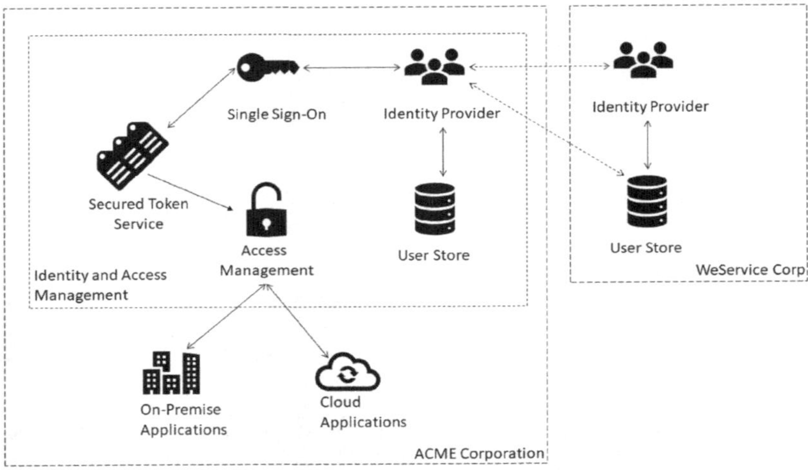

***Figure 5.1**: IAM with Partner Organization*

Identity and Access Management (IAM) systems of ACME corporation trust the IDP or User Store of WeService Corp to provide access to its employees. However, challenges are complex in the era of social networking. Enterprises want to trust a temporary worker without adding her to their IAM systems. They are open to letting the worker log in to a social network site, like Google, LinkedIn, Facebook, or GitHub. The worker wants not all of the information they have in the social network to be accessible to their employers. In this chapter, we will work with many such complex access and data management scenarios.

Structure

In this chapter, we will cover the following topics:

- Authentication vs authorization
- OAuth protocol
  - 3 – Legged OAuth Protocol
  - Cross-Site Request Forgery (CSRF) Protection
  - Web application displaying GitHub user data
  - Limited capability device
  - Native applications
  - Token issuance
- OpenID Connect (OIDC)

- Using OAuth for Authentication
- Identity Token
- JSON Web Token
- Login with Google

Authentication vs authorization

In *Chapter 1, Introduction to Web Authentication*, we looked at authentication. The users provide their credentials, and someone validates credentials in the backend; on successful validation, users are treated as the persons they claim to be. The process of authentication does not entrust any rights. It just identifies the person. The SAML assertion we discussed in the previous chapter had such characteristics. The Subject and NameID entries were authentication parameters. The attributes or claims gave differential rights to the user, namely, **hradmin** or **users**. These differentiated rights are essentially the function of authorization.

Let us pick up an example from the non-IT world. Some advanced cars have valet keys. The regular owner key gives access to the boot space, gloves compartments, and so on. A valet key lets access to the driver's side door and drive around only a small distance for a limited period. Now you go to a restaurant and give the valet the key to park the car. You may not authenticate the valet, but by her standing in front of the restaurant, you will trust her and give her the valet key authorizing her to use the car for a specific purpose. In some sense, you gave the key to the restaurant and let the restaurant provide the key to a bona fide staff. The IAM world picked up this pattern which we will discuss in this chapter. We are still discussing an authorization problem but something that is well beyond the scope of claims and attributes we discussed in the previous chapter. Here the bearer of the valet key is the valet. There is no additional authentication needed for him. HTTP authorization headers with bearer tokens pretty much follow the same pattern.

Social networking has changed the authentication and authorization landscape. Some of the networks have become ubiquitous. There is hardly a user who does not have an account in at least one of Google, Facebook, X (Twitter), LinkedIn, and the like. All these platforms have spent and advertised their Identity platforms extensively; they support multifactor authentication. They have a substantial number of personally identifiable information (PII) securely stored. Now, a service provider can access all this information by obtaining consent from the user while the user authenticates to an identity platform like Google or Facebook. As an exercise, we request the readers to try this:

- Create a new Google account.
- Now, go to **https://linkedin.com** and use this new account to access LinkedIn.
- A LinkedIn account will be created while associating it with the Google Account.

It reduces the need for the user to remember a password or credential for LinkedIn. *Will LinkedIn be able to access the user's Google password?* All the federated authentication schemes establish a one-on-one linkage between the user and the IDP. Hence, the service provider cannot access the credentials like passwords or OTPs. Moreover, for a service provider like LinkedIn, accessing the user's complete address book from Google is an option if the user permits. Against this backdrop, the industry conceived the OAuth protocol. There are more use cases we will discuss as we explore further.

Social networking brought a revolution in content mashups. You create content on one platform and reuse it on another platform. For example, you want to show your X (Twitter) feeds or Instagram reels on your webpage, at least a snippet as an advertisement. You want a few lines from your LinkedIn biodata on your web page. Your blog roll should show up on another page of yours. All these are examples of mashups. While some of these may not need any authorization, some websites will like the user to authorize this access by a third party. Let us say you want to show the basic profile of **GitHub** on your webpage. Here is what you will do:

- You will log in once to **GitHub** from your website.
- You will consent on **GitHub** that your website will request **GitHub** for your user profile.
- **GitHub** will provide a token or ticket that your website can store and request from **GitHub** the profile.

OAuth protocol

The protocol designers explain the protocol in this way[1]:

An open protocol to allow secure authorization in a simple and standard method from web, mobile, and desktop applications.

Not limited to only web applications, the protocol encompasses devices of varying form factors. The expanse of the protocol has made it a de facto standard for web authorization today. With REST APIs being the most common means of

1 As mentioned in: **https://oauth.net**

application development, there is a lot of focus on protecting API endpoints with tokens generated from OAuth protocols. OAuth 2.0 was developed as RFC 6749[2] in 2012 with a proposal from Microsoft Inc. It obsoletes the earlier version of OAuth 1.0 (RFC 5849[3]). With such a long involvement of OAuth in the industry, we will only be discussing OAuth 2.0 here. Moreover, there is no 3.0 version of OAuth[4] proposed in the market. Version 2.1 is in the draft stages[5]. Our focus will be on understanding and using the protocols rather than stringent adherence. General confusion exists regarding OAuth 2.0 and OpenID Connect (OIDC) 1.0 protocols. While both have very similar roots, OAuth is an authorization protocol, while OIDC is an authentication protocol. The OAuth framework is the basis of the OIDC protocol, but there are some differences. We will review these distinctions as part of this chapter. A programmer should understand these differences and use effective protocols and associated libraries.

3-legged OAuth protocol

At an abstract level, an OAuth workflow is the following diagram[6]:

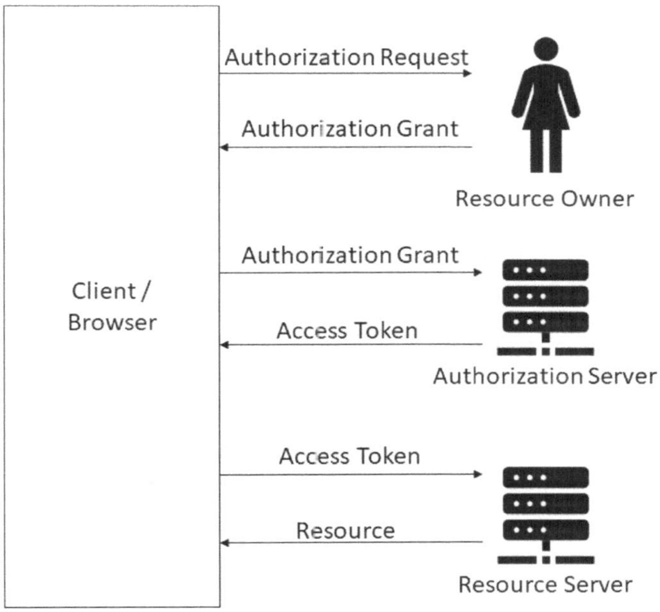

Figure 5.2: *OAuth 2.0 Abstract Protocol Flow*

2 The OAuth 2.0 Authorization Framework: **https://datatracker.ietf.org/doc/html/rfc6749**
3 The OAuth 1.0 Protocol: **https://datatracker.ietf.org/doc/html/rfc5849**
4 **https://oauth.net/3**
5 **https://oauth.net/2.1**
6 Abstract Protocol Flow, Figure 1, Section 1.2, supra 2.

While the above is a simplistic explanation of OAuth 2.0 flow, it is far from how an actual browser workflow behaves. The browser is on the end user's device. Such devices are considered unsecured and not trustworthy. However, web browsers can interact with any other server over the internet. Hence, the user can directly interact with the authorization server and present their credentials for obtaining the authorization code. While interacting in the web framework, we will split the client into two parts, the browser, and a web integration server. Let us relook at the preceding workflow with the new components.

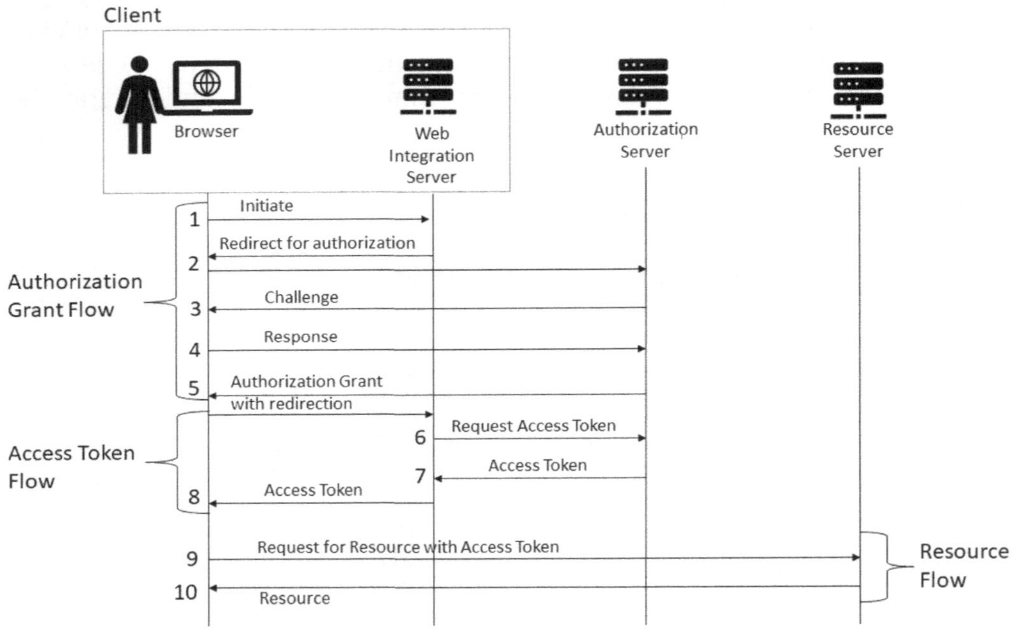

Figure 5.3: *OAuth in the web workflow*

1. The user initiates some activity that triggers authorization.
2. The integration server redirects the user to the authorization server for user consent. The integration server may set a **`scope`** for the access request.
3. The user gets a challenge on the browser based on the **`scope`** and the policy configured in the authorization server. This challenge depends on the kind of credentials; for example, it can be a username and password, OTP, biometric credential, and so on.
4. The user responds to the challenge with the credential details.
5. Upon successful validation, the authorization server sends an authorization code and redirects the browser to the **`redirect_uri`** of the integration server.

6. The integration server requests an **access_token** from the authorization server by providing the **client_id**, **client_secret,** and authorization **code**.
7. When the client credentials and the authorization code are validated, the authorization server issues an **access_token**.
8. The integration server can set the **access_token** as a browser cookie for subsequent resource requests.
9. The browser sends the **access_token** to the resource server to request the resource.
10. The resource server responds with the resource.

Such a complex web workflow for the seemingly simple OAuth workflow can be confusing. There are a couple of reasons for the same.

1. A user's device is amenable to attacks and cannot be trusted. Hence, we do not store **client_id** and **client_secret** on such devices.
2. The authorization server must reach the client. Inbound connections are not available with the end user devices. Through the **redirect_uri**, the authorization server can contact the client through a browser redirect.
3. The integration server ensures web security. The workflow expects a TLS channel setup between every communication end-point. A hacker cannot orchestrate a man-in-the-middle attack.
4. The integration server can set the tokens as cookies on the browser with additional protection like **HttpOnly** and **Secure** flags. The browser will send these cookies only over TLS connections and cannot use JavaScript to read and analyze the cookie.

Cross-Site Request Forgery (CSRF) Protection

In *Figure* 5.3, OAuth in the Web Workflow step 2, the web browser is redirected from the web integration server. *Is this step required?* If you follow the subsequent steps, the user interacts with the authorization server directly and obtains an authorization code. In step 6, the integration server gets the **access_token** by providing the authorization **code**, **client_id**, and **client_secret** as the inputs. Technically, a malicious actor can hijack step 2 through CSRF and obtain an authorization code for the scope of her choice from the user. Then she can use the **redirect_uri** of the integration server and submit an **access_token** request, thus elevating or reducing privileges. In the previous chapter, we suggested an SP must sign **AuthnRequest** for SAML workflows. There is no provision for signing the request here. *How do we ensure the actual request originated from the web integration server?*

In step 2, when the integration server creates a request for redirection to the authorization server, it adds a request parameter **state=<<A RANDOM VALUE>>**. In step 5, when the authorization server redirects to the **redirect_uri**, it sends the same value for the **state** parameter. The integration server ensures the **state** parameter obtained in step 5 is the same that it had added in step 2. The **state** parameter can help maintain the state before and after authentication to continue processing, like **RelayState** used in the SAML framework.

Web application displaying GitHub user data

Our web application displays a GitHub user's data. In this application, we redirect the user to the GitHub website and ask for her consent to access the user data. On her approval, we render the data in our application. Before we build our application, we register a new application in GitHub.

GitHub Configurations

1. Log in to your GitHub account.
2. Navigate to **https://github.com/settings/developers**. You can also reach here from user **Settings** -> **Developers** -> **OAuth Apps**.
3. Register a new application.
4. Click on the general tab on the newly registered application and generate a new client secret. Make sure to save the value of the secret. The secrets cannot be recovered later.

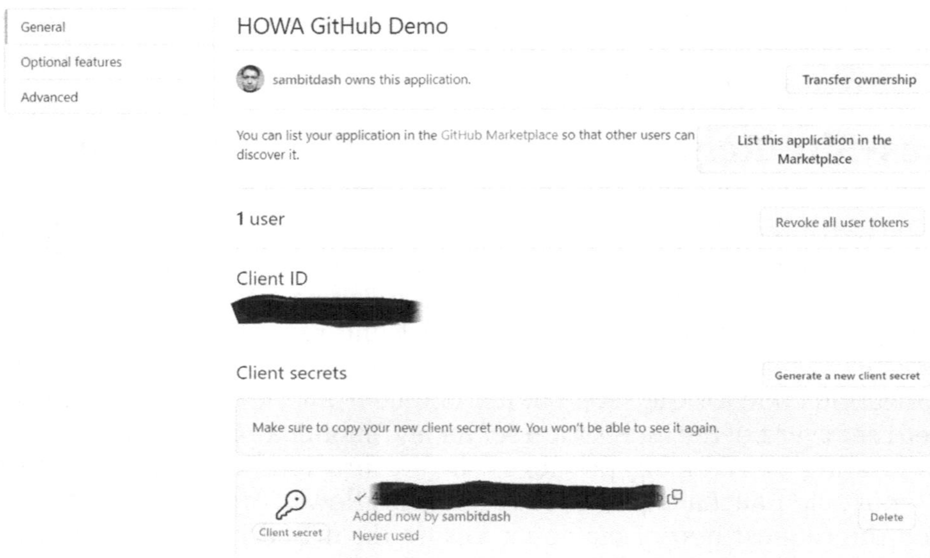

Figure 5.4: *Adding a new client secret for the OAuth application in GitHub*

5. Copy the **`client_id`** and **`client_secret`** and store them in a safe place.
6. Configure the authorization callback URI

   https://mysrv.local:8443/oauth/callback

Note

`client_id` and **`client_secret`** values are confidential. Do not check into the public code repositories. You can use the environment variables to use them in the continuous integration or development (CI/CD) pipelines. Device authorization does not require **`client_secret`**.

Setting up the web integration server

Our web integration server is the OAuth client configured at **https://mysrv.local:8443** and serves the Flutter web front end at the root folder. It has two endpoints for OAuth.

- **`/oauth/login`** - Handles step 2 in *Figure* 5.3 OAuth in the web workflow.
- **`/oauth/callback`** - Handles step 5 in *Figure* 5.3. When the authorization code is issued, it handles the token workflow.

Lastly, it has a **`/resource`** endpoint that queries the GitHub API to collect the user data for rendering the front end using the **`access_token`**.

The `main` function

In the **`main`** function, we set up an HTTP server over TLS. We serve the front-end static files from the root virtual. We have reviewed this code several times earlier. I will request readers to look at: **`chapter-5/github/authcode.go`**. We will only elaborate **`addOAuthHandlers`** here.

Oauth handlers for GitHub access

We use the **`oauth2`** library[7] that handles all the OAuth 2 network and transport. First, we configure a **`Config`** object providing it OAuth 2 specific parameters. There is also a preconfigured Endpoint for GitHub[8] which we use here.

```
conf := &oauth2.Config{
  ClientID:     client_id,
  ClientSecret: client_secret,
  Scopes:       []string{"user"},
  Endpoint:     github.Endpoint,
}
```

---

7 **https://pkg.go.dev/golang.org/x/oauth2**

8 **https://pkg.go.dev/golang.org/x/oauth2/github**

We configure the **/oauth/login** handler. The handler takes a request from a browser or HTTP client, fills up all the relevant parameters, and redirects it to the actual GitHub authorization server. **oauth2.AuthCodeURL** function formulates the redirection URL by taking two parameters **state** and **access_type**. We create a unique ID with the UUID method and provide that as the input for the state parameter. For **access_type**, we input **AccessTypeOffline**. We will discuss this parameter in a later section. We store the **state** parameter in a map[9]. Thus, we can query its availability when the redirection comes back from the authorization server after user consent. It confirms the request originated from the integration server.

```
http.HandleFunc("/oauth/login", func(w http.ResponseWriter,
                                     req *http.Request) {
  state := uuid.New().String()
  _setState(state)
  url := conf.AuthCodeURL(state, oauth2.AccessTypeOffline)
  log.Print(fmt.Sprintf("Redirecting to: %s", url))
  http.Redirect(w, req, url, http.StatusFound)
})
```

Next, we configure the **/oauth/callback** handler. In this handler, we first check for the **state** parameter in the collection and ensure it is one of the values we created. If found, we delete it from the map to avoid the possibility of a replay attack. If the request does not contain errors, it has the authorization code. We pick up the authorization code and exchange it for the access token by calling **conf.Exchange()** function. The access token is set as a cookie for resource access.

```
http.HandleFunc("/oauth/callback", func(w http.ResponseWriter,
                                        req *http.Request){
  state := req.FormValue("state")
  if _existsState(state) {
    _deleteState(state)
  } else {
    log.Println("Invalid state parameter")
    http.Error(w, "Invalid state parameter", http.StatusBadRequest)
  }
  if err := req.FormValue("error"); err != "" {
    desc := req.FormValue("error_description")
    http.Error(w, desc, http.StatusUnauthorized)
  }
```

9 If you have multiple integration servers, you can persist the values in a shared database. We used **_setState, _deleteState,** and **_existsState** as placeholders. Since several threads can access the **state** concurrently, proper access locking must be performed.

```
  if code := req.FormValue("code"); code != "" {
    token, _ := conf.Exchange(context.Background(), code)
    http.SetCookie(w, &http.Cookie{
      Name:     "token",
      Value:    token.AccessToken,
      HttpOnly: true,
      Secure:   true,
      Path:     "/",
    })
    http.Redirect(w, req, "/", http.StatusFound)
  } else {
    http.Error(w, "Invalid code parameter", http.StatusUnauthorized)
  }
})
```

We add a **/oauth/logout** handler where we delete the access token cookie.

```
http.HandleFunc("/oauth/logout", func(w http.ResponseWriter,
                                     req *http.Request) {
  http.SetCookie(w, &http.Cookie{
    Name:     "token",
    Value:    "deleted",
    HttpOnly: true,
    Secure:   true,
    Path:     "/",
    Expires:  time.Now().Add(-5 * time.Minute),
  })
  http.Redirect(w, req, "/", http.StatusFound)
})
```

Lastly, we configure the **/resource** handler. The handler takes the cookie from the request and creates a **Token** object. The **conf.Client** method takes the token and returns an ***http.Client**. The returned **http.Client** connects to the user endpoint of GitHub and obtains the response. The Flutter front end renders this data in the browser.

```
http.HandleFunc("/resource", func(w http.ResponseWriter,
                                 req *http.Request) {
  cookie, err := r.Cookie("token")
  if err != nil {
    http.Error(w, "User not authorized.", http.StatusUnauthorized)
  }
```

```
  client := conf.Client(context.Background(), &oauth2.Token{
    AccessToken: cookie.Value,
    TokenType:   "Bearer",
  })
  var (
    user_uri = "https://api.github.com/user"
    req      *http.Request
    res      *http.Response
  )
  if req, err = http.NewRequest("GET", user_uri, nil); err == nil {
    req.Header.Add("Accept", "application/vnd.github+json")
    if res, err = client.Do(req); err == nil {
      if res.StatusCode == 200 {
        defer res.Body.Close()
        b, _ := ioutil.ReadAll(res.Body)
        w.Header().Set("Content-Type", "application/json")
        w.Write(b)
      }
    } else {
      log.Printf(err.Error())
      http.Error(w, err.Error(), http.StatusInternalServerError)
    }
  }
})
```

User Interface

Note

Enter the **`frontend`** folder and run **`flutter build web`** to build the front-end code.

The user interface is rudimentary. The Flutter web application tries to access the **`/resource`** endpoint for user information as a JSON object. Based on the availability of the cookie with the access token, the UI can access the data and render it. When the data is not available, the login button shows up. When the user clicks on it, the application tries to open **`/oauth/login`**, which triggers the authentication workflow. When the user data is displayed, a logout button shows up. On clicking that button, you will delete the access token cookie. In the interest of space, we do not show the Flutter web sources here. We suggest the readers review the code at **chapter-5/github/frontend/library/main.dart**.

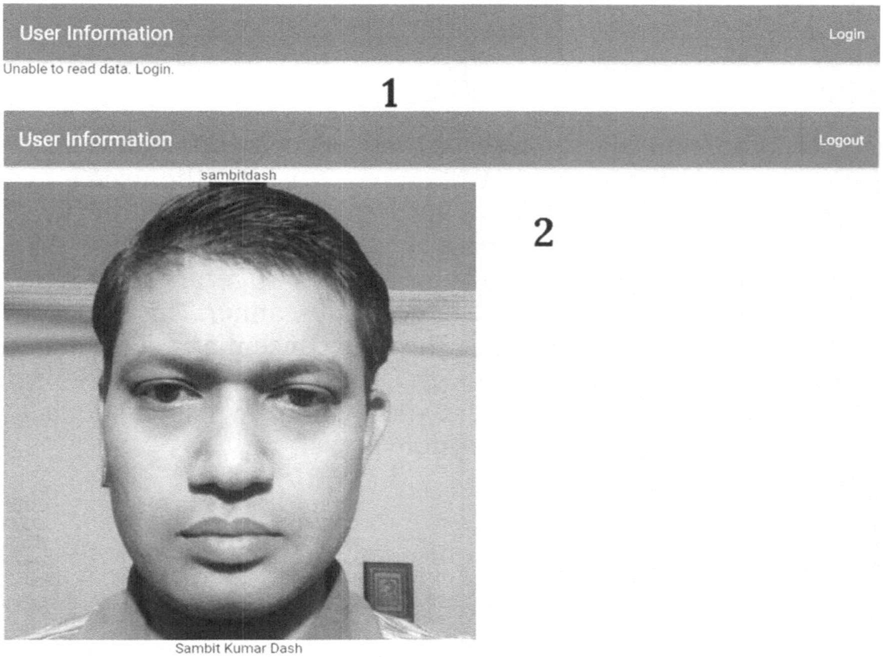

***Figure 5.5**: User interface with and without data access*

When you click the login button, following activities are triggered. These are captured from the developer tools of the browser.

1. The browser navigates to **https://mysrv.local:8443/oauth/login**
2. The integration server in turn redirects to **https://github.com/login/oauth/authorize?access_type=offline&client_id=<<GH_CLIENT_ID>>&response_type=code&scope=user&state=ba6f0890-0b54-4395-a78f-6d6302d08fcc**

   The parameter values are incidental and can change from session to session. If you do not have an active GitHub session, you must log in to GitHub here to proceed.
3. On successful authentication, GitHub will redirect the browser to **https://mysrv.local:8443/oauth/callback?code=<<b4c93e8...63c26>>&state=ba6f0890-0b54-4395-a78f-6d6302d08fcc**

   The **state** parameter is the same value received by GitHub in step 2.
4. The integration server requests the token using the **code** in step 3. And the value is set as a cookie **token=gho_d7WbWL...vYP21D0s0; Path=/; HttpOnly; Secure.**

5. To render the user interface, the integration server redirects the browser to **`https://mysrv.local:8443/`**.

Limited capability device

Internet is not confined to computer or browser-compatible devices only. The devices connect to the internet, yet they may not have the user interface for rendering the browser. Some may not have user-friendly input devices for text and biometry. For example, typing a password with a television remote or pointer can be cumbersome. A TV remote may not have a fingerprint scanner, while a mobile phone has a FIDO2-compatible fingerprint scanner. This protocol enables such devices to access resources while the user consent and authentication can be place-shifted to a separate device with UI and input capability. The protocol is known as OAuth 2.0 Device Authorization Grant[10], while colloquially, terms like device flow and device grant are synonymous.

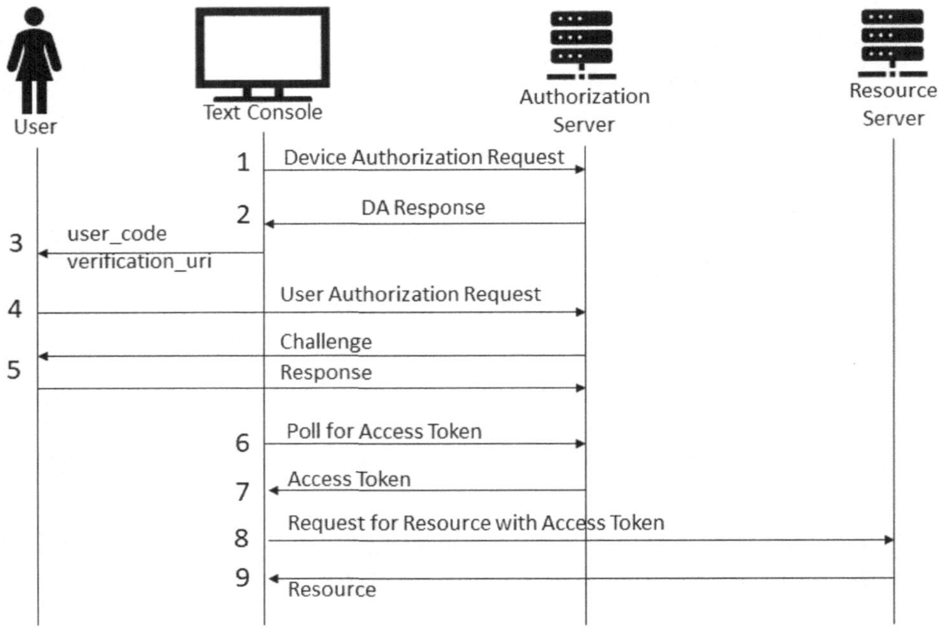

***Figure 5.6**: Device Authorization Grant*

Let us say a device requires a service registration. For example, when you use your TV to connect to Amazon Prime Video or Google TV, or you have developed a command-line tool that requires GitHub access, and so on.

10 **https://datatracker.ietf.org/doc/html/rfc8628**

Note:

Steps 3, 4, and 5 run in parallel to step 6.

1. The device contacts the authorization server with a **`client_id`** and the **`scope`** (the level of access required).
2. The authorization server responds with a **`device_code`**, a **`user_code`**, a **`validation_uri`**, an **`expires_in`** (the authorization will expire after these seconds), and an **`interval`** (time that should elapse before the client polls for the access token while waiting for the user).
3. The device retains the device code. It shows the user a validation URI and asks to access the URI on a web browser and enter the user code there.
4. The user initiates the user authorization request on a web browser and provides the **`user_code`**.
5. The authorization server can authenticate the user by challenging her for credentials, taking her consent for the request, and so on. If the authorization is approved, the authorization server can issue an access token for the transaction.
6. In the meantime, the client provides the **`client_id`**, **`device_id`**, **`grant_type`** (**`urn:ietf:params:oauth:grant-type:device_code`**) and polls for the access token.

    a. The client should wait for the **`interval`** number of seconds before polling again.

    b. A busy server can issue a **`slow_down`** error. In that case, the client should add another 5 seconds to the wait time interval.

    c. The client stops polling for **`expires_in`** seconds when it continues to get **`authorization_pending`** or **`slow_down`** as an error code.
7. If the client gets any other error, it stops execution. When the client receives an access token, it can stop polling.
8. Now that the client has the access token, it can send it to the resource server as an Authorization bearer token in the HTTP header.

    ```
    Authorization: Bearer <token>
    ```
9. The client receives the relevant resource requested.

Device workflow specification just came out in 2019. Hence, not all client libraries implement it. Some libraries have partial implementations waiting in pull requests. It is easy and may need about a hundred lines of client code with Golang. In our example, we will write a command line application to obtain user information from GitHub.

Command line utility for GitHub

Our command line utility is a perfect example of a limited capability device as it cannot show a browser for user consent. Hence, we obtain the user code and validation URI and show it to the user. The user can access the browser, provide the user code, and complete user consent. However, we need to configure this OAuth App on the GitHub Account.

GitHub Configurations

1. Log in to your GitHub account.
2. Navigate to **https://github.com/settings/developers**. You can also reach here from user **Settings** -> **Developers** -> **OAuth Apps**.
3. Register a new application and make sure to select **Enable Device Flow**.

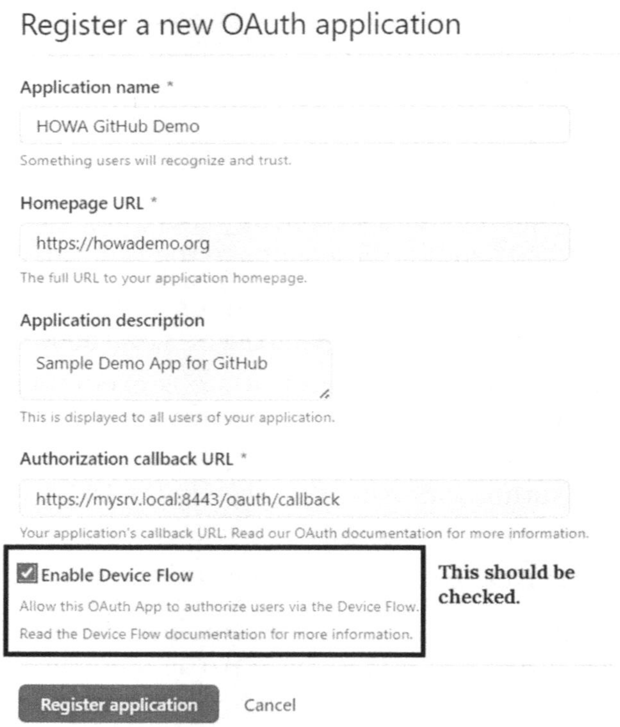

***Figure 5.7**: Registering OAuth App for GitHub*

4. Copy the **client_id** and keep it in a safe place.

   First, we obtain the device authorization information.

```
type DeviceAuthResponse struct {
  VerificationURI string
  DeviceCode      string
  UserCode        string
  ExpiresIn       time.Duration
  Interval        time.Duration
}

func get_device_authorization(device_uri string, client_id
string, scope []string)
  (devres *DeviceAuthResponse, err error) {

  var res *http.Response
  if res, err = http.PostForm(device_uri, url.Values{
    "client_id": {client_id},
    "scope":     scope,
  }); err != nil {
    log.Fatal(err)
  } else {
    if res.StatusCode == 200 {
      defer res.Body.Close()
      var (
        b  []byte
        vs url.Values
      )

      if b, err = ioutil.ReadAll(res.Body); err == nil {
        if vs, err = url.ParseQuery(string(b)); err == nil {
          interval, _ := strconv.ParseInt(vs["interval"][0], 10, 0)
          expires_in, _ := strconv.ParseInt(vs["expires_in"][0], 10, 0)
          devres = &DeviceAuthResponse{
            VerificationURI: vs["verification_uri"][0],
            DeviceCode:      vs["device_code"][0],
            UserCode:        vs["user_code"][0],
            ExpiresIn:       time.Duration(expires_in *
                                int64(time.Second)),
            Interval:        time.Duration(interval * int64(time.
                                Second)),
          }
        }
      }
    }
  }

  return

}
```

When we get the authorization response, we poll for the access_token.

```
func get_device_flow_access_token(c map[string]string)
  (access_token string, err error) {
  var devres *DeviceAuthResponse
  if devres, err = get_device_authorization(
    c["device_uri"],
    c["client_id"],
    []string{c["scope"]}); err == nil {
    println("Using a browser on another device, visit: ")
    println(devres.VerificationURI)
    println("")
    println("And enter the code: ")
    println(devres.UserCode)
    access_token, err = poll_for_access_token(
      c["token_uri"], c["client_id"], devres)
  }
  return
}
```

Here are some characteristics of the polling:

1. The polling happens for 900 seconds (**devres.ExpiresIn**) till we reach **expire_time**.
2. The client contacts the server every 5 seconds. However, if the server responds with a **slow_down** error, we increment the interval by another 5 seconds.
3. The response returned with an **access_token** or an error other than **authorization_pending** or **slow_down** stops the polling.

```
func poll_for_access_token(token_uri string, client_id string,
  devres *DeviceAuthResponse) (access_token string, err error) {

  var res *http.Response
  expire_time := time.Now().Add(devres.ExpiresIn)

  for {
    if res, err = http.PostForm(token_uri, url.Values{
      "client_id":   {client_id},
      "device_code": {devres.DeviceCode},
      "grant_type":
        {"urn:ietf:params:oauth:grant-type:device_code"},
    }); err == nil {
      if res.StatusCode == 200 {
        defer res.Body.Close()
        var (
```

```
                b  []byte
                vs url.Values
              )
              if b, err = ioutil.ReadAll(res.Body); err == nil {
                if vs, err = url.ParseQuery(string(b)); err == nil {
                  if reason, ok := vs["error"]; !ok {
                    access_token = vs["access_token"][0]
                    break
                  } else if reason[0] != "slow_down" {
                    devres.Interval += (5 * time.Second)
                  } else if reason[0] != "authorization_pending" {
                    err = fmt.Errorf(vs["error_description"][0])
                    break
                  }
                }
              }
            }
          }
          log.Println("Waiting for user consent...")
          time.Sleep(devres.Interval)
          if time.Now().After(expire_time) {
            break
          }
        }
        return

      }
```

Once we obtain the **access_token**, we can query for the user info from the REST end-point and print it.

```
func print_user_info(access_token string) (err error) {
  var (
    user_uri = "https://api.github.com/user"
    req      *http.Request
    res      *http.Response
  )
  if req, err = http.NewRequest("GET", user_uri, nil); err == nil {
    req.Header.Add("Accept", "application/vnd.github+json")
    req.Header.Add("Authorization",
                   fmt.Sprintf("Bearer %s", access_token))
    if res, err = http.DefaultClient.Do(req); err == nil {
      if res.StatusCode == 200 {
        defer res.Body.Close()
        b, _ := ioutil.ReadAll(res.Body)
        var dst bytes.Buffer
        json.Indent(&dst, b, "", "  ")
        log.Print(dst.String())
```

```
            }
        }
    }
    return
}
```

Here is the output from the run. Make sure to initialize the **`GH_CLIENT_ID`** environment variable with your application client ID.

```
PS C:\work\HOWA\chapter-5\github> $env:GH_CLIENT_ID='<<YOUR CLIENT ID>>'

PS C:\work\HOWA\chapter-5\github> go run ./device.go
Using a browser on another device, visit:
https://github.com/login/device

And enter the code:
63EC-119A

2023/05/06 10:15:18 Waiting for user consent...
2023/05/06 10:15:33 Waiting for user consent...
2023/05/06 10:15:53 Waiting for user consent...
2023/05/06 10:16:19 Waiting for user consent...
```

As the application waits, the user accesses the URL through a browser and submits her **`user_code`**. To complete the authentication, the user must log in to GitHub with her password and/or OTP (if configured).

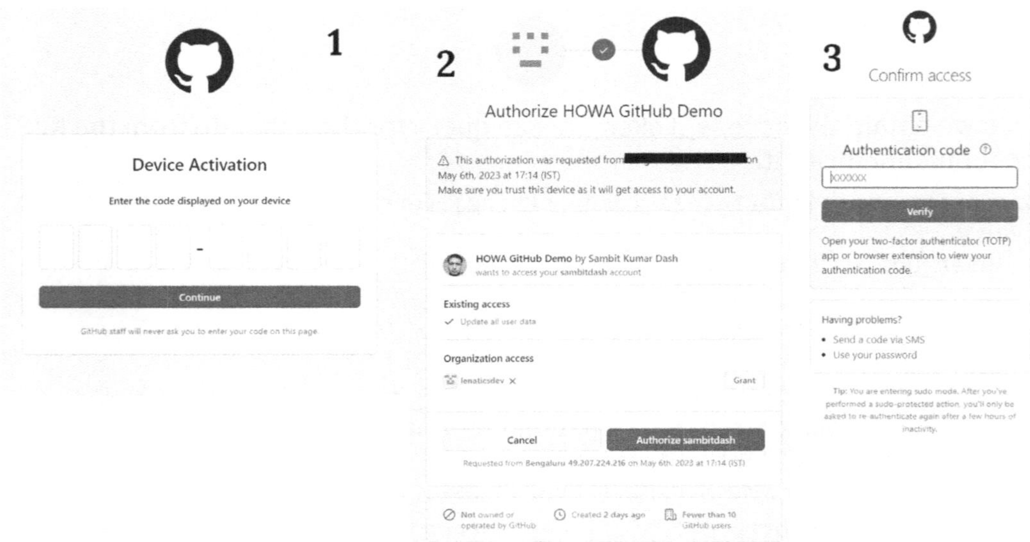

***Figure 5.8**: User completing authorization on the browser*

When the authorization is complete, the application will receive the **access_token** to obtain the logged-in user's information.

```
2023/05/06 10:16:19 Contacting the resource server for user info...
{
   "login": "sambitdash",
…
   "url": "https://api.github.com/users/sambitdash",
   "html_url": "https://github.com/sambitdash",
   "followers_url": "https://api.github.com/users/sambitdash/followers",
   "subscriptions_url": "https://api.github.com/users/sambitdash/
subscriptions",
   "organizations_url": "https://api.github.com/users/sambitdash/orgs",
   "repos_url": "https://api.github.com/users/sambitdash/repos",
   "events_url": "https://api.github.com/users/sambitdash/events{/
privacy}",
…
   "type": "User",
   "site_admin": false,
   "name": "Sambit Kumar Dash",
   "company": null,
…
}
```

We authorized a web application and an application with a command line with a limited user interface. Next, we authorize a thick client or mobile app to request resources.

Native applications

What makes a web application secure? The server, the browser, and the associated ecosystem ensure such a system remains secure. Here are some things to remember from *Figure 5.3 OAuth in the web workflow.*

- The redirection in Step 2 happens over HTTPS through the browser. So, no one can read the **state** parameter.
- The redirection in Step 5 also has the same **state** parameter. Hence, there was no CSRF attack involved.
- In Step 6, the request has a **client_secret**. A shared secret cannot be on multiple devices as it is vulnerable to stealing by a malicious actor.
- The integration server sets the access token as a cookie as **HttpOnly** and **Secure**. Thus, the cookie is transported over HTTPS; JavaScript on a browser cannot manipulate it. The browser honors it by design.

For a native application, like a desktop or mobile app, one can place-shift the authorization operation to a browser and obtain the authorization code. The native application uses this authorization code to request the access token. The complete scheme is shown in *Figure* 5.9:

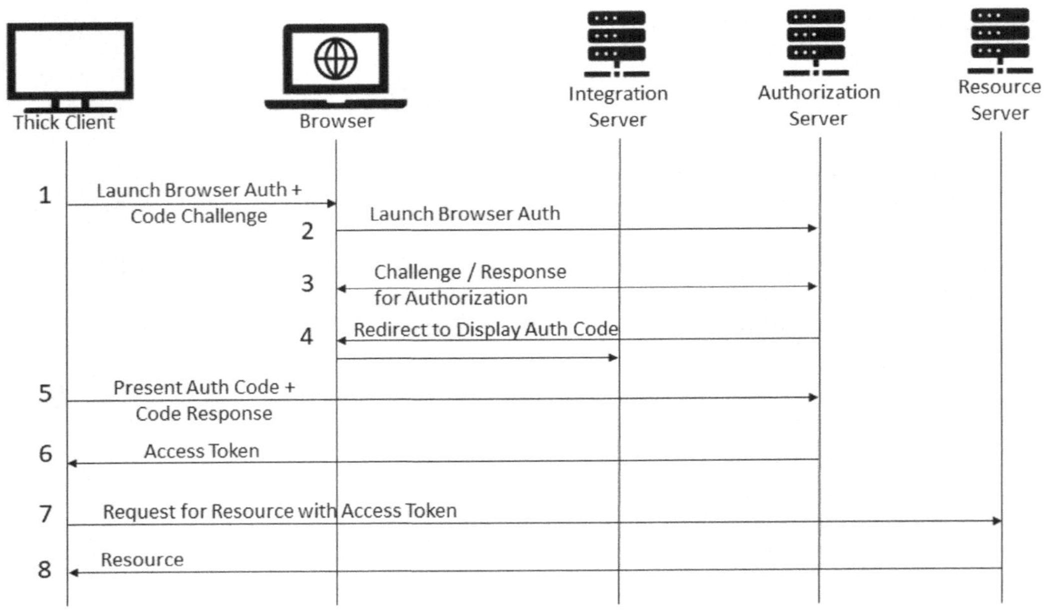

***Figure* 5.9**: PKCE *workflow*

In *Figure* 5.9, PKCE *workflow* Step 1, the native application utilizes the operating system process launcher to pass parameters to the browser. Process listing with a command like **`ps`** can expose the **`state`** parameter. An exposed **`state`** parameter makes the CSRF attack a possibility. Proof Key for Code Exchange (PKCE)[11] extends authentication for native clients. Here is a possible workflow that ensures secure authentication without the **`state`** and **`client_secret`** parameters:

1. The client creates a **`code_challenge`** and sends it as a parameter to the launch URL for the browser to navigate.

11 Proof Key for Code Exchange by OAuth Public Clients, **https://datatracker.ietf.org/doc/html/rfc7636**

Note:

The client generates the **code_challenge** from the **code_verifier** using the **code_challenge_method** algorithm. In an implementation, you may see:

- The **code_verifier** is a 256-bit random byte array that is base64 encoded with URL encoding.
- The **code_challenge** is the SHA-256 hash (**code_challenge_method=S256**) of **code_verifier** that is again base64 encoded with URL encoding.
- The browser URL has two parameters, **code_challenge** and **code_challenge_method**.
- Since **code_challenge** is a hash, no one other than the client knows the **code_verifier**.

  code_challenge_method=plain is another valid value. However it is not enough protection against eavesdropping as the **code_challenge** is transmitted in plain text.

1. The browser launches an authorization workflow for the user to approve over an HTTPS channel.
2. The authorization server and the user will exchange challenges and responses to authenticate and authorize.
3. The authorization server redirects to the integration server to display an **authorization_code** on the browser.
4. The user types the authorization code into the native client. The client sends a **code_verifier** for the **code_challenge** to authenticate to the server. over an HTTPS channel.
5. When the authorization server validates the **code_verifier** with the **code_challenge**, it delivers the access token for resource requests.
6. The client sends the access token for the resource.
7. The resource server delivers the requested resource.

Can we use PKCE *for native web clients*? With reactive clients like Flutter or React Native, the usage is easy.

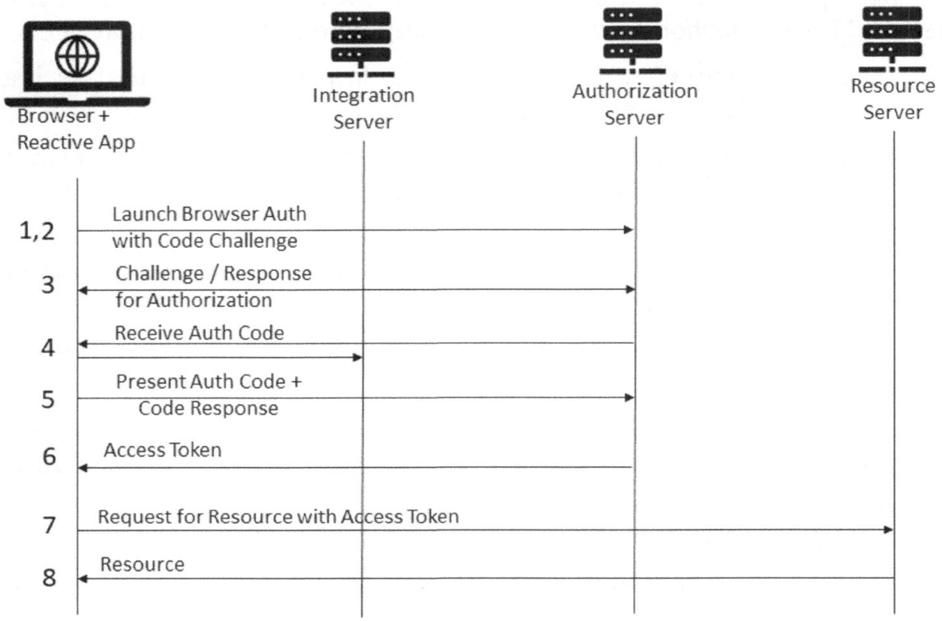

***Figure 5.10**: PKCE for Web Clients*

- The browser will generate the **`code_challenge`** using JavaScript. And request the authorization server for access. Hence, steps 1 and 2 are fused.
- Steps 4 and 5 can be a **`GET`** redirect or a form **`POST`** request. The server can specify the **`authorization_code`** as part of the redirect URL, or the client can extract the **`authorization_code`** with JavaScript and submit the **`POST`** request. The integration server can host the necessary JavaScript for the client.

There are no changes to the other steps. However, the **`access_token`** will be delivered to the client directly. The browser should take all the precautions to secure the access token. In the case of *Figure* 5.3 OAuth in the web workflow, the integration server receives the access token and sets it as a cookie with the browser. The cookie property **`HttpOnly`** did not permit the browser to access the cookie with JavaScript. With this workflow, this protection will not be available. The browser must take all precautions to keep the access token safe. PKCE is a new protocol. Many servers do not implement the specification. The GitHub server does not support it. Hence, we use a Golang-based custom OAuth server in our example.

Authorization server

You can find the sample code for the server in **`chapter-5/idp`**. You can open the command window with **`chapter-5/idp`** as the working directory and type **`go run ./idp.go`** to launch the application. The server configures an HTTPS connection at **https://idp.local:8443** using the certificate and private key in the **`chapter-5/certs`** folder. The **`idp.local`** DNS entry is added to the **`/etc/hosts`** file with a mapping to the loopback address. The following code initializes the TLS Server.

```
...
tlsserver := setupTLSServer("../certs/idp.local.p12", "idp.local")
log.Fatal(tlsserver.ListenAndServeTLS("", ""))
```

We use **`go-oauth2/oauth2`** for the OAuth2 server[12]. The server provides methods and objects to manage and orchestrate OAuth2 requests over an HTTPS channel. Two significant classes are the **`Manager`** and **`Server`**. The **`Manager`** class maintains the storage and configuration for the clients and tokens. The **`Server`** class has the logic for the actual OAuth2 connections. We use the following code to initialize and configure the **`Manager`** and the **`Server`**.

```
...
manager := manage.NewDefaultManager()
manager.SetAuthorizeCodeTokenCfg(&manage.Config{
  AccessTokenExp:    time.Second * 30,
  RefreshTokenExp:   time.Hour,
  IsGenerateRefresh: true,
})
manager.MustTokenStorage(store.NewMemoryTokenStore())
manager.MapAccessGenerate(generates.NewAccessGenerate())
clientStore := store.NewClientStore()
clientStore.Set("222222", &models.Client{
  ID: "222222",
  Domain: "https://mysrv.local:8444"
})

manager.MapClientStorage(clientStore)
srv := server.NewServer(&server.Config{
  TokenType:            "Bearer",
  AllowedResponseTypes: []oauth2.ResponseType{oauth2.Code, oauth2.Token},
  AllowedGrantTypes: []oauth2.GrantType{
    oauth2.AuthorizationCode,
    oauth2.PasswordCredentials,
    oauth2.ClientCredentials,
```

12 We have taken the example from the library and modified it to support PKCE. The library can be found at **https://pkg.go.dev/github.com/go-oauth2/oauth2/v4**.

```
    oauth2.Refreshing,
  },
  AllowedCodeChallengeMethods: []oauth2.CodeChallengeMethod{
    oauth2.CodeChallengePlain,
    oauth2.CodeChallengeS256,
  },
}, manager)
```

For a PKCE server, setting **oauth2.AuthorizationCode** for **AllowedGrantTypes** and **[oauth2.CodeChallengePlain,auth2.CodeChallengeS256]** for **AllowedCodeChallengeMethods** is important. The Oauth2 client is configured with **ID: 22222** and **Domain: "https://mysrv.local:8444".**

Refer to *Figure* 5.9 PKCE workflow, Step 2. The authorization server has a **/oauth/authorize** endpoint to accept the PKCE authorization request. Here is the relevant code for the same.

```
http.HandleFunc("/oauth/authorize", func(w http.ResponseWriter,
                                         r *http.Request) {
  if dumpvar {
    dumpRequest(os.Stdout, "authorize", r)
  }
  store, err := session.Start(r.Context(), w, r)
  if err != nil {
    http.Error(w, err.Error(), http.StatusInternalServerError)
    return
  }
  var form url.Values
  if v, ok := store.Get("ReturnUri"); ok {
    form = v.(url.Values)
  }
  r.Form = form
  store.Delete("ReturnUri")
  store.Save()
  err = srv.HandleAuthorizeRequest(w, r)
  if err != nil {
    http.Error(w, err.Error(), http.StatusBadRequest)
  }
})
```

The server initializes the **store** and searches an earlier successful authentication. If no data is found, **srv.HandleAuthorizeRequest(w, r)** is called. It triggers user authorization by invoking **userAuthorizeHandler(w http.ResponseWriter, r *http.Request)**. This handler verifies if there is a logged-in user. If no user is found, the user is redirected to **/login** for authentication.

```
func userAuthorizeHandler(w http.ResponseWriter, r *http.Request)
  (userID string, err error) {
…
  store, err := session.Start(r.Context(), w, r)
  if err != nil {
    return
  }
  uid, ok := store.Get("LoggedInUserID")
  if !ok {
    if r.Form == nil {
      r.ParseForm()
    }
    store.Set("ReturnUri", r.Form)
    store.Save()
    w.Header().Set("Location", "/login")
    w.WriteHeader(http.StatusFound)
    return
  }
  userID = uid.(string)
  store.Delete("LoggedInUserID")
  store.Save()
  return
}
```

Redirection to the **/login**, displays a form where the user authenticates with login: **alice** and password: **password**. The **loginHandler** function renders the form and addresses the authentication.

```
func loginHandler(w http.ResponseWriter, r *http.Request) {
…
  store, err := session.Start(r.Context(), w, r)
  if err != nil {
    http.Error(w, err.Error(), http.StatusInternalServerError)
    return
  }
  if r.Method == "POST" {
    if r.Form == nil {
      if err := r.ParseForm(); err != nil {
        http.Error(w, err.Error(), http.StatusInternalServerError)
        return
      }
```

```
    }
    store.Set("LoggedInUserID", r.Form.Get("username"))
    store.Save()
    w.Header().Set("Location", "/auth")
    w.WriteHeader(http.StatusFound)
    return
  }
  w.Write([]byte(`
  <html><body>
      <h1>Login In</h1>
      <form action="/login" method="POST">
        <label for="username">Username</label>
        <input type="text" name="username" required
             placeholder="username">
        <label for="password">Password</label>
        <input type="password" name="password" placeholder="password">
        <button type="submit">Login</button>
      </form>
  </body></html>`))
}
```

On successful authentication, the user is asked to authorize the transaction. The URL for authorization can be accessed from **`/auth`**. The **`authHandler`** function provides the necessary logic. The function looks for a **`LoggedInUserID`**, if not found the user is redirected to login.

```
func authHandler(w http.ResponseWriter, r *http.Request) {
…
  store, err := session.Start(r.Context(), w, r)
  if err != nil {
    http.Error(w, err.Error(), http.StatusInternalServerError)
    return
  }
  if _, ok := store.Get("LoggedInUserID"); !ok {
    w.Header().Set("Location", "/login")
    w.WriteHeader(http.StatusFound)
    return
  }
  w.Write([]byte(`
    <html><body>
      <form action="/oauth/authorize" method="POST">
        <h1>Authorize</h1>
        <p>The client would like to perform actions on your behalf.</p>
        <p><button type="submit">Allow</button></p>
```

```
        </form>
    </body></html>`))
}
```

Lastly, we configure the endpoint **/oauth/token** for issuing access tokens. You require the **client_id**, **authorization_code**, **scope**, and **code_verifier** for valid token issuance. In PKCE, the authorization server does not require **client_secret** to validate the client. Hence, an end-user device can directly request a token.

```
http.HandleFunc("/oauth/token", func(w http.ResponseWriter,
                                       r *http.Request) {
…
  err := srv.HandleTokenRequest(w, r)
  if err != nil {
    http.Error(w, err.Error(), http.StatusInternalServerError)
  }
})
```

The method **srv.HandleTokenRequest(w, r)** extracts all the relevant parameters from the HTTP Request. It uses the **client_id** and **authorization_code** to identify the session. It validates the session with the **code_verifier** and **scope**.

Integration and Resource Server

We have configured the integration and resource server at **https://mysrv.local:8444** and have assigned **mysrv.local** to the loopback address in the **/etc/hosts** file. The sources are available in the **chapter-5/pkce/resource** folder. It can be launched with the command **go run ./server.go** from the command line.

When no **redirect_url** is specified in an OAuth authorization request, the authorization server contacts the client at the domain URL (**https://mysrv.local:8444/**). We have configured the handler for the root path **(/)** as shown:

```
http.HandleFunc("/", func(w http.ResponseWriter, r *http.Request) {
  if r.Form == nil {
    r.ParseForm()
  }
  if r.Form.Has("error") {
    http.Error(w, r.Form.Get("error_description"), http.StatusUnauthorized)
  } else {
    code := r.Form.Get("code")
    w.Write([]byte(fmt.Sprintf(`
```

```
        <html><body>
          <h1>Code</h1>
          <p>%s</p>
        </body></html>
        `, code)))
      }
    }
)
```

The code merely renders the value of the **code** parameter on the HTML page.

The resource server is a handler at **/resource** that takes the access token as a bearer token in an HTTP Authorization header, extracts the token, and passes it to the IDP server (**https://idp.local:8443/test**) to test its validity. If the token is valid, the resource server receives properties like the **user_id**, **expires_in**, and **client_id**. The resource server relays those back to the client.

```
if auth_headers, ok = r.Header["Authorization"]; ok {
  if req, err = http.NewRequest("GET",
    "https://idp.local:8443/test", nil); err == nil {
    req.Header.Add("Authorization", auth_headers[0])
    if res, err = http.DefaultClient.Do(req); err == nil {
      defer res.Body.Close()
      if data, err = ioutil.ReadAll(res.Body); err == nil {
        w.Write(data)
      }
    }
  }
}
```

We have all the backend code in place. We need to develop the frontend application and authenticate with the OAuth server.

Native client using Flutter

We have the server components in place. Now, we develop the native frontend application using Flutter for Windows and Linux operating systems. We open three command line windows and launch the services as shown here.

IDP Service

```
HOWA\chapter-5\idp> go run ./idp.go
2023/05/25 13:18:51 Dumping requests
2023/05/25 13:18:51 Server is running at 8443 port.
2023/05/25 13:18:51 Point your OAuth client Auth endpoint to
https://idp.local:8443/oauth/authorize
2023/05/25 13:18:51 Point your OAuth client Token endpoint to https://
idp.local:8443/oauth/token
```

Integration and Resource Services

```
HOWA\chapter-5\pkce\resource> go run ./server.go
```

Flutter UI

```
HOWA\chapter-5\pkce\client> flutter run
Launching lib\main.dart on Windows in debug mode...
Building Windows application...                                    28.0s
√  Built build\windows\runner\Debug\client.exe.
Syncing files to device Windows...                                180ms

Flutter run key commands.
r Hot reload. 🔥🔥🔥
R Hot restart.
h List all available interactive commands.
d Detach (terminate "flutter run" but leave application running).
c Clear the screen
q Quit (terminate the application on the device).

A Dart VM Service on Windows is available at: http://127.0.0.1:57199/
a6P0fj6Bpg0=/
The Flutter DevTools debugger and profiler on Windows is available at: ht
tp://127.0.0.1:9100?uri=http://127.0.0.1:57199/a6P0fj6Bpg0=/
```

The following UI appears on the screen.

Figure 5.11: *Launching the PKCE Client*

Clicking on the lock icon on the top-right corner launches the browser with the authorization URL for the user to authorize.

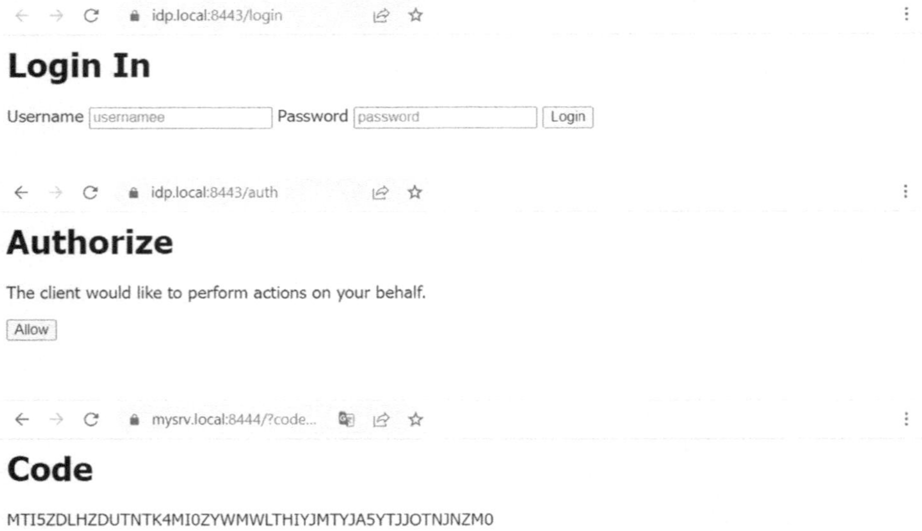

Figure 5.12: *Browser workflow to obtain authorization code*

The user uses the name **`alice`** and password to authenticate. She authorizes the transaction and gets the authorization code in the browser. She enters the code in the client application to obtain the access token.

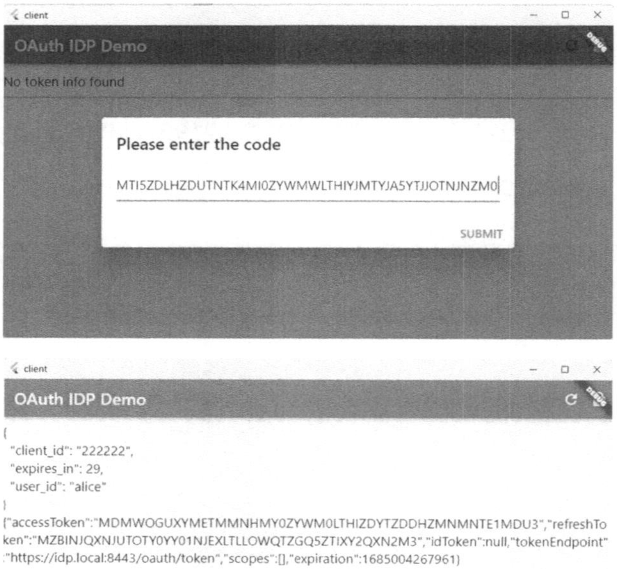

Figure 5.13: *Access token, refresh token, and the expiration details received by the client*

getOAuthClient handles almost all the OAuth token acquisition activity.

```
Future<oauth2.Client?> getOAuthClient(BuildContext context) {
  final grant = oauth2.AuthorizationCodeGrant(
    "222222",
    Uri.parse("https://idp.local:8443/oauth/authorize"),
    Uri.parse("https://idp.local:8443/oauth/token"),
    httpClient: Provider.of<http.Client>(context, listen: false),
    codeVerifier:
      base64Url.encode(List<int>.generate(32, (i) => _random.
                                                   nextInt(256))),
  );


  final authURI =
    grant.getAuthorizationUrl(Uri.parse("https://mysrv.local:8444/"));
  return launchUrl(authURI).then((ok) {
    return showDialog<String>(
      context: context,
      builder: (context) {
        return AlertDialog(
          title: const Text("Please enter the code"),
          content: TextField(autofocus: true, controller: dlgCtrl),
          actions: [
            TextButton(
              onPressed: () => Navigator.of(context).pop(dlgCtrl.text),
              child: const Text("SUBMIT"),
            )
          ]);
      },
    );
    }).then((code) {
      return ((code == null) || (code == ""))
        ? Future.value(null)
        : grant.handleAuthorizationCode(code);
    });
}
```

Following are the steps in the function:

1. We create an **AuthorizationCodeGrant** object with a client ID, authorization URL, token URL, an HTTP client, and a 32-byte code verifier.
2. The **grant.getAuthorizationUrl(redirectUrl)** generates the following URL and we launch the browser with the URL.

```
https://idp.local:8443/oauth/authorize?response_type=code&client_
id=222222&redirect_uri=https%3A%2F%2Fmysrv.local%3A8444%2F&code_
challenge=zf0q689C2YbepoOxN5dmuth5Lgnn4AqIBvOpxilUwRY&code_
challenge_method=S256
```

The **code_challenge** is generated from the **code_verifier** after applying the **code_challenge_method**.

3. The user completes the authorization on the browser window and receives the **authorization_code**.
4. She enters the authorization code in the dialog box on the client and submits it.
5. The **grant.handleAuthorizationCode(code)** method reaches the token endpoint on the authorization server and obtains the token. Here is the request dump from the authorization server.

```
token:
POST /oauth/token HTTP/1.1
Host: idp.local:8443
Accept-Encoding: gzip
Content-Length: 210
Content-Type: application/x-www-form-urlencoded; charset=utf-8
User-Agent: Dart/3.0 (dart:io)


grant_type=authorization_code&code=YTMZMWMWOWQTYJBIYS0ZNDA1L-
WI5NTETYWI1YTAYNDGYZJDH&redirect_uri=https%3A%2F%2Fmysrv.lo-
cal%3A8444%2F&code_verifier=ckUCagObNWMJRUa14shQ7pD0CuY8u5f42R-
t03U3us10%3D&client_id=222222
```

6. **getOAuthClient** returns an **oauth2.Client** object. This can be used as an HTTP Client to request for resources.

Here is the **OnPressed()** method on the lock **IconButton**.

```
onPressed: () {
  getOAuthClient(context).then((client) {
    oauth2Client = client;
    return oauth2Client;
```

```
    }).then((client) {
      return client != null
      ? client.get(Uri.parse("https://mysrv.local:8444/resource"))
      : Future.value(null);
    });
  ...
  }
```

The client is used to request the resource. From the server dump, you can see the authorization header is auto-populated by the library.

```
resource:
GET /resource HTTP/1.1
Host: mysrv.local:8444
Accept-Encoding: gzip
Authorization: Bearer MDMWOGUXY...MDU3
User-Agent: Dart/3.0 (dart:io)
```

The resource server sends the token to the test endpoint of the authorization server. It receives the following information about the validity of the token and relays it back to the client. The client displays the result with the client ID (**222222**), user ID (**alice**), and no of seconds (**29**) to go before the token expires.

Token issuance

All the hard work for the issuance of tokens, yet we have not delved much into them. As per the OAuth specification[13], an access token has the following characteristics:

- It acts as a credential to access a resource.
- It is opaque to the client and only understood and interpreted by resource and authorization servers.
- The tokens are valid for a specific scope and only during a specific time window.
- Access tokens can be of different formats and types. One such format is a bearer token. The bearer token gives the possessor access rights to the resource. No further proof of possession is needed.

13 Access Token, Section 1.4, Supra 2.

RFC 6750[14] talks about the usage of bearer tokens. An application can present a bearer token in one of the following ways:

1. An HTTP header that looks like **Authorization: Bearer <<token>>**
2. An HTTP form parameter in a post request:

```
{
...
        access_token: <<token>>,
...
}
```

3. An HTTP URL encoded parameter in a GET request, like **https://server/resource?access_token=<<token>>**

We have used the first option in our samples.

Note:

- Bearer tokens are secret information. Anyone in possession of such a token can access resources. You should avoid printing[15] tokens in log files, consoles, and other places. A stolen bearer token can present significant security risks.
- Tokens should be valid only for a short duration. Tokens valid for long durations introduce revocation requirements; hence should not be used.
- An access token withstands clock skews of client, authorization, and resource servers. They are valid only for a few minutes, for example, 5 mins.

A token response has the following:

- **access_token** - The token used to access resources, for example, **MGM5NDJHZDITODQ5YY0ZZMZLLTK3OTGTYTU4NZY2ZTC2NMJH**
- **refresh_token** - The token the system can use to request a new access token when the old access token expires, for example, **NZNKZTHMMWUTNZDKMS01ZJDILTG3ODYTYZBIZTEZMDQ2YZEZ**
- **expires_in** - The token is valid for these many seconds, for example, **29** seconds

14 Authentication Requests, Section 2, The OAuth 2.0 Authorization Framework: Bearer Token Usage, **https://datatracker.ietf.org/doc/html/rfc6750**

15 We have printed tokens on the consoles and user interfaces to explain concepts and help you understand the authorization process. They are not the code for a production server.

- **scope**: The scope of the token. The authorization server can narrow the authorization scope from the original request.
- Additional optional parameters

The dart **oauth2** package aggregates these values in the **credential** attribute of the **oauth2.Client** object. We display this object in the UI as a JSON.

```
onPressed: () {
  getOAuthClient(context).then((client) {

    …

  }).then((res) {
    bodyCtrl.text = "${res?.body ?? "No token info found\n"}"
    bodyCtrl.text += "${oauth2Client!.credentials.toJson()}\n";

    …

  });
```

Next, we study how to effect single sign-on while using short-lived tokens.

Token expiry

The authorization server issues token for a short duration of time. The client that receives this token can use it to request resources. The client can discard the token. Even though eavesdroppers steal this token, the token expiry limits the attack window. Short-duration tokens need user authorizations in a few minutes and are not friendly for user experience. OAuth addressed this by issuing a refresh token. The refresh token has a long expiry period (a few hours to several days). The client can request a new access token using the refresh token and use it for another purpose.

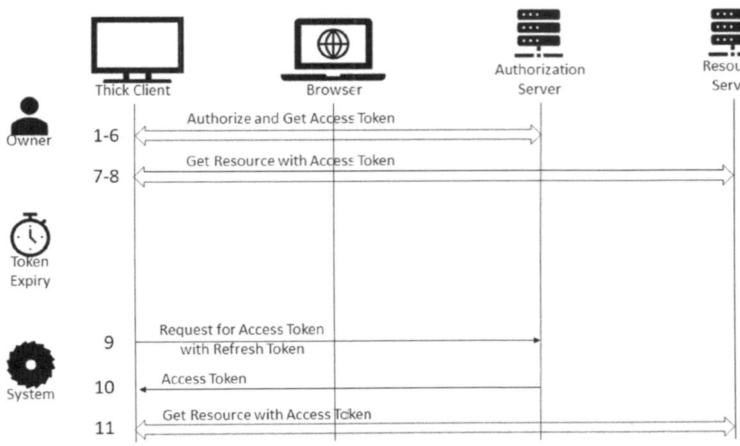

Figure 5.14: *Using the refresh token to obtain a new access token*

In *Figure* 5.14, we have already seen steps 1–8. If the access token expires, the client can request a new one at step 9. It does not require user authorization; the refresh token is used as a credential to issue the access token. We have set up the following parameters while initializing the authorization server.

```
...

manager.SetAuthorizeCodeTokenCfg(&manage.Config{
  AccessTokenExp:     time.Second * 30,
  RefreshTokenExp:    time.Hour,
  IsGenerateRefresh: true,
})
...
```

The access token is valid for 30 seconds, and the refresh token for one hour. In real life, the validity period of access tokens is set for 5–10 minutes to compensate for clock skews on the internet. Moreover, we configured regenerating the refresh token on every token refresh. Let us understand the security implications of using bearer tokens.

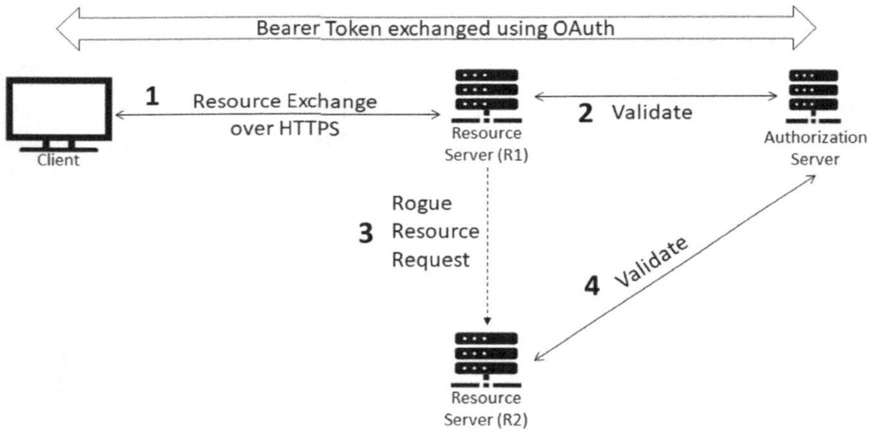

***Figure* 5.15**: *A rogue resource server can be a source of man-in-the-middle attack*

A secret transferred over the wire can become a target for eavesdropping and man-in-the-middle attacks. An encrypted channel minimizes such attacks when a client sends a bearer token to a resource server. We assume all the connections in *Figure* 5.15 are HTTPS-based.

1. The client embeds the bearer token in the HTTP header and sends it to the resource server (R1).

2. R1 validates the bearer token with the authorization server. This validation scheme is not part of the OAuth 2 specification, and the authorization servers can design the methods that the resource servers adhere to.
3. R1 can potentially cache the bearer token and request a resource from the server R2 impersonating the user.
4. The validation is successful when R2 presents the bearer token to the authorization server.

A rogue resource server can orchestrate a man-in-the-attack if the token issuance is not well thought-out. Here are some of the remedial policies that the authorization server can undertake.

- Only authenticated resource servers can validate tokens with the authorization servers. The authorization server will maintain the trusted resource server in its metadata for the issued access token.
- If the server R1 and R2 have different scopes, then the access token issued for R1 cannot be used by R2.
- An access token can be for one-time use by an authorization server policy. Once R1 has validated the access token in *Figure* 5.15 Step 2, R1 cannot present it to R2 in Step 3.

In the PKCE client, we request the access token. The client obtains the access token and waits for it to expire. After expiry, it refreshes the user interface and activates the refresh icon. The code can be seen in **chapter-5/pkce/client/lib/main.dart**.

```
IconButton(
  onPressed: () {
    getOAuthClient(…).
      then((res) {
        bodyCtrl.text = ${oauth2Client!.credentials.toJson()}\n";
        final wait = oauth2Client!.credentials.expiration!
          .difference(DateTime.now()) +
          const Duration(seconds: 1);
          Future.delayed(wait, () {setState(() {});});

      });

  },

  icon: const Icon(Icons.lock)…
);
```

Clicking on the refresh icon obtains a fresh access token. The UI again waits for the access token to expire. When the authorization server issues the access token, it sends a new refresh token.

```
IconButton(
  onPressed:(oauth2Client != null) && (oauth2Client!.credentials.
isExpired)
    ? () {
      oauth2Client!.refreshCredentials().then((_) {
        bodyCtrl.text += "${oauth2Client!.credentials.toJson()}\n";
        setState(() {});
      })…
    : null,
  icon: const Icon(Icons.refresh),
)
```

`oauth2Client!.refreshCredentials` method is the client call for refreshing the token. This, in turn, requests the **`/oauth/token`** endpoint on the authorization server with the following payload:

```
grant_type=refresh_token&refresh_token=NJM5NGIZM…ZDMWZJHI&client_
id=222222
```

Here is how the user interface looks like.

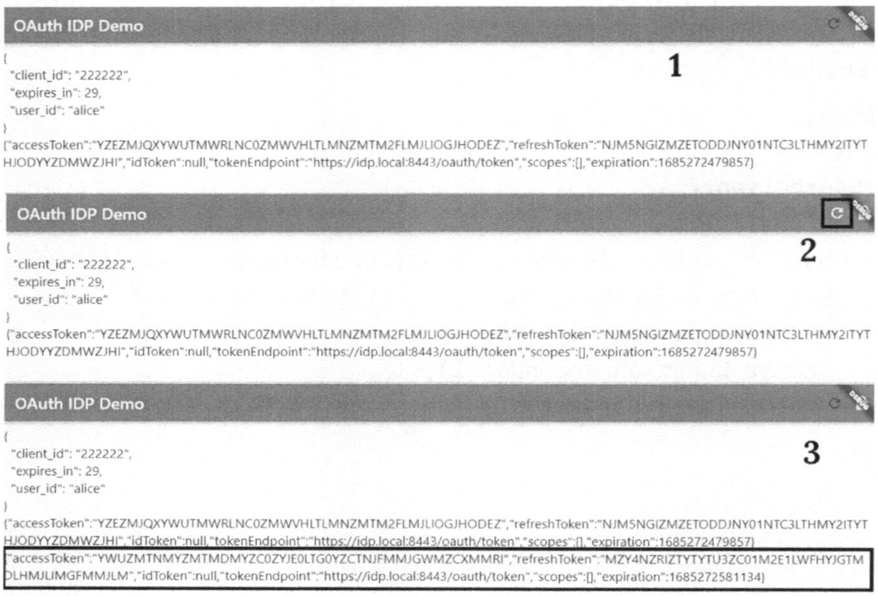

Figure 5.16: *Refreshing the access token from the PKCE client*

While we show the examples of token refresh with the PKCE client, the behavior on other clients is very similar.

Scopes

Scopes are mnemonics for an authorization level. The client fills in the scope for an authorization request URL and redirects the user to the browser. Based on the value of the **scope** parameter, the user consents to various elements of the scope. Scopes can be hierarchical and one scope can cover multiple underlying scopes. In the GitHub examples, we requested for authorization code with the **scope=[user]**. This in turn authorizes the following activities[16]:

user	Grants read/write access to profile info only. Note that this scope includes **user:email and user:follow**
read:user	Grants access to read a user's profile data.
user:email	Grants read access to a user's email addresses.
user:follow	Grants access to follow or unfollow other users.

***Table 5.1**: Hierarchical scopes in GitHub*

Here is the code snippet from **chapter-5/github/authcode.go**:

```
http.HandleFunc("/oauth/login", func(w http.ResponseWriter, req *http.
                                              Request) {
  state := uuid.New().String()
  _setState(state)
  conf.Scopes = []string{"user"}
  url := conf.AuthCodeURL(state, oauth2.AccessTypeOffline)
  log.Print(fmt.Sprintf("Redirecting to: %s", url))
  http.Redirect(w, req, url, http.StatusFound)
})
```

We are rendering the user's read-only data in the browser. Hence, we can request the **read:user** scope for the token. Since **read:user** is part of the scope **user** hierarchy, the authorization server will issue the token if the authorization code is used. That is how we have coded.

16 Scopes of OAuth Apps in GitHub, **https://docs.github.com/en/apps/oauth-apps/building-oauth-apps/scopes-for-oauth-apps**

```
http.HandleFunc("/oauth/callback",
  func(w http.ResponseWriter, req *http.Request) {
...
    if code := req.FormValue("code"); code != "" {
      conf.Scopes = []string{"read.user"}
      log.Printf("Reducing token scope to: %v\n", conf.Scopes)
      token, _ := conf.Exchange(context.Background(), code)
      http.SetCookie(w, &http.Cookie{
        Name:     "token",
        Value:    token.AccessToken,
        HttpOnly: true,
        Secure:   true,
        Path:     "/",})
      http.Redirect(w, req, "/", http.StatusFound)
    }
...
)
```

This ensures the token's scope is limited and not misused for accessing a resource for writing. The user has given consent for both read and write access. Hence if write access is required, the client can use the refresh token, request for a token with **scope=[user]**, and enable write access with the new access token.

OpenID Connect (OIDC)

OAuth 2.0 has established itself as an authorization protocol that provides access to a specific resource. *Can we use it for authentication?* In *Chapter 4, Federated Authentication - I*, we discussed SAML. In the SAML protocol, the service provider (SP) trusts the Identity Provider (IdP), and the IDP trusts all the SPs. While this is true for an enterprise, in social networks end-user decides the IdP. For example, we want all the Google, Meta, X (Twitter), and so on. users to access the e-retail site that we developed. Based on our experience with GitHub data access, we use the following OAuth workflow:

Our retail portal redirects the user to GitHub.

1. The user provides her credentials and consents to obtain the email address from GitHub.
2. A code generated is provided in the token workflow to request an access token.
3. The retail site presented the access token to obtain the user's email address from the GitHub resource server.

4. The email obtained is the username for the retail portal.

We achieved login with GitHub; we want to replicate the same with LinkedIn, Meta, and so on. Many libraries provide custom login APIs to support users authenticating using an OAuth 2.0 workflow. However, steps 4 and 5 vary depending on the social network used and the application integrating such authentication. In the meantime, OpenID Authentication Framework was already underway to provide a user-oriented identity provider. The OpenID consortium archived OpenID 2.0 and introduced OpenID Connect 1.0, an identity framework built over OAuth 2.0.

Using OAuth for Authentication

OpenID Connect (OIDC), built on the OAuth 2.0 framework, can be shown in the following diagram:

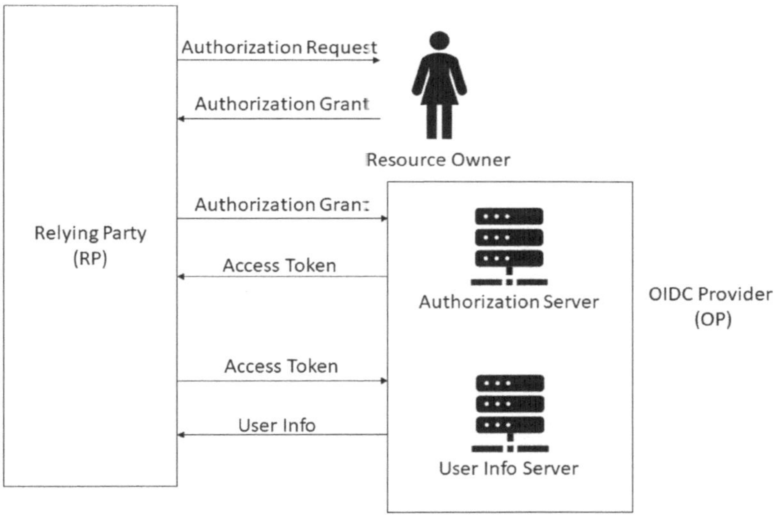

Figure 5.17: *OIDC Architecture*

The client is the Relying Party (RP). The OIDC provider (OP) comprises the authorization server and a user info resource provider. The token response for OIDC includes three tokens.

1. **`access_token`**: Opaque token to query user info.
2. **`refresh_token`**: Opaque token to refresh the **`access_token`** on expiry.
3. **`id_token`**: A token containing user information. This token is in the JSON Web Token (JWT) format and can be signed to ascertain the source. The

token is like **`Assertion`** in a SAML response, with claims regarding the user signed by the issuer.

We draw your attention to the SAML Metadata for IDP. OPs publish similar directory information. You can see one for Google that we will use in a later section. However, there is no additional metadata requirement for the relying party. An OP administrator configures an RP with the following details like all OAuth clients:

- Client ID
- Client Secret
- Redirect URL
- A domain of the RP for exclusion in CORS policies.

Identity Token

ID tokens provide user information as claims. They have very similar characteristics to SAML Assertions we have seen already. Here are the claims[17] that are in the ID token.

iss	The issuer, or signer, of the token. For Google-signed ID tokens, this value is **https://accounts.google.com.**
aud	Optional. Who the token was issued to.
azp	The audience of the token. The value of this claim must match the application or service that uses the token to authenticate the request. Typically, the client ID of the OIDC connection.
sub	The subject: the ID that represents the principal making the request.
iat	Unix epoch time when the token was issued.
exp	Unix epoch time when the token expires.

Table 5.2: *Most commonly used claims in an ID token*

While these are only the mandatory claims for the issuer and audience, there are also user information claims like name, email, picture, and so on. We will see some of them in the example in the section Login with Google. The token is presented as a JSON Web Token (JWT). Secondly, ID tokens are only one of the ways to request user information. The OPs also expose a service endpoint to request user information using the access token. In the default configuration, the

17 Taken from Google Cloud documentation. **https://cloud.google.com/docs/authentication/token-types**

user information endpoint and ID token provide similar claims in the response. Some OPs allow configuring them independently.

JSON Web Token

JSON Web Tokens (JWT) is a compact URL-safe approach to exchange claims information across systems[18]. While we have just discussed receiving claims data as a response in the form of ID Tokens. the OIDC protocol allows JWTs used as requests[19]. JWTs can be signed or even encrypted; when they are encrypted, signing precedes encryption. We will discuss JSON Web Signatures (JWS) here[20], which is the formatting for the signed JWTs.

***Figure 5.18**: JSON Web Signature Format*[21]

JWS begins with a JSON Object Signing and Encryption (JOSE) header. Following are some of the registered parameters used commonly.

- **`alg`**: Algorithm used to sign the JWS. **`HS256`** and **`RS256`** are commonly used values. Both signing schemes utilize the **`SHA-256`** hash of the data. **`HS256`** uses the HMAC-based signing with a shared secret, while **`RS256`** uses a RSA key pair.
- **`typ`**: Typically, JWT.
- **`kid`**: The ID of the key used in the signature. Although the specification allows public keys in the JOSE headers, most OPs publish them through

18 RFC 7519, JSON Web Token, **https://datatracker.ietf.org/doc/html/rfc7519**

19 Section 6, OIDC Core 1.0 Specification, **https://openid.net/specs/openid-connect-core-1_0.html#JWTRequests**

20 RFC 7515, JSON Web Signature, **https://www.rfc-editor.org/rfc/rfc7515.html**

21 Data used from RFC 7515

the OpenID directory. **`kid`** provides a mechanism to search such a directory and locate the key.

We apply **`Base64URL`** encoding on the header followed by a dot **`(.)`** character. The claims are put inside a JSON object format and encoded using **`Base64URL`** encoding; this is the payload of the JWS. The combined data is signed using the algorithm specified in the header (**`alg`**) with the relevant key. The resultant signature is encoded using **`Base64URL`** encoding. Another dot **`(.)`** is added after the payload. The encoded signature is placed right after it.

The combined token looks like:


```
eyJ0eXAiOiJKV1QiLCJhbGciOiJIUzI1NiJ9.

yJpc3MiOiJqb2UiLCJleHAiOjEzMDA4MTkzODAsImh0dHA6Ly9leGFtcGxlLmNvbS9pc19y-
b290Ijp0cnVlfQ.tzxo0VemMte9T1bdN1r3qh8PWYnsa3bP9dbzWkidVao
```


The following symmetric key[22] was used to sign the payload using **`HS256`** algorithm.


```
{"kty":"oct",
 "k":"AyM1SysPpbyDfgZld3umj1qzKObwVMkoqQ-EstJQLr_T-1qS0gZH75aKtMN3Yj0iPS
4hcgUuTwjAzZr1Z9CAow"}
```


Here is the process to decode a JWT:

1. Take the first two parts, including the delimiter dot (.).
2. Compute the signature using the shared secret in `HS256` or RSA public key in the case of `RS256`.
3. Generate the `Base64URL` encoding from the signature.
4. The encoded signature should match the third part of the token.
5. Decode the first and second parts of the JWT using `Base64URL` encoding.

While the process is simple, good online resources are available to decode JWTs[23]. We decode the above token using the **https://jwt.io** debugging tool.

---

22 The data is provided in RFC 7515, Appendix-A.1, **https://www.rfc-editor.org/rfc/rfc7515.html#appendix-A.1**

23 jwt.io, **https://jwt.io**

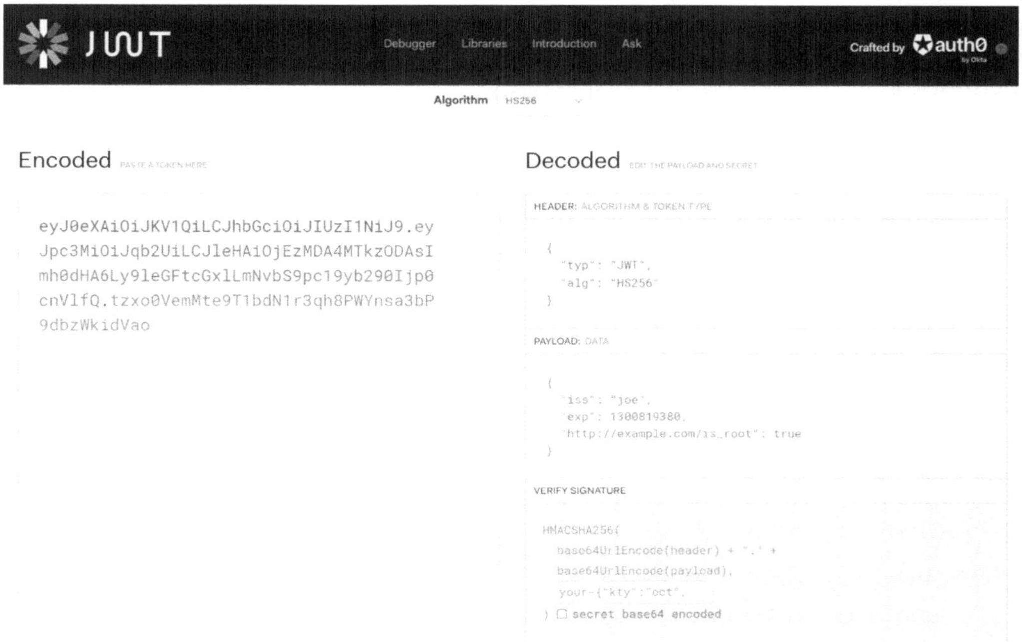

Figure 5.19**: Decoding of JWT using* ***https://jwt.io

Some header and payload parameters are public and registered with the Internet Assigned Numbers Authority (IANA). However, you can use private parameters as well. You should provide it as a URL with your domain, for example, **http://example.com/is_root.**

Login with Google

The OIDC providers are certified and listed on openid.net[24]. The IAM vendors have embraced the protocol and providing certified products and solutions. Only a handful of social networking giants have shown any interest in it. Most social networking providers: LinkedIn, Meta, X (Twitter), and so on., provide OAuth-based user information APIs; we can tune for user authentication, but they do not implement the OIDC standard. Our GitHub sample using OAuth (above) for authentication is a case in point. Microsoft and Google provide extensive OIDC support due to their interest in cloud computing and focus on enterprise IAM. Google Federated Identity got certification as an OP in 2015. We will review Google's OIDC implementation to a limited extent. OIDC is a collection of profiles. Google has been certified in four of the profiles. IAM products work with other products; some work as IDPs to other Identity Management systems. In such an interconnected world, adherence to standards makes the solutions

24 **https://openid.net/certification/**

useful for easier adoption. OpenID Federation (OIDF) provides this certification process for vendors to register and comply. Certification gives better visibility in vendor evaluation in enterprise selling.

We will connect to the Google Cloud Platform (GCP) using an OIDC client library. As the user authenticates, we collect the ID Token and show the content on the screen. We also query the user info endpoint of the OP and present the received data on the screen juxtaposed to the data received from the ID Token.

Configuring the Google Cloud Platform

To configure the Google Cloud for OIDC authentication, follow the steps below:

1. Open the Google Cloud Console at: **https://console.cloud.google.com**.
2. Create a new project if you already do not have one.
3. Click on the APIs and Services Tab.
4. If you do not have an OAuth consent screen configured, you must configure one to proceed. You will also add the test user accounts who can use the client for authentication.
5. Now click on the credential in the navigation pane and configure a new OAuth 2.0 Client ID. On completion of this step a new client ID and secret will be created.
6. You can download the client details of client ID and secret and keep them in a safe place[25].

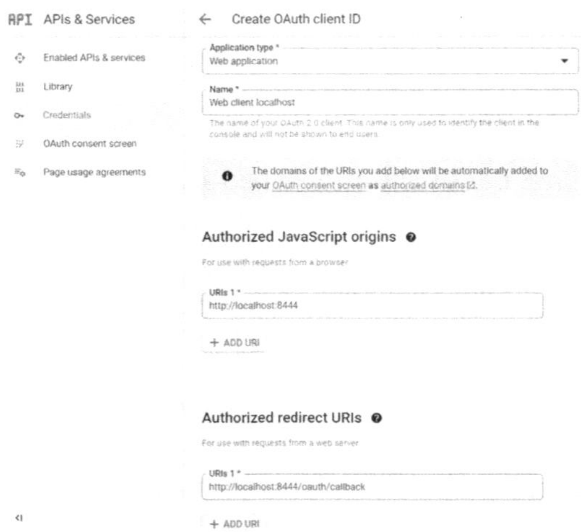

***Figure 5.20**: Creating OAuth 2.0 client credentials*

25 Do not check-in client ID and the secret to any source control system as it can be accessed by an unauthorized person.

In the sample code, we use **GOOGLE_CLIENT_ID** and **GOOGLE_CLIENT_SECRET** environment variables to pass the OIDC Client ID and Secret into our application. While configuring OAuth credentials, you cannot use domain names that do not have a valid top-level domain (TLD). For example, you cannot configure **mysrv.local** as a test domain. You can use **localhost** as a test domain.

You can find the code in **chapter-5/google**. Enter this directory in a shell and set the environment variables **GOOGLE_CLIENT_ID** and **GOOGLE_CLIENT_SECRET**. Launch the OIDC client application with **go run ./oidc.go**.

User Experience

The application is a simple demo. We show you the screens the user will be interacting with.

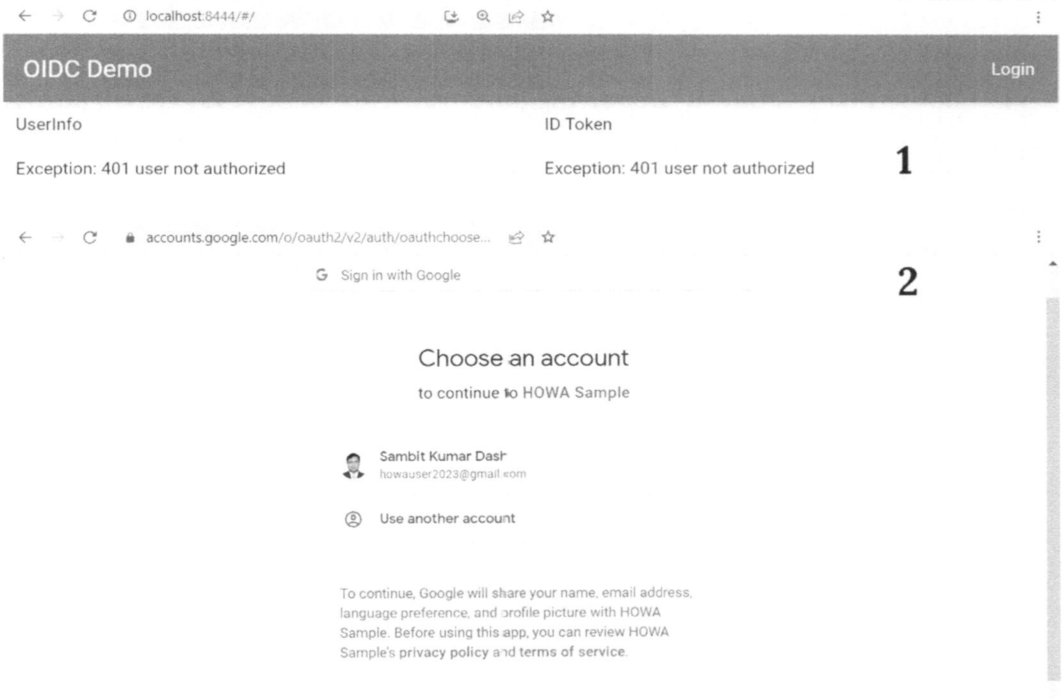

Figure 5.21: *Authenticate with Google using OIDC*

Launch the browser and go to the URL **http://localhost:8444/**.

1. The browser shows the login button with both User Info and ID Token section stating no user has authenticated.

2. On clicking the Login button, the browser is opens **/oauth/login** which redirects to:

   ```
   https://accounts.google.com/o/oauth2/v2/auth?access_
   type=offline&client_id=<<CLIENT_ID>>&redirect_
   uri=http%3A%2F%2Flocalhost%3A8444%2Foauth%2Fcallback&response_ty
   pe=code&scope=openid+profile+email&state=f97379cd-be86-4b6b-bbbe-
   3711cc860ae0
   ```

   The URL is very similar to an OAuth redirect with scopes **`openid`** and **`profile`** added. The scope **`openid`** is mandatory and it suggests claims based on the scopes will be added. For example, a **`profile`** scope adds **`name, picture, locale, etc.`** properties to the claims. The scope **`email`** adds **`email`** and **`email_verified`** to the claims.
3. Google will authenticate the user and redirect the browser to **`/oauth/callback`** with the authorization code to complete the token issuance workflow. We have already seen this in the context of OAuth.
4. In the token request, the relying party receives an **`access_token`**, an **`id_token`**, and a **`refresh_token`**. We create a **`session`** cookie and associate these tokens with the session.
5. When the tokens are issued, the browser is redirected to **`http://localhost:8444`** which in turn contacts the **`/userinfo`** and **`/idtoken`** endpoints to request for that information and render the UI with the details.

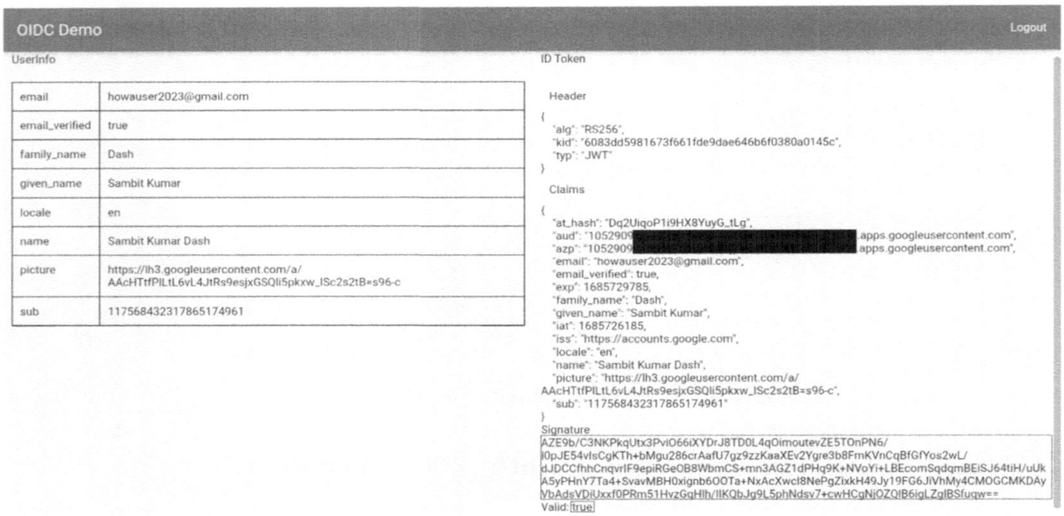

***Figure 5.22**: User info and ID token data presented through UI*

6. Lastly, the Login button changes to Logout.

We use the **coreos/go-oidc**[26] library for the backend tasks in Golang. We set up an HTTP server at port **8444** and assigned the Flutter web frontend at the root (/) virtual.

```
func main(){
  addOIDCHandlers()
  http.HandleFunc("/", func(w http.ResponseWriter, r *http.Request) {
    http.FileServer(http.Dir("frontend/build/web")).ServeHTTP(w, r)
  })
  server := &http.Server{Addr: ":8444"}
}
```

In the **addOIDCHandlers** we initialize the provider object with the OIDC discovery metadata.

```
func addOIDCHandlers() {
  provider, _ := oidc.NewProvider(context.Background(),
    "https://accounts.google.com")
…
  verifier := provider.Verifier(&oidc.Config{ClientID: client_id})
…
  conf := &oauth2.Config{
    ClientID:     client_id,
    ClientSecret: client_secret,
    Endpoint:     provider.Endpoint(), // Obtained from the OIDC
directory
    Scopes:       []string{oidc.ScopeOpenID, "profile", "email"},
    RedirectURL:  "http://localhost:8444/oauth/callback",
}
```

The OIDC directory for Google is available at: **https://accounts.google.com/.well-known/openid-configuration**. The directory provides paths and capabilities supported by the server. Parts of the information provided by the directory are shown below.

```
{
  "issuer": "https://accounts.google.com",
  "authorization_endpoint": "https://accounts.google.com/o/oauth2/v2/auth",
…
```

26 Package oidc implements OpenID Connect client logic for the **golang.org/x/oauth2** package. **https://pkg.go.dev/github.com/coreos/go-oidc/v3/oidc**

```
  "token_endpoint": "https://oauth2.googleapis.com/token",
  "userinfo_endpoint": "https://openidconnect.googleapis.com/v1/
userinfo",
  "revocation_endpoint": "https://oauth2.googleapis.com/revoke",
  "jwks_uri": "https://www.googleapis.com/oauth2/v3/certs",
…
  "scopes_supported": ["openid","email","profile"],
  "claims_supported": ["aud","email","email_verified","exp","family_
name",
     "given_name","iat","iss","locale","name","picture","sub"],
…
}
```

The **/oauth/login** handler is like what we have already seen in the GitHub example (above). We redirect to the **authorization_endpoint** to authenticate with Google.

```
http.HandleFunc("/oauth/login", func(w http.ResponseWriter, req *http.
Request) {
  state := uuid.New().String()
  _setState(state)
  url := conf.AuthCodeURL(state, oauth2.AccessTypeOffline)
  log.Printf("Redirecting to: %v", url)
  http.Redirect(w, req, url, http.StatusFound)
})
```

The **/oauth/callback** handler is not far from the GitHub example as well. Removing the error handling and state management code, the token workflow is shown.

```
http.HandleFunc("/oauth/callback", func(w http.ResponseWriter, req
*http.Request){
…
  if code = req.FormValue("code"); code != "" {
    if token, err = conf.Exchange(req.Context(), code); err == nil{
      log.Printf("The token is expiring at: %v", token.Expiry)
      if err = _saveToken(w, token); err == nil {
        http.Redirect(w, req, "/", http.StatusFound)
      }
    }
  }
})
```

The **exchange** method returns three tokens, namely, **access_token**, **id_token**, and **refresh_token** as part of the **token** object. It also has the expiry time of the **access_token**. In the function **_saveToken**, we create a session cookie and associate the token object to the session. We also verify the **id_token** and the **access_token**.

```
_saveToken := func(w http.ResponseWriter, token *oauth2.Token) (err
error) {
…
  if idToken, err = verifier.Verify(context.Background(),
    idTokenStr); err == nil {
    if err = idToken.VerifyAccessToken(token.AccessToken); err == nil {
      uuidstr := uuid.NewString()
      muToken.Lock()
      defer muToken.Unlock()
      tokens[uuidstr] = token
      _setCookie(w, "session", uuidstr, false)
    }
  }
  return
}
```

Following are a few checks carried out on the **id_token**. One can look at the specification for an elaborate list of checks[27].

1. **Issuer**: The issuer exists and is well formatted and is matching the issuer of the provider in the configuration.
2. **Audience**: The audience (**aud**) record of the token must the client ID.
3. **Expiry**: Ensure the token has not expired. The current time is within the not before (**nbf**) and expiry (**exp**) time. Google does not provide a not before (**nbf**) value by default.
4. **Signature**: Verify the signature of the JSON Web Signature (JWS) token. While the method **Verify** keeps the certificate extraction transparent from the developer, we will discuss this in some detail later.

27 Section 3.1.3.7. ID Token Validation, **https://openid.net/specs/openid-connect-core-1_0.html#IDTokenValidation**

In OAuth 2.0, the **access_token** is verified at the authorization server. It increases network round-trip time. To overcome this limitation, a hash of the **access_token** is embedded in the ID token as the **at_hash** parameter[28]. The method **idToken.VerifyAccessToken** implements this scheme.

Token Security

Access tokens could be random strings containing no Personally Identifiable Information (PII). So, they are safe to be passed on to clients like a browser cookie. *What if an embedded JavaScript in the page extracted the token and accessed the resource server?* You can secure the cookies by marking them **HttpOnly**, and the browser JavaScript cannot access them. The browser shows a UI element by querying the server REST API. The REST APIs can provide access by analyzing the submitted cookie. *Should ID tokens be sent to the browser as a cookie?* Some implementations set complete ID tokens as cookies. We will suggest you be judicious in your application. Suppose ID token claims contain the group information of the user. The UI rendering does not require this information, yet, it flows down to the client's device. In a security-compromised browser, a hacker can access the groups the user belongs to. For better security, keep data transmission to the minimum and only when required. In this sample, we do not expose the ID token through a cookie but return the contents as a REST API for the client to render. We provide two REST API endpoints, **/idtoken** and **/userinfo**, to convey the ID token and the user info, respectively.

Token Expiry

Access tokens are issued only for a short period. Google access tokens are valid for 60 mins. However, refresh tokens can be for longer durations, or they may not expire. In such cases, the user can revoke the refresh tokens. Checking for the expiry of access tokens can be a cumbersome code. The **oauth2** library provides a **TokenSource** wrapper that refreshes the access token when the caller calls its **Token()** method.

```
...

ts = conf.TokenSource(r.Context(), token)
if ntoken, err = ts.Token(); err == nil {
  if ntoken != token {
    log.Println("Refreshed the token and saving...")
    err = _saveToken(w, ntoken)
  }
}
...
```

28 Section 3.1.3.8 Access Token Validation, **https://openid.net/specs/openid-connect-core-1_0.html#CodeFlowTokenValidation**

Service Endpoints

If we had to implement the querying of Userinfo, we would have followed the following steps.

1. Find the "**userinfo_endpoint**" from the OP directory, i.e., **https://openidconnect.googleapis.com/v1/userinfo**.
2. Create an HTTP query with the **access_token** as the Bearer token in the authorization header and the **userinfo_endpoint** as the URL.

provider.Userinfo method carries out all this tasks and obtains the data.

```
...
if ui, err = provider.UserInfo(r.Context(), ts); err == nil {
  claims := make(map[string]interface{}
  if err = ui.Claims(&claims); err == nil {
    w.Header().Set("Content-Type", "application/json")
    enc := json.NewEncoder(w)
    enc.SetIndent("", "  ")
    enc.Encode(claims)
  }
}
...
```

For **/idtoken**, we take the ID token string and convert it to a JWT token structure.

```
claims := jwt.MapClaims{}
idTokenStr := token.Extra("id_token").(string)
if idtoken, err := jwt.NewParser().ParseWithClaims(
  idTokenStr, &claims, _keyFunc); err == nil {
  w.Header().Set("Content-Type", "application/json")
  enc := json.NewEncoder(w)
  enc.SetIndent("", "  ")
  enc.Encode(idtoken)
}
```

The **ParseWithClaims(idTokenStr, &claims, _keyFunc)** method decodes the three parts of the ID token we discussed earlier. The **_keyFunc** function provides the necessary public key to verify the signature. Here is the relevant logic implemented in the **_keyfunc** method.

1. Search the OP directory for the **jwks_url** and obtain the public keys from Google.
2. Find the key whose key id (**kid**) matches the key id (**kid**) mentioned in the JWT header.
3. The key is in the JSON web key format. Convert the key to the RSA key format.

In the interest of space, we suggest the users review the **_keyFunc** at **chapter-5/google/oidc.go**.

Web front end

Note:

Enter the **frontend** folder and run **flutter build web** to build the front-end code.

The web front end is straightforward. It tries to access the **/userinfo** and **/idtoken** endpoints.

```
late Future<String> userinfo;
late Future<String> idtoken;

@override
void initState() {
  super.initState();
  userinfo = getInfo(Uri(scheme: "http", path: "/userinfo"));
  idtoken = getInfo(Uri(scheme: "http", path: "/idtoken"));
}

Future<String> getInfo(Uri uri) async {
  var res = await http.get(uri);
  if (res.statusCode == 200) {
    return res.body;
  } else {
    throw Exception("${res.statusCode} ${res.body}");
  }
}
```

If the user has authenticated, it receives the userinfo as a JSON object which it renders in a tabular form.

```
  Widget getUserInfo(BuildContext context) {
```

```
  return FutureBuilder(
    future: userinfo,
    builder: (BuildContext ctx, AsyncSnapshot<String> sn) {
      if (sn.hasData) {
        List<TableRow> trs = [];
        Map<String, dynamic> m = jsonDecode(sn.data!);
        m.forEach((k, v) {
          trs.add(TableRow(children: [
            Padding(
              padding: padding,
              child: Text(k),
            ),
            Padding(
              padding: padding,
              child: Text(v.toStr ing()),z              ),
          ]));
        });
        return Table(
          defaultColumnWidth: const IntrinsicColumnWidth(),
          children: trs,
          border: TableBorder.all(),
        );
      } else if (sn.hasError) {
        return Text(sn.error.toString());
      } else {
        return const Text("Reading data...");
      }
    },
  );
}
```

For the ID token, the UI receives the JSON structure. It renders the header, claims, signature, and validity of the signature.

```
Widget getIDToken(BuildContext context) {
  return FutureBuilder(
    future: idtoken,
    builder: (BuildContext ctx, AsyncSnapshot<String> sn) {
      if (sn.hasData) {
        Map<String, dynamic> m = jsonDecode(sn.data!);
        const encoder = JsonEncoder.withIndent("    ");
        final headerPretty = encoder.convert(m["Header"]!);
        final claimsPretty = encoder.convert(m["Claims"]!);
        final signature = m["Signature"]!;
        final valid = m["Valid"]!;

        const padding = EdgeInsets.all(10);
        return Column(
          crossAxisAlignment: CrossAxisAlignment.start,
          children: [
            const Padding(
              padding: padding,
              child: Text("Header"),
            ),
            Text(headerPretty),
            const Padding(
              padding: padding,
              child: Text("Claims"),
            ),
            Text(claimsPretty),
            const Text("Signature"),
            Text(signature),
            Text("Valid: ${valid.toString()}"),
          ],
        );
      } else if (sn.hasError) {
        return Text(sn.error.toString());
```

```
        } else {
          return const Text("Reading data...");
        }
      },
    );
  }
```

If the user has authenticated, the Login button changes to a Logout button.

```
  Widget getLoginButton(BuildContext context) {
    return FutureBuilder(
      future: userinfo,
      builder: (BuildContext ctx, AsyncSnapshot<String> sn) {
        final path = sn.hasData ? "/oauth/logout" : "/oauth/login";
        final btnTxt = sn.hasData ? "Logout" : "Login";
        return TextButton(
          onPressed: () => launchUrl(Uri(scheme: "http", path: path),
              webOnlyWindowName: "_self"),
          child: Text(btnTxt, style: const TextStyle(color: Colors.
white)),
        );
      },
    );
  }
```

A Scaffold class places the preceding UI elements in the designated locations.

Conclusion

We reviewed the IAM infrastructure of an enterprise and identified the need for daisy chaining of IDPs. We looked at the social networking world of sharing content and the need for authorization beyond groups and attributes. We reviewed the OAuth 2.0 specification and various grant types required for the secure delivery of access tokens. Then we looked at the rationality of developing an OIDC protocol and how OIDC provides the capabilities of an IDP through ID tokens. We reviewed the JWT format in the context of using them as ID tokens. We discussed how to keep the tokens secured in exchanges. However, we have not discussed the credentials to authenticate with the authentication or authorization servers. We discussed passwords in the context of cryptography. In the next chapter, we will go beyond passwords as credentials or authenticators.

Questions

1. Pick up an open-source Identity and Access Management product. Write an OIDC application and authenticate with the IAM system. Configure some claims and verify them in your application.
2. What are the differences between the tokens in OAuth 2.0 and OIDC 1.0?
3. In Figure 4.17: Identity and Access Management, we discussed the role of SAML IDPs. How will OAuth or OIDC-based systems integrate into that architecture?
4. While SAML **`AuthnRequests`** are signed to ascertain the requester, no signing is carried out in OAuth. Is OAuth secured enough?
5. Can PKCE and Device Grant protocols be used interchangeably? Are there cases where both protocols are needed to be used together?

CHAPTER 6
Multifactor Authentication

Introduction

In the chapters on federated authentication, we looked at how service providers can present the identity providers with an authentication request and how identity providers can respond with a successful or a failed response. We did not focus on the interaction between the user and the identity provider. In its simplest form, the identity provider challenges the user to provide her credentials to validate. The user submits her credentials; the identity provider authorizes access if the credentials are validated. We have seen some examples with usernames and passwords as credentials. We talked about how to keep passwords safe on the server. We also suggested some best practices for managing passwords. Whatever you do, passwords are cumbersome; enterprises spend billions of dollars managing passwords[1]. With mobile devices and biometric scanners becoming ubiquitous, industries are looking for credentials beyond passwords. We will look at some of those in this chapter.

Structure

In this chapter, we will cover the following topics:

1 Enterprises spent over two billion USD managing passwords in 2022-23. **https://www.statista.com/statistics/1300988/global-password-management-market-revenue/**

- Factors of authentication
- OTP-based authentication
- Fast Identity Online (FIDO)
- Bringing it all together

Factors of authentication

We have already seen passwords in previous chapters. Passwords have been in use since the inception of computers. While they are one of the most common authentication credentials, fingerprints, access cards, USB tokens, etc., are used as authentication mechanisms.

***Figure 6.1**: Authentication factors*

NIST classified these credentials into three factors of authentication.

1. **Something You Know**: Here are some of the most common credentials in this category
    - **Passwords**: We have discussed them at length and found them hard to manage, yet they are most prevalent. Personal Identification Numbers (PINs) used on phone interfaces are similar.
    - **Questionnaire**: These are trivia-like facts known about a person, e.g., date of birth, mother's maiden name, the first school you went to, etc. There is not much variation in the answers for an individual. Multiple websites can use similar questions. For example, many websites store the date of birth or mother's maiden name. In the era of social networking, observing a person's profile can answer many such questions.

- **Patterns**: These are commonly used in mobile screen locking. The number of combinations is limited.

All knowledge-based credentials are vulnerable to social engineering attacks. For example, a malicious actor can ask a few questions in an unrelated context, and the user divulges private information without realizing his security is compromised. In a phishing attack, a malicious actor can present the user with a lookalike website. The user innocently enters his knowledge information and exposes the data. A malicious actor can harvest the knowledge information once and use it several times later.

2. **Something You Have**: This authentication factor ensures the user has a physical token or gadget. Here are a few commonly used tokens:

    - **Key fob**: A device generates a temporary password that the user can use only once within a specified period to authenticate. We will discuss this further in a later section.
    - **USB Dongle/Common Access Cards**: These devices have asymmetric cryptography-based keypairs. When a user wants to authenticate, the operating system sends these devices signing requests. Once signed, the user is validated.
    - **Mobile Devices**: Everyone today has one or more mobile devices. When the user tries to authenticate, the user receives a one-time password. He uses this password to log in. The mobile device can have an authenticator app that will receive a notification when a user tries to log in to a website. The user can access the website only when she approves the authentication request on her mobile. The mobile device may have an application that generates an OTP, like a key fob discussed earlier.

A user can get locked out if the device is lost. A stolen device can give the malicious actor access to the authentication platform. Hence, some of these devices require a PIN to access the device, or in a mobile phone, the user must lock the screen. The malicious actor can sit in line, harvest the credentials, and submit on behalf of the user as a man-in-the-middle (MiTM) during the transaction; but, an attacker cannot save the one-time password and use it later[2]. However, there is no protection against a man-in-the-middle attack unless you use a server authentication scheme, like Transport Layer Security (TLS).

2 When you know the internal working of OTP algorithms, you can generate OTPs ahead of time and save them; you can use them later. We will discuss these cases in a later section.

- **FIDO Devices and WebAuthn**: TLS is one proven defense against MiTM attacks. Since the communication channel is encrypted end-to-end, no malicious actor can access any credential data. Mutual TLS (m-TLS) provides secured client authentication and defense against MiTM attacks. However, m-TLS is cumbersome to use and is not browser-friendly.Certificate-based authentication (CBA) with a web browser either uses a Java-Applet[3] or requires a helper application to access the client certificates on a desktop. WebAuthn workflow with FIDO devices provides a user-friendly authentication scheme and is supported on all modern browsers. FIDO devices can integrate biometric authentication into the same workflow as well. We will discuss this in a later section.

3. **Something You Are**: These authentication factors are associated with a person's physical attributes. Most of these are biometric characteristics of a person, e.g., face, fingerprint, heartbeat, voice, iris/retina, etc. A sensor captures these parameters and passes them over the internet for validation. Some malicious actors capture these biometric data and reuse them in another context. Stolen biometric information can be detrimental as there is no way to create new biometric information. Most biometric authentication schemes verify if the person presenting the biometric data is alive. These checks are known as liveness checks. Some authentication experts insist biometry data not be transmitted over the wire. In such cases, the biometric data is validated in the device of capture, like the mobile device, and a signed response is sent to the authentication server confirming biometric data validation. We will discuss this further in the context of WebAuthn in a later section.

OTP-based authentication

Passwords are shared secrets between the server and the user, yet they have these limitations:

- A user must remember them. So, they are associated with the user's past experiences and knowledge.
- They cannot be of arbitrary binary values. They are valid words or close derivatives of them. So, they cannot be as random as binary data of the same length.

3 All browsers, like Google Chrome, Microsoft Edge, Apple Safari, etc., have discontinued support for Java applets over the past several years. Hence, running a helper application alongside the web browser is the only option for supporting CBA with browsers.

- While password policies insist on higher complexity, they make the passwords hard to remember.
- The servers do not store the password in clear text. They derive a key from the password and save the key. However, the user sends the password in clear text through the authentication channel. If the channel is unsecured, the password is compromised.
- Once compromised, a hacker can use the password later.

To overcome the shortcomings described above, we introduce the following scheme. The server publishes a book of random numbers and provides that to the user. While authenticating, the user shall present one random number from the book in a specific sequence, say left to right and top to bottom.

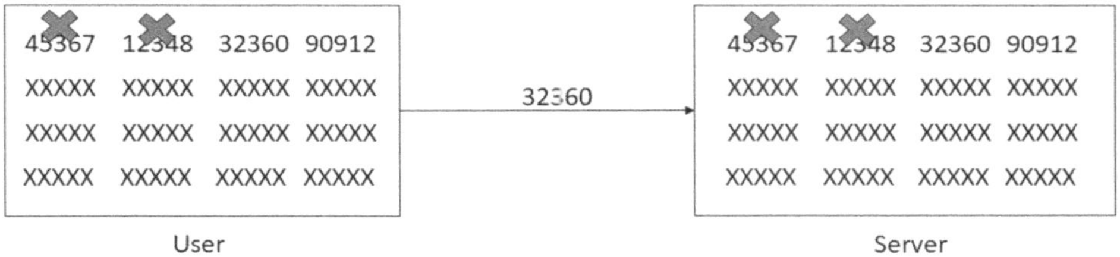

Figure 6.2: *A book of random numbers*

Once the server accepts the random number, the client and server will mark the number as used (**`45367`** and **`12348`**). The user will send the next number in the sequence (**`32360`**) in the subsequent authentication attempt. If the server can provide such a book to every user independent of the book given to another user, we can overcome all the limitations we saw with the passwords. The one-time password concept came from this idea. The practical implementation looks like this:

1. The server and the device share a shared secret (`K`). In the case of a hard token, the manufacturer burns it into the chip. In the case of a soft token or mobile application, we use an out-of-band transmission mechanism.
2. The user clicks a button on the device to increment a counter (`C`).
3. The client generates an **`HMAC_SHA1(K, C)`**. The generated string is 160 bits (20 bytes) long.
4. The device truncates the string to a 31-bit value or a positive 4-byte integer. The device divides the integer by 10^6 and shows the user the

6-digit one-time password. If required, the device can generate 7 or 8-digit numbers as options.

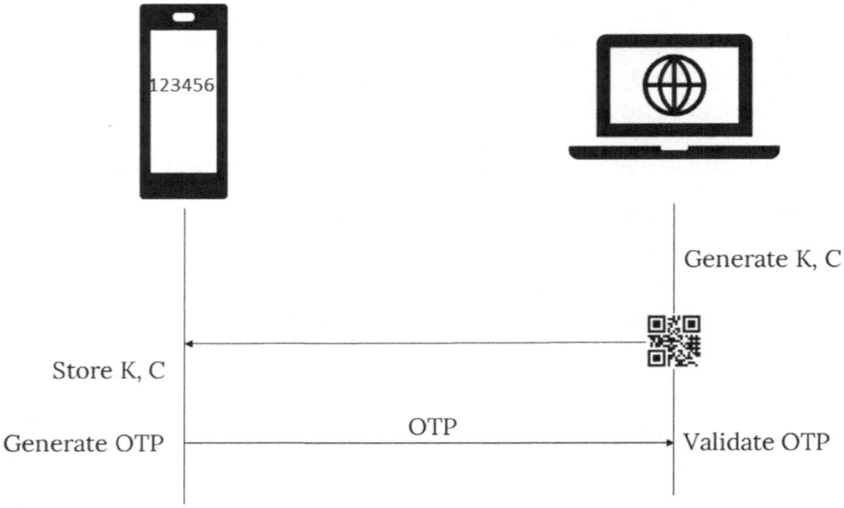

***Figure 6.3**: HMAC-based OTP workflow schematic*

5. The user presents the value to the server.
6. The server follows steps 2–4 to generate the OTP. If the OTP generated at the server matches the password sent by the user, the validation is successful.
7. On a successful match, the server stores the incrementedcounter. This step ensures the password is only valid for one time.

The HMAC-based OTP (HOTP) algorithm[4] expects the shared secret to be random and should be at least 128 bits long. It does not define the exchange workflow. In the figure, we have shown a QR code-based exchange of the credential information.

HOTP Sample

We provide a sample code to understand the HOTP framework and would like you to review it alongside reading the book.

1. Go to the **`Chapter-6/otp/frontend`** folder. Run **`flutter build web`** to build the front end.

4 The complete specification is documented in RFC 4226 **https://www.ietf.org/rfc/rfc4226.txt**

2. Go to the parent directory (**`Chapter-6/otp`**) and launch the server using the command **`go run ./otp.go`**.
3. Now open the browser and go to the URL: **https://mysrv.local:8443/**

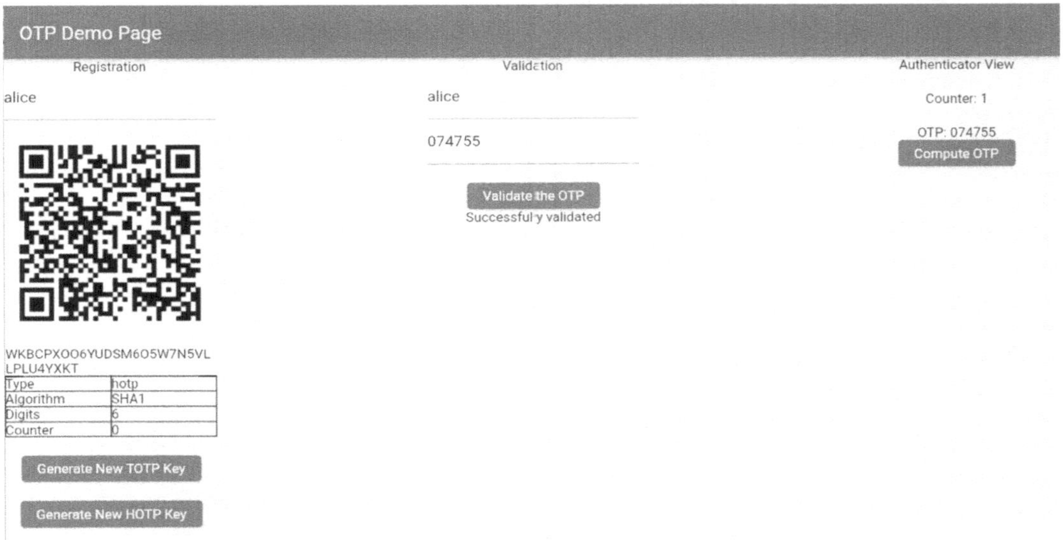

***Figure 6.4**: HOTP workflows in one screen*

Figure 6.4 is composed of three parts.

- **Registration**:
  - When you enter a user name and click the generate new HOTP key button, you see a new secret and QR code. You can view the parameters of the credentials in a tabular form.
  - If you have Google Authenticator installed on your mobile device and scan the QR code, Google Authenticator will prompt you if you want to add the credential to your device. Alternatively, you can manually add the secret to the Google Authenticator.
  - The shared secret is in a base32 encoded form.

  If you decipher the QR code, you will find a URL[5] in the format shown below:

```
otpauth://hotp/mysrv:alice?issuer=mysrv&secret=WKBCPXOO6YUDSM6O5W7N5VLLPLU4YXKT
```

5 The complete format of the URL for **`otpauth`** can be seen at: **https://github.com/google/google-authenticator/wiki/Key-Uri-Format**

For the HOTP, the optional parameters are **digits** and **counter**. If we include them, the URL will be as shown.

otpauth://hotp/mysrv:alice?issuer=mysrv&secret=WKBCPXOO6YUDS M6O5W7N5VLLPLU4YXKT&counter=0&digits=6

Under the hood, we implement a **/register** endpoint with a handler for the following steps.

- Create a cryptographically secure random number and encode it using base32 encoding.
- Formulate the **otpauth** URL using the format guide we discussed above.
- Create a new OTP secret key object from the URL.
- Collect all the parameters from the key and form a JSON object for the response.
- Generate the QR code and add its path to the response object.

The error handling has been removed for better readability of the code.

```
http.HandleFunc("/register",
                func(w http.ResponseWriter, r *http.Request) {
        username := r.FormValue("username")
        otptype := r.FormValue("type")
        secret_bytes := make([]byte, 20)
        rand.Read(secret_bytes)
        secret := base32.StdEncoding.EncodeToString(secret_bytes)
        url := fmt.Sprintf(
                  "otpauth://%s/mysrv:%s?issuer=mysrv&secret=%s",
          otptype, username, secret)
        key, _ := otp.NewKeyFromURL(url)
        keyinfo := map[string]string{
          "secret":    key.Secret(),
          "type":      key.Type(),
          "algorithm": key.Algorithm().String(),
          "digits":    key.Digits().String(),
        }
```

```
    img, _ := key.Image(200, 200)
    var imgbuf bytes.Buffer
    png.Encode(&imgbuf, img)
    keyinfo["image"] = base64.StdEncoding.
                         EncodeToString(imgbuf.Bytes())
    w.Header().Set("Content-Type", "application/json")
    jsonResp, _ := json.Marshal(keyinfo)
    log.Printf("new %s key provisioned for the user %s",
      key.Type(), username)
    w.Write(jsonResp)
    users[username] = &_userData{
      Type:    key.Type(),
      Secret:  key.Secret(),
      Counter: 1,
    }
  })
```

The user interface is straightforward. It obtains the parameters for the credential and renders:

- The QR Code
- Base32 encoded secret
- Other parameters in a tabular form.
- A button for the user to trigger the provisioning of a new key.

We suggest the readers review **RegistrationView** in **frontend/lib/main.dart**.

- **Validation**

  The validation endpoint (**/validate**) receives the username and the OTP. The method **hotp.Validate** call takes the shared secret, counter, and OTP as inputs. If the OTP matches, the validation is considered successful. The handler is shown below:

```
http.HandleFunc("/validate",
              func(w http.ResponseWriter, r *http.Request) {
    username := r.FormValue("username")
    otp := r.FormValue("otp")
```

```
        authdata, _ := users[username]
        if authdata.Type == "hotp" {
          ok = hotp.Validate(otp, authdata.Counter, authdata.Secret)
          if ok {
            authdata.Counter++
          }
        }
        if ok {
          log.Printf("User %s authenticated successfully", username)
           return
        } else {
           http.Error(w, "invalid username or otp", http.
StatusUnauthorized)
           log.Print("invalid username or otp")
        }
      })
```

- **Authenticator**

  The authenticator code is all dart-based and rendered in the browser. It does not require any backend REST APIs. The package '**`otp/otp.dart`**' is used for computing the OTP values.

  - **`OTP.generateHOTPCodeString(widget.secret, counter, isGoogle: true)`** computes the OTP value.
  - A trigger button is provided to increment the counter.

We suggest the readers review **`AuthenticatorView`** in **`frontend/lib/main.dart`**.

Synchronization of the counter

Synchronization of the counter across the server and authenticator device is a challenge. Let us say a user received a hard token and left it unattended. A kid in the house got hold of the device and kept pressing the trigger button. Such a device is out of sync with the server. Some devices ask for a protection PIN before they increment the counter. However, that makes it harder for the user. *Can some steps be taken at the server?*

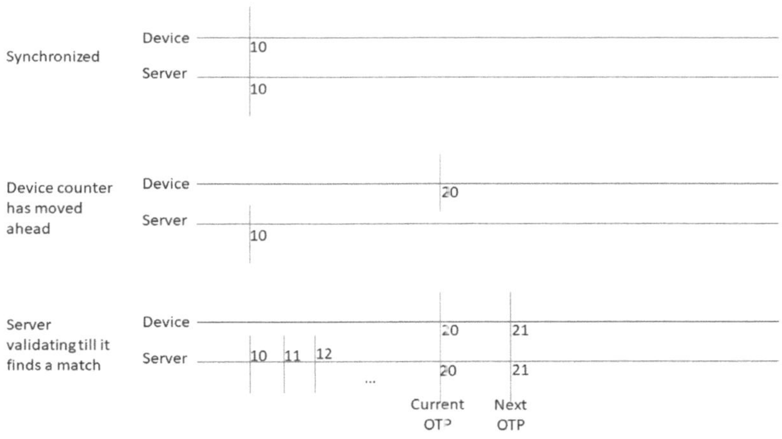

Figure 6.5: *HOTP device and server counter synchronization*

When a server cannot validate an OTP, it can look ahead to ten counter values to find a potential match. Once an OTP match exists, the server will ask the user to present the next OTP value. If that OTP matches, the synchronization is completed. In *Figure* 6.5, the device counter was 20, and the server was 10. When the user presents the OTP, the server increments the counter till it reaches 20. Then the server asks the user to submit the OTP for counter 21. If the server can validate, the server sets the counter value to 21. How reliable is such a scheme? The probability of a random 6-digit number being a valid OTP is 10^{-6}. The probability of two such consecutive values being valid is $10^{-6} \times 10^{-6} = 10^{-12}$. At this small probability, it is more likely to assume the user owns the device.

Unattended HOTP devices

Suppose Alice leaves her HOTP authenticator unattended, and a malicious user (Mallory) gets access to it. Mallory can harvest a few OTPs from the device and record them in a notebook. At her convenience, Mallory can access the server and authenticate as Alice. The OTPs are for one-time use only, but they never expire. Hence, some devices insist the user uses a PIN to access the OTP. There are only 10^6 possibilities of OTP values. In such cases, one can orchestrate a brute-force attack. A server should only allow limited authentication attempts for a user at any specific instance and lock the account if such a limit is exceeded.

Time-based OTP

Synchronizing the counter across the device and the server can be cumbersome. Secondly, we did not want OTPs to be valid for an indefinite amount of time.

What if the moving factor or the counter is time-dependent? These led to the development of the standard for time-based one-time passwords.

$$Counter(C) = \frac{Unix\ Time^{6}\ in\ Sec}{Step\ in\ Sec}$$

The default step is 30s.

While developing the TOTP standard[7], SHA-1 is no longer considered secure enough as a hash algorithm. Hence, HMAC_SHA256, HMAC_SHA512, etc., became additional valid hash algorithms. However, the HMAC_SHA1 algorithm is safe for OTP generation with no known vulnerabilities and is the default algorithm for the standard. We use the package **`totp`** of the **`github.com/pquerna/otp`** library for developing the backend code. The code is very similar to what we have seen for the **`hotp`** implementation. We use the same dart library: **`otp/otp.dart`** for front-end development.

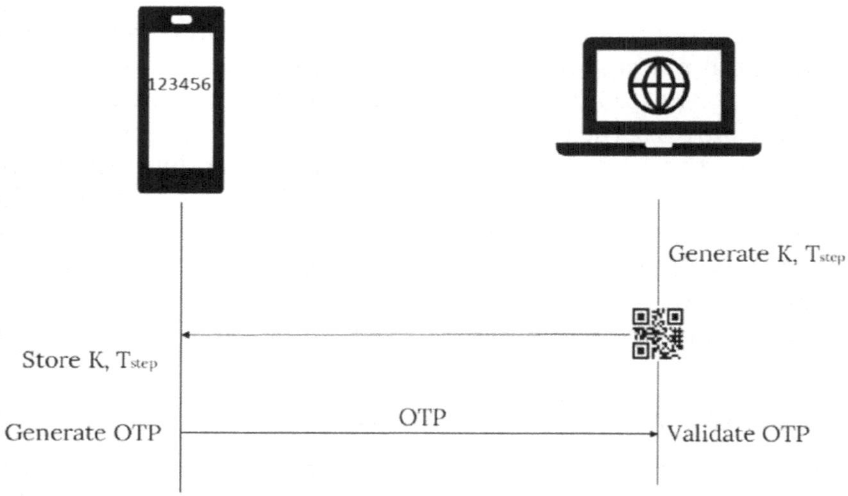

***Figure 6.6**: TOTP workflow as a schematic. The QR code contains the time step instead of the counter.*

If you click on the button to generate a new TOTP secret, the authenticator view will change to a TOTP counter with time remaining to refresh the OTP. The QR code will have a new URL:

6 Time elapsed since January 1, 1970, 00:00:00 UTC. **https://pubs.opengroup.org/online-pubs/9699919799/basedefs/V1_chap04.html#tag_04_16**

7 TOTP: Time-Based One-Time Password Algorithm, RFC-6238, **https://datatracker.ietf.org/doc/html/rfc6238**

```
otpauth:
//totp/mysrv:alice?issuer=mysrv&secret=NWIEBQGRXFVV23DZACSGOYWK5B22MT37
```

We use the default step size 30s and digits of length 6. Hence, they do not show up explicitly in the URL.

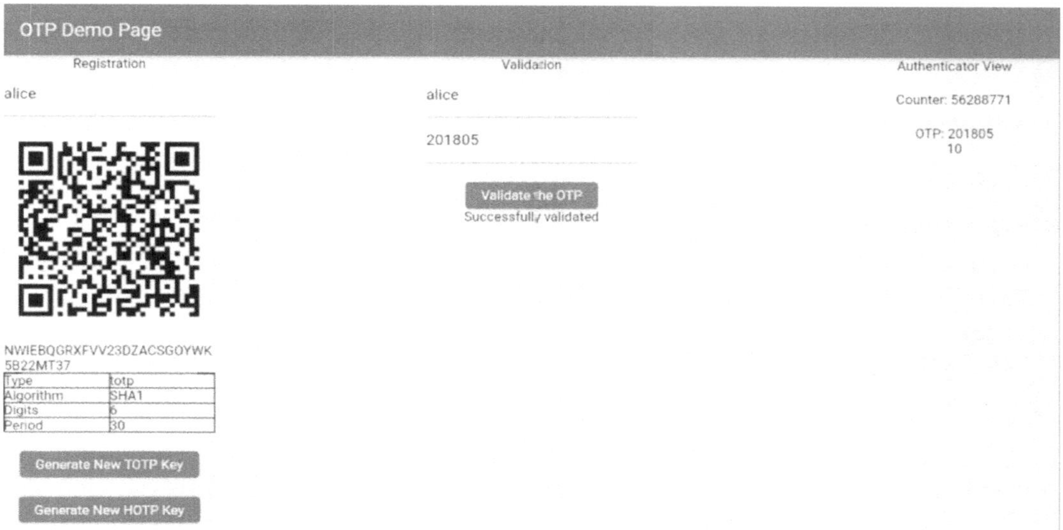

Figure 6.7: *TOTP workflows in one screen*

Registration

We have already seen the code for registration. In the case of TOTP, the **`period`** parameter is sent in place of the **`count`** parameter.

```
http.HandleFunc("/register",
                func(w http.ResponseWriter, r *http.Request) {

…

if otptype == "totp" {

  keyinfo["period"] = fmt.Sprint(key.Period())

}
…
})
```

Validation

The TOTP validator takes the OTP and the secret as input.

```
http.HandleFunc("/validate",
                func(w http.ResponseWriter, r *http.Request) {
```

```
…
if authdata.Type == "totp" {
  ok = totp.Validate(otp, authdata.Secret)
}
…
})
```

Authenticator

We use the method:

```
OTP.generateTOTPCodeString(
  widget.secret,
  DateTime.now().millisecondsSinceEpoch,
  algorithm: Algorithm.SHA1,
  isGoogle: true,
);
```

to generate the OTP. The user interface has a step-down timer, providing the remaining time before the next OTP will be computed. The full code can be seen in the **`frontend/lib/main.dart`** file.

Synchronization of time

TOTP is not entirely devoid of synchronization challenges. A user picked up an OTP at time 00:00:05 hours. This device computed this OTP at 00:00:00 hours. Suppose the user sent the code to the server at 00:00:08 hours. The server validated the OTP. At 00:00:15 hours, the user wants to authenticate again. *Can she send the same* OTP? That will fail the basic premise of OTP being a one-time password[8]. The user must wait for the OTP period to expire (30 sec) for a new OTP. Most APIs, including our examples, do not check if the code has already been used. Maintaining the context requires a database or local store to hold the context information. We have avoided context tracking to keep the code simple. However, that makes the implementation incomplete. The code is valid for 30 seconds and is invalidated on use.

8 Section 5.2, Supra 4

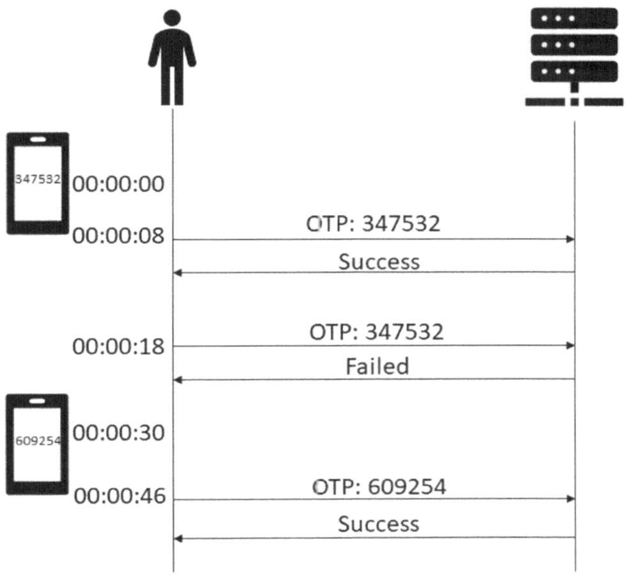

Figure 6.8: *TOTP is a one-time password*

We have a few conditions where synchronization brings additional challenges.

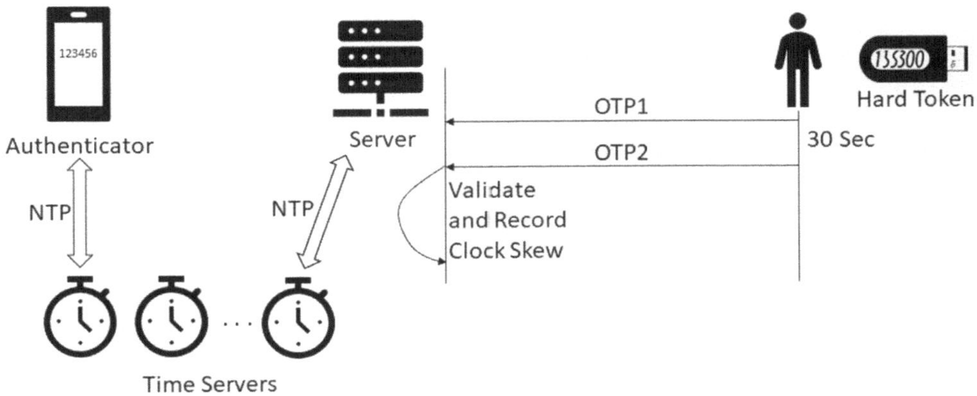

Figure 6.9: *TOTP clock synchronization*

In *Figure 6.9 TOTP clock synchronization*, we show authenticators generating OTPs and validating servers validating OTPs. General-purpose computing devices like mobile phones can synchronize time with a time server using the Network Time Protocol (NTP), while hard tokens cannot synchronize with a time server; yet, the code generated should be in sync with the server. To compute the clock skew, the user must present two consecutive OTPs to the server. The server must start searching for the OTPs generated in the past, let us say from the past several hours. All hardware OTP generators have an internal battery; with aging, these device batteries lose power, and the clocks run slowly. If you have an old TOTP generator, you may need to conduct these calibrations several times a year. Most hard tokens have a shelf life of 3–5 years. They are tamperproof and are not amenable to battery replacement or other maintenance activities.

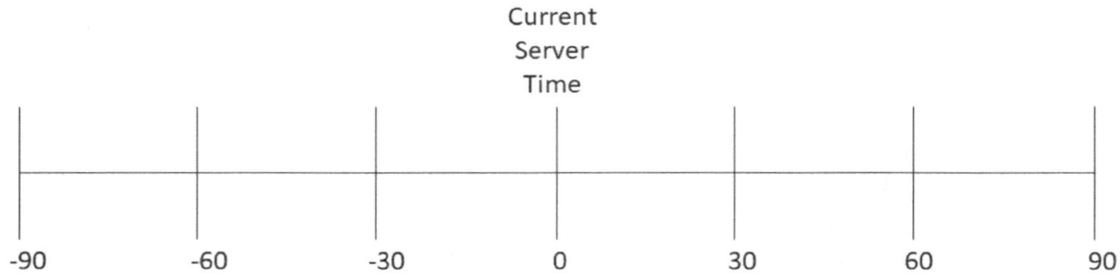

Figure 6.10: *Several TOTPs are valid at the time*: T=0

You are trying to log in to a site and get challenged to provide an OTP. You open the authenticator app. You look at the OTP and realize a good 15 seconds have passed. There are only 15 seconds left to enter it on your desktop browser, and you are running against time, you make mistakes, fat-fingered while typing, etc. That is where the servers will be more tolerant and allow OTPs 2 or 3-time steps older. User experience takes priority over security. In *Figure* 6.10 Several TOTPs are valid at the time: T=0, we allow seven OTPs to be valid. *Why future?* While most synchronization is for OTPs generated in the past, there are cases when the authenticator runs on a device with a clock ahead of time. Hard token authenticators, if not calibrated, can have the internal clock running ahead of the server. Considering all these, it is better to be tolerant on both sides.

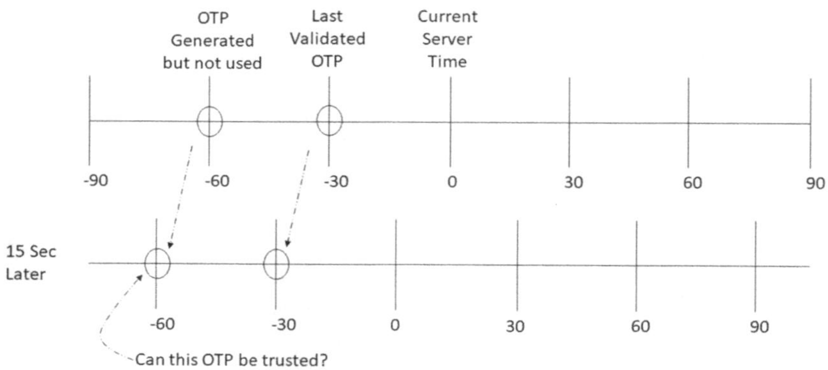

Figure 6.11: *Validity of past TOTP when a future OTP has been validated*

Alice read the OTP from the device (T=–60) and wanted to enter it in the authentication screen but missed it. So, she used the subsequent OTP generated at (T = –30) and managed to log in. At this time, Eve saw the OTP generated at (T=–60) through a spy camera mounted over Alice's head. Fifteen seconds have elapsed. *Can Eve use the OTP generated at T=–60 and impersonate Alice?* Any time a server validates a TOTP successfully, it must mark all older OTPs invalid. So as soon as the OTP at T=–30 is validated, the OTP generated at T=–60 becomes an invalid OTP. It ensures OTPs cannot be harvested and used within the extended validity period developed for convenience.

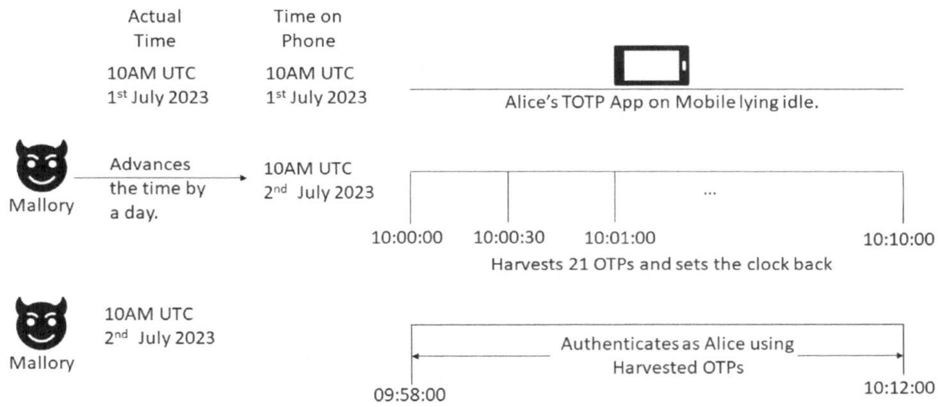

Figure 6.12: *Harvesting TOTP from a future time*

Alice left her unlocked phone on the desk and went on a short errand. Mallory took the opportunity, advanced the clock by a day, and harvested the OTPs from 10:00 a.m. to 10.10 a.m. The next day sitting at her home, Mallory impersonates herself as Alice and accesses Alice's bank account. With 21 harvested OTPs, she can virtually carry out any bank transaction in a 15-minute window. It is not easy to carry out this attack on a hard token as clock manipulation will require one to break open the device and destroy it as such devices are tamperproof. But this attack can be carried out on a mobile app authenticator. Hence, some authenticator apps detect clock manipulations and reset the authenticator. They notify the user and contact the server so that no further authentication is permitted for the authenticator.

In addressing the counter-synchronization issues of HOTP, we introduced the TOTP systems. Now, we realize TOTP-based systems have their share of synchronization requirements. The standard, while providing guidance, does not solve the synchronization issues. The shared secret is the core of the OTP systems. Is *the key exchange as a QR code safe enough?*

Exchanging shared secret

QR code is a mere visual encoding of data. It does not add any security or encryption by default. Any QR code scanner can decipher the content with ease. The QR code we used base32 encoded text of the secret; technically, you see a bare shared secret on the screen. If you use TLS to access the website, you are sure the QR code did not transmit over an unsecured network. With security cameras all around, in workplaces, shopping malls, etc., *can you be sure a security camera did not capture the QR code or the screen?* We propose an alternative to the original QR code algorithm.

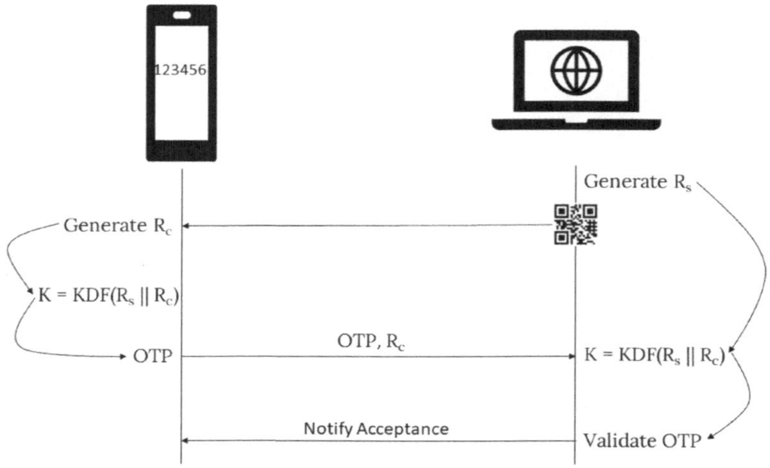

***Figure 6.13**: Using key derivation function to generate a shared secret*

In *Figure 6.13 Using key derivation function to generate a shared secret*, the server presents only a server random (R_s) in the QR code. The client creates a client random (R_c), uses the received server random (R_s), and uses a key derivation function (KDF) to generate the secret (K). It generates an OTP and sends it alongwith the client random (R_c) to the server. The server generates the same shared secret (K) using the server random (R_s) and client random (R_c) using the key derivation function (KDF). Now, the server can validate the OTP and ensure proof of possession of the exchange. While we present only the outline, a detailed specification can be seen from the Dynamic Symmetric Key Provisioning Protocol (DSKPP)[9].

Cryptography experts are generally paranoid about the safety of shared secrets, application keys, passwords, etc. Here are some guidelines that should be adhered to

9 Dynamic Symmetric Key Provisioning Protocol (DSKPP), RFC 6063, **https://datatracker.ietf.org/doc/html/rfc6063**

- When transmitted over the wire, channel encryption like TLS must be used.
- If practical, use a key derivation function to generate by exchanging the seeds between the client and the server.
- Avoid duplicating the key on another device or maintaining a backup of the keys. The existence of such a backup has led to several security attacks, the most notorious one being the RSA breach[10] of 2011.

Keeping the shared secrets on a mobile application can be a significant challenge. Some applications use device hardware parameters[11] that are hard to replicate to cloak the shared secret and store the cloaked value on the device. Modern applications prefer special-purpose secured computing elements to store and compute cryptographic operations. We will discuss some of these in a later section. Authenticator apps by almost all vendors are providing OTP wallets. You can provision multiple TOTPs using QR codes and generate codes. You can use the code on any validation server. Moreover, some authenticators provide backup and restore of the credentials. You can get the OTPs on your new phone and discard the old phone. A couple of things to remember, if your backup system is hacked, hackers can access your OTPs using the same technique. Secondly, when you discard the old phone, ensure the OTP application data is cleared and deleted. If not, a mere reinstallation can provide access to the previously cached data. Again, these are implementation-dependent and vary from application to application. We suggest that users choose the safest authenticator that addresses these issues. We do not recommend any specific vendor[12].

Other OTP-like authenticators

Almost all authentication methods backed by a shared secret, using a key derivative to authenticate, have similar cryptographic strengths. For example, a 6-digit OTP is weaker than 8-digit for a brute force attack. However,the attack vectors needed to exploit both OTPs can be very similar. If someone manages

10 The Full Story of the Stunning RSA Hack Can Finally Be Told, **https://www.wired.com/story/the-full-story-of-the-stunning-rsa-hack-can-finally-be-told/**

11 Protecting cryptographic secrets using file system attributes, **https://patents.google.com/patent/US9171145B2/en**

12 We have referred to Google Authenticator at places in this chapter. Google Authenticator is one of the most popular authenticator applications; it quickly helps readers connect to the concept. Secondly, it introduced the QR code and `otpauth` URL provisioning. What we discussed applies to all the authenticators having similar capabilities. Our statements should not be considered an endorsement for Google.

to steal the shared secret, a 6 vs. 8-digit OTP will not significantly affect the security. The protection against brute force attacks is a rate limitation, like allowing only five failed attempts for a credential. Server-generated OTPs are the most common method of OTP used in the industry. The authentication server generates the OTP and sends it to the user over email, SMS, enterprise messaging services, or even consumer-encrypted messaging services like WhatsApp and Signal. More than the OTP, the transport is open to attacks. Email and SMS channels are unreliable and are potentially susceptible to eavesdropping. Some encrypted channels for message exchange eavesdrop and analyze messages. Technically, they can access the OTPs as well. Some authenticators embed the authentication code as a session ID and share it as a magic link over SMS or email. All these have a similar cryptographic strength, but some need lesser user involvement than others. If SMS OTP is considered unsecured as the SMS channel can be attacked, all other message-based channelsshould be evaluated for a similar breach possibility. Hence, it is ideal to understand the underlying technology and find the weakest link in the authentication workflow rather than be carried away with the associated marketing claims of the authenticators.

Fast Identity Online (FIDO)

Passwords are inherently cumbersome and unsecured. Shared secret-based OTP systems can be hard to manage. They are secured to a great extent if the secrets need not be stored, archived, moved around, etc. *Can public key cryptography and digital certificates provide a better security framework*? The answer is yes, but they are not private enough. Let us assume,that to use an Amazon Kindle device; I need a digital certificate. I logged into the Amazon Kindle device and requested a certificate from DigiCert. DigiCert now knows I have a Kindle device. *Should DigiCert know that*? Alternatively, DigiCert can issue me a certificate based on my tax filing ID. If I use that certificate to authenticate to Amazon, Amazon will know my tax filing ID. Some privacy is lost when an attesting authority issues a certificate as the certificate is issued to some form of Personally Identifiable Information (PII) like, email ID, tax filing ID, etc. Secondly, mutual TLS (m-TLS) is a network protocol. When authentication fails due to an improper client certificate, the browser reports it as a connection failure. The web application will not be aware of this failure as there is no network connection. Other certificate-based authentication (CBA) schemes are not browser-friendly as they require additional helper applications. Thirdly, the architecture of issuing a certificate to a user is cumbersome and requires a savvy user to download the certificate safely to the device or a USB trust store.

Industry experts from companies like Google, Microsoft, Apple, Yubico, etc., reviewed the complex authentication landscape and decided to use Public Key Infrastructure (PKI) as the authentication mechanism. PKI asymmetric cryptography is a keypair but does not mandate the public key has to be attested by a trusted attorney if the contract is between only two parties. As shown in *Figure 2.10: Signing using asymmetric cryptography*, for trusted communication between Alice and Bob, there is no need for a Trent if Bob and Alice know each other. As in password authentication, you do not need a Certificate Authority to validate. Bob maintains the directory of public keys and validates Alice against the directory.

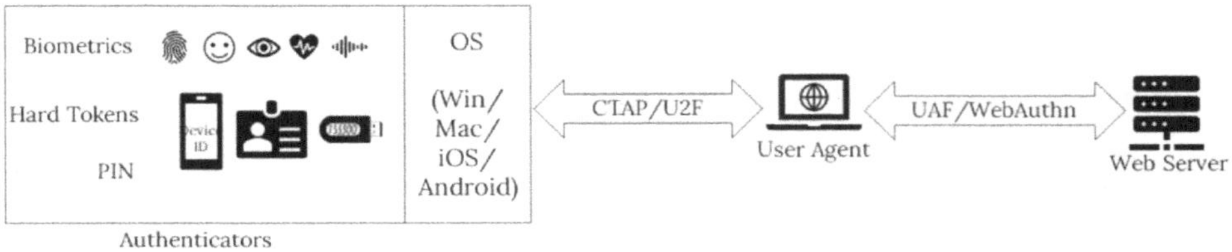

Figure 6.14: *Scope of FIDO Authentication Framework*

The industry experts formed a consortium called Fast Identity Online (FIDO)[13]. The FIDO consortium has vendors across the spectrum; authenticator device manufacturers, OS and browser vendors, IAM vendors, and even relying parties. It splits the communication into two parts. Browser to a relying party (RP) and Brower to the authenticator device.Protocols like client-to-authenticator protocol (CTAP) and universal second factor (U2F) provide the conduit for the user agent to the authenticator device. Universal Authentication Framework (UAF) and its web equivalent WebAuthn, are protocols for the browser to the relying party. In this chapter, our focus will be the communication from the browser to the relying party. The authenticators perform all the PKI operations like keypair creation or payload signing. WebAuthn only provides a secure channel to pass this information to the server. The metadata info for keypairs associated with a user and a website is cached in the browser as passkeys. Just like autofill options with passwords, modern browsers can suggest them to authenticate.

What is a passkey[14]?

Passkeys are like passwords but better. They are better because they arenot created insecurely by humans and because they use public key cryptography to create much more secure experiences.

But passkeys arenot a new thing. It is just a new name starting to be used for WebAuthn/FIDO2 credentials that enable fully passwordless experiences. These types of credentials are also called discoverable credentials or sometimes resident credentials.

13 FIDO Alliance, **https://fidoalliance.org/**

14 Quoted from: **https://passkey.org/ last accessed: 11th July 2023**

We will discuss introductory concepts of WebAuthn and leave the advanced topics for the readers to explore as they get familiar with the technology.

There are two workflows for WebAuthn.

- **Registration**: In this workflow, we create a keypair in a device and associate it with a user.
- **Authentication**: Once a user association is there for keypair, we can authenticate the user by signing some payload.

Both the workflows have a begin and finish step.

Registration

The registration workflow is as shown.

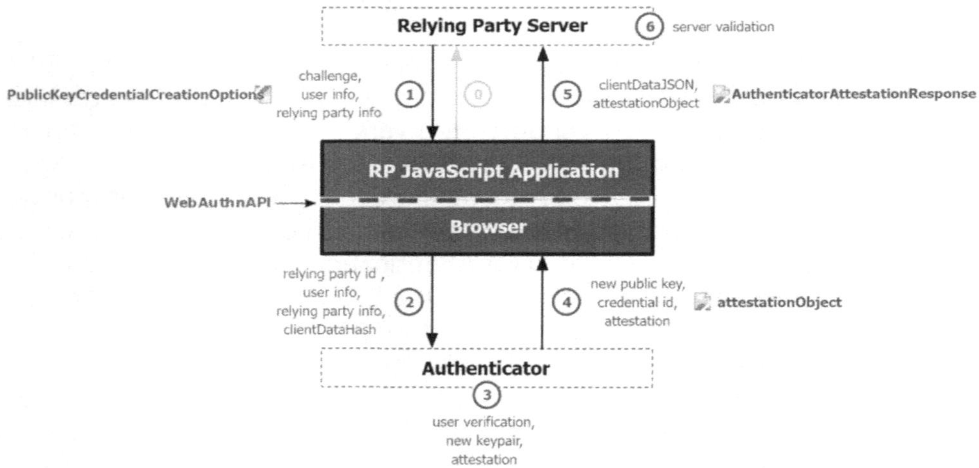

Figure 6.15*: WebAuthn credential registration workflow*[15]

The workflow steps are:

0. The browser requests the relying party (RP) for the credential creation options.
1. The RP sends the RP ID, the user information, the challenge to be signed, and public key algorithms to be trusted. We choose only RS256 and ES256 as valid public key algorithms. Here is a sample `PublicKeyCredentialCreationOptions`.

15 Figure 1 Registration Flow, WebAuthn Specification, **https://www.w3.org/TR/webauthn-2/#fig-registration**

```
{
  "publicKey": {
    "rp": {
      "name": "HOWA Webauthn",
      "id": "mysrv.local"
    },
    "user": {
      "name": "alice",
      "displayName": "alice",
      "id": "P4HRxVLRhlC...-f6DftobVe_DzK7FOSXEAxq7-Q2v5gWW-r7c1w"
    },
    "challenge": "M2TWgXNr4KuwFcgYMp8py3qxwtM-kIReQzRyuN6dmpU",
    "pubKeyCredParams": [
      {
        "type": "public-key",
        "alg": -7
      },
      {
        "type": "public-key",
        "alg": -257
      }
    ],
    "timeout": 300000,
    "authenticatorSelection": {
      "requireResidentKey": false,
      "userVerification": "preferred"
    }
  }
}
```

2. The browser invokes the **window.navigator.credentials.create** to generate a passkey in a FIDO 2-compliant device.
3. The device verifies the user before the keypair is generated. The verification can be a biometric or PIN verification. It also generates an attestation[16] for the device that generates the key pair.
4. The browser receives the public key, a credential ID, and the attestation information.
5. The browser encapsulates the data into an **AuthenticatorAttestation Response** and sends it to the server. Here is a sample response:


```
{
  "CollectedClientData": {
    "type": "webauthn.create",
    "challenge": "M2TWgXNr4KuwFcgYMp8py3qxwtM-kIReQzRyuN6dmpU",
    "origin": "https://mysrv.local:8443"
  },
  "AttestationObject": {
    "AuthData": {
      "rpid": "oJPAfsVbMMryZe5na+tp9WdzjjSy5jwSrFc+xWjL8q4=",
      "flags": 69,
      "sign_count": 0,
      "att_data": {
        "aaguid": "AAAAAAAAAAAAAAAAAAAAAA==",
        "credential_id":
"VzGuzbEqdqS1N5ZHtRGFjg7CpThjPVfNPPdv+wpph9s=",
 "public_key": "pAEDAzkBACBZAQDBDOf…RhIUMBAAE="
      },
      "ext_data": null
    },
    "authData": "oJPAfsVbMMryZe5na+…RhIUMBAAE=",
    "fmt": "none"
```


16 The attestation here is for the device and not the user. It is a statement like, the keypair was generated on a YubiKey device model number: AA001. It contains no user PII.

```
    },
    "Transports": null
  }
```

6. The server validates the response with the challenge it generated in step 1.

The APIs we have used in the code have aggregated these seven steps in three API calls.

1. Begin registration includes steps 0 and 1.
2. Steps 2, 3, and 4 are part of the WebAuthn JavaScript API call.
3. Finish registration including steps 5 and 6.

Authentication

The authentication workflow is as shown:

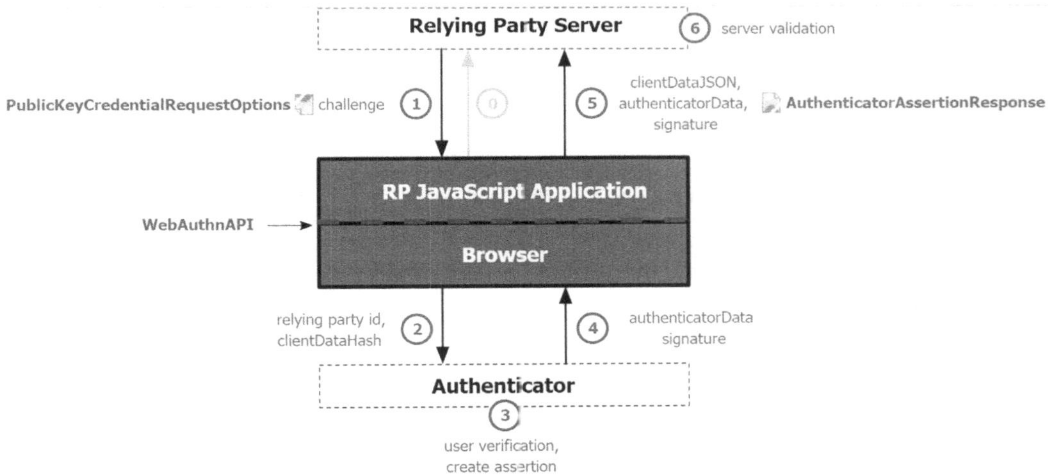

***Figure 6.16**: WebAuthn authentication workflow*[17]

0. The browser requests the relying party (RP) for the credential for signing options.
1. The RP sends the RP ID, the user information, the challenge to be signed, and a list of credentials for signing. Here is a sample **`PublicKeyCredentialRequestOptions`**.

17 Figure 2 Registration Flow, WebAuthn Specification, **https://www.w3.org/TR/webauthn-2/#fig-authentication**

```
{
  "publicKey": {
    "challenge": "fg8DIlb7mtNxRfcnwT1CgjRr8W0KsgjOebyk2RM9lkM",
    "timeout": 300000,

    "rpId": "mysrv.local",
    "allowCredentials": [
      {
        "type": "public-key",
        "id": "VzGuzbEqdqS1N5ZHtRGFjg7CpThjPVfNPPdv-wpph9s"
      }
    ],
    "userVerification": "preferred"
  }
}
```

2. The browser invokes the **`window.navigator.credentials.get`** to access the passkey in a FIDO 2-compliant device.
3. The device verifies the user before the keypair is generated. The verification can be a biometric or PIN verification. It also generates an assertion that contains the signature for the challenge.
4. The browser receives the public key, a credential ID, and the assertion information.
5. The browser encapsulates the data into an **`AuthenticatorAssertionResponse`** and sends it to the server. Here is a sample response:

```
{
  "CollectedClientData": {
    "type": "webauthn.get",
    "challenge": "fg8DIlb7mtNxRfcnwT1CgjRr8W0KsgjOebyk2RM9lkM",
    "origin": "https://mysrv.local:8443"
```

```
    },
    "AuthenticatorData": {
      "rpid": "oJPAfsVbMMryZe5na+tp9WdzjjSy5jwSrFc+xWjL8q4=",
      "flags": 5,
      "sign_count": 1,
      "att_data": {
        "aaguid": null,
        "credential_id": null,
        "public_key": null
      },
      "ext_data": null
    },
    "Signature": "Nlt41J9VgUew5gkev…ktAkfvADYbYrUAT7A==",
    "UserHandle": null
  }
```


6. The server validates the response with the challenge it generated in step 1.

The APIs we have used in the code have aggregated these seven steps in three API calls.

1. Begin login includes steps 0 and 1.
2. Steps 2, 3, and 4 are part of the WebAuthn JavaScript API call.
3. Finish login including steps 5 and 6.

Sample code and user interface

We implemented these workflows; the code is available in the folder **`chapter-6/webauthn`**.

- Go to the **`frontend`** folder and run **`flutter build web`** to build the front end.
- Go back to the parent directory and launch the WebAuthn server by typing the command: **`go run ./webauthn.go`**

You can access the server at: **https://mysrv.local:8443/**

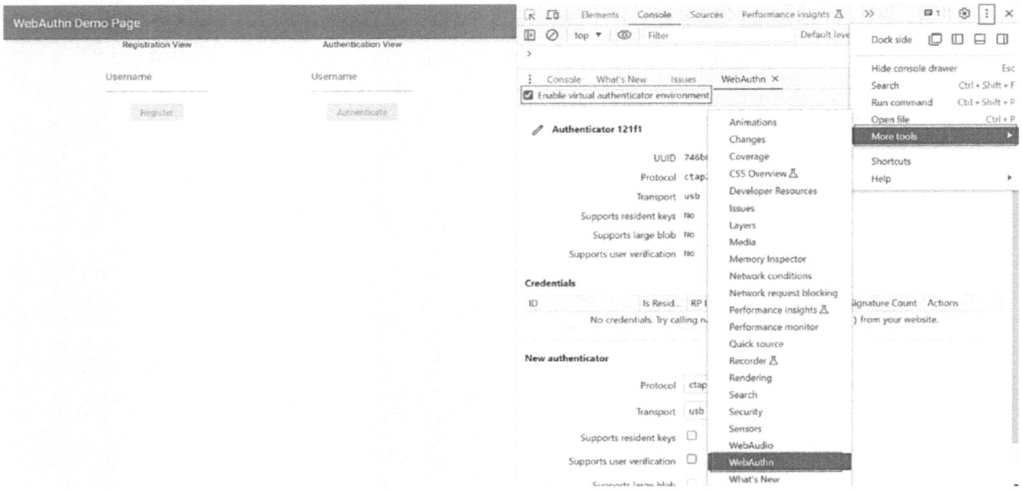

Figure 6.17: *The test site opened on a Google Chrome browser with the developer tools*

In *Figure* 6.17 The test site opened on a Google Chrome browser with the developer tools, using the highlighted user elements to create a WebAuthn credential in the virtual credential environment. In the Registration View, provide the username **`alice`** and click on the **`Register`** button.

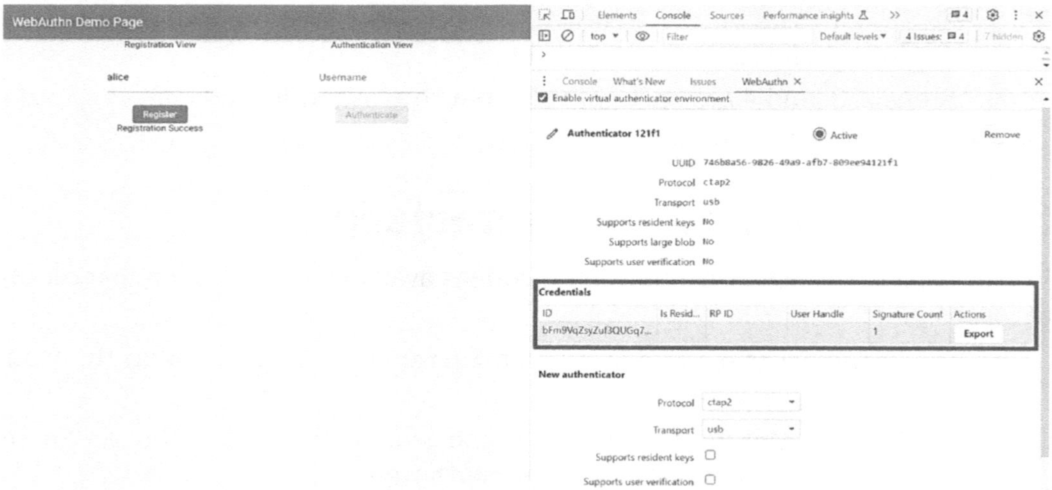

Figure 6.18: *Credential created for* ***`mysrv.local`***

The highlighted credential was created in the virtual authenticator environment for **`mysrv.local`**. If we go to the Authentication View and authenticate using the credential, we will see the signature count is incremented.

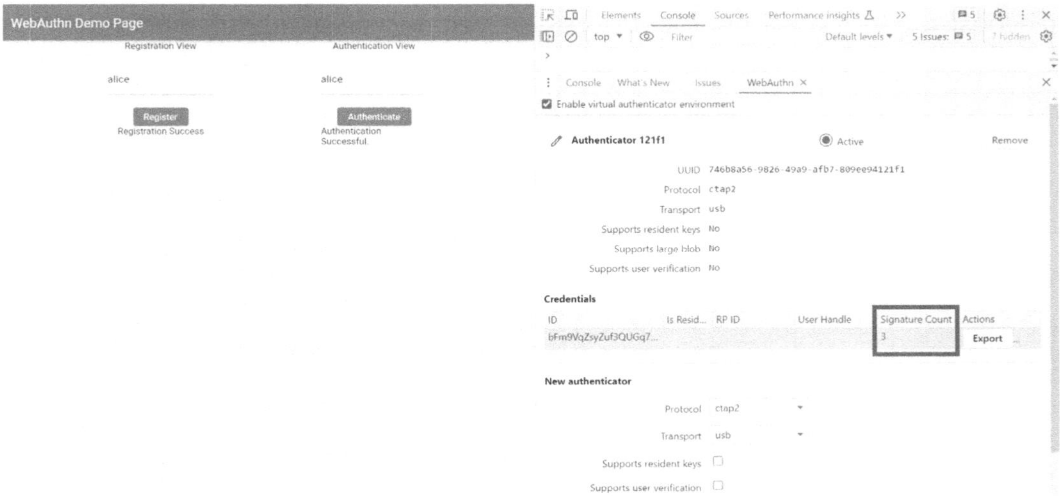

Figure 6.19: *WebAuthn authentication in virtual authentication environment of Chrome*

If you have a fingerprint scanner configured with Microsoft Windows Hello or have an Android or iOS phone, you can use them as passkey providers.

Selection of FIDO 2 Devices

If you look at the credential creation options, the server is looking for credentials of type **`public-key`** supporting algorithms of type RS256 (**`-257`**) or ES256 (**`-7`**)[18]. We do not specifically mention where to look for the security keys. In such a condition, if your desktop has Windows Hello configured, Windows will prompt for your fingerprint, PIN, Selfie, etc.

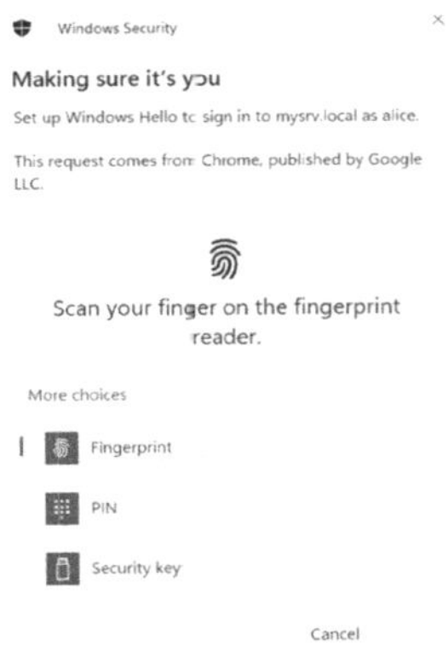

Figure 6.20: *Windows Hello prompt for fingerprint*

18 Some Windows 10 or 11 devices may consider SHA-1 unsecured. Not providing a list of supported algorithms may fail credential registration.

If a local security key is not found, Google Chrome will ask you to pair an Android or iOS device using a QR Code.

Figure 6.21: *Google Chrome pairing with a phone using QR code and NFC, USB, or BLE*

1. Google Chrome asks the user to register a phone or tablet.
2. The browser prompts the user to read the QR code[19] using his mobile camera.

19 The QR code contains a URL **`FIDO:/08071528303820966389…321447142660`**

3. On a scan, a mobile app asks for the user's permission to connect the phone.
4. The mobile device waits for the user to provide her approval with a fingerprint, PIN, or Selfie.
5. On success, the phone creates a passkey and notifies the browser over a BLE or NFC connection per the CTAP-2 protocol[20].

If WebAuthn is about PKI-based signing, how come all the discussions in real-life examples are focused on biometric authentication? Most FIDO-compliant devices store the private key in a secured store. Any access or operation that uses the private key requires user validation; a user's biometry, a device PIN, etc. There is a two-factor authentication inherent in this approach. One factor is the PKI-key validated at the server. The second factor is locally validated in the device while accessing the private key. Since the biometry information never leaves the FIDO device, the potential stealing of biometry is minimal. We will conceptually discuss this in the next chapter when we discuss identity in detail. Providing access to the private key only on user authentication is also known as **user presence**.

Front end for registration

The front-end code is available at **`chapter-6/webauthn/frontend/lib/main.dart`**

1. In the **`RegistrationView`**, we contact the REST API at **`/webauthn/register/begin`** to obtain the credential creation parameters along with the challenge to sign.
2. We pass the parameter to the **`window.navigator.credentials.create()`** method to create the credential.
3. The results of the credentials are submitted to the **`/webauthn/register/finish`** for the server to validate the attestation data and record the registration status.

We have discussed the JSON payload in the earlier sections.

```
class _RegistrationViewState extends State<RegistrationView> {
  final TextEditingController userCtrl = TextEditingController();
  String regStatus = "";
  @override
  Widget build(BuildContext context) {
```

20 The artwork is taken from: **https://fidoalliance.org/design-system/content/#pass-wordless-registration-success**

```
return Column(
  children: <Widget>[
    const Text("Registration View"),
    padding,
    TextField(
      decoration: const InputDecoration(
        border: UnderlineInputBorder(),
        hintText: 'Username',
      ),
      controller: userCtrl,
    ),
    padding,
    ValueListenableBuilder(
      valueListenable: userCtrl,
      builder: (context, uctrl, child) {
        return ElevatedButton(
          onPressed: uctrl.text.isEmpty
              ? null
              : () async {
                  try {
                    final state = const Uuid().v4();
                    final res = await httpPost(
                        "/webauthn/register/begin",
                        {
                          "username": userCtrl.text,
                          "state": state,
                        },
                        null);
                    final publicKey = res["publicKey"];
                    if (publicKey == null ||
                        !publicKey.containsKey("challenge")) {
                      return;
                    }
```

```
final challenge = publicKey["challenge"];
res["publicKey"]["challenge"] = str2buffer(challenge);
final uid = publicKey["user"]["id"];
res["publicKey"]["user"]["id"] = str2buffer(uid);
final cred =
    await window.navigator.credentials?.create(res);

if (cred == null) {
  throw Exception("Failed to acquire credentials.");
} else {
  var obj = {
    "id": cred.id,
    "rawId": buffer2str(cred.rawId),
    "type": 'public-key',
  };

  obj["response"] = {
    "attestationObject":
       buffer2str(cred.response.attestationObject),
    "clientDataJson":
       buffer2str(cred.response.clientDataJson),
  };

  final res1 = await httpPost(
      "/webauthn/register/finish",
      {
        "username": userCtrl.text,
        "state": state,
      },
      obj);
  setState(() {
    regStatus = res1["message"];
```

```
                    });
                  }
                } catch (e) {
                  setState(() {
                    regStatus = e.toString();
                  });
                }
              },
          child: const Text("Register"),
        );
      },
    ),
    Text(regStatus),
  ],
 );
}
}
```

The data obtained from the Golang layer is in the **base64url** encoding, while the browser expects the data in a byte array format. We use the helper method **str2buffer** for the same. Similarly, when we pass information from the browser to the REST APIs, we convert the byte arrays to **base64url** encoding using the **buffer2str** function.

```
ByteBuffer str2buffer(String s) {
  var r = 4 - s.length.remainder(4);
  while (r > 0) {
    s += "=";
    r--;
  }
  return base64Url.decode(s).buffer;
}

String buffer2str(ByteBuffer buf) {
  return base64UrlEncode(buf.asUint8List());
}
```

We look at the REST APIs for beginning and finishing registration next.

REST APIs for registration

The rest APIs are built using the **go-webauthn/webauthn**[21] library. We have developed two APIs. The **begin** API provides the credential creation parameters and the **finish** API provides the response from the browser back to the server to verify and associate the registered credential with the user. Both APIs have a **username** and a **state** parameter for tracking the sessions across the API calls.

```
http.HandleFunc("/webauthn/register/begin",
  func(w http.ResponseWriter, r *http.Request) {
    username := r.FormValue("username")
    state := r.FormValue("state")
    user := datastore.GetUser(username)
    options, session, _ := wauthn.BeginRegistration(user,
      webauthn.WithCredentialParameters(
        []protocol.CredentialParameter{
        {
           Type:      protocol.PublicKeyCredentialType,
           Algorithm: webauthncose.AlgES256,
         },
         {
          Type: protocol.PublicKeyCredentialType,
           Algorithm: webauthncose.AlgRS256,
         },
        },
      ))
    datastore.SaveSession(state, session)
})
```

The **begin** API[22] invokes the **BeginRegistration** API with the **user** object and credential parameters and generates the credential creation options for the browser. We use the **datastore** map object to track the **session** information.

---

21 Go WebAuthn, **https://pkg.go.dev/github.com/go-webauthn/webauthn**

22 The error handling and logging code segments are not shown.

The **finish** REST API is shown here:

```
http.HandleFunc("/webauthn/register/finish",
  func(w http.ResponseWriter, r *http.Request) {
    username := r.FormValue("username")
    state := r.FormValue("state")
    ccr, _ := protocol.ParseCredentialCreationResponse(r)
    session := datastore.GetSession(state)
    if ccr.Response.CollectedClientData.Challenge != session.Challenge {
      http.Error(w, "Internal Server Error", http.StatusBadRequest)
      log.Print("invalid session or client")
      return
    }
    user := datastore.GetUser(username).(userImpl)
    credential, _ := wauthn.CreateCredential(user, *session, ccr)
    user.AddCredential(credential)
    datastore.SaveUser(user)
    log.Printf("User: %s registered a WebAuthn credential.", username)
  },
)
```

We used the **ParseCredentialCreationResponse**[23] method to collect the credential information. We check for the **Challenge** parameter with the parameter in the **session** object to ensure, that the **begin** and **finish** calls maintain the session state across the call. Finally, we create the credential using the **CreateCredential** call and associate the same with the **user** object.

The authentication REST APIs are like the registration APIs. There is a **begin** and a **finish** call. The **begin** API generates the challenge. A FIDO 2 credential signs the challenge. The signed response is sent to the server using the **finish** API. The session management in login is like what we have seen in the registration APIs. We suggest the readers review the handlers for **/webauthn/login/begin** and **/webauthn/login/finish**.

---

23 There is a **FinishRegistration** method available that carries out the end-to-end validation.

Device Attestation

In our examples, we used FIDO 2 devices for registration and authentication. We accept any form of FIDO 2 device in the sample code. However, think of a bank (RP) that has issued Google Titan Security devices to its customers to authenticate. They would like to ensure the customer is using such devices only. In such cases, the registration process mandates an **`attestationConveyancePreferenceOption`** to **`enterprise`**. The device attestation **`AAGUID`** will be sent to the RP. The attestation statement is signed by the manufacturer certificate confirming the device belongs to the manufacturer. FIDO Alliance provides a metadata service[24] with information regarding all registered FIDO 2 devices. The RP can use this information to verify the attestation data obtained from the device. The Google Titan Security device metadata is presented here for reference.

```
{"aaguid": "42b4fb4a-2866-43b2-9bf7-6c6669c2e5d3",
  "metadataStatement": {
    "legalHeader": "… https://fidoalliance.org/metadata/metadata-legal-
terms/.",
    "aaguid": "42b4fb4a-2866-43b2-9bf7-6c6669c2e5d3",
    "description": "Google Titan Security Key v2",
    "authenticatorVersion": 1,
    "protocolFamily": "fido2"
    "schema": 3,
    …
    "authenticationAlgorithms": ["secp256r1_ecdsa_sha256_raw"],
    "publicKeyAlgAndEncodings": ["ecc_x962_raw","cose"],
    "attestationTypes": ["basic_full"],
    "userVerificationDetails": [
      [{
        "userVerificationMethod": "passcode_external",
        "caDesc": {"base": 10, "minLength": 4, "maxRetries":
0,"blockSlowdown": 0}
       },
…
      ],…
    ],
    "keyProtection": ["hardware", "secure_element"],
    "matcherProtection": ["on_chip"],
    "cryptoStrength": 128,
    "attachmentHint": ["external", "wired", "wireless", "nfc"],
```

```
    "tcDisplay": [],
    "attestationRootCertificates": ["MIICMjCCAdmgA…vlW/yBqza/AdS0Sq6Q="],
    "icon": "data:image/png;base64,…=",
    "authenticatorGetInfo": {
      "versions": ["FIDO_2_0", "U2F_V2"],
      "extensions": ["credProtect","hmac-secret"],
      "aaguid": "42b4fb4a286643b29bf76c6669c2e5d3",
      "options": {"rk": true, "clientPin": false},
      "maxMsgSize": 2200,
      "pinUvAuthProtocols": [1]
    }
  },
  "statusReports": [{
    "status": "NOT_FIDO_CERTIFIED", "effectiveDate": "2023-06-15"
  }],
  "timeOfLastStatusChange": "2023-06-15"
},
```

The metadata has extensive information on the hardware's capabilities. RPs can use this information to whitelist or blacklist devices.

Device Security

The metadata provided above contains **`keyProtection`** with **`hardware`** and **`secure_element`**. Cryptographic secrets like private keys in the case of asymmetric algorithms or shared secrets in the case of symmetric algorithms require the highest level of protection. In the token in the discussion, such a computing chip is available in the hardware for storing the private key and computing signatures. Even in the case of general-purpose operating systems like Android or iOS, there are Trusted Execution environments (TEE) that run parallel to the operating systems. Only trusted or signed applications can run in such environments. The TEE is not accessible to a regular app on a mobile device. Thus, the cryptographic operations remain secluded from other apps running in the system. The user interface for sensitive data like passwords can be in the secured user interface region backed by the TEE. Secure Enclave on iPhones provides an encrypted computation environment on a part of the processor. The purpose is to keep access to sensitive data and computation isolated from the rest of the computational surroundings. While we will not be delving into the details of developing FIDO 2 authenticators as part of this book, we discussed authenticator development in the context of OTPs. Some apps write the keys on a **`KeyStore`** or **`KeyChain`** on Android and iOS platforms. Sometimes the keys are protected by locking the device. Most passkey interfaces on Android, document unlocking the device provide access to the private keys. It also simplifies the user experience. FIDO devices can communicate in pairs over proximity technologies like NFC, Bluetooth LE, or USB-like technologies. With varied kinds of hardware devices involved in cryptographic operations, there is a need to standardize their capabilities. It helps decide the class of devices fit for a particular environment for their cryptographic protection strength that can be tested and certified. The US Federal Information Processing Standard Publications (FIPS) publishes the standard FIPS-140-2[25] that standardizes security requirements for cryptographic modules. They describe a four-level classification.

- **Level-1**: Lowest level of cryptographic hardware that can run one approved cryptographic function. A PC encryption board can be an example of such a system.
- **Level-2**: The cryptographic module can run on general-purpose computing hardware, but it must have some evidence of tampering embedded in it. A minimum role-based authorization is needed for the operator to access the device.
- **Level-3**: This cryptographic module must resist tampering. Physical barriers can be present to make the system tamperproof. The module should have identity-based authentication and role-based authorization mechanisms for the operators. The plaintext CSPs should have separate paths from other data processed in the system. All critical security parameters entering or leaving the system must be encrypted. Many security fob devices fall into this category.
- **Level-4**: The highest level of security that provides active tamper protection and evidence reporting. The physical operating environment is protected. The system is isolated from external disturbances; it should be fault tolerant.

Physical security devices or hard tokens still play a significant role in high-security environments like financial, banking, defense, etc. As technologies are maturing in this area, we see the interaction of the user and devices becoming more seamless.

25 FIPS-140-2 specification, **https://csrc.nist.gov/publications/detail/fips/140/2/final**, though the FIPS-140-3 specification is available, the adoption will take some time.

Bringing it all together

In the previous two chapters, we reviewed SAML, OAuth 2, and OIDC used extensively in federated authentication. However, we used a password-based authentication mechanism in our samples. *Can we use other forms of authentication we studied in this chapter*? We have developed an integrated sample code to take care of this. You can go to the folder `chapter-6/integrated`.

In this folder, we have developed two servers: `idp.go` and `mysrv.go`.

1. `idp.go` is an authentication server that provides OAuth 2 authorization. We launch it with the command: `go run ./idp.go`.
2. `mysrv.go` is a service provider (SP) that provides access to basic user information based on this authorization. We build the front end from the folder `mysrvfront` with the command: `flutter build web`. We launch the server with the command `go run ./mysrv.go`.
3. Open the browser and go to the URL: **https://mysrv.local:8444/**.

You will see the screen as shown in step 1 of *Figure* 6.22 Integrated sample for SP and Server. The user has no access to the user information as she has not logged in. Now if you click on the `Login` button on the top right corner of the page, you will be redirected to **https://idp.local:8443/login.**

Authorization policy

Identity and Access Management (IAM) systems control user authentication behaviors through authentication and authorization policies. We have developed a simple authorization policy here. The policy is in the function `applyLoginPolicy`. In our sample, there is only one user alice.

- If the user alice does not have a TOTP credential or a WebAuthn credential, we redirect the user for password-based authentication. The password is associated with the user object as a field `password`.
- If the user has a TOTP credential, we redirect the user to authenticate with it.
- If the user has a WebAuthn credential, we redirect the user to authentication with WebAuthn.
- If the user has no TOTP credential configured, we redirect the user to register the TOTP credential.
- If the user has no WebAuthn credential configured, we redirect the user to register the WebAuthn credential.

- If all the authentication steps are complete, we ask for the user's consent for authorization.

We suggest the readers review the function to understand the exact authentication sequence. An industry-grade IAM system will have a rules-based engine to configure this policy rather than to write code in if loops.

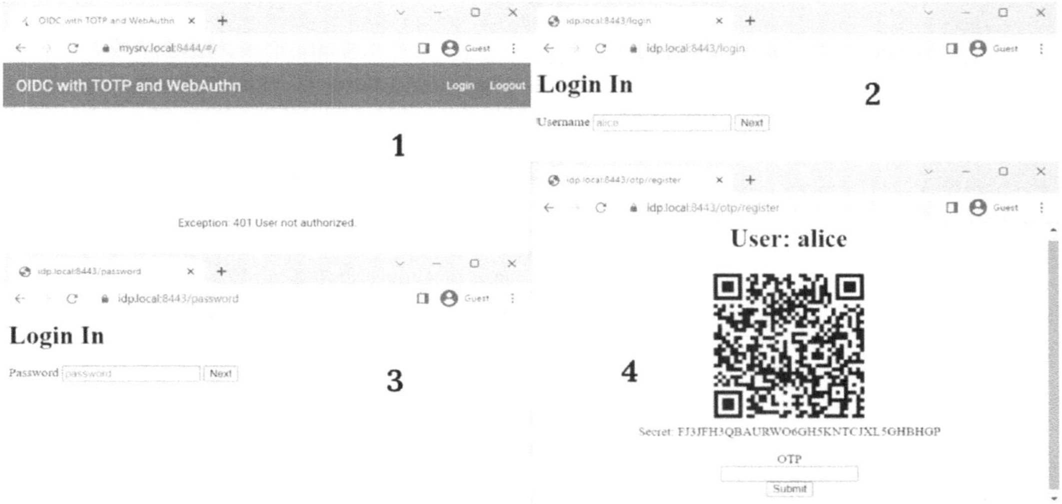

***Figure 6.22**: Integrated sample for SP and Authorization Server*

Server-rendered authentication forms

In *Figure* 6.22 Integrated sample for SP and Authorization Server, when the user clicks the Login button, he is redirected to **https://idp.local:8443/login** URL. If the user has no registered authenticators, the server redirects to the password page **https://idp.local:8443/password**. In the section on WebAuthn, we split the registration and authentication workflows into two REST APIs, namely, **`begin`** and **`finish`**. The SPA client would contact these services over a REST API, render the UI, and pass on the user response to the **`finish`** API. Contrast it to authentication pages rendered by the server based on the request parameters (**`begin`**), and the user responds as a form submit (**`finish`**). This is annotated in the handler for the **`/password`** page.

```
http.HandleFunc("/password", func(w http.ResponseWriter, r *http.
Request) {
...
  if store, err = sess.Start(r.Context(), w, r); err == nil {
    if r.Method == "POST" && r.Form == nil {
```

```
      defer applyLoginPolicy(w, r)
      u, _ := store.Get("LoggedInUser")
      if err = r.ParseForm(); err == nil {

/*** The finish block ***/

        if pw = r.Form.Get("password"); pw == u.(*userImpl).password {
          store.Set("PasswordPassed", true)
          store.Save()
        }
        return
      }
    }
  }
…
/*** The begin block ***/
w.Write([]byte(`
<html>
<body>
<h1>Login In</h1>
<form method="POST">
<label for="password">Password</label>
<input type="password" name="password" placeholder="password">
<button type="submit">Next</button>
</form>
</body>
</html>
    `))
})
```

In **`idp.go`**, you will find all the handlers are written in this manner. In the interest of space, we will not quote code blocks here. We encourage readers to review the authentication handlers.

1. **`/password`** – for password-based authentication.
2. **`/webauthn/register`** and **`/webauthn/login`** – for WebAuthn
3. **`/otp/register`** and **`/otp/login`** – for TOTP

Since the code is rendered by the server, we use hand-coded HTML and JavaScript templates. In Step 3, when the password authentication is completed, the server redirects to the OTP registration page in Step 4.

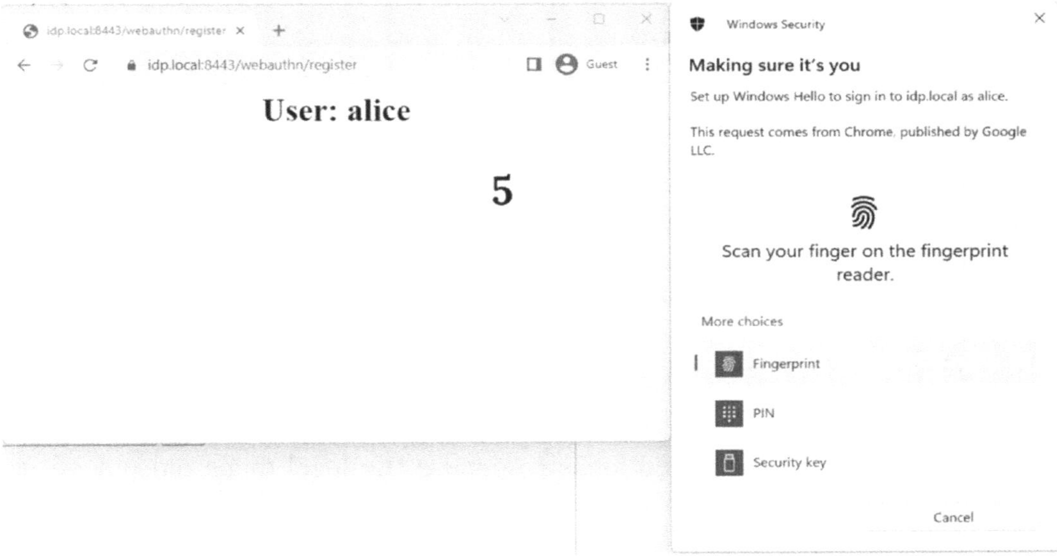

***Figure 6.23**: WebAuthn registration in the authorization flow.*

When the OTP registration is complete, the policy is verified again. The policy router routers to the WebAuthn registration as shown in step 5.

User consent

Before a user accesses the service provider, the authorization server must apprise the user of the information shared with the SP and should proceed only when the user consents. Consent plays a crucial legal requirement in certain circumstances. The intent is for the user to pause and take stock of the situation and not proceed if not required to continue. We provide a simple consent screen with an **Allow** button, but ideally, there should also be a cancel button.

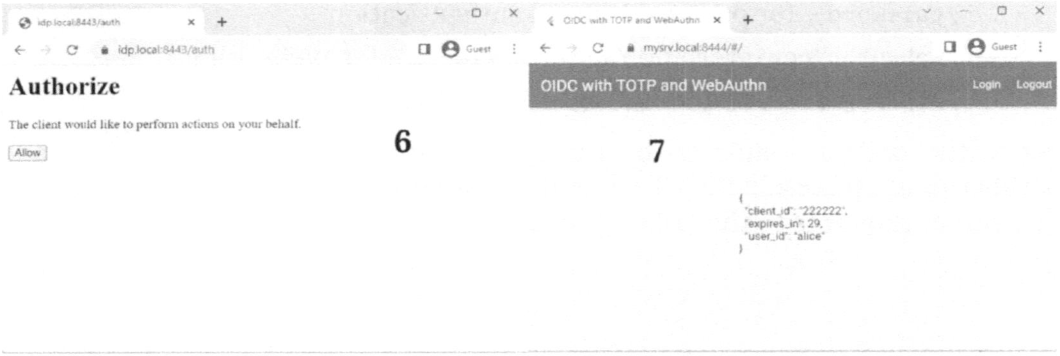

Figure 6.24*: User explicitly consenting to proceed*

The user consent should follow authentication. It ensures the user consenting is a verified user. Once the user consents, the authorization server redirects to the service provider and the results are shown in step 7.

Session Management

In the previous chapters, we used a combination of cookies and local maps for session management. We used locks to ensure the local maps did not get to a race condition. All these were useful for learning. For production use, you can use the **go-session/session**[26] package. The package maintains a cookie for tracking purposes only. The data is stored in local maps, RDBMS, in-memory databases, etc., based on configuration. For clustering of application servers, it will be helpful. In our example, we use local maps as storage which is the default.

```
http.HandleFunc("/password", func(w http.ResponseWriter, r *http.
Request) {
...
  if store, err = sess.Start(r.Context(), w, r); err == nil {
    if r.Method == "POST" && r.Form == nil {
      defer applyLoginPolicy(w, r)
      u, _ := store.Get("LoggedInUser")
      if err = r.ParseForm(); err == nil {
        if pw = r.Form.Get("password"); pw == u.(*userImpl).password {
```

26 session, An efficient, safely and easy-to-use session library for Go (sic.), **https://pkg.go.dev/github.com/go-session/session**

```
          store.Set("PasswordPassed", true)
          store.Save()
        }
        return
      }
    }
  }
...
}
```

`sess.Start()` function finds the cookie from the request and finds out the associated storage. **`store.Get("LoggedInUser")`** finds the user object from the local store. Once authentication is successful, we store the flag "**`PasswordPassed`**" for future reference. **`store.Save()`** commits the update to the underlying database. We have followed the above approach with all the authenticators.

Post Registration

You can use the **Logout** button on the SP to terminate the active sessions. Now, **Login** again. Once the WebAuthn and OTP credentials are registered, the server challenges the WebAuthn and OTP authentication. The password challenge is not there. You can think of this as a temporary password to bind a strong credential. Like administrators sending users a temporary password for the user to set a stronger password, we used the temporary password to achieve passwordless authentication for the user.

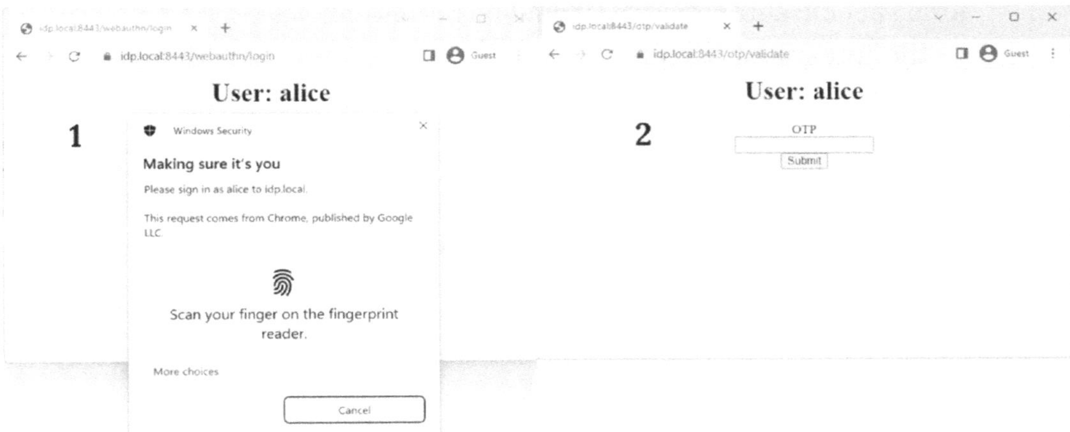

Figure 6.25: *Passwordless authentication*

Now, the user can authenticate using WebAuthn (step 1) followed by OTP (step 2) to reach the consent screen. Although oversimplified in approach, we discussed a few critical components of an IAM system for Web Authentication, authorization server, service provider, authentication policies and routing, consent management, etc.

Conclusion

It has been a long journey, starting with simple web architecture, qualitative aspects of cryptography, applying it to web security, introducing federated authentication, and taking asymmetric cryptography to passwordless authentication. Our technology pursuits around authentication have reached a logical closure. *How do we know the person presenting the authenticator is truly human? Does he have the right to own and submit the authenticator*? In real life, our businesses are facing this challenge regularly. Banks address these with Know Your Customer (KYC) with government-supplied documents. The whole class of such problems is called identity proofing. With the advent of Artificial Intelligence (AI), ID proofing is getting automated. There is a need to link the authenticators to identity as well. In the next chapter, we will review some of these aspects.

Questions

1. In the integrated example of OAuth2, TOTP, and WebAuthn, add a configuration policy to use a HOTP authenticator.
2. In the integrated sample code, no limits are there on the number of authentication failures. Add code such that no more than three failures for a specific authenticator should be permitted.
3. In the integrated sample, there are no restrictions on the number of attempts to register a credential type. Ensure a user gets only three attempts to register a credential.
4. With the integrated sample code, allow specific types of **`AAGUID`**s for WebAuthn authentication.
5. Implement the counter synchronization for a HOTP device and the authentication server.

CHAPTER 7
Advanced Trends in Authentication

Introduction

So far, we have looked at the technologies of authentication. We developed a sample code and applied it to solve some simple applications around authentication. This chapter goes beyond technology and code. It is about the business problems authentication addresses, new biometric authentication trends, fundamental cryptography changes, and so on. Authentication is associated with Identity and Access Management (IAM), yet we have not even introduced identity properly. *What is the true identity of a person? Can there be one authoritative identity for a person? Does the association of biometric data of users to identity make them foolproof? What kind of biometry is good to be captured?* Like most industries, AI will disrupt user authentication as well. Is *quantum computing posing authentication challenges*? All these will be subject matters of discussion for this chapter.

Structure

In this chapter, we will cover the following topics:

- Digital identity
- Biometric authentication

- Post-quantum cryptography
- Zero trust architecture
- Conclusion

Digital identity

Human identity is a complex phenomenon and is artificially assigned by fellow humans. A person gets an identity from the social network she keeps. For example, when a child is born, the parents provide a name for the child. The visual appearance of the human being is associated with the name. We use this correlation to identify the person. In most cultures, there are family names of a person and a public name by which she is known outside. The family name is the identity within the family group, while the external name is the identity in the larger generic world. When people make their friend circles, they call each other nicknames that could be different from names kept by their parents. No one understands such names outside the friend circle. But, those names generally uniquely identify each person in the group. The soldiers use nicknames to communicate with each other and hide their actual names during a mission.

We need identities to recognize someone **uniquely**. It was not hard to realize that names do not fit into unique definitions. Two persons can have the same name. Two Alice join the same class in the school. To break such barriers, we introduced roll numbers identifying each student in a class. From names, we started diversifying into numbers. These schemes meet the purpose of uniqueness in the functional context of the classroom. Hence, the roll number is a **functional identifier** of a student in a classroom. A running serial number for a group of people can be a great identifier in ledger books.

Proliferation of identities

Every functional activity of a person introduces a new identity. Let's consider a bank. You have a savings or checking account for day-to-day transactions, several deposit accounts, loan accounts, and so on. Each activity provides a new account number as a new identifier. Very soon, you realize you have a plethora of identifiers, and it all becomes hard to track. The banks understood this issue and introduced a customer relationship number. The customer relationship number became the central entity to link and track all accounts. Banks can now send consolidated account statements intermittently for all the services the customer is availing.

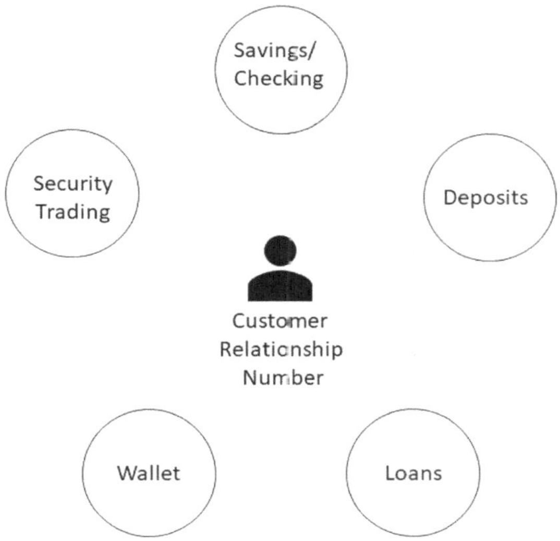

Figure 7.1: *Customer relationship number* (CRN) *provides a holistic view of all the banking activities*

CRN solved the tracking problem for the customer, but not for the bank. Suppose the loan is issued to the customer on some special occasion on a discounted scheme; there are several such customers the bank wants to notify for revision of interest rate. The bank needs to keep identifiers for all the loan accounts. There is a functional need to keep an identifier. The introduction of CRN does not make the functional identifiers redundant. All the customers, irrespective of the service, have CRN. So, the bank may want to associate some of the customer-specific properties with the CRN in the master data.

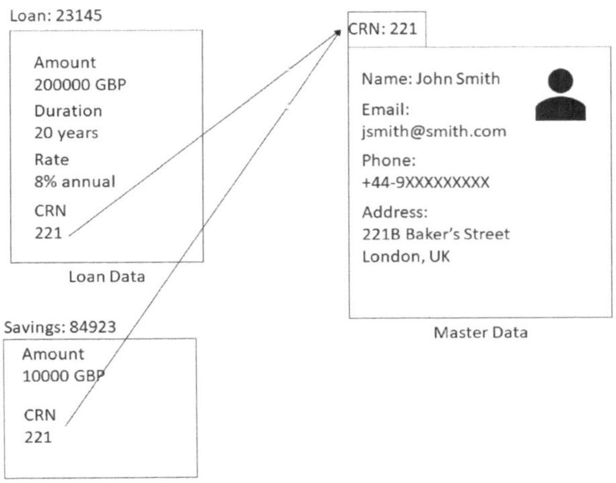

Figure 7.2: *Banking accounts linked to the CRN*

The bank need not keep the user information against all the accounts and can refer to the user's master data when such information is required. All the user's data can be kept at one location and is the foundation for a person to be a bank customer. So CRN can be considered a **foundational identity** of a person maintained by the bank.

Foundational identity

Let's extend the identities from a state perspective. Every resident service requires an identity of its own. Here are some of the identity cards in use in India.

- Passport - is used for Indian citizens to travel abroad,
    - OCI and PIO cards for non-Indian citizens of Indian descendants,
- Voter's ID card - is only issued to citizens to exercise their adult franchise,
- Ration Card - to receive food or necessities through the government public distribution scheme; issued to a family with photographs of every member,
- MNREGA Card - to receive employment under social welfare schemes,
- Personal Account Number (PAN) card - to pay income tax,
- Permanent Retirement Account Number (PRAN) card - is used for linking the pension accounts of an individual,
- Motor Driving License – is used for identifying an authorized motorist, and so on.

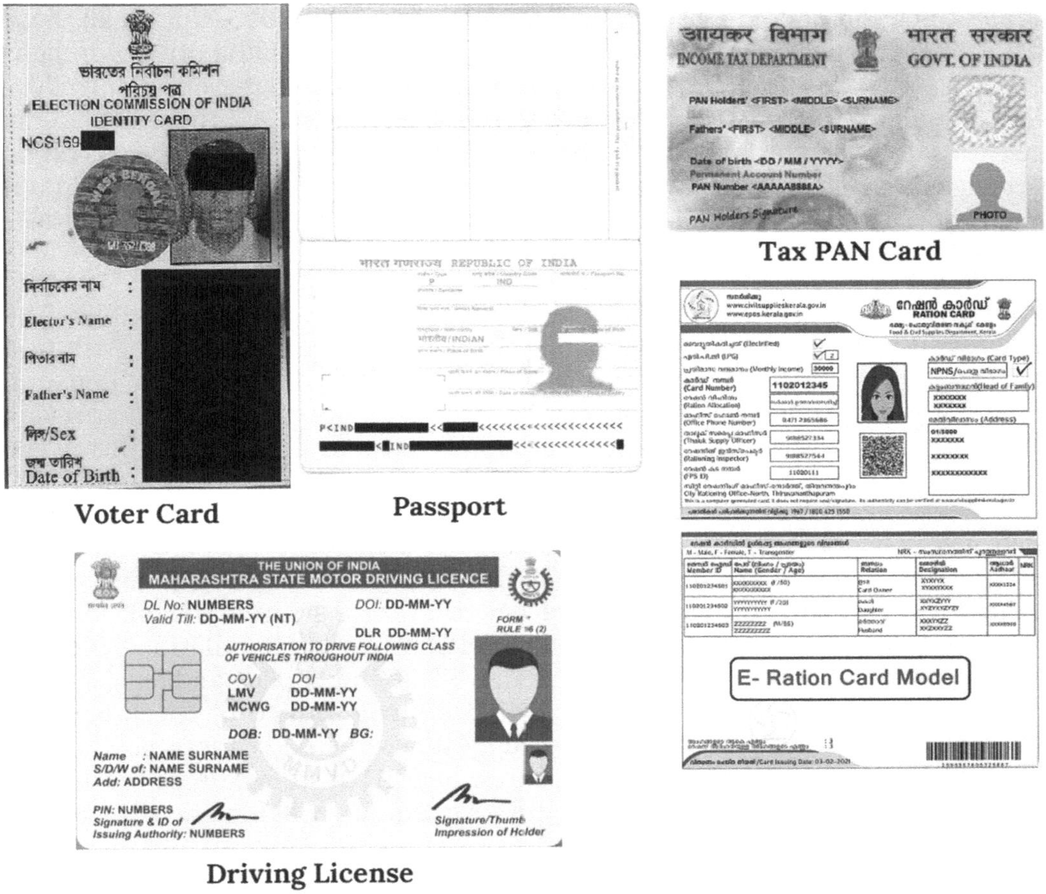

***Figure 7.3**: A collection of Indian identity documents*[1]

You realize all these documents, even in their simplest credit card form factors, are a pain to carry. Some of them have a manual signature; some have photographs as biometric identities. Some have demographic information about the person's date of birth, parent's name, and address. Indian Govt realized the need to have

1 All ID cards are taken from **https://www.wikipedia.org**, the Driving License template from the article: **https://www.cars24.com/blog/driving-licence-online-apply-in-maharashtra-mh-dl/**

an identification document for every resident of India and link that to all these other forms of identification. That became the foundational identity of Indians or Aadhaar[2]. *Is the proliferation of identities a significant reason to introduce elaborate identity management schemes*? The answer is no. All these functional identities do not cover the population of a country of the size of India. When no identity is associated with the people, the benefits and social initiatives do not reach the target audience. This is the real reason for an initiative of massive-scale identity drives[3].

While the Indian national ID initiative is only a decade old, countries like the USA have the Social Security Numbers (SSN), Singapore National Registration Identity Cards (NRIC), French National ID Cards, and so on, for several decades. As digital presence increases, national IDs are no longer passive cards carrying information; the service providers can validate them online with the user's consent. There are several levels of validation possibilities, like demographic data, OTPs over SMS and email channels, and biometrics of the users. The transition from a manual or machine-verifiable card to a digitally verifiable identifier makes digital identifiers a compelling proposition. Moreover, inclusiveness, technology-focused design, and governance are considered the pillars of a national identity development process. Developing a good foundational identity system is not just technology; it requires a well-defined policy and legal system to back it up. World Bank initiative ID4D took cognizance of these and has developed a practitioner's guide[4]. We suggest interested readers go through it for a thorough understanding of the National ID systems. Since we realize the national ID system is a digital identity system, we will look at what digital identity platforms should have.

Digital identity

The National Institute of Standards Technologies (NIST) is a U.S. federal agency that studies various Information and Communications Technologies (ICT) and proposes guidelines for their use for the U.S. government to follow. While their recommendations are normative and mandatory for the US government and private enterprises, other countries look up to them for reference material to build their policies. Digital Identity Guidelines[5] on computer security are the subject matter of discussion for us in this section.

2 Aadhaar in many Indian languages means foundation.

3 Identity for Development, ID4D, World Bank, Principles on Identification for Sustainable Development, **https://id4d.worldbank.org/guide/1-principles**

4 ID4D version 1, Practitioner's Guide, © 2019 International Bank for Reconstitution and Development/The World Bank 1818 H Street, NW, Washington, D.C., 20433

5 NIST Special Publication 800-63 Revision 3, **https://pages.nist.gov/800-63-3/**

As per NIST:

Digital identity is the unique representation of a subject engaged in an online transaction. A digital identity is always unique in the context of a digital service, but does not necessarily need to uniquely identify the subject in all contexts. In other words, accessing a digital service may not mean that the subject's real-life identity is known.

There are three distinctive processes for identity:

1. **Identity Proofing -** Identity proofing establishes that a subject is who they claim to be.
2. **Authentication -** Digital authentication establishes that a subject attempting to access a digital service is in control of one or more valid authenticators associated with that subject's digital identity. For services in which return visits are applicable, successfully authenticating provides reasonable risk-based assurances that the subject accessing the service today is the same as that which accessed the service previously.
3. **Identity Federation -** Federation is a process that allows for the conveyance of authentication attributes and subscriber attributes across networked systems. In a federation scenario, the verifier or Credential Service Provider (CSP) is referred to as an identity provider or IdP. The RP is the party that receives and uses the information provided by the IdP.

NIST provided recommendations for all possible IT infrastructure that require user identity. Some systems can be as simple as a web page or as complex as a national ID infrastructure. Hence, it classified the identity-proofing activities at three assurance levels. They are called **Identity Assurance Levels (IAL)**.

- **IAL-1**: is the lowest level of assurance with the user providing her information. No linkage is needed to establish the user's digital persona to any real-life identity. A user registers to a website and fills out the profile information in an IAL-1 compliant system. No document verification is needed.
- **IAL-2**: The user's digital persona has to be linked to a real-life identity, either remotely or in person.
- **IAL-3**: The user has to physically appear in front of authorized personnel to establish a linkage between the digital personal and real-life identity. Biometric data collection is a must for these highest assurance level identity proofing systems. For enrollment into a national ID database, the user may need this level of assurance.

Once an identity is established by a **credential service provider (CSP)**, a credential is issued to the user. The user can use the credentials to authenticate and access the system later. The assurance levels required for authentication are different from the assurance level needed for identity proofing. They are called the **Authentication Assurance Levels (AAL)**. The assurance levels establish how strongly the claimant owns the authenticator.

- **AAL-1**: A single-factor or multi-factor authentication can be used by the claimant to establish proof of possession of the credential using a secure authentication protocol.
- **AAL-2**: At least two factors of authentication are needed to establish proof of possession of the claimant over the account. Only FIPS or NIST-approved algorithms have to be used for authentication.
- **AAL-3**: is the highest level of assurance needed for authentication. Two factors of authentication using approved algorithms have to be used, as we have seen with AAL-2. The verifier should use hardware-based authenticators. The authenticators should be verifier impersonation resistant.

In *Chapters 4 and 5 Federated Authentication: I and II*, we discussed federated authentication. The Identity Provider (IdP) provided user assertions to other relying parties (RPs). The Federated Assurance Levels (FALs) govern the exchange of such assertions between IdP and RP. Just like IAL and AAL, there are three levels here as well.

- **FAL-1**: RPs receive signed assertions from IdPs using approved algorithms. We have seen this in the examples in earlier chapters.
- **FAL-2**: RPs should receive encrypted assertions that they only can decrypt.
- **FAL-3**: Encrypted and signed assertions to be exchanged with additional proof of possession of a subscriber cryptographic key. These high-security data exchanges keep the user information secured and private in agency communications.

We stated only the overview of assurance statements. The NIST specifications describe detailed procedures to comply with the assurance levels. The codification of assurance levels makes it easier to formulate identity requirements for policy enforcement. Let's say an e-commerce platform like Amazon will create a service that is just IAL-1 for its customers. But, when it comes to vendors, they may prefer an IAL-2 assurance. They may want to know if the vendor is a serious business person and not some fly-by-night operator. For their employees who have access to the data center, they may prefer an IAL-3 needing biometric evidence in person. Why such varying assurance levels for different stakeholders? Every assurance level introduces cost and complexity for the user. If your user account creation requires document evidence for enrollment, the user may find this cumbersome and shift to another vendor. The identity assurance level should be just right to ensure security, yet the process is not cumbersome for the average user. Only a small set of trained people can access the core needing the highest level of assurance. This principle applies to authentication and federation assurance as well. Assurance levels provide a concise way to communicate and document security policies. Although defined by NIST, other security standards of other countries also formulate similar constructs for their jurisdictions.

Indian National Foundational Identity (Aadhaar)

We discussed foundational identities as well as digital identities. Indian foundational ID system Aadhaar merged both. In the crudest of forms, one can say Aadhaar is a unique 12-digit number issued to every resident of India above a certain age. To enroll in Aadhaar, a person has to go to designated Aadhaar enrollment centers or Aadhaar Seva Kendra. There are about 35,000 such centers around India. Mobile enrollment drives are conducted by the government when needed for remote locations. The enrollment process involves collecting some demographic data about the user.

- Name
- Parent's name
- Date of birth
- Address
- Mobile number
- Email address

Biometric information collected at the center:

- All ten fingerprint
- Iris data
- Photograph

On successful validation and verification, an Aadhaar letter is sent to the user by post.

निर्देश

- आधार ओळखीचे प्रमाण आहे, नागरीकतेचे नाही.
- ओळखीचे प्रमाण ऑनलाइन ऑथेन्टीकेशन द्वारा प्राप्त करा.
- कोणत्याही प्रकारच्या मदतीकरिता :–

फोन नं. 1800 180 1947 वर संपर्क करा, किंवा
पी. ओ. बॉक्स नं. 1947, बैंगलुरू–560001 वर पत्र पाठवा, किंवा
help@uidai.gov.in वर ईमेल करा.

नोंध: मुलांचे 15 वर्षाचे वय झाल्यानंतर बायोमेट्रिक वैशिष्ट्यांचे नूतनीकरण अवश्य करून घ्या.

INSTRUCTIONS

- Aadhaar is proof of identity, not of citizenship.
- To establish identity, authenticate online.
- In case any help is required :

Call 1800 180 1947 or;
Write to P.O. Box No. 1947, Bengaluru - 560 001 or;
Email at help@uidai.gov.in

Note: Children on attaining 15 years of age need to update biometric information.

भारतीय विशिष्ट ओळख प्राधिकरण
UNIQUE IDENTIFICATION AUTHORITY OF INDIA

Address: 1st Floor,
Salarpuria Touchstone,
Marathahalli Sarjapur,
Outer Ring Road,
Bengaluru - 560087

Aadhaar - Aam Aadmi Ka Adhikaar

आधार

भारत सरकार
Unique Identification Authority of India
Government of India

Enrollment No 1190/11450/02075

To,
Deepak Vasant Surve
S/O Vasant Surve
Hendre Buldg No.17,Room no.3,Groundfloor
D.N.Singh Road
Hathibaug Mazgaon
Mumbai
Mumbai
Maharashtra 400010
9969651728

Ref: 290 / 25A / 90679 / 90694 / P

SAMPLE

आपला आधार क्रमांक / Your Aadhaar No. :

3977 8800 0234

आधार – सामान्य माणसाचा अधिकार

भारत सरकार
GOVERNMENT OF INDIA

Deepak Vasant Surve
Year of Birth : 1967
Male

3977 8800 0234

आधार – सामान्य माणसाचा अधिकार

Figure 7.4: *A sample Aadhaar letter*[6]

Validation

Authentication and credential validation are used synonymously.

- A relying party of Aadhaar would like to know if Ashok Kumar, S/o Ramesh Kumar, Age: 40 has Aadhaar number **XXXX XXXX 1234**. The Aadhaar system will validate this information and report positive or negative. It is called **demographic validation**. Partial matching of demographic data can be used to validate addresses.

6 **https://www.uidai.gov.in/images/Aadhaar_letter_large.png**

- Aadhaar supports OTPs being delivered over **SMS** and **emails**.
- In biometric authentication, Aadhaar supports **face**, **fingerprint**, and **iris** images. Only approved devices can be used to capture biometric data.
- Lastly, Aadhaar supports shared secret-based OTPs generated on **mobile authenticator** applications.
- For manual validation, the **Aadhaar letter** can be used.
- The authentication API supports the validation of multiple authenticators simultaneously.

Ecosystem

API access to the Aadhaar ecosystem is available to registered entities only. There are three categories of Aadhaar servers.

- Central Identity Repository (CIDR) - All the Aadhaar user data is available at the CIDR at a central location. Only authorized services have access to this epository.
- Authentication Service Agency (ASA) - Can contact the CIDR over a VPN network.
- Authentication User Agency (AUA) - Provides user services based on Aadhaar authentication. These can be banks, government departments, and so on.

A user or a kiosk operator on behalf of the user contacts an AUA. The AUA makes an authentication request to the CIDR directly if it has access or contacts an ASA to complete the request. Some of the scenarios are shown in *Figure* 7.5.

While this is not true federated access, only limited and registered agencies can contact the Aadhaar database for identity information.

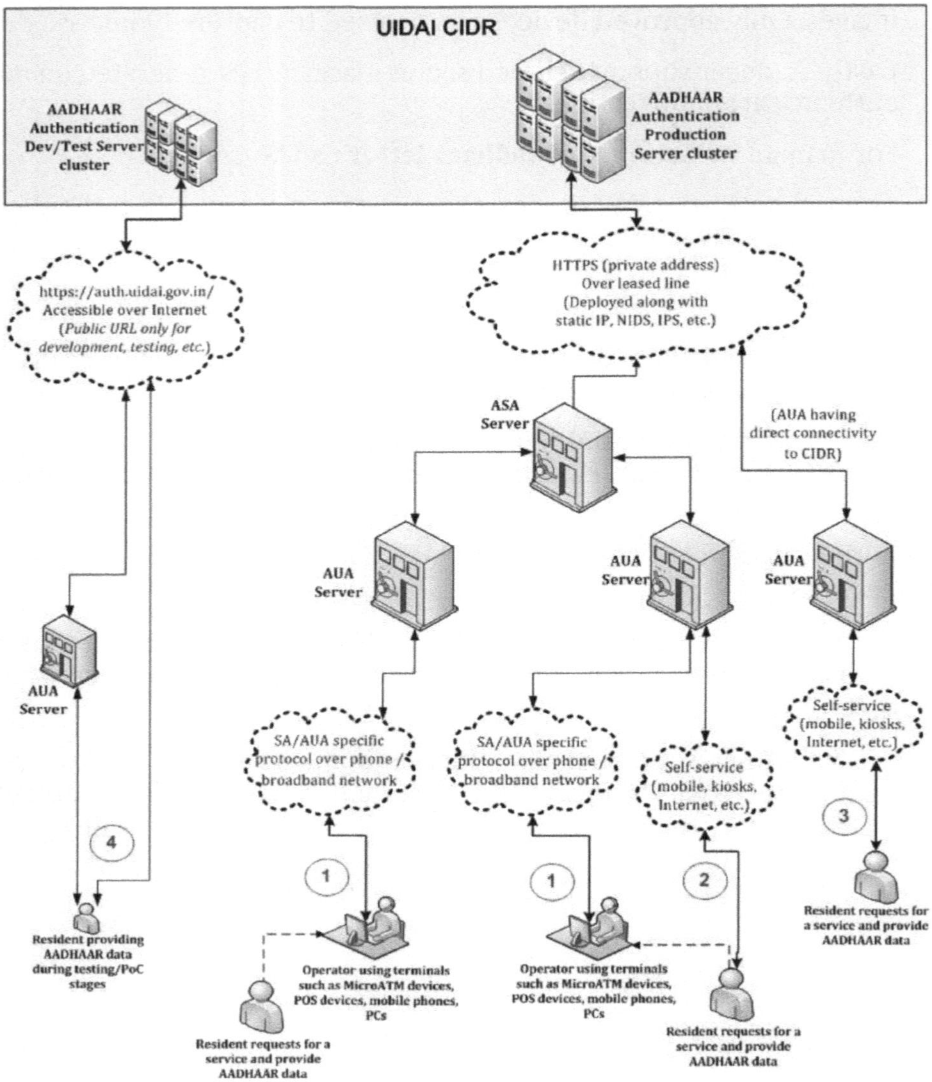

Figure 7.5: *Aadhaar authentication flow under various scenarios*[7]

Aadhaar provides development and test server access to the public to test their solution during active development. Once they are convinced their solution is working well, they can migrate to the product setup through an AUA or ASA.

7 *Figure* 1, Aadhar Authentication API Specification - version 2.5 (revision-1) January-2022

Beyond India (MOSIP)

Aadhaar was a historical milestone. Creating the foundational ID for over a hundred billion people in a developing nation with significant resource constraints created confidence. Can such a model be replicated for other nations as well? IIIT Bangalore took the initiative to build an open-source platform with funding from Bill and Melinda Gates Foundations, Omidyar Networks, and Tata Foundations for the global public good. Such a system has to consider all the use cases of Aadhaar yet be customizable to the requirements of other nations and constraints. Welcome Modular Open Source Identity Platform (MOSIP). Some even call MOSIP Aadhaar in a Box[8].

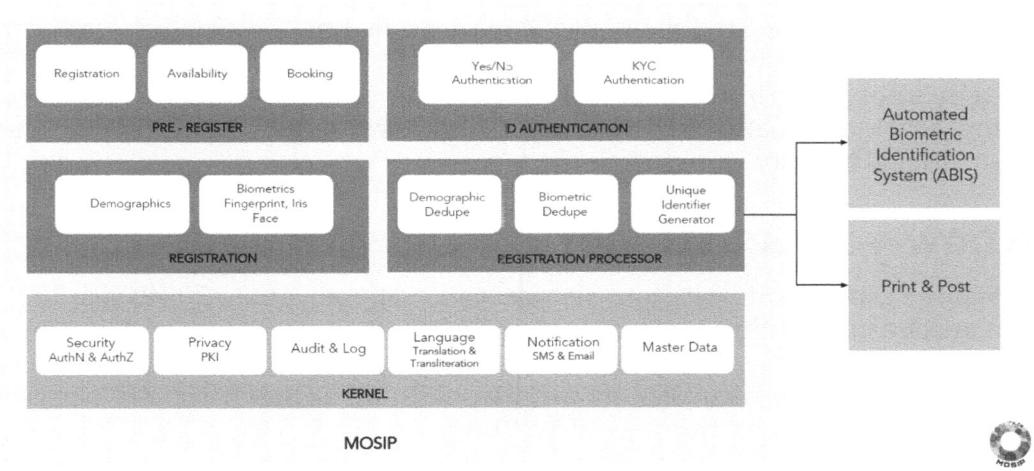

Figure 7.6: *MOSIP Functional Architecture*[9]

At a functional level, MOSIP has a kernel that provides these capabilities:

- Pre-registration - Think of a user who wants to register herself. She goes to a portal, finds the availability of the enrollment center, and books a slot.
- Registration - She provides the demographic data with proof which will be recorded. She also provides her biometric data. The system should be flexible enough to interface with all possible biometric sensors.

8 Flanagan, Heather, ed. "Government-Issued Digital Credentials and the Privacy Landscape." OpenID Foundation, May 4, 2023. **https://openid.net/Government-issued-Digital-Credentials-and-the-Privacy-Landscape-Final**

9 MOSIP 101, **https://mosip.io/uploads/resources/5cb55cb4092b4MOSIP%20101.pdf**

- Registration Processor - In the backend, the demographic data collected is verified from the provided documentary evidence. The biometric data is compared with all the data collected for uniqueness. This layer requires integration with available third-party biometric engines. MOSIP does not provide any biometric engine but provides interfaces for integration.
- ID Authentication - Yes and No authentication that approves or rejects the user. KYC authentication provides the data associated with the user like demographic and address information.

The kernel provides system management capabilities like, authentication and authorization for management tasks, PKI for privacy, audit and logging, language and translations, notifications, and master data management. The system can integrate with automated biometric identification systems, printing and postal systems for dispatch, and so on. The modular aspects of MOSIP ensure the system is not prescriptive, and deployment can be configured to specific needs. Many developing nations in Asia and Africa have deployed MOSIP for their foundational identity.

Know your customer

In *Figure* 7.1, a bank offers various services to a customer. About 30-40 years back, you needed an introduction letter to open a bank account. Another customer of the branch or your company signed the letter. Since the number of customers was small, the branch manager or official would know all the customers in person, so this system of operation was okay. Today we hardly visit branches for cash withdrawals. We seldom go to the branches as most transactions are completed online. So many transactions we do on the banking channels that it may not be practical to go to the bank for them. You can walk into any branch of the bank for transactions. There is no designated home branch as such. So no one recognizes you there. Against this backdrop, how does a bank identify its customers? Even if they could somehow identify the customer, do they know the financial aspects of the person? A letter of introduction never gave that confidence. Moreover, financial guarantee from friends and family in nuclear families is hard to obtain, which is very common in city living. So banks are relying on data more than interpersonal relationships of the customer with the staff. Hence, banks need identity information that is accepted by everybody.

Let's understand how governments are benefiting their citizens. In India, the government has started disbursing monetary benefits directly to citizens and not to contractors for social benefit schemes.

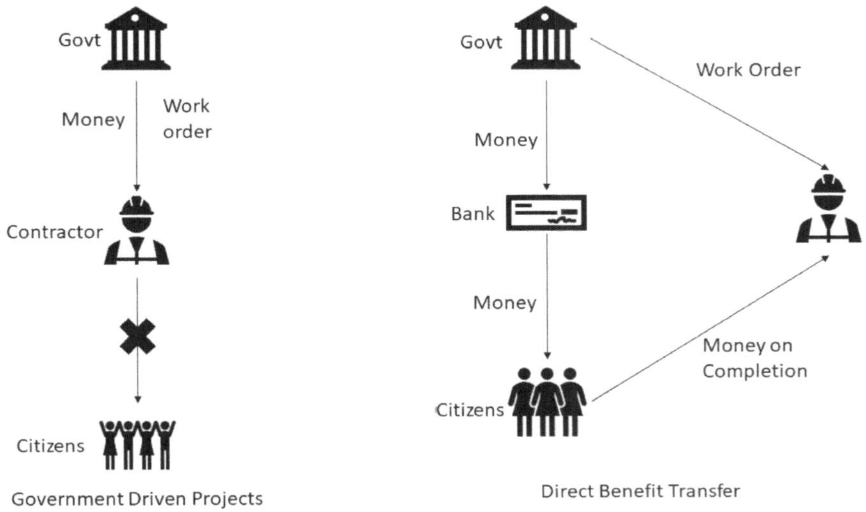

Figure 7.7: *Direct benefit transfers making contractors responsible*

When the government was developing the whole project, the contractor used to get the funds. However, without delivering the benefits to the customer, he would submit a report to the officials. Some officials will receive bribes and approve the projects when no quality work gets delivered to the citizens. Today the money moves through the citizen's bank account. The government deposits the funds into the citizen's bank account. Only on completion of work does the contractor get paid by the citizen. The funds the citizen receives are fixed by the government scheme, yet he can add his funds for additional customizations. It is also beneficial for the contractor as he can provide better service and get a better price for the customization he contributes. In India, the Govt. has opened 480 million bank accounts for citizens. There is a balance of 22 billion dollars USD worth of funds in them by 30th Dec. 2022[10]. The government has claimed to have transferred 37 billion USD with direct benefit transfer[11]. These schemes are achievable as citizens can be tracked consistently with Aadhaar-like foundational identities, and banks get the confidence to issue saving accounts to individuals with just their identity.

Since we have elaborated on Aadhaar earlier, let's see what information Aadhaar shares for KYC[12]. They are:

---

10 Jan Dhan accounts total balance surge to □1.80-lakh cr in Dec 2022 **https://www.thehindubusinessline.com/money-and-banking/jan-dhan-accounts-total-balance-surge-to-180-lakh-crore-in-december/article66365089.ece**

11 Direct Benefits Transfer, Government of India, **https://dbtbharat.gov.in/**

12 Aadhaar eKYC API Specification – Version 2.0 May 2016

- Proof-of-Identity (POI) - Name, DOB, Gender, Phone, Email
- Proof-of-Address (POA) - Components of Address of the person
- Photo of the user
- A rendered image of a printable Aadhaar letter

This information is issued only when a user authenticates and provides her consent using a strong credential like biometry or shared secret-based OTP. Aadhaar does not provide KYC information to all the AUAs or ASAs. Specifically approved KYC User Agencies (KUAs) that work with KYC Service Agencies (KSAs) who can request such data from the Aadhaar CIDR (*Figure* 7.5).

Beyond identity

Based on the information in Aadhaar, a bank only issues a customer relationship number or a basic savings bank account. But, it gives no financial information about the person. *Can such a person be provided with a credit card or a personal loan? If so, how much of a credit limit is safe for such a person?* Today, banks want to access such information online from trusted sources. They are not looking at someone walking up to a branch with documents as evidence. They expect the customer to upload the documents as electronic images. The data can be extracted from the submitted images by AI-based systems. The banks want to contact the tax filings and obtain the income potential. They have a rules engine to approve the loans. So from the customer applying for the loan to document and database evidence collection to approval, all the steps can be completed within a few hours of application.

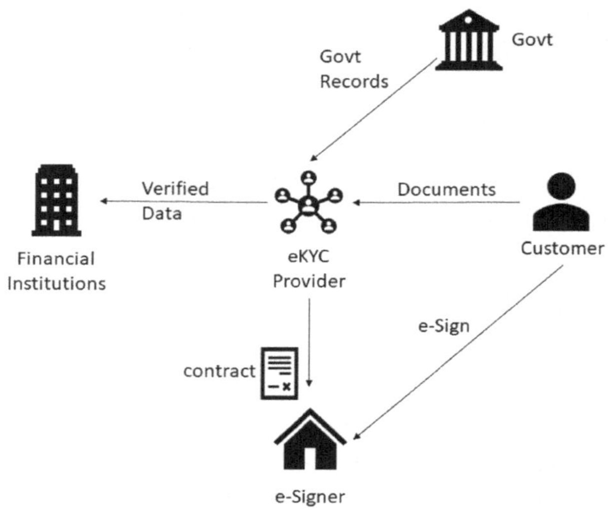

Figure 7.8: *e-KYC provider at work*

Hence, this has become a repeatable business requirement in the financial market, and some organizations are providing such services for banks and non-banking financial institutions (NBFC). They understand workflows and provide the necessary user interface for identity and documentary evidence. The customer approves such transactions by providing necessary supporting documentation. Financial institutions extract the information, verify it, and enable the service for the customer.

e-Signing

In a traditional certificate signing infrastructure, the user has to request a certificate from a certifying authority. The CA validates the user and issues a certificate. We discussed this in detail in *Chapter 2: Fundamentals of Cryptography*. The user must keep the certificate and the private key in a hardware token. The user will sign a digital contract by applying her digital signature only. It requires every user should have a certificate, she is involved in signing the contract, and there is no flexibility in the workflow. A technically savvy user can obtain a certificate for herself.

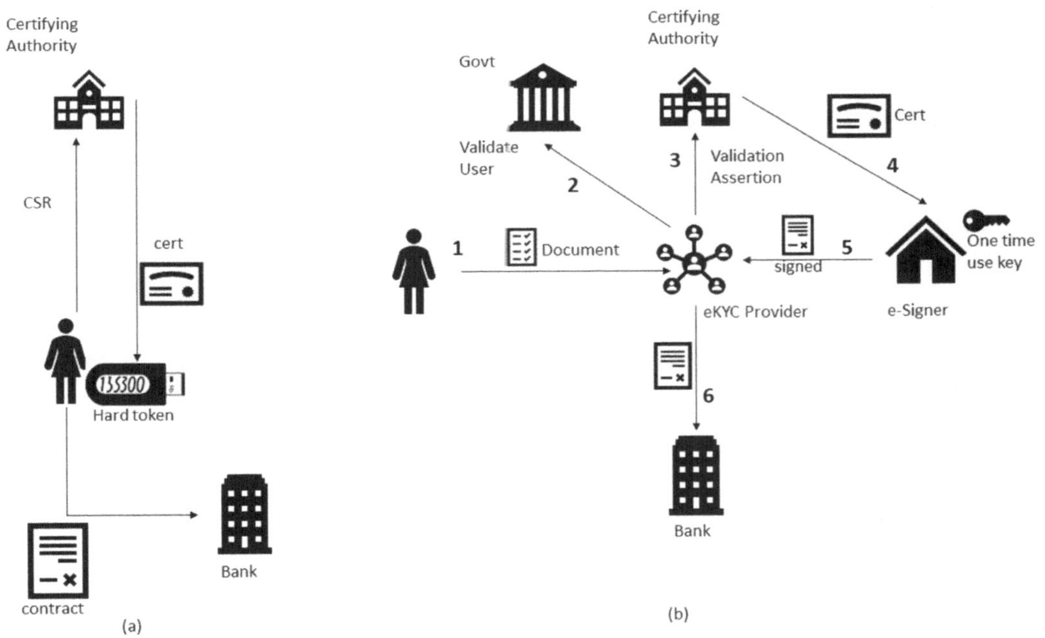

Figure 7.9: *(a) Traditional signing vs (b) e-Signing better workflow integration*

Contrast this to the e-signing workflow.

- The user submits a document to the eKYC provider.

- The eKYC provider authenticates the user with the government ID database (Aadhaar) and obtains all the user information.
- The eKYC provider presents the user details to the CA as a registration agent (RA) to issue a certificate to the e-signer when needed.
- The e-signer generates a one-time use keypair for the user and obtains a certificate for the user from the CA.
- The e-signer obtains the document from the eKYC provider, applies the digital signature, and sends it to the eKYC provider. The private key is not stored but deleted after signing.
- The e-KYC provider submits the document to the bank.

The user can sign a document as part of a larger document workflow of e-KYC. The user does not have to maintain the key in secured hardware. We discussed a simplified functional form of the Cloud Signature Consortium API[13]. The exact technical workflow can vary substantially.

Identity Wallets

Foundational identities provide a mechanism to identify a citizen. The KYC processes obtain verified information about a user from many validated databases. However, all these systems will like to authenticate the user subsequently. They can issue a credential, and the user carries one for each service provider. Here is a personal experience. Many establishments in the USA where they serve alcohol insist patrons produce valid identity cards certifying they are of the age of majority. A USA citizen presents her driver's license typically. As a foreigner, I showed my passport. The person running the establishment had never seen an Indian passport. So, he looked into further details, like the visa pages, and ensured I was a bonafide traveler. In doing so, he discovered I had visited several times, the specific dates of my travel, and so on. Let us understand some terminologies from the context.

- **Credential** - The passport is the credential.
- **Issuer** - The Government of India is the issuer.
- **Holder** - I was the holder of the credential.
- **Verifier** - The person at the establishment is the verifier.

13 Architectures and protocols for remote signature applications, **https://cloudsignatureconsortium.org/resources/download-api-specifications/**

- **Private data** - my travel dates from and to the USA, the ports of entry, how long I stayed, who has sponsored my VISA, how long it is valid, my parents' names, my spouse's name, and everything else that goes into a passport.
- **Claim** - The information that I was above the age of majority (18 or 21 years).

In producing a simple identity to enter a business establishment, I had to expose all this privacy information. The verifier did not recognize the issuer (Indian Government) hence all this confusion. He was convinced by the VISA issued by a USA authority. In the digital world, we will have this further aggravated as there may not be human verification. For a verification system to work, a basic trust between the holder, issuer, and verifier must exist.

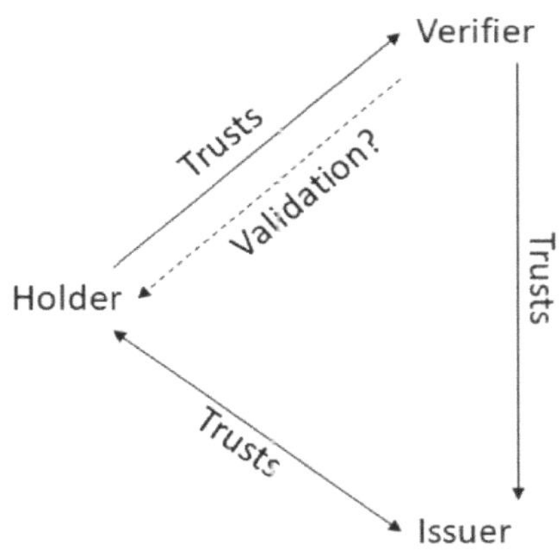

Figure 7.10: *Existing trust relationship before validation*

In a credential verification setup, the following trusts exist:

1. The holder and the issuer trust each other.
2. The verifier trusts the issuer.
3. The holder trusts the verifier and presents the credentials issued by the issuer to verify.

In the passport example, the verifier did not trust the issuer. Let us relook at the same problem with digitally verifiable credentials.

1. At the port of entry, I present my e-passport and e-visa from my mobile application to the USA border protection office.

2. The USA border protection verifies:
    a. Indian Government has issued the passport.
    b. The USA Immigration office has issued the visa.
    c. The in-built technologies ensure that they do not have to contact the issuers to validate.
3. Once USA border protection is convinced, they issue me a new credential on my mobile device. The credential has the following claims:
    a. Name
    b. Date of Birth
    c. Time of Entry into the USA
    d. Permitted time of exit from the USA
    e. Country of Citizenship
4. When I enter the business establishment, I present the credentials issued by the USA border protection service. The establishment trusts it and lets me in. The presentation and trust mechanism are cryptographic operations, like signing.

ID	Type	Issuer	Basis	Claims
101	e-Aadhaar	Govt. of India	Foundation	Sensitive
102	e-Passport	Govt. of India	101	Sensitive
103	e-VISA	USA Immigration	102	Sensitive
104	e-I94	USA Border Control	102, 103	Name, Age, Validity, and so on.

***Table 7.1**: The credentials in an identity wallet*

The above is one of many use cases Identity Wallets can address. There are several credentials listed in the identity wallet of the user. The user will authenticate with the appropriate credential trusted by the verifier. W3C consortium has developed a Verifiable Credentials Data Model[14] that addresses some of these use cases and much more. As digital identities proliferate, users will use credential wallets and exchange information cryptographically. The credential model also talks about verifiable data registries maintained over distributed databases and ledgers like blockchains.

14 Verifiable Credentials Data Model 1.0, **https://www.w3.org/TR/vc-data-model-1.0/**

Biometric authentication

In *Chapter 6: Multifactor Authentication*, we talked about biometry under the something you are category. We will delve deeper into understanding biometric authentication in this chapter. Considering digital IDs are validated using biometric identification techniques, it is in our interest we realize their capabilities and limitations. For a biometric technology to be relevant, it should be[15]:

- **Universal**: available on most normal populations.
- **Unique**: The characteristic must be unique to a person, and no two persons should have similar characteristics.
- **Measurability**: It should be easy to pick the characteristics of a person.
- **Permanence**: The characteristics must be permanent and stand the passage of time.
- **Performance**: They must perform accurately and consistently on time.
- **Acceptable**: The population should be comfortable presenting the sample.
- **Circumvention**: It should not be easily replicated by some digital means.

With all the advances in biometric recognition technologies and their ubiquitous usage in the industry, NIST does not seem to consider a compelling need to use it for authentication. Here are some of the cited reasons[16]:

- The False Match Rate (FMR) does not provide the necessary confidence in the system.
- The techniques are statistical, while cryptographic or password systems are deterministic.
- Biometric templates, when compromised, are hard to replace. Techniques have improved, yet, the usage is still limited.
- Some characteristics like photographs, and so on, can be easily acquired.

Biometric systems can be an additional factor of authentication in a multifactor authentication system when:

- A what-you-have credential is additionally available,
- A channel authentication should be before biometric collection,

15 Jain, A., and A. Ross, "Introduction to Biometrics," in Handbook of Biometrics, A. Jain, P. Flynn, and A. Ross, (eds.), New York: Springer, 2008, pp. 1–22.

16 SP-800-63B, section 5.2.3, Digital Identity Guidelines - Authentication and Lifecycle Management, **https://pages.nist.gov/800-63-3/sp800-63b.html#sec5**

- The False Match Rate (FMR) should be better than 1 in 1000[17],
- The system should be resilient to 90% of the presentation attacks,
- The comparison of biometric data on the local devices is preferred, and so on.

While NIST has not been encouraging about using biometric data for authentication, there is a deferring viewpoint on identity proofing. Here are some of the salient points[18].

- It can be collected for non-repudiation and reproofing the identity.
- In IAL3, biometrics can be used in deduplicating enrollments, thus restricting fraudulent enrollments. At IAL3, biometric collection is a mandatory requirement.
- Document used for identity evidence must contain a photograph or an identity template. Without the presence of such information, the evidence is considered unacceptable.
- Similarly, while verifying evidence if the biometrics is not compared with the actual, such verification is marked weak or unacceptable.
- While ID proofing is in person, the biometrics should be collected firsthand from the user and not from another source.

Now that we understand the scope of biometrics, let us look at some of the common biometric authentication techniques.

Fingerprint

Human skin is not smooth. It has undulations and ridges that are unique to every individual. These ridges are called papillary or friction ridges. This fundamental property is used as a mechanism to identify a person. Crime investigators have been using fingerprints from time immemorial. Ink-smeared fingerprints are applied on documents as a person's signature and are considered an identifying attribute. So the interest in using it for digital identity is quite understandable.

Fingerprint scanners are tactile sensors and not always optical sensors like cameras. Some of them are earlier than digital camera sensors. It is one of the reasons we see the adoption of fingerprints in digital identity alongside storing images of human beings. Here are some of the fingerprint sensor technologies:

- Inked capture - used on legal documents

17 Revised to 1 in 10000 in the 4th revision of SP-800-63B. This revision is still under review.

18 SP-800-63A, Digital Identity Guidelines - Enrollment and Identity Proofing Requirements, **https://pages.nist.gov/800-63-3/sp800-63a.html**

- Latent fingerprint - used in forensics
- Optical sensors - the cameras cannot capture the undulations with regular lighting
- Solid state capacitive sensors - swipe motion sensors on laptops and mobiles are parts of these
- RF sensors - resilient to epidermal changes in the skin
- Thermal fingerprint sensors
- Multispectral image sensors
- Ultrasonic and piezoelectric sensors

While laptop and mobile devices use capacitive sensors for fingerprint acquisition, optical sensors are used for multiuser fingerprint acquisition. Training capacitive sensors require several iterations of providing the fingerprint, which is okay for a personal device. However, the acquisition of fingerprints for several users at a kiosk or public authentication device is optical sensor-based. The optical sensors use specialized illumination to ensure accurate image capture.

Fingerprint analysis has a history spanning over a century. Just like signature analysis, dermatoglyphics has been an area of research. Some technologies, like Galton's minutiae, Henry's classifications, and so on, are popular. Today Automated Fingerprint Identification Systems (AFIS) handle all forms of fingerprint images. One can consider these as specialized image processing techniques. Finger images are known to be stored in monochromatic and greyscale forms as well. In extremely large-scale databases, like national IDs, multiple fingerprint captures per person are taken[19]. For example, for a USA visa or Indian Aadhaar enrollment, all ten fingers are taken. Fingerprint quality may deteriorate as a person ages. Hence, fingerprints may need re-enrollment for the aging population.

Face biometry

While optical sensors were available long back, face feature extraction technologies were not as developed. Modern face detection technologies matured post-deep learning era. Social networking giants like Google and Meta developed compelling face recognition technologies for automatically tagging users in photographs. FaceNet by Google[20] can be considered one of the early innovations that revolutionized face detection. While other heuristics and

19 Shimon K. Modi, Biometrics in Identity Management Concepts to Applications, 2011, Artech House

20 FaceNet: A Unified Embedding for Face Recognition and Clustering, **https://arxiv.org/abs/1503.03832**

face feature identification existed earlier, machine learning and deep learning techniques are the most common in face detection today.

We use the open-source library **`Kagami/go-face`**[21] to compare two face images and provide the code for the same. The library internally utilizes **`Dlib`**[22] for face recognition. For authentication tasks, we use a 1:1 face match.

- We take two images.
- Extract the mathematical face descriptors as a vector of 128 floating point numbers.
- Find the Euclidean distance between the two face descriptors.
- If the distance is less than 0.6, there is a likely chance that the faces belong to the same person 99.37% of the time[23].

The following is the source code that translates the workflow mentioned earlier into the Go language.

```
http.HandleFunc("/compare", func(w http.ResponseWriter, r *http.Request)
{
  if r.ParseForm() == nil {
    img1 := r.Form.Get("img1")
    img2 := r.Form.Get("img2")
    imgbuf1, _ := base64.URLEncoding.DecodeString(img1)
    imgbuf2, _ := base64.URLEncoding.DecodeString(img2)
    face1, _ := rec.RecognizeSingleCNN(imgbuf1)
    face2, _ := rec.RecognizeSingleCNN(imgbuf2)
    dist := face.SquaredEuclideanDistance(face1.Descriptor, face2.
Descriptor)
    msg := fmt.Sprintf("The square euclidean distance is: %f", dist)
    log.Println(msg)
    w.Write([]byte(msg))
  } else {
    msg := "Internal server error"
    log.Println(msg)
    http.Error(w, msg, http.StatusInternalServerError)
  }
})
```

21 go-face, go-face implements face recognition for Go using `dlib`, a popular machine learning toolkit, https://pkg.go.dev/github.com/Kagami/go-face

22 Dlib C++ Library, Dlib is a modern C++ toolkit containing machine learning algorithms and tools for creating complex software in C++ to solve real world problems. **http://dlib.net/**

23 **http://dlib.net/face_recognition.py.html**

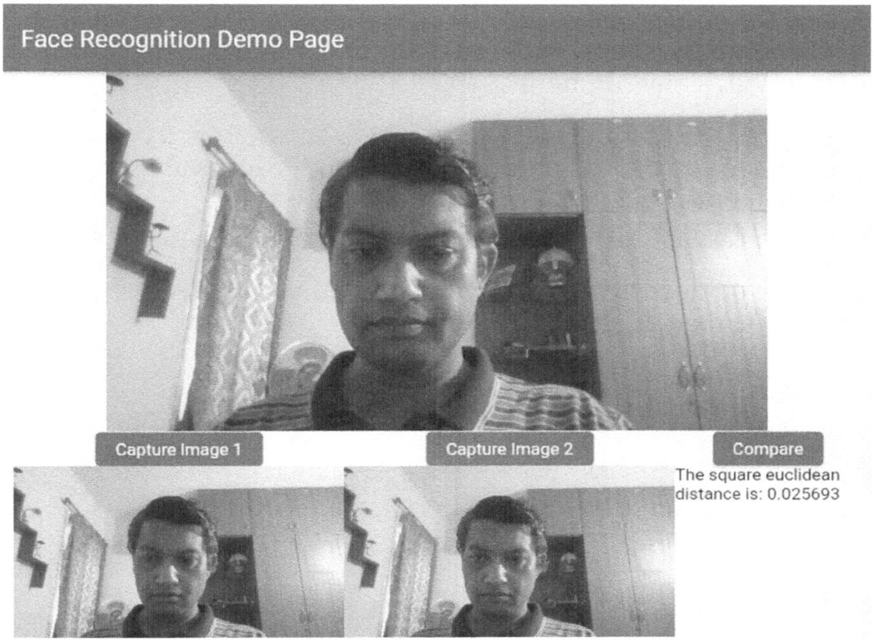

***Figure 7.11**: The comparison of two selfies of the author*

We provide a flutter-based front end to capture two images of a user and pass them to the back end to compute the Euclidean distance. We obtained 0.16[24] as the observed Euclidean distance. The code can be found in **`chapter-7/frontend`**.

Setting up the sample application in a Linux operating system is simple, as **`Dlib`** and its associated libraries are available by default in most Linux distributions. The author used the Windows Subsystem for Linux (WSL2) running Ubuntu to develop the application.

- Enter the **`chapter-7/frontend`** folder and build the front end with the command: **`flutter build web`**. You can run this step in Windows PowerShell if Flutter is not there for the WSL2 environment.
- Start a WSL 2 session and install the dependencies for **`Dlib`**.
  ```
  sudo apt-get install libdlib-dev libblas-dev libatlas-base-dev
  liblapack-dev libjpeg-turbo8-dev
  ```
- Make sure you have the **`g++`** compiler in the WSL 2 environment. If not available, install it with **`sudo apt install g++`**
- Set up the go language environment in WSL 2.

24 The API reports the square of this value.

- Enter the folder **`chapter-7`** and launch the backend by running the application: **`go run ./face.go`**. The service starts running on **`port 8080`** of the WSL 2 environment.
- However, the running server is not accessible from the Windows browser. You have to forward the port to be accessible from a Windows environment. On an admin shell on Windows run:

  ```
  netsh interface portproxy add v4tov4 8080 localhost 8080
  ```

- Now, if you access **http://localhost:8080** you will see the UI appearing on your screen as shown in *Figure* 7.11.

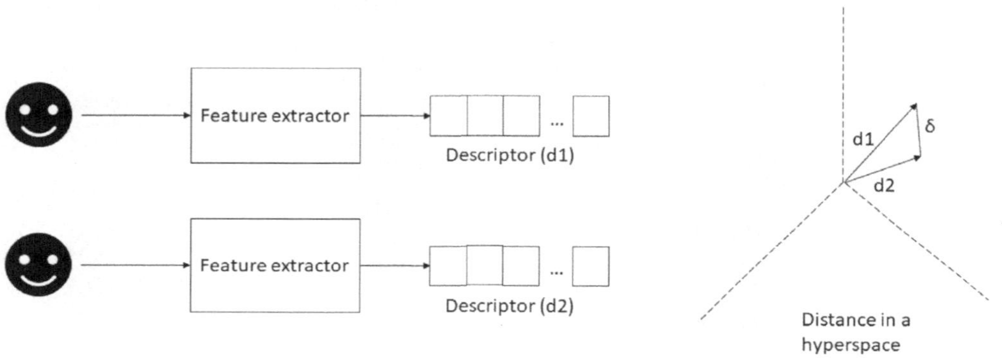

***Figure 7.12**: 1:1 face matching architecture used for go-face*

The libraries and models are not state-of-the-art. Hence, not advised for use in production-ready authentication systems. It is merely for training and understanding. The model uses a modified version of ResNet and fits each identity into a ball of 0.6 radii. We leave the details for the readers to review the works of Davis King[25]. While this exposure is good for learning, we draw the reader's attention to two reports.

- Papers with Code reports on open-source face verification results[26].
- NIST Face Recognition Vendor Test (FRVT) 1:1 face match result[27].

25 dlib_face_recognition_resnet_model_v1.dat, **https://github.com/davisking/dlib-models**
26 **https://paperswithcode.com/task/face-verification**
27 **https://pages.nist.gov/frvt/html/frvt11.html**

The MobileFaceNet-based model proposed in 2022 has a TAR@FAR[28]=10^{-6} of 90.24%. The FaceNet model that was state-of-the-art in 2015 had a TAR @FAR=0.01 of only 67% on the IJB-C dataset. There have been significant improvements in face verification approaches. Transfer learning is used from one model to be reviewed and improved over using another model to better the base results. From the vendor test data released by NIST, one can see an FNMR of 0.0016 with an FMR[29] of 10^{-6} for the US VISABORDER dataset. Moreover, NIST test results provide geographical diversity-based NFMR results. One should understand the NIST dataset is not comparable to the datasets against which the open-source results are tested.

Face biometrics has many facets beyond the face verification or matching we discussed. Here are some of them:

- **1:N face match** – typically used by search engines to locate a face in a database. Some applications include searching for an image from a known criminal database, social media tagging, and so on.
- **Emotion detection** – body language and facial expressions detection help identify the general attitude of persons for recruitment.
- **Parts of facial features** – locating eyes, ears, nose, and so on, when a face is partly occluded due to sunglasses or headgear, this helps identify the person. In geographies where partially covering the face is customary, these technologies are helpful in person identification.
- **Identification of demographic attributes** – age, sex, ethnicity, etc. can be inferred from face biometrics.

While other biometric techniques are well-developed and can provide better accuracy, face recognition is still one of the preferred choices. Here are some of the reasons.

- The input to the human and computer is the same. So, in case an automated process fails, a human being can take over and complete the task.
- The sensors are available and ubiquitous. Today cameras are everywhere on every mobile device. So, data acquisition is easy.
- The technology of automated face identification has improved substantially.
- Since a human being can see the input to the system, she can help in debugging and forensic analysis in case of a breach or failure.

28 True Acceptance Rate at False Acceptance Rate – When you tighten the false acceptance rate (a wrong user is identified less), the acceptance rate for the real user will go down. That means some authentications will fail.

29 False Non-match Rate at False Match Rate – the complement of TAR@FAR.

Face recognition also poses challenges for authentication.

- The capturing of the facial image is passive. Anyone can pick up a facial image. Someone can steal this information with ease.
- A person's photograph is available easily. So, one can collect such information and present it for authentication (presentation attacks). Liveness detection is a must when someone is using a face authentication system.
- Substantially overlapping facial attributes like identical twin images can affect face recognition[30].

We suggest the readers undertake a thorough investigation of the technologies available before deciding on a face verification technology for their user authentication needs.

Other biometric technologies

Our emphasis on fingerprint and face recognition is understandable as they are available on all end-point devices like laptops, mobile phones, and so on. Yet, people have used other technologies for digital identity. Here are a few others:

- Iris recognition
- Handshape
- Speaker
- Vascular pattern
- Dynamic signature
- Keystroke, retina, DNA, gait, and so on.

Each biometric technology provides capabilities that are different from the capabilities of the other technologies. Mohammad Al Rousan and Benedetto Intrigila analyze biometric technologies in ten different parameters and classify their suitability in three levels of rankings, high, medium, and low.

30 Vendor test data for identical twins can show a false match rate of over 99% per NIST reports. **https://pages.nist.gov/frvt/html/frvt_twins_demonstration.html**

Biometric identifier	Distinctiveness	Complexity	Universality	Quantifiability	Performance	Comparison	Collect capacity	Acceptance	Cost	Use
Fingerprint	M	L	H	H	M	H	H	H	M	H
Iris	H	M	H	H	H	H	H	H	H	M
Facial	M	M	H	H	M	M	H	H	M	M
Palm	M	H	H	H	M	M	L	L	H	M
Ear	M	H	H	H	L	L	L	L	H	L
Footprint	M	H	M	M	L	L	L	L	H	L
Finger vein	H	H	H	L	H	H	L	L	H	L
Voice	M	H	H	M	M	M	L	L	H	L
Signature	L	H	H	H	L	L	M	H	L	L
Keystroke dynamics	L	M	M	L	L	L	L	L	H	L

H = High; M = Medium; L = Low

***Figure 7.13**: A comparison of biometrics types based on the characteristics of biometric entities*[31]

Iris scanning can have an FAR of 10^{-7} with an FRR of 10^{-4} with a very low possibility for spoofing[32]. This makes it a compelling technology for national ID databases[33]. In the next section, we will study if the biometric authentication should be carried out in a local end-user device or a remote server.

Local vs. server authentication

NIST encourages comparing biometric characteristics on a local device over sending to a central server. It reduces the potential for attacks on a larger scale. Even if there is a need to send the data to a central server, NIST recommends the following[34]:

- Only approved devices that can attest biometric data for source identification should be used.
- The transmission should occur on an encrypted channel.
- Standards-based biometric template revocation should be implemented.

The FIDO alliance also focused on a similar path in their biometric strategy. The FIDO 2 devices transmit signed data from the devices using PKI crypto operations. Biometric authentication provides access to the private keys to sign the data for authentication. The device can sign the data in a secured enclave that another application running in the device cannot access. We discussed some of these aspects in *Chapter 6: Multifactor Authentication*. Windows Hello[35] supports

31 Mohammad Al Rousan and Benedetto Intrigila, A Comparative Analysis of Biometrics Types: Literature Review, Journal of Computer Science 2020, 16 (12): 1778.1788, DOI: 10.3844/jcssp.2020.1778.1788 (Table 1)

32 Otti, Csaba. (2016). Comparison of biometric identification methods. 339-344. 10.1109/SACI.2016.7507397.

33 Iris is used as one of the supported biometric types with Aadhar, **https://uidai.gov.in/en/ecosystem/authentication-devices-documents/biometric-devices.html**

34 Supra 2

35 **https://learn.microsoft.com/en-us/windows/security/identity-protection/hello-for-business/hello-biometrics-in-enterprise**

face, iris, and fingerprint identification as part of its technology stack. Devices store all the data in encrypted format or special purposed trusted platform modules (TPM) where available. Application developers cannot access the raw capture of biometric data. For biometric authentication for a web application, you can use FIDO 2 with WebAuthn. We have already implemented some of these in *Chapter 6: Multifactor Authentication* in the section on WebAuthn. If a centralized comparison is necessary for implementations, the end-user device should implement stringent encryption methods like certificate and public key pinning[36] for additional security over TLS. However, certificate pinning makes it harder when changing server certificates.

Digital non-repudiation has some challenges with the local validation of biometrics. Suppose a bank wants customers to use a FIDO 2 authenticator on a WebAuthn channel. When a customer registers her mobile device as an authenticator, the bank has no mechanism to verify the device and the biometry used to unlock the phone. In such cases, the bank can procure FIDO 2 hard tokens from suppliers like YubiKey and send them to the customers to use. That way, the bank can ascertain the devices used are actual devices assigned to the customer. Any hard token introduces an additional device the customer has to carry, reducing the convenience. Suppose the bank captures the user's face on the same mobile phone and validates it on the server while enrolling the user's passkey on the mobile phone through WebAuthn; this will ensure the mobile phone belongs to the user. If the face image could be signed with the FIDO 2 private key, there would be stronger proof-of-possession evidence. Server-based biometric validation can enroll subsequent FIDO 2 authenticators for future use. The workflow is for remote credential enrollment improving user convenience.

Liveness and antispoofing mechanisms

Fingerprints have been in use for authentication for several decades. Hackers have also faked fingers using various synthetic materials like latex, Play-Doh, wood glue, gelatin, eco-flex, platinum-catalyzed silicone, modasil, and so on. It is crucial for a system to identify the use of such fake material and not permit authentication even when such fingers generate a similar impression as the original finger on a sensor. Hardware and software both work in tandem to identify such fakes. Hardware-based systems can rely on finger temperature, odor, heartbeat, pulse oximetry, and so on. Image processing is the dominant technology in software-based systems. Some characteristics captured are skin deformity, texture features, pores features, and so on. Pores in the fingerprint provide the most predictable results. The perspiration emanating from pores

36 Certificate and Public Key Pinning, **https://owasp.org/www-community/controls/Certificate_and_Public_Key_Pinning**

and the density of pores on the ridges are analyzed for liveness detection. Researchers have used various machine learning statistical techniques like wavelets, SVM, CNNs, deep neural networks, and so on[37].

While providing a fingerprint requires a positive activity from a human being, someone can pick up a person's photograph without the person being aware. A malicious person can coerce a person to provide her biometry. Liveness detection ensures a person is conducting herself in absolute control of her actions. Someone can pick up some liveness characteristics from one frame of a picture. If a person's eyes are closed in an image capture, possibly the image capture was not with the person's consent. We looked at a systematic literature review[38] conducted by some researchers on liveness detection; we present some of their findings in this section.

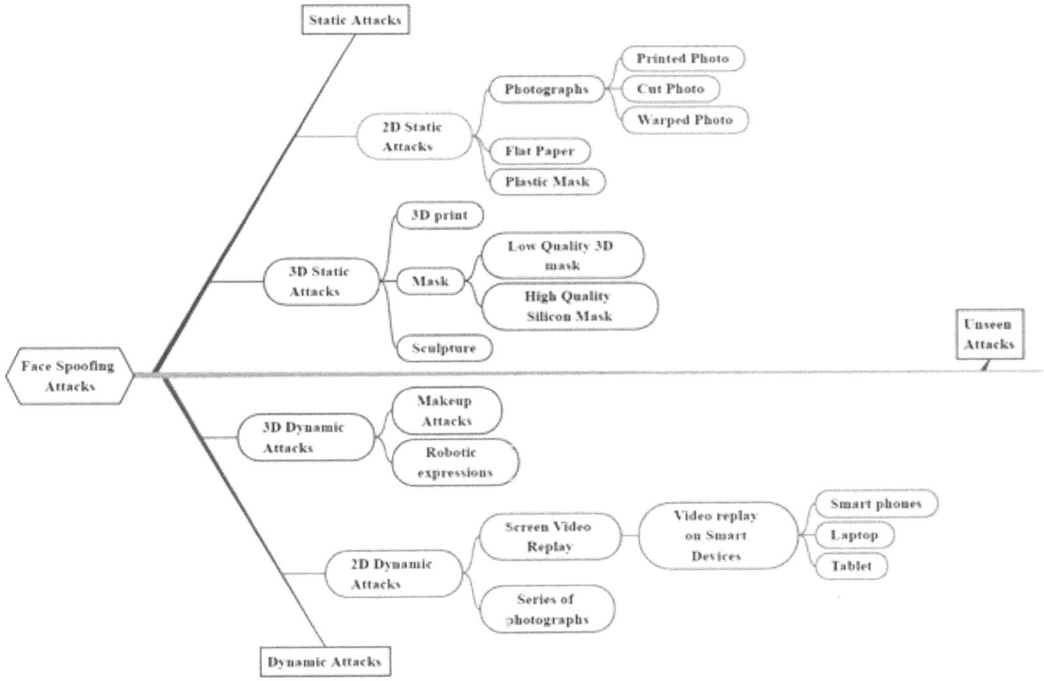

Figure 7.14: *Categorization of Face Spoofing Attacks and Spoof Instruments*[39]

37 D. Agarwal and A. Bansal, Journal of King Saud University – Computer and Information Sciences 34 (2022) 4089–4098

38 Smita Khairnar, Shilpa Gite, Ketan Kotecha, and Sudeep D. Thepade, Face Liveness Detection Using Artificial Intelligence Techniques: A Systematic Literature Review and Future Directions, Big Data Cogn. Comput. 2023, 7, 37. **https://doi.org/10.3390/bdcc7010037**

39 Figure 5, Ibid.

We present modalities of face spoofing attacks in *Figure* 7.14. With sophisticated anti-spoofing measures, the attackers are resorting to more complex attacks. For example, static images are prone to an image of printed photo-based attacks. When technology improves to recognize those, people resort to 3-D masks. Infrared cameras are good at capturing the material difference in skin vs. an artificial face mask. Newer materials for masks make infrared-based detection redundant. In such cases, video-based face feature extraction can add to the protection. Hackers are using video replays to attack. As a protection mechanism, the system may ask the user to read something from the screen that changes in every session. In short, anti-spoofing can involve both voice and video from pure video. Every anti-spoofing measure increases cost and complexity[40]. Hence, NIST recommends that anti-spoofing measures should be capable of handling at least 90% of the cases.

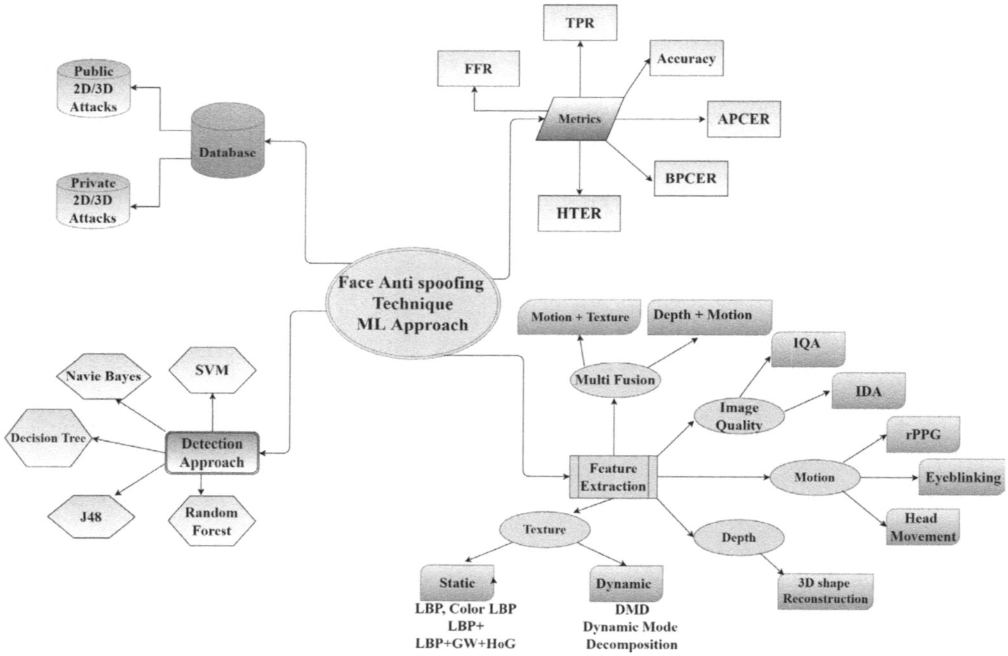

Figure 7.15: *Face anti-spoofing techniques using a machine learning approach*[41]

40 Windows Hello only allows face recognition when the system has an IR camera. **https://learn.microsoft.com/en-us/windows/security/identity-protection/hello-for-business/hello-biometrics-in-enterprise#facial-recognition-sensors**

41 Figure 7. Supra 24.

Today most anti-spoofing measures are based on machine learning algorithms, like, Convolutional neural networks (CNN), support vector machines (SVM),

random forest, naïve Bayes, decision trees, J48, and so on. They work on public and private actual and spoof data samples and try to optimize the metrics. Some of the metrics are:

- Accuracy
- False recognition rate (FRR)
- Total positive rate (TPR)
- Attack presentation classification error rate (APCER)
- Bonafide presentation classification error rate (BPCER)
- Half total error rate (HTER)

Features are extracted from the images to assess image quality (IQA) or distortion (IDA) and study eye-blinking, head movement, or blood circulation using photoplethysmography (rPPG). Analysis of motion, texture, and depth can provide cues to the liveness of the person. When multiple views like video or stereo camera are present, 3D faces can be constructed from the data for better liveness extraction.

Post-quantum cryptography

Explaining quantum computers is beyond the purview of this book. However, we present the concepts in an oversimplified manner. Bits can be in two states, 0 or 1. Quantum bits (Qubit) can be 0 and 1 at any instance with varying probability. However, the state is internal. When you observe, they collapse to either 0 or 1. Qubits get entangled with one another. So, two qubits can inherently store $2^2 = 4$ values. Thus, N qubits can retain 2^N values. But, when you observe, they all collapse to one number of N values. If you can manipulate the internal probabilities by some computational means, and when you observe, you can get the desired outcome of N-values. This one-step reduction from exponential to linear values gives enormous power to quantum computing. While there has been significant research in the field, researchers from various private organizations in the last decade have shown results of commercial possibilities. Google has claimed to have solved a problem in a few minutes using a quantum computer which otherwise would have taken thousands of years in traditional computing, thus, establishing quantum supremacy[42].

42 Quantum supremacy is proof that quantum computers are better at solving certain problems faster than normal computers.

Not all algorithms are suitable for a quantum computer, nor are all the algorithms to be rewritten for their quantum computing equivalents. Traditional computing will still be there. However, some algorithms are better suited for quantum machines. When quantum computers were still in their conceptual phases, Shor showed that integer factorization and discrete logarithms in the quantum computing world are not hard problems. A quantum-resistant RSA algorithm has to have parameters of the length of a terabyte[43]. It is impractical to use the RSA kind of algorithm. A few years later, Grover showed the searching keys with 2^N possibilities would take 2^{N-1} operations, while on a quantum computer, the same operations can take 2^{N-2} operations. Thus, symmetric key encryption of 128-bit will require 2^{64} operations. AES-256-GCM in place of AES-128-GCM will be a preferred choice. Similarly, SHA-3-512 will be chosen over SHA-3-256 in the post-quantum world.

Current status

The National Institute of Standards and Technology (NIST) has set up a committee of experts to finalize technologies safe for the post-quantum phase. They have submitted the report from the third round of the standardization process[44]. The committee accepts CRYSTALS-Kyber as one of the Key Exchange Methods (KEM). Similarly, CRYSTALS-Dilithium can be used for digital signatures. Falcon and SPHINCS+ will be standardized for digital signatures. BIKE, Classic McEliece, HQC, and SIKE are considered for evaluation in the next round for KEM. NIST is diversifying its signature portfolio with non-structured lattice signature schemes as these schemes are safe under quantum computing. As can be seen, the process is ongoing for an authoritative list. As standardization is in full swing, the implementations are not far behind. The open-source open quantum-safe (OQS) project[45] is developing the quantum-safe version of OpenSSL 1.1.1[46]. However, they released the last stable version in the line in July 2023. The subsequent versions will be available as a single shared library provider[47] on OpenSSL 3.0. Digital certificate vendors are updating their plans to launch PQC certificates with regular announcements.

Zero trust architecture

Discussion of Zero Trust in a book on web authentication in specific may not be very relevant, yet, if one delves deeper, most authentication vendors speak

43 David Wong, Real-World Cryptography, Copyright © 2021 Manning Publications Co.

44 Status Report on the Third Round of the NIST Post-Quantum Cryptography Standardization Process, NIST IR 8413-upd1, July 2022

45 **https://openquantumsafe.org/**

46 **https://github.com/open-quantum-safe/openssl/**

47 **https://github.com/open-quantum-safe/oqs-provider/**

about zero trust in some of their communications. So, we decided to include it here as a concept for us to be aware of. With enterprises distributing their cloud workloads across multiple data centers, employees, or external contractors accessing enterprise data from anywhere, the earlier access control mechanisms of trusted access to on-premise locations are no longer viable options. The earlier assumption that anyone within the perimeter is trustworthy vs. anyone outside of the perimeter is no longer a valid paradigm for access control. The earlier enterprise security models, like the castle-and-mort and related network security equipment, like firewalls, intrusion detection systems, and so on, are no longer relevant.

IT Analyst company Forrester was the first to define a zero implicit trust model[48] that insisted -

- Ensuring all resources are accessed securely, regardless of the location of the user or resource
- Logging and inspecting all traffic
- Enforcing the principle of least privilege

In the meantime, Google proposed HTTPS and SSH-based access to the enterprise from anywhere under an architecture BeyondCorp[49] as its internal network architecture. Today, it has productized the architecture for external use. IT Analyst Gartner developed a Continuous Adaptive Risk and Trust assessment (CARTA)[50] approach to zero trust. The framework suggests a Policy Decision Point (PDP) and Policy Enforcement Point (PEP) to manage a zero-trust network. Gartner introduced terms like Zero Trust Network Access (ZTNA) for user-to-server security and Zero Trust Network Segmentations (ZTNS) for server-to-server security. While most of the architectures were discussing the principles of Zero Trust, the Cloud Security Alliance, while defining the Software Defined Perimeter (SDP), presented the topological view of Zero Trust Architecture. It defined an mTLS peer-to-peer network for secured communication across various topological arrangements for data exchange while a centralized controller manages the policies. Some of the topological deployments[51] are:

- Client-to-Gateway
- Client-to-Server

---

48 SDP Working Group Software-Defined Perimeter Architecture Guide © Copyright 2019, Cloud Security Alliance. All rights reserved.

49 Rory Ward and Betsy Bayer, BeyondCorp – A New Approach to Enterprise Security, DECEMBER 2014 VOL. 39, NO. 6, ;login:, **www.usenix.org**.

50 Nike Andravous, Zero Trust Security–A Complete Guide, Copyright © 2022 BPB Publications, India

51 Supra 7

- Server-to-Server
- Client-to-Server-to-Client
- Client-to-Gateway-to-Client
- Gateway-to-Gateway

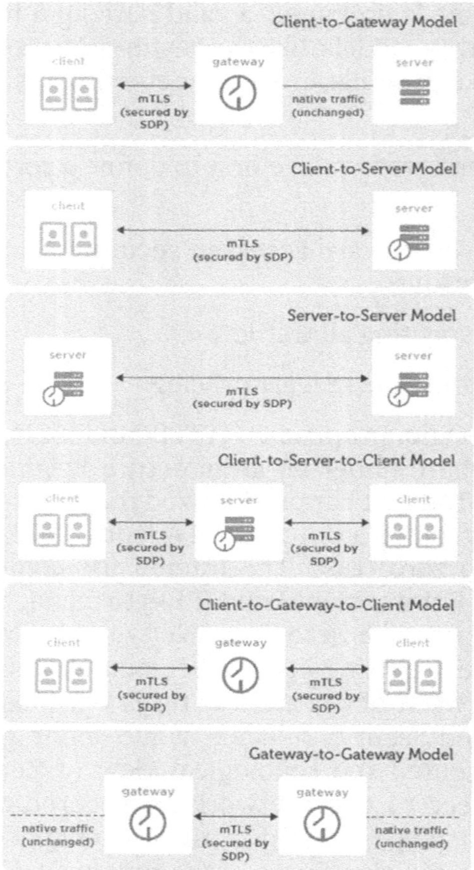

***Figure 7.16**: Connections secured by SDP deployment model*[52]

The SDP architecture was inclusive of the enterprise security systems already present. It established a significant role for the **Identity and Access Management (IAM)** systems and brought them to a central component for the policy management and controller framework.

52 Figure 8, Ibid.

Standardization

NIST white paper on Zero Trust Architecture[53] has accepted the enterprise architecture complex; yet has defined the principles as follows:

Zero trust (ZT) provides a collection of concepts and ideas designed to minimize uncertainty in enforcing accurate, least privilege per-request access decisions in information systems and services in the face of a network viewed as compromised. Zero trust architecture (ZTA) is an enterprise's cybersecurity plan that utilizes zero trust concepts and encompasses component relationships, workflow planning, and access policies. Therefore, a zero-trust enterprise is the network infrastructure (physical and virtual) and operational policies that are in place for an enterprise as a product of a zero-trust architecture plan.

The whitepaper defines a set of components that should be present to make the ZTA implementations work. Identity Management and PKI play a significant role there. Both these systems are parts of user authentication as well.

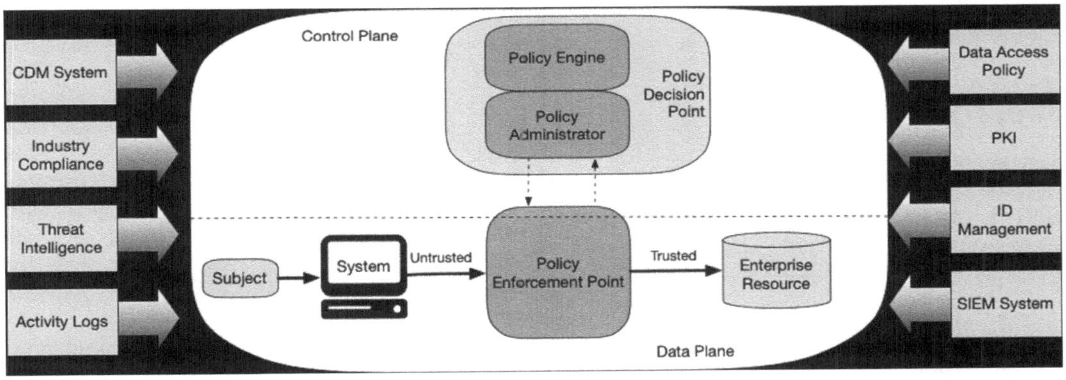

Figure 7.17: *NIST core zero trust logical components*[54]

Like the SDP architecture, the NIST ZTA also elaborates on topological models of ZTA. Cybersecurity and Infrastructure Security Agency (CISA) presents a maturity model[55] for the Zero Trust Architecture adoption. As per the model, **Identity**, **Devices**, **Networks**, **Applications & Workloads**, and **Data** are the building pillars for the enterprise. Those are to be considered under these cross-cutting capabilities: **Visibility and Analytics**, **Automation and Orchestration**, and **Governance**.

53 Zero Trust Architecture, NIST Special Publication 800-207, August 2020

54 Figure 2, ibid.

55 Zero Trust Maturity Model, CISA, April 2023

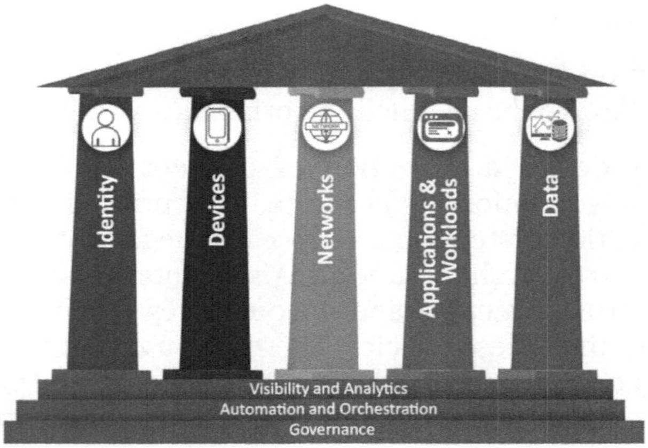

Figure 7.18: CISA ZTA *maturity model components*[56]

There are four levels of maturity discussed as part of the model:

- Traditional
- Initial
- Advanced
- Optimal

The Identity pillar includes the following functional decompositions:

- Authentication
- Identity stores
- Risk assessment
- Access management
- Visibility and analytics capability
- Automation and orchestration capability
- Governance capability

Controls are defined against each functional characteristic for the classification under the maturity levels. For authentication, at a traditional maturity level, one of the password or multifactor authentication technologies can be used. The agency may include locale or activity-based authentication at an initial maturity level. Similarly, the agency can consider phishing-resistant FIDO2 or PIV cards as authentication mechanisms to achieve an advanced level of maturity. Continuous authentication will provide an optimal level of ZT maturity.

56 Figure 1, Ibid.

To summarize, irrespective of how the access management and architectures change, the Zero Trust principles will always consider Identity a central piece of the paradigm. While we discussed the theoretical principles and architectures for Zero Trust, such systems require massive peer-to-peer encrypted networks for communication. Client-to-gateway-to-client architectures may need peer nodes on every network element connecting to other ends using mTLS connections for the data network. Open-source technologies like Wireguard[57] are becoming the backbones of upcoming next-generation access management tools.

Conclusion

We discussed a few trends in user authentication. However, we did not explicitly talk about the effect of artificial intelligence (AI). AI has been the new electricity affecting almost every field. All biometric inference networks are on Machine Learning (ML) principles. We did not talk much about passwordless authentication in future trends because we have discussed that as part of WebAuthn. Passwordless authentication schemes include local biometry validation on desktops, laptops, or mobile devices. In technology, predicting future trends is like soothsaying and is best avoided. We have discussed technologies that are being adopted by the vendors who are supplying user authentication solutions and products. There are 200+ multi-factor authentication products[58] in the market. There has been an explosion of IAM and associated products, yet, it is not a mature market because there has been a continuous infusion of new ideas and concepts and newer application landscapes. Technology companies are refreshing older technologies and introducing newer ones. For example, network integration technologies like RADIUS have taken a backseat, and web-based authentication frameworks are central to all authentication platforms. Manual identity proofing has almost shifted to complete automation or assistive technologies. Again, we have discussed the application of technologies and kept academic research outside of this book. We hope we did justice in introducing you to the overall authentication landscape. Every field we explained here has a lot of research, policies, and documentation available to explore. We suggest you expand your horizons per your needs and interests.

57 Wireguard, **https://www.wireguard.com/**

58 Best Multi-Factor Authentication (MFA) Software, G2, **https://www.g2.com/categories/multi-factor-authentication-mfa#grid**

Questions

1. Design an identity wallet to keep multiple certificates on a mobile device. How will you authenticate using the wallet?
2. In *Chapter 6: Multifactor Authentication*, we developed a sample application for TOTP and WebAuthn. Extend the sample application to include a 1:1 face verification for authentication.
3. Study some anti-spoofing mechanisms and analyze how to incorporate them into your face authentication system.
4. Set up a TLS server using Open Quantum-Safe enabled OpenSSL server. Now, connect to it from a compliant client.
5. Review the network access of servers in your organization and propose how to bring zero trust access to such an environment.

Appendix A

The Go Programming Language Reference

Introduction

In this appendix, we introduce some salient features of the Go programming language. People conversant with the language may skip. Most of our examples are simple and cater to the needs of a new programmer. We will focus on aspects we have used in this book.

Installation

1. Go to **https://go.dev/dl/**
2. Download the package relevant to your operating system.
3. Follow the installation instructions on the web page **https://go.dev/doc/install** for the operating system of your choice.

The Go Play Ground

The Go language maintainers provide a website to run simple Go programs and learn the language quickly. It is called The Go Playground. You can access it at **https://go.dev/play**. The following pieces of code are already available as examples in the playground. You may have to modify them at places as suggested in this appendix.

Hello World

It is a simple piece of code that prints a Unicode string. The code is available as an example in the Go Playground.

```
package main
import "fmt"
func main() {
	fmt.Println("Hello, 世界")
}
```

We use a function **Println** that is defined in the library **fmt**. So, we had to import it.

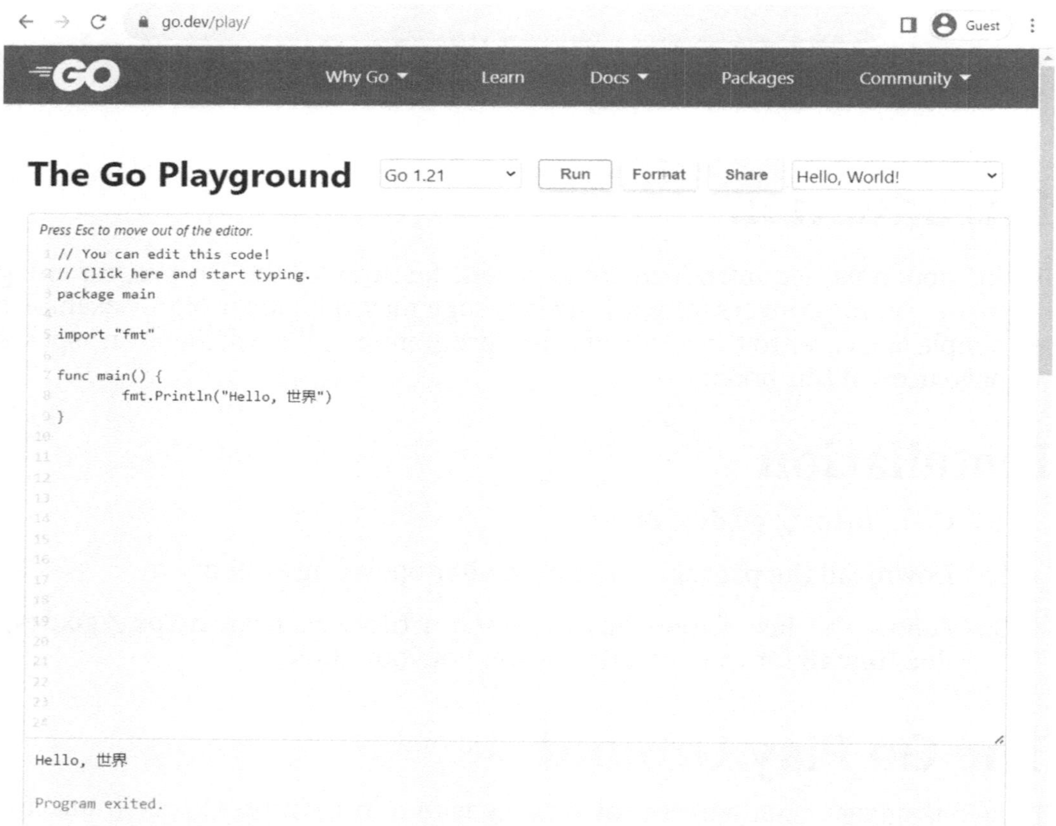

Figure A.1: *Hello World example on Go Playground*

We modify the previous code slightly and introduce a simple function next.

Simple function

We add two integers in a function and invoke it from the **main** method.

```
package main
import "fmt"
func sum(a, b int) int {
	return a + b
}
func main() {
	fmt.Println(sum(1, 2))
}
```

This prints 3 in when run. We can also define sum() inside the main() function.

```
func main() {
	var sum func(int, int) int
	sum = func(a, b int) int {
		return a + b
	}
	fmt.Println(sum(1, 2))
}
```

sum is not a function. It is a variable that is assigned an anonymous function. You can declare and assign in one compact statement with `:=`.

```
func main() {
	sum := func(a, b int) int {
		return a + b
	}
	fmt.Println(sum(1, 2))
}
```

Closure

In the playground, select the **Fibonacci Closure** code. A function defines a variable and returns a function. When the returned function is invoked, the variable is manipulated. The concept is called a closure. The behavior is similar to using static variables. With closures, you can create complex constructs.

```
// fib returns a function that returns
// successive Fibonacci numbers.
func fib() func() int {
	a, b := 0, 1
	return func() int {
		a, b = b, a+b
		return a
	}
}
func main() {
	f := fib()
	// Function calls are evaluated left-to-right.
	fmt.Println(f(), f(), f(), f(), f())
}
```

This prints **1 1 2 3 5**. Every time you call **f()**, the values of **a** and **b** change.

HTTP server

In the Go playground, select **HTTP Server**.

We use the **net/http** package to start an HTTP server.

```
package main
import (
	"fmt"
	"io"
	"log"
	"net"
	"net/http"
	"os"
)
```

We create a handler for the server to listen on. The handler runs at the endpoint **/hello**.

```
func main() {
	http.HandleFunc("/hello", func(w http.ResponseWriter, r *http.
Request) {
		fmt.Fprint(w, "Hello, playground")
	})
```

We create a listener that runs at port 8080.

```
	log.Println("Starting server...")
	l, err := net.Listen("tcp", "localhost:8080")
	if err != nil {
		log.Fatal(err)
	}
```

We spawn another Golang lightweight process and run the HTTP server listening on port 8080. The server keeps running in the background but relinquishes the control for the client code to run next.

```
	go func() {
		log.Fatal(http.Serve(l, nil))
	}()

	log.Println("Sending request...")
```

We contact the server using a client call. Go client calls and waits for the response to arrive.

```
	res, err := http.Get("http://localhost:8080/hello")
	if err != nil {
		log.Fatal(err)
	}
```

We copy the response body to the standard output.

```
	log.Println("Reading response...")
	if _, err := io.Copy(os.Stdout, res.Body); err != nil {
		log.Fatal(err)
	}
}
```

We see **Hello, playground** as the output. What happens when another client contacts the server at the **/hello** endpoint?

The HTTP server spawns another lightweight process and runs the registered handler. The implementation of **net/http** module takes care of the management of connection handlers. Thus, one client accessing the server does not stop another client from accessing it.

Built-in data types

Like other programming languages, Go has several **built-in** data types. We state only a few that we have used in this book.

- **int**: Integral numbers like **1, 35, -45, 0,** etc.
  - They can be further classified as signed, unsigned, and with bit sizes, like, **int32**, **uint32**, **int64**, **uint8**, etc.
- **float**: Floating point numbers like **0.0, 1.0e6, 3.2e-6, -5.4,** etc.
  - Floating point numbers can have bit sizes specified, like, **float32**, **float64**, etc.
- **string**: Text strings are represented between two double quotes, like, **"Hello World."** Multiline preformatted text can be written within backticks (**`**) as shown:

  ```
  fmt.Println(` This is
      a multiline text
  formatting is preserved.`)
  ```

- **bool**: Boolean data type. It can be either **true** or **false**. These variables are used extensively in conditions and branching.
- **rune**: it is a 32-bit integer data type used to represent character values. **'a', 'b', '5',** etc. are runes.

Variables

Variables can be declared as shown:

```
var i int
i = 10
```

or

```
i := 10
```

Even functions can be assigned to variables. Please review the preceding **Closure** example.

By default, a zero value is assigned to a variable.

Pointers

We want to change the value of a parameter passed to a function. We introduce a function **incr** which increments the input parameter by one.

```
package main
import "fmt"
func incr(a *int) {
        *a++
}
func main() {
        i := 3
        incr(&i)
        fmt.Println(i)
}
```

4 will be printed.

a in the function is a pointer of type **int**. To the function, we pass the address of **i**; the value of **i** gets incremented.

A pointer variable is assigned a **nil** value by default.

Global vs. local

When variables by the same name are declared in multiple scopes, the variable in the current scope is used.

```
var i = 4
func main() {
        i := 3
        fmt.Println(i)
}
```

3 will be the output from this code.

Control flow

Like most structured programming languages, Golang supports many control flow primitives. We start with the conditional **if…else** loop.

```
func main() {
	i := 5
	k := 0
	if i < 1 {
		k = 1
	} else if i < 10 {
		k = 2
	} else {
		k = 3
	}
	fmt.Println(k)
}
```

The output is **2**.

switch is a compact way of representing a long **if…else** loop.

```
func main() {
	switch i := 3; i {
	case 1:
		fmt.Println("One")
	case 2:
		fmt.Println("Two")
	default:
		fmt.Println("Default")
	}

	for i := 0; i < 10; i++ {
		fmt.Printf("%d ", i)
	}
}
```

i defined in the **switch** statement is not available to the **for** loop. As expected, this code will print the following output.

```
Default
0 1 2 3 4 5 6 7 8 9
```

The **for** loop has other forms that can behave like a **while** loop of other languages. Golang has no **while** keyword.

```
func main() {
	i := 0
	for i < 10 {
		fmt.Printf("%d ", i)
		i++
	}
}
```

What about **do...while** loop of other languages? We will emulate the same using a **for** loop. The previous loop can be rewritten as shown.

```
func main() {
	i := 0
	for ok := true; ok; ok = (i < 10) {
		fmt.Printf("%d ", i)
		i++
	}
}
```

You can use a **break** to terminate a **for** loop. The following code does the same task as the previous one. We use **break** to end the infinite **for** loop.

```
func main() {
	i := 0
	for {
		if i >= 10 {
			break
		}
		fmt.Printf("%d ", i)
		i++
	}
}
```

Error handling

Other programming languages provide specialized control flows for error handling. Golang does not provide any such control flows. The errors are returned as additional values in functions. Let us review it with some examples. A **map** is an inbuilt data type in Golang that maps one value to another. In the following example, we map a **string** to an **int**.

```
func main() {
	m := map[string]int{"one": 1, "two": 2, "three": 3}
	str := "two"
	if v, ok := m[str]; !ok {
		fmt.Printf("Mapping for %s not found.", str)
	} else {
		fmt.Printf("Mapping for %s is %d", str, v)
	}
}
```

Accessing **m[str]** returns values **v** and **ok**. **v** contains the mapped value and **ok** is **true** if a mapping exists and **false** when no mapping exists. If we use the expression **v := m["two"], v** will be assigned **2.** If we want to collect the value of **ok** only, we can use the expression: **_, ok := m["two"].** We realize multiple values can be returned and apply the same principles to a function.

```
package main
import (
	"fmt"
	"math"
)
func mysqrt(a float64) (float64, error) {
	if a < 0 {
		return 0.0, fmt.Errorf("No square root for negative 
numbers: %f", a)
	} else {
		return math.Sqrt(a), nil
	}
}
func main() {
	a := -36.0
	if sa, err := mysqrt(a); err != nil {
		fmt.Println(err)
	} else {
		fmt.Println(sa)
	}
}
```

In the preceding function **mysqrt()** , we returned two values; one for success with the actual square root, and the other value has the error information. In the main function, we take the appropriate action based on the error. Golang functions have a substantial portion of the code handling errors from called methods.

User-defined data types

When you must describe a complete record, simple built-in types may not be sufficient. Let us define a **Rectangle** structure.

```
type Rectangle struct {
	a, b float64
}
func Square(a float64) *Rectangle {
	return &Rectangle{a: a, b: a}
}
func main() {
	r := Square(5)
	fmt.Println(r)
}
```

We defined a **Rectangle** with two sides as **float64**. The function **Square()** takes a parameter of one side and constructs a special constrained **Rectangle**. So **Square** is a constructor for a **Rectangle** object. Constructor is a function that instantiates a new object and returns the pointer to the object.

```
func (r Rectangle) Area() float64 {
	return r.a * r.b
}
func (r *Rectangle) Set(a, b float64) {
	r.a = a
	r.b = b
}
func main() {
	r := Square(5)
	fmt.Println(r)
	fmt.Printf("Area: %f\n", r.Area())
	r.Set(5, 6)
```

```
        fmt.Println(r)
}
```

We added an **Area()** method to the **Rectangle**. We added a **Set()** method that can change the sides of the **Rectangle**. For a method to change the values of a type, the method must be defined for the pointer type.

```
type Ranges float64
func (r Ranges) String() string {
        if r < 0 {
                return "small"
        } else if r < 100 {
                return "medium"
        } else {
                return "large"
        }
}
func main() {
        r := Ranges(1000.0)
        fmt.Println(r)
}
```

We have decomposed the floating-point range into three parts and will output it based on the value. We create a new type **Ranges** based on **float64**. We have defined the **String** method for it. When the object is printed the **Ranges.String()** method is called. While **String()** is used to export values from a user-defined type, sometimes we need to export the values as JSON objects. We take the same **Rectangle** example and convert it to JSON.

```
import (
        "encoding/json"
        "fmt"
        "os"
)
type Rectangle struct {
        W float64 `json:"width"`
        H float64 `json:"height"`
}
func main() {
```

```
        r := Rectangle{W: 5, H: 6}
        fmt.Println(r)
        if js, err := json.Marshal(&r); err == nil {
                os.Stdout.Write(js)
        }
}
```

While defining the Rectangle we annotate that during conversion to JSON, the parameter **W** will be named as **"width"** and the parameter **H** will be named as **"height."** We marshal the structure using the method **json.Marshal()**. The output is as shown:

```
{5 6}
{"width":5,"height":6}
```

Interface

Let us look at the following code:

```
package main
import (
        "fmt"
        "math"
)
type NumberError struct {
        A float64
}
func (e NumberError) Error() string {
        return fmt.Sprintf("The number is negative: %f", e.A)
}

func mysqrt(a float64) (float64, error) {
        if a < 0 {
                return 0.0, NumberError{a}
        } else {
                return math.Sqrt(a), nil
        }
}
```

```
func main() {
	a := -36.0
	if sa, err := mysqrt(a); err != nil {
		fmt.Println(err)
	} else {
		fmt.Println(sa)
	}
}
```

The output is:

```
The number is negative: -36.000000
```

We define a new type **NumberError**. We define a function **Error()** for the type. With these changes, we can use an instance of **NumberError** for the return type **error**. **error** is an interface defined as shown:

```
type error interface{
	Error() string
}
```

A type implements an interface when it has all the methods of the interface defined for it. Here **NumberError** has the method **Error()** defined for it. Hence, **NumberError** implements the **error** interface.

Exporting methods and variables

Every function or variable defined in a package is visible within the package. However, when you define a function or variable with the first letter capitalized, it is exported. Such a function or variable can be accessed from outside the package. Here are some examples of exported symbols.

```
package main
import (
	"fmt"
	"howa.in/geom"
)
func main() {
	r := geom.Rectangle{A: 5.0, B: 6.0}
	fmt.Println(r.A, " ", r.B)
}
-- go.mod --
module howa.in
```

```
-- geom/geom.go --
package geom
var A = 5
type Rectangle struct {
	A, B float64
}
```

The symbols **A** and **Rectangle** can be accessed outside of the package **geom**. If you instantiate an object of type **Rectangle**, you can access its members as well in another package **main**. This code will output:

```
5   6
```

If you have **Rectangle** defined with parameters in lowercase **a** and **b**, you cannot access them from the package **main**. However, you can define a constructor for Rectangle objects.

```
package main

import (
	"fmt"

	"howa.in/geom"
)

func main() {
	r := geom.NewRectangle(5, 6)
	fmt.Println(r)
}
-- go.mod --
module howa.in
-- geom/geom.go --
package geom
var A = 5
type Rectangle struct {
	a, b float64
}
func NewRectangle(a, b float64) *Rectangle {
	return &Rectangle{a: 5.0, b: 6.0}
}
```

The Go playground can run a multifile code. You specify a new file by providing the name of the file delimited by two dashes (--).

Resolving package dependencies

Note

This example must be run locally on a desktop or laptop. You should not run it on the Go Playground. You need to install the Golang development environment.

In the folder **appendix-a**, try to run the sample code **sudoku.go**[1] with the command: **go run ./sudoku.go**. The execution will fail with the following error:

```
sudoku.go:6:2: no required module provides package github.com/gonutz/sudoku: go.mod file not found in current directory or any parent directory; see 'go help modules'
```

Modules provide an easy way to create package dependencies.

1. We will create a module with the command: **go mod init howa.in/sudoku**
2. Resolve the package dependencies using the command: **go mod tidy**
3. If you run the code using: **go run ./sudoku.go**, you will see the following output.

```
631 784 925
894 265 713
527 913 684

965 427 138
712 836 459
483 159 276

378 692 541
256 341 897
149 578 362 <nil>
```

1 This is the example code of the package **gonutz/sudoku** **https://pkg.go.dev/github.com/gonutz/sudoku**

We see two files:

- `go.mod`: has the direct package dependencies and version dependency on Golang.
- `go.sum`: has the indirect package dependencies with version information.

Conclusion

We just scratched the surface of the programming language. There are deeper concepts and constructs available with the language. Refer to the Golang documentation at: **https://go.dev/doc/** for a detailed understanding of the language.

Appendix B
The Flutter Application Framework

Introduction

In this appendix, we introduce some salient features of the Flutter Application Framework. People conversant with the framework may skip. Most of our examples are simple and cater to the needs of a new programmer. We will focus on aspects we have used in this book. Flutter helps you build applications for Windows, Linux, Mac OS, iOS, Android, and the Web. Most of our samples in this book are built for the web platform.

Installation

1. Go to **https://docs.flutter.dev/get-started/install.**
2. Download the package relevant to your operating system.
3. Follow the installation instructions on the web page for the operating system of your choice.

DartPad

The Dart programming language is used to develop in Flutter Application Framework. The maintainers of the Dart programming environment provide

DartPad, a web-based IDE to try the Dart code and test their results. This environment accepts Flutter UI code and displays the output side-by-side. For this appendix, you can use that environment. Flutter development may require you to understand a variety of concepts. We will discuss some of them in this chapter.

As a programming language, Dart is structurally comparable to other front-end development languages like **JavaScript** or **TypeScript**. If you are familiar with them, you will find similar concepts here. Hence, we will not delve much into the syntax and semantics of the language but focus on a few sample programs available at **https://dartpad.dev**.

Hello World

On DartPad, select the sample **Hello World**. You will see the following piece of code.

```
void main() {
  for (var i = 0; i < 4; i++) {
    print('hello $i');
  }
}
```

Dart's entry point is a **main** function. Here we print hello four times in a loop as shown.

```
hello 0
hello 1
hello 2
hello 3
```

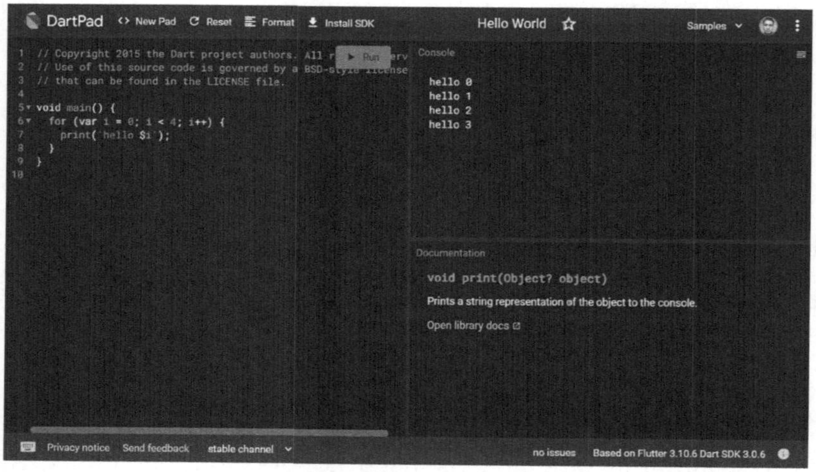

Figure B.1: Hello World in DartPad

The **print()** function takes a string in this case. The string can be quoted in a single quote (') or double quote ("). A variable with **$** is computed and the value is embedded in the string. This is called **interpolation**. You can also interpolate an expression like **${2*i}**. The expression must appear within curly braces. **var i = 0** initializes a variable for the **for** loop. The variable **i** is not visible outside of the **for** loop.

Fibonacci function

On DartPad, select the **Fibonacci** sample. The code is presented as follows:

```
void main() {
  var i = 20;
  print('fibonacci($i) = ${fibonacci(i)}');
}
/// Computes the nth Fibonacci number.
int fibonacci(int n) {
  return n < 2 ? n : (fibonacci(n - 1) + fibonacci(n - 2));
}
```

It outputs the 20th number from the Fibonacci series.

```
fibonacci(20) = 6765
```

The **fibonacci** function is recursive. We also see the ternary (**?:**) operator here. String interpolation is used to create the output for printing.

Futures

In the browsers, the front-end JavaScript code runs as a single thread. However, there are code blocks that contact the back-end REST APIs. Those can block the execution of the user interface and provide an unacceptable user experience. A cooperative multitasking framework has been introduced in JavaScript (Promise) to address this. The framework is called a Future in Dart. We will review Futures in this section.

```
Future<int> delay(int id) {
  return Future.delayed(const Duration(seconds: 1), () {
    print('id: $id');
    return id;
  });
}
```

In the function **delay**, we have an identifier (**id**) as an argument. The code calls the system method **Future.delayed**. **Future.delayed**, waits for a second, prints the **id**, and returns the value of the **id**. The returned value is wrapped inside a **Future<int>** as **id** is of type **int**. A **Future** returned essentially means the execution is not over yet. However, if you want to wait for the execution to be over, you can invoke a **then** function on it and compute the subsequent step inside the argument function. The result wrapped in the **Future** is the argument to the function parameter in the **then** method.

```
Future<int> delayGroup(int id) {
  return delay(id).then((i) {
    return delay(i + 1);
  }).then((i) {
    return delay(i + 1);
  }).then((i) {
    return delay(i + 1);
  });
}
```

In the preceding function, we have taken four **delay()** functions and chained them with **then()**. The output of the previous method is incremented by one and passed to the subsequent **delay()** function. All these evaluations should happen in series, yet we do not want the execution to halt for 4s. We invoke the **delayGroup()** function twice, once with id **10** and another time with the id of **20**.

```
void main() {
  delayGroup(10);
  delayGroup(20);
}
```

The output is as follows:

```
id: 10
id: 20
id: 11
id: 21
id: 12
id: 22
id: 13
id: 23
```

The execution can be explained by the following illustration.

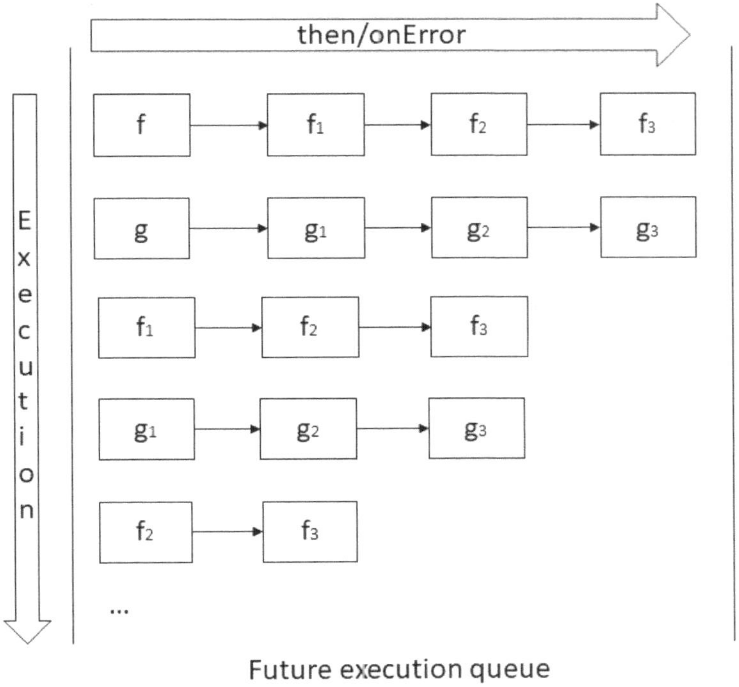

***Figure B.2**: Futures are placed on a queue. Execution is carried out by one **then** block at a time*

In this case, two future chains are executing, for example, **f** and **g**. Once f is executed the next in the **then** block is placed in the execution queue. So instead of executing $\mathbf{f_1}$, **g** is executed. Similarly, after **g** is executed, $\mathbf{g_1}$ is placed in the queue, and so on. This way **f** and **g** run in parallel, yielding to each other at every **then** block. Some people find this syntax cumbersome. Hence, Dart (also JavaScript) provides an **async/await** notation for the same. Here is **delayGroup()** with **async/await** syntax.

```
Future<int> delayGroupAsync(int id) async {
  var i = await delay(id);
  i = await delay(i + 1);
  i = await delay(i + 1);
  i = await delay(i + 1);
  return i;
}
```

Just like **then()** for successful execution, you can add a **catchError()** method to handle exceptions with **Future**.

HTTP Requests

On DartPad, select the **HTTP Requests** sample code.

```
import 'dart:convert' as convert;
import 'package:http/http.dart' as http;
void main(List<String> arguments) async {
  // This example uses the Google Books API to search
  // for books about HTTP. For details, see
  // https://developers.google.com/books/docs/overview
  final url = Uri.https(
    'www.googleapis.com',
    '/books/v1/volumes',
    {'q': '{http}'},
  );
  // Await the HTTP GET response, then decode the
  // JSON data it contains.
  final response = await http.get(url);
  if (response.statusCode == 200) {
    final jsonResponse = convert.jsonDecode(response.body);
    final itemCount = jsonResponse['totalItems'];
    print('Number of books about HTTP: $itemCount.');
  } else {
    print('Request failed with status: ${response.statusCode}.');
  }
}
```

We access the Google Books API to download information regarding the books on HTTP. The downloaded data is in JSON format. We convert the JSON data to equivalent Dart constructs and access the total number of books. Since the data is dynamic, the results may vary from the data reported in the book.

```
Number of books about HTTP: 2395.
```

Here are the steps taken by the code:

- We form a URI for the API.

- We request async **`http.get()`** on the URL.
- On successful completion of the get request, we convert the request body to a dictionary by using the **`jsonDecode`** function.
- We read the number of books in the result from the dictionary.

User interface

The Flutter framework is a representation of the MVVM architecture. You can think of the client Flutter code as a View that updates on changes with the View Model represented by a REST API.

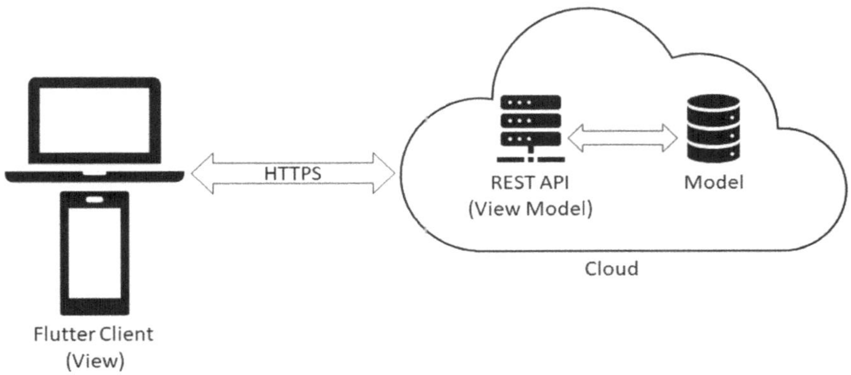

***Figure B.3**: Flutter client in the MVVM architecture*

If you look at the examples discussed in the book, we have used the MVVM architecture extensively. The REST APIs are in the Golang in these examples. The flutter code accesses the REST API using the **`http.get`** method or the **`HttpClient`** object. We will focus on the client-side rendering code in the following sections.

Stateless vs stateful widgets

Unlike MVC architectures, where the view gets updated based on a trigger from the controller, a change in the view model rebuilds the views in MVVM architectures. When we talk about building the UI, it is not always that every UI internal component is redrawn from scratch. The framework has avenues to track changes and reconstruct where necessary. However, from a code standpoint, the **`build`** method is invoked several times.

A UI element in Flutter is a Widget. Pretty much everything is a widget. It starts with an application at the highest level to a static text widget at the lowest level.

A **StatelessWidget** has no state information. It is instantiated by the framework and built. For any reason, if you refresh the widget, you will have to rebuild it again. At the highest level, the application is a **StatelessWidget**, that instantiates a **MaterialApp**. The **MaterialApp** does not have any state information but has configuration and style information only. The app has a home page or the first screen to be shown.

```
import 'package:flutter/material.dart';
void main() => runApp(MyApp());
class MyApp extends StatelessWidget {
  @override
  Widget build(BuildContext context) {
    return MaterialApp(
      title: 'Flutter Demo',
      debugShowCheckedModeBanner: false,
      theme: ThemeData(
        colorScheme: ColorScheme.fromSeed(seedColor: Colors.deepPurple),
        useMaterial3: true,
      ),
      home: const MyHomePage(title: 'Flutter Demo Home Page'),
    );
  }
}
```

The app instantiates a **MyHomePage** class. This class builds all the visible UI. The visible UI has the following components:

- An application toolbar containing a title.
- The body area shows a numeric counter.
- A floating button, when clicked, increments a number shown in the body area.

Hence, the class has a state of a numeric counter. When the numeric counter changes, we need to update the user interface.

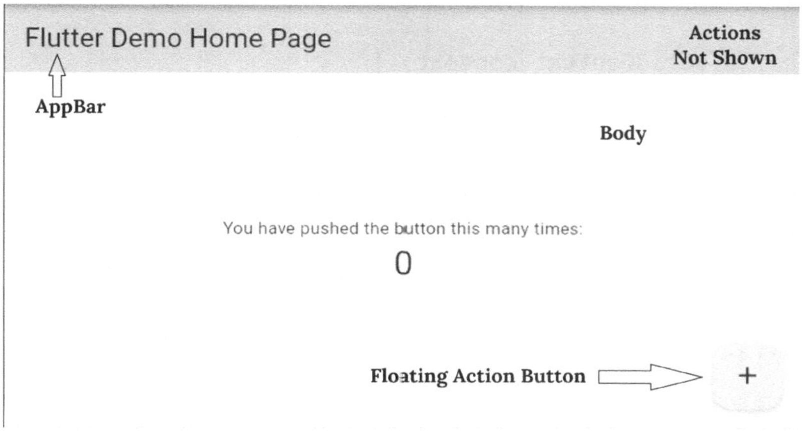

***Figure B.4**: Scaffold widget and its components*

Hence, we create **MyHomePage** as a **StatefulWidget**. A **StatefulWidget** has an associated **State** object that will maintain the counter. When the value of the counter changes, the **setState** method is invoked; it builds the **StatefulWidget**.

```
class MyHomePage extends StatefulWidget {
  final String title;
  const MyHomePage({
    Key? key,
    required this.title,
  }) : super(key: key);
  @override
  State<MyHomePage> createState() => _MyHomePageState();
}
```

The associated **_MyHomePageState** class has a **_counter** member. Clicking on the floating action button invokes the **_incrementCounter()** method. **setState()** method updates the **_counter** member. The UI reflects the new value of the **_counter** on rebuild.

```
class _MyHomePageState extends State<MyHomePage> {
  int _counter = 0;
  void _incrementCounter() {
    setState(() {
      _counter++;
    });
  }
```

```
  @override
  Widget build(BuildContext context) {
    return Scaffold(
      appBar: AppBar(
        backgroundColor: Theme.of(context).colorScheme.inversePrimary,
        title: Text(widget.title),
      ),
      body: Center(
        child: Column(
          mainAxisAlignment: MainAxisAlignment.center,
          children: [
            const Text(
              'You have pushed the button this many times:',
            ),
            Text(
              '$_counter',
              style: Theme.of(context).textTheme.headlineMedium,
            ),
          ],
        ),
      ),
      floatingActionButton: FloatingActionButton(
        onPressed: _incrementCounter,
        tooltip: 'Increment',
        child: const Icon(Icons.add),
      ),
    );
  }
}
```

When a lot of data changes in a localized part of a UI due to a change in a view model, **StatefulWidgets** are very useful. What about the cases where a view model affects small changes at various parts of UI? For example, the user has added new items to the shopping cart, a new message has come, and so on. Change notifications are ideal for such scenarios.

Providers and change notifications

We reimplement the previous example using **StatelessWidget** and **ChangeNotifier**. We retain the state of the counter outside the UI widget and associate it with the application. We associate a change notifier with the state of the counter so that the UI that needs an update can be notified.

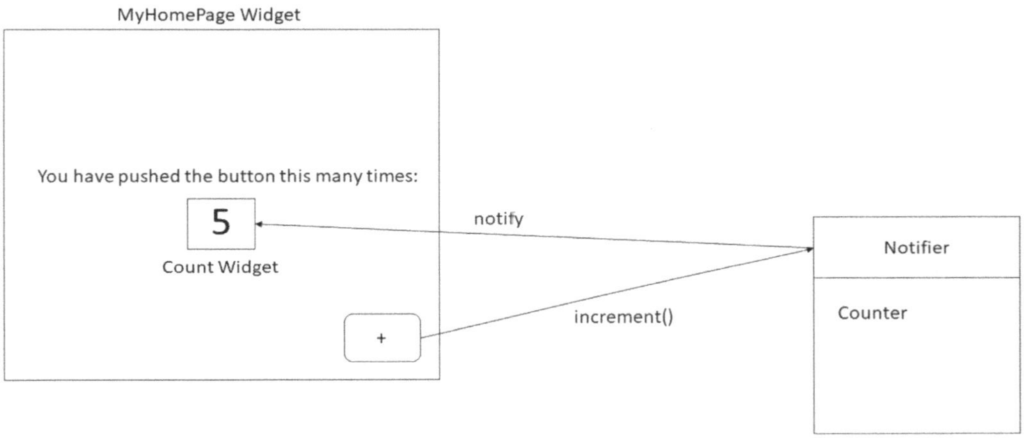

***Figure B.5**: Change notifier in action*

Here are some of the proposed changes:

- Since there is no state information with the widgets, all the UI widgets are stateless.
- We introduce a new Count widget that listens for updates when the counter increments.
- The floating button widget will send the notifier an increment message.
- The notifier will notify the Count widget of the incremented counter.

How can the widgets find the notifier object? Who maintains the lifecycle of the notifier object? The application object holds a **ChangeNotifierProvider** that can provide access to the **ChangeNotifier**.

```
import 'package:flutter/material.dart';
import 'package:provider/provider.dart';
void main() {
  runApp(
    MultiProvider(
      providers: [
```

```
        ChangeNotifierProvider(create: (context) => Counter()),
      ],
      child: const MyApp(),
    ),
  );
}
```

The **Counter** class is the **ChangeNotifier**.

```
class Counter with ChangeNotifier {
  int _count = 0;
  int get count => _count;
  void increment() {
    _count++;
    notifyListeners();
  }
}
```

There is hardly any change to the **MyApp** class.

```
class MyApp extends StatelessWidget {
  const MyApp({Key? key}) : super(key: key);
  @override
  Widget build(BuildContext context) {
    return MaterialApp(
      theme: ThemeData(
        colorSchemeSeed: Colors.blue,
        useMaterial3: true,
      ),
      home: const MyHomePage(),
    );
  }
}
```

MyHomePage is a **StatelessWidget**. It instantiates the **Scaffold** class.

```
class MyHomePage extends StatelessWidget {
  const MyHomePage({Key? key}) : super(key: key);
  @override
  Widget build(BuildContext context) {
```

```
    return Scaffold(
      appBar: AppBar(
        title: const Text('Provider example'),
      ),
      body: const Center(
        child: Column(
          mainAxisSize: MainAxisSize.min,
          mainAxisAlignment: MainAxisAlignment.center,
          children: <Widget>[
            Text('You have pushed the button this many times:'),
            Count(),
          ],
        ),
      ),
      floatingActionButton: FloatingActionButton(
        key: const Key('increment_floatingActionButton'),

        onPressed: () => context.read<Counter>().increment(),
        tooltip: 'Increment',
        child: const Icon(Icons.add),
      ),
    );
  }
}
```

There are two significant changes:

- There is a **Count** class instantiated in the body for showing the counter value.
- The **onPressed** method of the floating action button. The method invokes **context.read<Counter>()**. The notifier is searched from the widget hierarchy and the **increment** method is invoked on the notifier object. The **read** method ensures the widget only sends messages to the notifier and does not listen to the notifier updates.

The following code describes the **Count** class:

```
class Count extends StatelessWidget {
  const Count({Key? key}) : super(key: key);
  @override
  Widget build(BuildContext context) {
    return Text(
      '${context.watch<Counter>().count}',
      key: const Key('counterState'),
      style: Theme.of(context).textTheme.headlineMedium,
    );
  }
}
```

context.watch<Counter>() ensures the **Count** widget listens to notifications from the **Counter** notifier. When the count is incremented, the **Count** widget is only rebuilt. The other widgets are not updated. There are other concepts like **Consumer** which also can be used to listen to notifiers. We have used some of them in the examples.

Conclusion

We scratched the surface of the Flutter framework in this appendix, the bare minimum knowledge needed in Flutter to use this book. There are complex concepts and constructs available within the framework. Moreover, our focus was limited to building web applications using the framework. You can also develop platform native applications using the framework. Refer to the Flutter documentation at: **https://docs.flutter.dev/** for a detailed understanding. You may also refer to: **https://dart.dev/guides** for information on the Dart language.

Appendix C
TLS Certificate Creation

Introduction

In *Chapter 3: Authentication with Network Security*, we discussed certificate chains for TLS servers and clients. In this appendix, we provide the OpenSSL commands to create such certificates. We use an intermediate CA to sign the leaf certificate for the server. We use the root CA to sign the intermediate CA. The chain of trust is in *Figure 3.6: Server certificate hierarchy*.

Root certificate

The root CA is a self-signed certificate. While there are other quick ways to create self-signing certificates in OpenSSL[1], we use a similar process for all certificates. First launch OpenSSL with the **`openssl`** command and enter the OpenSSL command mode. On the **`OpenSSL>`** prompt:

1. Generate a Certificate Signing Request (CSR) along with generating an RSA-keypair.

   ```
   req -newkey rsa:2048 -days 365 -config ssl.cfg -keyout sroot.key
   -out sroot.csr
   ```

---

1 The samples are developed using OpenSSL 1.1.1

The file **sroot.csr** has the CSR for the certificate and **sroot.key** has the private key. The command will prompt for a password to protect the private key. The file **ssl.cfg** has the configurations needed for OpenSSL. We use the following file:

```
[root@controller certs_x509]# cat openssl.cnf
[ req ]
distinguished_name = req_distinguished_name
policy             = policy_match
x509_extensions = v3_ext

# For the CA policy
[ policy_match ]
countryName                = optional
stateOrProvinceName        = optional
organizationName           = optional
organizationalUnitName     = optional
commonName                 = supplied
emailAddress               = optional

[ req_distinguished_name ]
countryName                     = Country Name (2 letter code)
countryName_default             = IN
countryName_min                 = 2
countryName_max                 = 2
stateOrProvinceName             = State or Province Name (full
name) ## Print this message
stateOrProvinceName_default     = KA ## This is the default value
localityName                    = Locality Name (eg, city) ##
Print this message
localityName_default            = BANGALORE ## This is the
default value
0.organizationName              = Organization Name (eg, company)
## Print this message
0.organizationName_default      = HOWA ## This is the default
value
organizationalUnitName          = Organizational Unit Name (eg,
section) ## Print this message
```

```
organizationalUnitName_default  = Server Root ## This is the
default value
commonName                      = Common Name (eg, your name or
your server hostname) ## Print this message
commonName_max                  = 64
emailAddress                    = Email Address ## Print this
message
emailAddress_max                = 64

[v3_ext]
subjectKeyIdentifier = hash
authorityKeyIdentifier = keyid:always,issuer
```

The file defines the policies for certificate generation, for example, the parameters that should be prompted to generate the CSR, the size of the parameters, etc.

2. Sign the CSR using the private key.

```
x509 -in sroot.csr -days 365 -signkey sroot.key -CAcreateserial
-out sroot.crt -extfile ca.ext -req
```

We use the private key to sign the CSR. We use a file **ca.ext** to add a few extension parameters. The **ca.ext** file is as shown:

```
basicConstraints = critical,CA:true
```

3. Annotate the certificate with the textual content for readability.

```
x509 -in sroot.crt -text -out sroot.annot.crt
```

The file **sroot.annot.crt** has all the text content of the root certificate.

```
Certificate:
    Data:
        Version: 3 (0x2)
        Serial Number:

6b:2e:e7:96:f2:fb:da:55:74:73:23:fe:a2:a4:02:36:f9:21:2e:8e
        Signature Algorithm: sha256WithRSAEncryption
        Issuer: C = IN, ST = KA, L = BANGALORE, O = HOWA, OU =
Server Root, CN = sroot
```

```
        Validity
            Not Before: Aug 13 17:32:01 2023 GMT
            Not After : Aug 12 17:32:01 2024 GMT
        Subject: C = IN, ST = KA, L = BANGALORE, O = HOWA, OU =
Server Root, CN = sroot
        Subject Public Key Info:
            Public Key Algorithm: rsaEncryption
                RSA Public-Key: (2048 bit)
                Modulus:
                    00:a9:f9:9b:d5:f6:62:cd:3a:08:64:4c:3e:42:1a:
                    f4:3a:f3:3a:6d:97:79:33:40:e3:50:e2:81:8f:ba:
                    d2:c7:31:eb:07:b5:87:ef:64:f2:f5:67:0e:8b:37:
                    f3:df:05:20:81:39:9b:0e:e6:e2:14:e8:7a:a3:a7:
                    2b:03:3a:0a:87:94:08:1e:4e:32:66:d0:e1:e5:5e:
                    21:1c:88:d0:ed:c3:75:65:a7:6d:e1:5f:e6:ee:b5:
                    1b:b2:e7:31:ce:ca:7d:48:7b:15:44:4d:f4:1f:3e:
                    5b:67:29:5d:e1:e2:db:67:2c:39:bc:b2:bc:a9:7c:
                    a4:9d:b6:0c:f3:50:b7:46:c9:06:65:c2:0a:bd:23:
                    df:94:41:0d:84:fc:96:73:36:38:2f:68:9d:13:f4:
                    a8:bc:e2:02:00:77:89:91:67:2e:e1:69:3a:e2:d1:
                    ed:b4:75:87:4a:22:f2:fb:49:8f:d7:86:df:d5:e6:
                    77:40:b1:70:7b:94:c6:dc:27:d5:b3:67:60:cb:d3:
                    50:22:0a:3f:9e:c2:96:f2:6a:47:a7:55:8c:fc:52:
                    e1:e7:38:92:30:3a:24:94:16:e2:53:e2:30:0c:94:
                    7f:5e:1d:83:ea:cc:9f:48:c3:40:06:5e:c8:7f:6c:
                    0e:e4:02:76:4a:e2:91:e0:2f:39:65:42:6d:9c:a7:
                    a8:1b
                Exponent: 65537 (0x10001)
        X509v3 extensions:
            X509v3 Basic Constraints: critical
                CA:TRUE
    Signature Algorithm: sha256WithRSAEncryption
         9a:d2:8f:d7:c5:36:4c:6b:25:f5:1d:7c:e1:05:fb:60:fd:74:
         63:b8:21:34:98:8d:2f:a4:3e:f2:35:60:4b:32:f4:63:5a:d4:
         5d:d4:08:32:a3:63:aa:d2:d2:aa:70:54:3f:2b:a1:40:f7:30:
```

```
            71:74:75:83:18:8a:ed:23:7f:12:5e:f2:56:06:35:cc:b4:1a:
            0c:b5:b0:32:67:07:67:c7:21:cd:97:8d:f6:b6:2c:c0:57:a0:
            45:a7:fd:08:70:09:d9:f0:e2:48:c6:f8:be:5c:ea:3d:16:ea:
            12:c6:ba:75:d5:70:7a:32:b5:cf:0a:ec:15:0f:b2:d9:6d:aa:
            5d:4a:94:58:11:2d:cc:5b:93:c9:39:41:a0:a9:ed:63:87:0d:
            33:bb:92:b3:b5:48:cf:f1:0d:94:73:74:54:e4:ca:db:ac:ee:
            7d:96:6d:89:b3:48:d2:4e:72:3d:dd:73:6d:3c:87:fd:32:b1:
            b7:05:ca:a6:e5:0f:18:50:a7:a2:d3:94:0b:6c:02:d9:0e:41:
            5a:34:e6:5a:65:ca:31:98:6c:ff:fa:6c:f2:0b:67:ca:36:f2:
            aa:52:cc:4f:7b:ba:e1:50:29:08:c6:a8:d5:eb:7d:c9:1d:81:
            cf:a4:f0:e4:1c:3b:6f:3a:34:00:2a:ee:22:8c:6e:ef:e7:8a:
            95:a4:55:53
-----BEGIN CERTIFICATE-----
MIIDZzCCAk+gAwIBAgIUay7nlvL72lV0cyP+oqQCNvkhLo4wDQYJKoZIhvcNAQEL
BQAwYzELMAkGA1UEBhMCSU4xCzAJBgNVBAgMAktBMRIwEAYDVQQHDAlCQU5HQUxP
UkUxDTALBgNVBAoMBEhPV0ExFDASBgNVBAsMC1NlcnZlciBSb290MQ4wDAYDVQQD
DAVzcm9vdDAeFw0yMzA4MTMxNzMyMDFaFw0yNDA4MTIxNzMyMDFaMGMxCzAJBgNV
BAYTAklOMQswCQYDVQQIDAJLQTESMBAGA1UEBwwJQkFOR0FMT1JFMQ0wCwYDVQQK
DARIT1dBMRQwEgYDVQQLDAtTZXJ2ZXIgUm9vdDEOMAwGA1UEAwwFc3Jvb3QwggEi
MA0GCSqGSIb3DQEBAQUAA4IBDwAwggEKAoIBAQCp+ZvV9mLNOghkTD5CGvQ68zpt
l3kzQONQ4oGPutLHMesHtYfvZPL1Zw6LN/PfBSCBOZsO5uIU6HqjpysDOgqHlAge
TjJm0OHlXiEciNDtw3Vlp23hX+butRuy5zHOyn1IexVETfQfPltnKV3h4ttnLDm8
srypfKSdtgzzULdGyQZlwgq9I9+UQQ2E/JZzNjgvaJ0T9Ki84gIAd4mRZy7haTri
0e20dYdKIvL7SY/Xht/V5ndAsXB7lMbcJ9WzZ2DL01AiCj+ewpbyakenVYz8UuHn
OJIwOiSUFuJT4jAMlH9eHYPqzJ9Iw0AGXsh/bA7kAnZK4pHgLzllQm2cp6gbAgMB
AAGjEzARMA8GA1UdEwEB/wQFMAMBAf8wDQYJKoZIhvcNAQELBQADggEBAJrSj9fF
NkxrJfUdfOEF+2D9dGO4ITSYjS+kPvI1YEsy9GNa1F3UCDKjY6rS0qpwVD8roUD3
MHF0dYMYiu0jfxJe8lYGNcy0Ggy1sDJnB2fHIc2Xjfa2LMBXoEWn/QhwCdnw4kjG
+L5c6j0W6hLGunXVcHoytc8K7BUPstltql1KlFgRLcxbk8k5QaCp7WOHDTO7krO1
SM/xDZRzdFTkytus7n2WbYmzSNJOcj3dc208h/0ysbcFyqblDxhQp6LTlAtsAtkO
QVo05lplyjGYbP/6bPILZ8o28qpSzE97uuFQKQjGqNXrfckdgc+k8OQcO286NAAq
7iKMbu/nipWkVVM=
-----END CERTIFICATE-----
```

The PEM-encoded certificate is placed within the beginning and end block markers. Anything outside of the block is taken as comments.

Intermediate CA

The steps for the Intermediate CA are similar to as shown for the Root CA.

1. Generation of the RSA keypair and CSR.

   ```
   req -newkey rsa:2048 -config ssl.cfg -keyout sint.key -out sint.csr
   ```

   Provide a password to encrypt the **sint.key** file.

2. Signing the CSR using the private key of the Root CA.

   ```
   x509 -in sint.csr -CA sroot.crt -CAkey sroot.key -days 365
   -CAcreateserial -out sint.crt -extfile ica.ext -req
   ```

   We use the **-CA** and **-CAkey** parameters instead of the **-signkey** parameter. We used **ica.ext** for extensions. The contents of the file are as follows:

   ```
   basicConstraints = critical,CA:true,pathlen:0
   ```

3. Annotate the certificate with the textual content for readability.

   ```
   x509 -in sint.crt -text -out sint.annot.crt
   ```

We create the end-entity server certificate next.

TLS server certificate

In our example, the server certificate is meant for the DNS address **mysrv.local**. We follow similar steps as earlier.

1. Generation of the RSA keypair and CSR.

   ```
   req -newkey rsa:2048 -config ssl.cfg -keyout mysrv.local.key -out
   mysrv.local.csr
   ```

2. Signing the CSR using the private key of the Intermediate CA.

   ```
   x509 -in mysrv.local.csr -CA sint.crt -CAkey sint.key -days 365
   -CAcreateserial -out mysrv.local.crt -extfile server.ext -req
   ```

   The extensions for the server are as follows:

   ```
   basicConstraints = CA:false

   keyUsage =
   digitalSignature,nonRepudiation,keyEncipherment,dataEncipherment

   extendedKeyUsage = serverAuth
   ```

```
subjectAltName = DNS:mysrv.local
```

3. Annotate the certificate with the textual content for readability.

```
x509 -in mysrv.local.crt -text -out mysrv.local.annot.crt
```

Generating the PKCS-12 file

PKCS-12 format helps carry multiple certificates and private keys in one container in a secure manner. The container can be a file or a cryptographic device. As we need to carry the chain for convenience, we will concatenate all the CA certificates to the end entity certificates. Here are the commands.

- Windows PowerShell: `Get-Content .\sroot.annot.crt,.\sint.annot.crt,.\mysrv.local.annot.crt | Out-file .\mysrv.local.comb.crt`
- Linux: `cat .\sroot.annot.crt .\sint.annot.crt .\mysrv.local.annot.crt > .\mysrv.local.comb.crt`

We use the **pkcs12** command in OpenSSL to create the PKCS-12 file.

```
OpenSSL> pkcs12 -export -in mysrv.local.comb.crt -inkey mysrv.local.key
-out mysrv.local.p12
Enter pass phrase for mysrv.local.key:
Enter Export Password:
Verifying - Enter Export Password:
OpenSSL>
```

The same process can be followed to create the PKCS-12 files for the Intermediate CA and the Root CA certificates.

Client hierarchy

In *Figure 3.7: Client certificate hierarchy*, we showed a different chain for the client authentication certificates. The generation of the client certificates is very similar to the server certificates. We leave it here as an exercise for you. The client extensions are different from the server as shown.

```
basicConstraints = CA:false
keyUsage =
digitalSignature,nonRepudiation,keyEncipherment,dataEncipherment
extendedKeyUsage = clientAuth
subjectAltName = email:alice@mysrv.local
```

The **subjectAltName** has a format of an email. The extended key usage is for client authentication, and so on.

Index

P

R

S

T

U